EXPLORING GEOMETRY

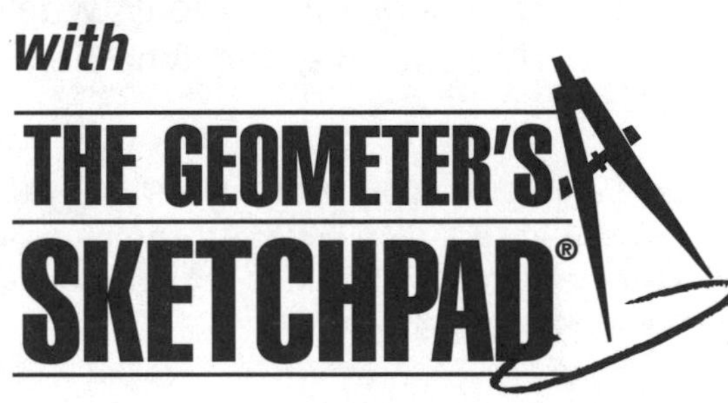

Revised for Use with Version 4

DAN BENNETT

Revision Editor	Steven Chanan
Production Editor	Christine Osborne
Copyeditor	Joan D. Saunders
Editorial Production Manager	Deborah Cogan
Production Director	Diana Jean Parks
Art and Design Coordinator	Caroline Ayres
Contributing Writer	Masha Albrecht
Cover and Chapter Opener Design	Kirk Mills
Cover Photographs	Images © 1997 Photodisc, Inc.
Prepress and Printer	Data Reproductions
Publisher	Steven Rasmussen

Special thanks to all the teachers and students who offered feedback on previous editions, who responded to surveys, and who field-tested activities for this edition.

Portions of this material are based upon work supported by the National Science Foundation under award numbers III-9203421 and DMI-9623018. Any opinions, findings, and conclusions or recommendations expressed in this publication are those of the author and do not necessarily reflect the views of the National Science Foundation.

®The Geometer's Sketchpad, ®Dynamic Geometry, and ®Key Curriculum Press are registered trademarks of Key Curriculum Press. ™Sketchpad is a trademark of Key Curriculum Press. All other brand names and product names are trademarks or registered trademarks of their respective holders.

Limited Reproduction Permission

© 2002 Key Curriculum Press. All rights reserved. Key Curriculum Press grants the teacher who purchases *Exploring Geometry with The Geometer's Sketchpad* the right to reproduce activities and example sketches for use with his or her own students. Unauthorized copying of *Exploring Geometry with The Geometer's Sketchpad* and of the *Exploring Geometry* sketches is a violation of federal law.

Exploring Geometry Sketches CD-ROM

Key Curriculum Press guarantees that the Exploring Geometry Sketches CD-ROM that accompanies this book is free of defects in materials and workmanship. A defective CD-ROM will be replaced free of charge if returned within 90 days of the purchase date. After 90 days, there is a $10.00 replacement fee.

Key Curriculum Press
1150 65th Street
Emeryville, California 94608
510-595-7000
editorial@keypress.com
http://www.keypress.com

10 9 8 7 6 5 4 06 05 ISBN 1-55953-581-4

Contents

© 2002 Key Curriculum Press

Chapter 3: Triangles

Chapter 4: Quadrilaterals

© 2002 Key Curriculum Press

Chapter 5: Polygons

Chapter 6: Circles

Chapter 7: Area

Chapter 8: The Pythagorean Theorem

© 2002 Key Curriculum Press

Chapter 9: Similarity

Chapter 10: Trigonometry and Fractals

Activity Notes

© 2002 Key Curriculum Press

Introduction

This introduction offers some background on Sketchpad™ and different ways to use it (some of which may be familiar from *Teaching Mathematics with The Geometer's Sketchpad,* which comes with the program) and some explanation of the ideas we had in mind when we created these activities.

Dynamic Geometry® and Change in Mathematics Teaching

The way we teach mathematics—geometry in particular—has changed. The rigidly deductive approach to teaching geometry is finally being seriously challenged, and alternatives are available after more than a century of failing to reach a majority of students. (The National Assessment of Educational Progress found in 1982 that proof was the least-liked mathematics topic of 17-year-olds, and less than 50% of them rated the topic as important.) An early example of one of these alternatives is the 1985 release of a landmark piece of instructional software called The Geometric Supposers, developed by Judah Schwartz and Michal Yerushalmy of the Education Development Center. This program encouraged students to invent their own mathematics by creating simple geometric figures and making conjectures about their properties.

By publishing the first edition of Michael Serra's *Discovering Geometry: An Inductive Approach* in 1989, Key Curriculum Press joined the forces of change. *Discovering Geometry,* a high school geometry textbook, takes much the same approach that the creators of The Geometric Supposers espoused: Students should create their own geometric constructions and themselves formulate the mathematics to describe relationships they discover. With *Discovering Geometry,* students working in cooperative groups do investigations, often using compass-and-straightedge constructions, to discover properties. Students look for patterns and use inductive reasoning to make conjectures. Proof is developed out of students' attempts to explain why their conjectures are true. Only at the end of book is proof formalized as a way to systematize knowledge. The third edition of *Discovering Geometry,* published in summer 2002, maintains a discovery approach while further integrating applications and tools, most notably The Geometer's Sketchpad.

The approach of The Geometric Supposers, *Discovering Geometry,* and The Geometer's Sketchpad is consistent with research done by the Dutch mathematics educators Pierre van Hiele and Dina van Hiele-Geldof. From classroom observations, the van Hieles learned that students pass through a series of levels of geometric thinking: visualization, analysis, informal deduction, formal deduction, and rigor. Standard geometry texts expect students to employ formal deduction from the beginning. Little is done to enable students to visualize or to encourage them to

© 2002 Key Curriculum Press

make conjectures. A main goal of The Supposers, *Discovering Geometry*, and The Geometer's Sketchpad is to bring students through the first three levels, encouraging a process of discovery that more closely reflects the way mathematics is invented: A mathematician first visualizes and analyzes a problem, making conjectures before attempting a proof.

In the meantime, in 1988, the National Council of Teachers of Mathematics (NCTM) published the *Curriculum and Evaluation Standards for School Mathematics* (the *Standards*), which called for significant changes in the way mathematics is taught. In the teaching of geometry, the *Standards* called for decreased emphasis on the presentation of geometry as a complete deductive system and a decreased emphasis on two-column proofs. The *Standards* called for an increase in open exploration and conjecturing and increased attention to topics in transformational geometry. In 2000, NCTM published *Principles and Standards for School Mathematics,* which further emphasized the important role that dynamic geometry software such as The Geometer's Sketchpad can play in geometry classrooms.

The Geometer's Sketchpad was among the first in the new generation of educational software, which has added to the momentum of change begun by The Geometric Supposers and spurred on by publications like *Discovering Geometry* and the NCTM *Standards*. Sketchpad brings geometry exploration tools to state-of-the-art hardware, enabling students to explore relationships dynamically so that they can see change in geometric figures as they manipulate them. Sketchpad combines this breakthrough with complete construction, transformation, and coordinate geometry capabilities and the extensibility offered by scripting, broadening the scope of what it's possible to do with geometry software to an extent never seen before.

Where Sketchpad Came From

The Geometer's Sketchpad was developed as part of the Visual Geometry Project, a National Science Foundation–funded project under the direction of Dr. Eugene Klotz at Swarthmore College and Dr. Doris Schattschneider at Moravian College in Pennsylvania. Sketchpad creator and programmer Nicholas Jackiw developed Sketchpad's first versions in an open, academic environment in which many teachers, researchers, and other users provided design input. Key Curriculum Press continues to study how Sketchpad can be most effectively used by schools. Funded in part by grants from the National Science Foundation, this research is reflected in these notes, in curriculum materials, and in the ongoing development of Sketchpad. By 1999, the *Teaching, Learning, and Computing* national teacher survey conducted by the University of California, Irvine, found that the nation's mathematics teachers rated Sketchpad the "most valuable software for students" by a large margin.

© 2002 Key Curriculum Press

Where Exploring Geometry Came From

From the time teachers and students first used Sketchpad, we've been soliciting feedback on what types of activities can be used most effectively in the classroom. Funding from the National Science Foundation's Small Business Innovation Research Program enabled us to visit classrooms and interview teachers and students. Our research continued after the release of the first edition of this book, and we collected an immense amount of valuable feedback from users of that edition. Three important messages came through in our research.

1. **Sketchpad's ease of use can best be taken advantage of if initial activities require only simple constructions.** With experience, Sketchpad's power enables students to create figures of arbitrarily great complexity. But students who are beginners at using the program grasp concepts best when their thinking is directed toward relationships, rather than constructions. For this reason, the activity notes for each of these activities specify the level of proficiency required (beginner, intermediate, or advanced), and the majority of the activities are designed for beginners. Introductory activities give students greater guidance with the program's user interface, and some rely on pre-made sketches so that students can focus on relationships instead of constructions.

2. **Sketchpad can integrate different geometry topics in ways textbooks don't.** For example, in a single Sketchpad triangle investigation, students might investigate line and angle relationships, area, transformations, symmetry, and coordinate geometry. The consequence of this finding is that, with few exceptions, the activities in this book don't follow a linear sequence. The book's organizational structure doesn't dictate a single "proper" order in which to use the activities.

3. **Opportunities for student insight come in many places throughout the course of an investigation, not just from dragging a completed construction.** For this reason, students are explicitly asked to drag parts of their figure during the course of a construction, and leading questions are interspersed throughout the activity. This is a change from previous editions, in which students were asked to respond to questions only at the end of the activity.

Ideas for these activities come from a variety of sources. We started with *Discovering Geometry,* where we found many discovery lessons that were easily adaptable to computer-based exploration. We also collected ideas from teachers we had contact with in our research. Finally, we studied other geometry books for topics that would make good Sketchpad investigations. *Geometry,* by Harold Jacobs (W. H. Freeman and Co., 1974), and *Geometry, An Investigative Approach,* by Don Chakerien et al. (Sunburst Communications, 1987), were valuable in this regard.

© 2002 Key Curriculum Press

Using Exploring Geometry Activities

Exploring Geometry was designed primarily for high school geometry classrooms. Other curriculum modules available from Key Curriculum Press address the specific needs of younger and older students. You will find, however, that many of the activities here will be useful if you teach middle school or college.

The activities in this book cover the core content of a typical geometry course (with the exception of some topics in three-dimensional geometry). Courses using an inductive approach could use Sketchpad nearly every day to discover geometric properties. Students in courses using a deductive approach could use Sketchpad to discover theorems they would then prove and to confirm and develop their understanding of theorems after they prove them. In short, these activities are here when you need them—for when you think a particular lesson is just right exploration on the computer or when your students start lobbying for a trip to the computer lab.

How Exploring Geometry Is Organized

The order of the activities in this book follows, more or less, the order of investigations in the text *Discovering Geometry: An Inductive Approach*, by Michael Serra. One important difference in the topics' order is that the Transformations chapter is found early in this volume. Sketchpad makes it easy to construct figures using transformations and to investigate symmetry. We recommend that you get students started early using Sketchpad's transformation capabilities so they can take advantage of these capabilities in their constructions.

The activities need not be done in any particular order. Every activity is self-contained. None relies on students' having done another activity. (The activity notes for some activities refer to related activities that might be helpful to do first.)

Introductory Activities

The following activities are designed for students with little or no experience using Sketchpad. Each comes at the beginning of a chapter. These activities either start with a pre-made sketch or offer more specific guidance on how to use Sketchpad. The geometry content of these activities is also introductory.

Chapter 1: Introducing Points, Segments, Rays, and Lines
Introducing Angles

Chapter 2: Introducing Transformations

Chapter 3: Defining Triangles

Chapter 4: Defining Special Quadrilaterals

Chapter 6: Introducing Circles

© 2002 Key Curriculum Press

Features of a Typical Activity

A typical activity has three sections: an introduction that describes the objective of the activity; a section titled Sketch and Investigate, in which students follow construction steps and answer questions; and a section titled Explore More, which lists possible extensions of the investigation.

Sketch and Investigate is the core of the activity. Construction steps are numbered. Questions are numbered Q1, Q2, and so on. These questions range from requiring short, fill-in-the-blank answers to requiring complete paragraphs. The activity page itself is the student's worksheet, with space for writing answers. In some cases, students may need a separate sheet of paper for their answers.

In nonintroductory activities, most construction steps are described in geometric terms, not in terms of Sketchpad commands and actions. That makes the directions concise, allowing students to focus on geometry instead of on software details that quickly become redundant. For those who do need extra help using the software, hints appear in the margins.

Explore More suggestions can be challenging. Students who finish an activity early can get started on Explore More activities, but you should expect many of these activities to turn into long-term projects. You might occasionally demonstrate one as a class wrap-up. For space reasons, many Explore More suggestions are collected together at the end of the book in the section titled Additional Explore More Suggestions.

Different Methods for Collecting Student Sketchpad Work

Method	Advantages	Disadvantages
Viewing student work on their monitors (and possibly signing off on it as you go around the room)	• Very simple, and you'll be doing it anyway.	• Minimal written record. • Often you don't get to every student during the class period.
Collecting completed photocopies of activity sheets	• Easy to collect and assess. • Worksheets are well structured to provide guidance to students.	• Result has no dynamic information. • Result has no constructions. • Worksheets can lack flexibility and don't allow as much exploration.

© 2002 Key Curriculum Press

Different Methods for Collecting Student Sketchpad Work (continued)

Method	Advantages	Disadvantages
Collecting printouts of student sketches	• Easy to collect and assess.*	• Depends on your printer availability (having the whole class trying to print at the end of the period can be a disaster). • Printout is not dynamic, so you can't tell whether the constructions are really correct.
Collecting student work on individual student disks	• Work that you assess is dynamic.* • Easy to organize: Each student is responsible for his/her own disk.	• It can be time-consuming to look through a pile of disks.
If you have a network, collecting work in student file folders	• You can collect dynamic work without using disks.*	• Requires a network.
Collecting student work on a teacher disk (or a couple of teacher disks)	• You need only look at a few disks. • The work is dynamic. • You don't need to deal with students who can't find their disks.	• Everyone might need to save at the same time (for instance, at the end of class), and you only have one or two disks to save on.

* On the following page is a blackline master you can display or distribute. It offers students guidelines and suggestions for presenting their work.

© 2002 Key Curriculum Press

Presenting a Sketchpad Sketch

You can use this list as a checklist to make sure you're presenting your sketch well. There may be additional requirements for particular assignments.

A *good* sketch has these features:

- ❑ It contains your name and the name of your class (use the **Text** tool to do this).
- ❑ It describes the problem or challenge you're exploring.
- ❑ It contains text explaining your mathematical observations and conjectures.
- ❑ It contains text explaining your construction.
- ❑ The sketch is correctly constructed (this means it does not fall apart if you drag any vertices or edges in the sketch).
- ❑ The sketch is not overconstrained (this means it can take on any of the necessary characteristics of the construction and is not limited to only a few cases).

An *excellent* sketch may have some of these additional features:

- ❑ It is in color, if possible.
- ❑ It offers unique or exceptional mathematical explanations or discoveries.
- ❑ It contains unique or informative constructions and illustrations.
- ❑ It includes a Show/Hide button that helps illustrate concepts in your sketch.
- ❑ It includes buttons that animate parts of your sketch to demonstrate your findings.

Reminders

If you're turning in your sketch electronically, make sure you save your file by the correct name and in the correct location.

If you're turning in your sketch as a printout, check **Print Preview** in the File menu before printing. Also, remember that colors will print in grayscale unless you have a color printer.

© 2002 Key Curriculum Press

Activity Notes

Notes for each activity are in the second-to-last section of the book. Here you'll find more information as to what prerequisite geometry facts and terms are assumed, what Sketchpad proficiency is required, how much class time to allow, what example or required sketches and custom tools accompany the activity, and possible answers to the Sketch and Investigate questions and the Explore More questions.

The necessary Sketchpad proficiency is specified using the terms *beginner, intermediate,* and *advanced.* All the activities, including those for beginners, assume very basic knowledge of how to use a computer in general and Sketchpad in particular: clicking and dragging (creating objects using the Toolbox), selecting (including multiple objects), using menus, and opening and closing documents ("sketches"). Introductory activities offer a little more help with some of these basics.

Intermediate users are able to do more complex constructions with hidden objects, create and use basic custom tools, use animation, and perform transformations. Activities designated for intermediate users are not necessarily difficult; you probably just don't want to use them with students who have never used Sketchpad. Users might be considered intermediate after just a few sessions with the program.

Advanced users know most Sketchpad features and can do complex constructions that require precise mouse manipulations, advanced use of custom tools, and keyboard shortcuts. Students needn't be advanced to try an advanced activity, but they may find that it takes a long time or is tedious because they lack the experience needed to do it efficiently.

How much class time your students spend on an activity depends largely on how much time you want them to spend writing about, talking about, or presenting their findings. None of the activities are designed to take longer than one 50-minute class period, but you could choose to spend days talking about one investigation. On the other hand, you might be able to do two or three activities in a single class period. The class time suggested in these notes includes time to do the construction, manipulate it, make some observations, think, and write down one or more conjectures. It does not include time for extended discussion, presentations, or extensions of the activity.

Using the Exploring Geometry Sketches CD-ROM

One or more sketches accompany nearly every activity in the book. These files can be found on a single CD-ROM that will run both on Macintosh computers and on computers operating with Windows 95 or later. You can open these sketches directly from the CD, or you can copy them onto one or more hard drives. Teachers who purchase this book are free to make as many copies of the sketches as needed for their students.

© 2002 Key Curriculum Press

The sketches require The Geometer's Sketchpad application to open. The CD does not contain the application itself. Read the Read Me file on the disk for more details.

The sketches fall into four general categories.

Example Sketches: In most activities, students do their own constructions, making their own sketches. No pre-made sketch is needed for these activities. However, example sketches do accompany these activities so that you can quickly see a finished construction like the one students are asked to make. On occasion, you may wish to use the pre-made sketches to speed up an investigation, especially with students who are just learning how to use the software.

Required Sketches: In some activities, students do start with a pre-made sketch (as named in the activity and in the Activity Notes). These sketches enable students to move straight to investigating relationships in complicated constructions.

Regular Polygon Custom Tools: Constructions of regular polygons, particularly squares, come up in several activities. It's handy to use custom tools for these. You may choose to have students make their own custom tools for at least a square and an equilateral triangle. Or you can have them use the tools in the sketch **Polygons.gsp,** included on the CD in several locations and with the application itself. (To use the tools in **Polygons.gsp** on a particular occasion, open the sketch, then access its tools from the Custom Tools menu of any other open sketch. To make these tools permanently available, move the **Polygons.gsp** file into the Tool Folder, which is located alongside the application itself on your hard disk.)

Demonstration Sketches: These sketches are related to concepts covered in the activities, but they're meant to be more or less self-explanatory, usually through the use of action buttons. They could be used with or without the activity worksheet. In activities for which a pre-made sketch is not required, you might have students do the constructions described in the activity, then use the demonstration sketch to summarize and review their findings. Students could open and explore these sketches themselves, or you or a student could present them with an overhead display.

Using Sketchpad in Different Classroom Settings

Different schools have different settings in which computers are used. Sketchpad was designed with this in mind, and its display features can be optimized for these various settings. Teaching strategies also need to be adapted to available resources. Here are some suggestions for teaching with and using Sketchpad in a classroom with one computer, one computer and a computer projection device, several computers, or in a computer lab.

© 2002 Key Curriculum Press

A Classroom with One Computer

Perhaps the best use of a single computer is to have small groups of students take turns using it. Each group can investigate or confirm conjectures they have made while working at their desks or tables using standard tools such as paper and pencil or graphing calculators. In that case, each group would have an opportunity during a class period to use the computer for a short time. Alternatively, you can give each group a day on which to do an investigation on the computer while other groups are doing the same or different investigations at their desks. A single computer without a computer projection device or large-screen monitor has limited use as a demonstration tool.

A Classroom with One Computer and a Computer Projection Device

Having a computer projection device considerably increases your teaching options. You or a student can act as a sort of emcee to an investigation, asking the class questions such as: "What should we try next?" "Which objects should I reflect?" "What do you notice as I move this point?" Sketchpad becomes a "dynamic chalkboard" on which you or your students can draw precise, complex figures that can be distorted and transformed in an infinite variety of ways. Watching someone use Sketchpad as a demonstration tool is a good way for students to learn some fundamentals of the program before they go to the computer lab. You can also model good Sketchpad presentation techniques for students. Use large and bold text styles and thick lines to make text and figures clearly visible from all corners of a classroom.

A Classroom with Several Computers

If you can divide your class into groups of three or four students and give each group access to a computer, you can plan whole lessons around computer investigations.

- Introduce to the whole class what it is they're expected to do.
- Provide students with some kind of written explanation of the investigation or problem they're to work on. It's often useful for that explanation to be on a piece of paper that leaves students room to record some of their findings. For some open-ended explorations, the problem or question could simply be written on the chalkboard or typed into the sketch itself. Likewise, students' "written" work could be in the form of sketches with captions and comments.
- Make sure students understand that everybody in a group needs the chance to actually operate the computer.
- Make sure that the students in a group who are not actually operating the computer contribute to the group discussion and give input to the student operating the computer.

© 2002 Key Curriculum Press

- Move among groups posing questions, giving help if needed, and keeping students on task.
- Summarize students' findings in a whole-class discussion to bring closure to the lesson.

A Computer Lab

Teachers using Sketchpad often find that even if enough computers are available for students to work individually, it's still best to have students work in pairs. Students learn best when they communicate about what they're learning, and students working together can better stimulate ideas and help one another. If you do have students working at their own computers, encourage them to talk about what they're doing and to compare their findings with those of their neighbors—they *should* peek over one another's shoulders. The suggestions above for students working in small groups apply to students working in pairs as well.

Exploring Geometry and Your Geometry Text

The variety of ways Sketchpad can be used makes it an ideal tool for exploring geometry, no matter what text you're using. Use Sketchpad to demonstrate concepts or example problems presented in the text. Or have students use Sketchpad to explore problems given as exercises. If your text presents theorems and proves them, give your students an opportunity to explore the concepts with Sketchpad before moving on to the proof. Working out constructions in Sketchpad will deepen students' understanding of geometry concepts and will make proof more relevant than it would be otherwise.

Sketchpad is ideally suited for use with books that take a discovery approach to learning geometry. In Michael Serra's *Discovering Geometry*, for example, students working in small groups do investigations and discover concepts for themselves before they attempt proof. Many of these investigations call for compass-and-straightedge constructions, any of which can be done in Sketchpad. Many other investigations involving measurements, calculations, and transformations can also be done effectively and efficiently with Sketchpad.

We wish to stress, however, that we don't advocate abandoning all other teaching methods in favor of using the computer. Students need a variety of learning experiences, such as hands-on manipulatives, compass-and-straightedge constructions, drawing, paper-and-pencil work, and discussion. Students also need to apply geometry to real-life situations and see where it is used in art and architecture and where it can be found in nature. While Sketchpad can serve as a medium for many of these experiences, its potential will be reached only when students can apply what they learn with it to different situations.

© 2002 Key Curriculum Press

Common Commands and Shortcuts

Below are some common Sketchpad actions used throughout this book. In time, these operations will become familiar, but at first you may want to keep this list by your side.

To undo or redo a recent action

Choose **Undo** from the Edit menu. You can undo as many steps as you want, all the way back to the state your sketch was in when last opened. To redo, choose **Redo** from the Edit menu.

To deselect everything

Click in any blank area of your sketch with the **Arrow** tool or press Esc until objects deselect. To deselect a single object while keeping all other objects selected, click on it with the **Arrow** tool.

To show or hide a label

Position the finger of the **Text** tool over the *object* and click. The hand will turn black when it's correctly positioned to show or hide a label.

To change a label

Position the finger of the **Text** tool over the *label* and double-click. The letter "A" will appear in the hand when it's correctly positioned.

To change an object's line width or color

Select the object and choose from the appropriate submenu in the Display menu.

To hide an object

Select the object and choose **Hide** from the Display menu.

To select an angle

Select three points, making the angle vertex your middle selection. Three points are the required selections to construct an angle bisector (Construct menu), to measure an angle (Measure menu), or to mark an angle of rotation (Transform menu).

To mark a center of rotation or dilation

Use the **Selection Arrow** tool to double-click the point. A brief animation indicates that you've made the mark.

To construct a segment's midpoint

Select the segment and choose **Midpoint** from the Construct menu.

To construct a parallel or perpendicular line

Select a straight object for the new line to be parallel/perpendicular to and a point for it to pass through. Then choose **Parallel Line** or **Perpendicular Line** from the Construct menu.

To construct a polygon interior

Select the vertices (points) of the polygon in consecutive order around the polygon. Then, in the Construct menu, choose **[Polygon] Interior.**

To reflect a point (or other object)

Double-click the mirror (any straight object) or select it and choose **Mark Mirror**. Then select the point (or other object) and choose **Reflect** from the Transform menu.

To trace an object

Select the object and choose **Trace** from the Display menu. Do the same thing to toggle tracing off. To erase traces left by traced objects, choose **Erase Traces** from the Display menu.

To use the Calculator

Choose **Calculate** from the Measure menu. To enter a measurement into a calculation, click on the measurement itself in the sketch.

Keyboard Shortcuts

Command	Mac	Windows
Undo	⌘+Z	Ctrl+Z
Redo	⌘+R	Ctrl+R
Select All	⌘+A	Ctrl+A
Properties	⌘+?	Alt+?
Hide Objects	⌘+H	Ctrl+H
Show/Hide Labels	⌘+K	Ctrl+K
Trace Objects	⌘+T	Ctrl+T
Erase Traces	⌘+B	Ctrl+B

Command	Mac	Windows
Animate/Pause	⌘+`	Alt+`
Increase Speed	⌘+]	Alt+]
Decrease Speed	⌘+[	Alt+[
Midpoint	⌘+M	Ctrl+M
Intersection	⌘+I	Ctrl+I
Segment	⌘+L	Ctrl+L
Polygon Interior	⌘+P	Ctrl+P
Calculate	⌘+=	Alt+=

Action	Mac	Windows
Scroll drag	Option+ drag	Alt+drag
Display Context menu	Control+ click	Right+ click
Navigate Toolbox	Shift+arrow keys	
Choose **Arrow**, deselect objects, stop animations, erase traces	Esc (escape key)	
Move selected objects 1 pixel	←, ↑, →, ↓ keys (hold down to move continuously)	

© 2002 Key Curriculum Press

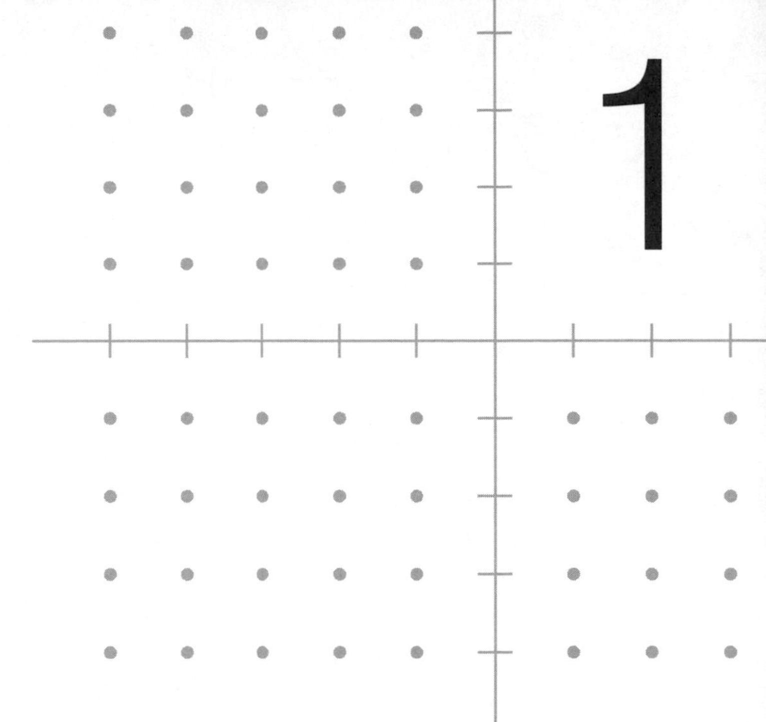

1

Lines and Angles

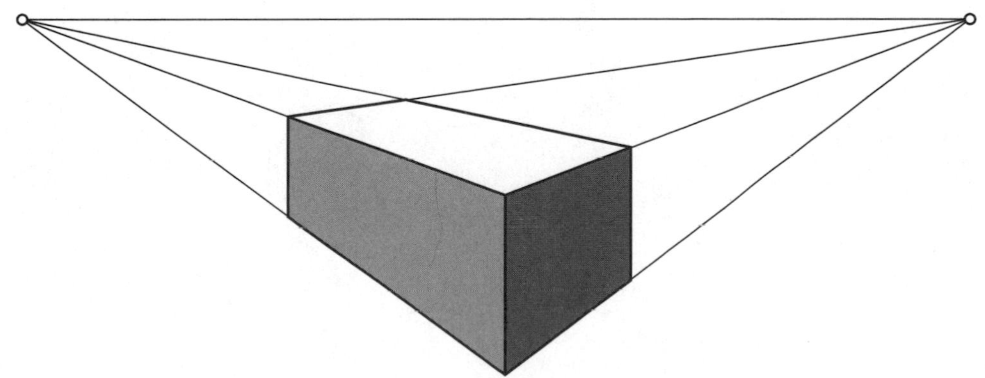

Introducing Points, Segments, Rays, and Lines

Name(s): ______________________

In this activity, you'll experiment with drawing, dragging, measuring, and labeling points, segments, rays, and lines. These objects, along with circles, are the building blocks of most geometric constructions.

Sketch and Investigate: Points and Segments

Note: If at any time you think you've made a mistake or you want to do something differently, you can always undo as many steps as you like. The **Undo** and **Redo** commands are in the Edit menu.

The **Point** tool

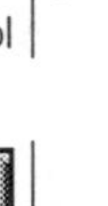

1. Choose the **Point** tool and click in the sketch to construct a point. Click again to construct a second point. Notice that the most recently constructed point is *selected*: It appears with an outline.

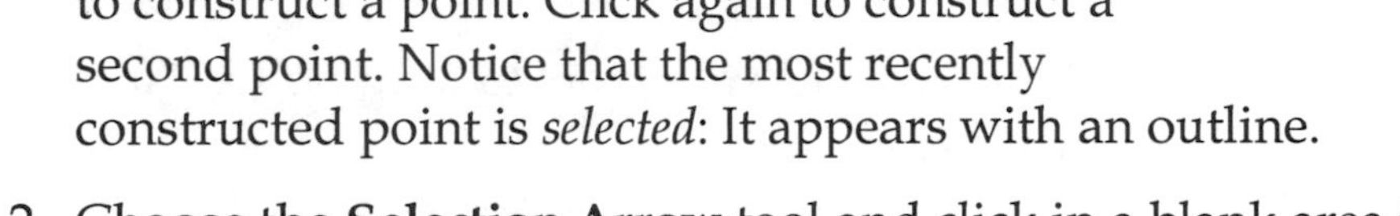

The **Selection Arrow** tool

2. Choose the **Selection Arrow** tool and click in a blank area in the sketch. This deselects everything.

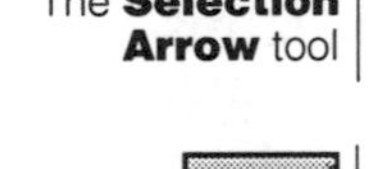

The **Text** tool

By default, point labels start with *A*.

3. Choose the **Text** tool. Position the finger over a point, then click to display that point's label. Display the other point's label, too.

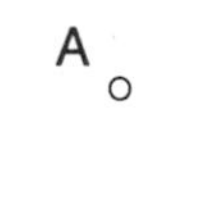

4. With the **Selection Arrow** tool, click on both points. Now both points should be selected.

5. In the Measure menu, choose **Distance**.

AB = 2.72 cm

6. Drag one of the points and observe the measurement.

A B

Q1 How can you make the distance between the two points zero?

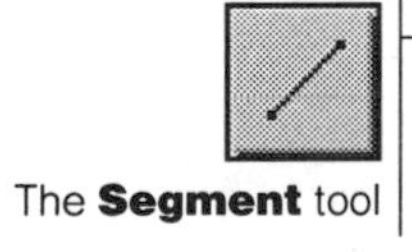

The **Segment** tool

7. Choose the **Segment** tool and draw a segment connecting the two points. You'll see a triple segment at first, indicating that the segment is selected.

8. With the segment selected, go to the Measure menu and choose **Length**.

9. Use the **Selection Arrow** tool to drag either endpoint of the segment.

© 2002 Key Curriculum Press

Q2 How does the length of a segment compare to the distance between its endpoints?

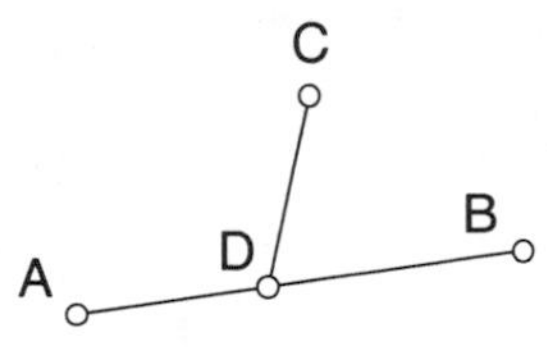

10. Use the **Segment** tool to construct a second segment with one endpoint attached to the first segment. To do this, click the mouse button first when the pointer is in a blank area of the sketch, then when it's directly on the original segment.
11. Use the **Text** tool to show the labels of this segment's endpoints.
12. Use the **Selection Arrow** tool to drag point D to confirm that it is attached to $\overline{AB}$.
13. Select $\overline{CD}$ (the segment, not its endpoints), then go to the Construct menu and notice what choices are available. Choose **Midpoint**.

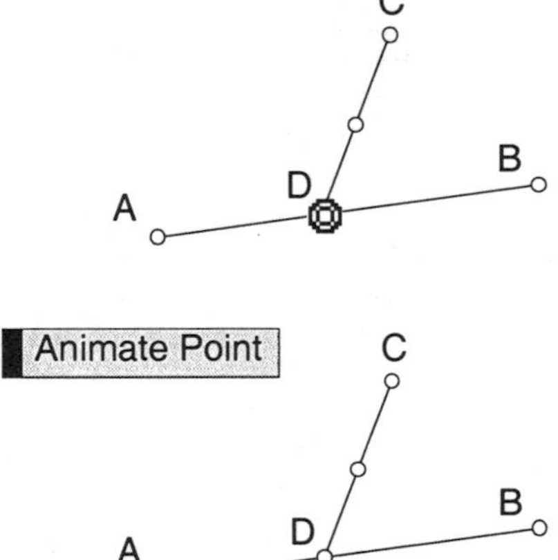

14. Click in a blank area to deselect everything.
15. Select point D.
16. In the Edit menu, drag to the Action Buttons submenu and choose **Animation**. You'll get a dialog box you can use to specify animation settings. To choose the default settings, click OK. You've created an Animation action button in your sketch.
17. Press the action button (by clicking on it) to start the animation.
18. Press the button again to stop the animation.
19. Select the midpoint; then, in the Display menu, choose **Trace Midpoint**.
20. Press the Animation button again and observe the path that the midpoint traces.

Q3 Describe the path that the midpoint traces as point D moves back and forth.

© 2002 Key Curriculum Press

Sketch and Investigate: Rays and Lines

21. In the File menu, choose **New Sketch**.

Straightedge tool palette

22. Press and hold down the mouse button on the **Segment** tool. A palette of **Straightedge** tools will pop out to the right. Drag right and choose the **Ray** tool.

23. Draw a ray in your sketch. Notice that the ray extends in one direction beyond the edge of your sketch window.

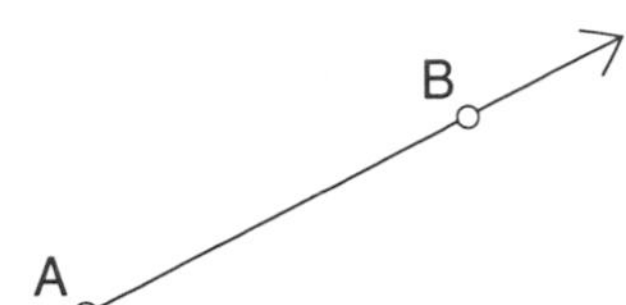

24. Use the **Text** tool to show the labels of the ray's control points.

25. Use the **Selection Arrow** tool to drag each point to observe how it controls the ray.

Q4 A ray with endpoint *A* that passes through a point *B* is called ray *AB* (represented symbolically as $\overrightarrow{AB}$). Could it also be called ray *BA*? Explain.

26. Select the ray and go to the Measure menu. Note that **Length** is grayed out.

Q5 Why do you think you can't measure the length of a ray?

27. With the ray still selected, go to the Construct menu and look at your choices. Choose **Point On Ray**.

Q6 Why can't you construct the midpoint of a ray?

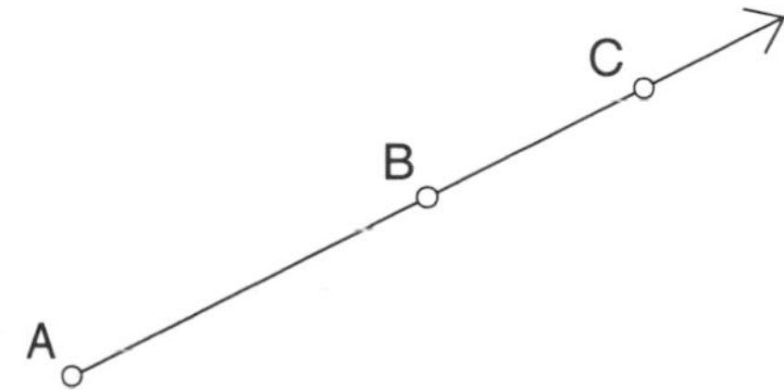

© 2002 Key Curriculum Press

28. Drag this new point to see how its behavior compares to that of the ray's two control points.

Q7 Give two different names to the ray shown at right. Use just two points in each name.

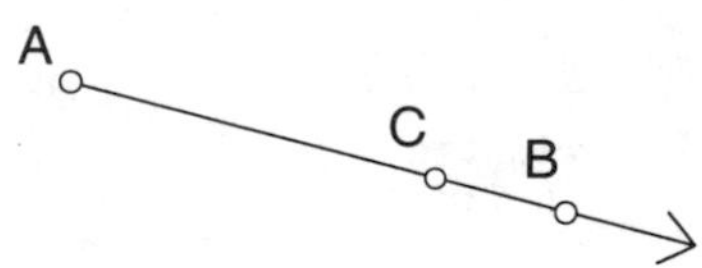

29. Press and hold down the **Ray** tool, then drag right to choose the **Line** tool.

30. Experiment with drawing lines in your sketch.

Q8 List all the similarities and differences you can between segments, rays, and lines.

Q9 Name two rays and a segment that lie on the line below.

Q10 In Sketchpad, construct a line without using the **Line** tool. Explain what you did. Does your line remain a line when you drag points?

© 2002 Key Curriculum Press

Introducing Angles

Name(s): ______________________

An *angle* is sometimes defined as two rays that share an endpoint. But two segments with a common endpoint also determine an angle. And we usually name an angle after three points. If that's not confusing enough, *angle measure* is usually considered something different from an angle. In this activity, you'll explore angles and angle measures with Sketchpad.

Sketch and Investigate

1. In the Edit menu, choose **Preferences**. Set the angle unit to degrees with precision to the nearest tenth.

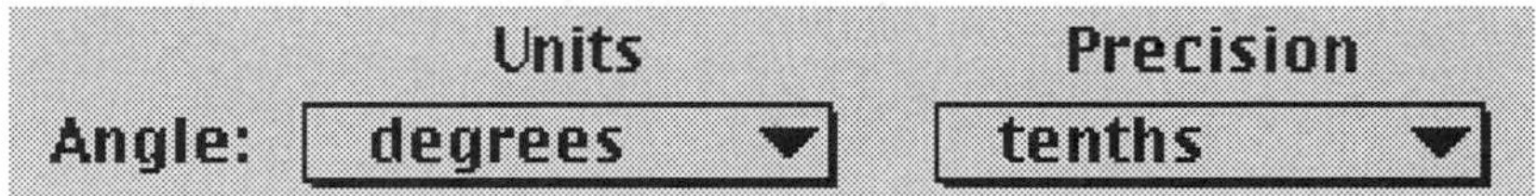

Angle Units and Precision menus from the Preferences dialog box

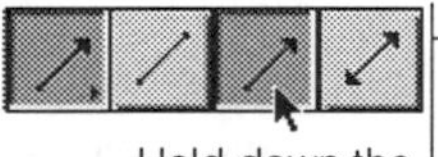

Hold down the mouse button on the active **Straightedge** tool to see the Straightedge tool palette, then drag to choose the **Ray** tool.

2. Use the **Ray** tool to construct $\overrightarrow{AB}$.
3. Construct another ray, $\overrightarrow{AC}$, with the same endpoint A.
4. Drag each of the three points to make sure the two rays always share a common endpoint (point A).

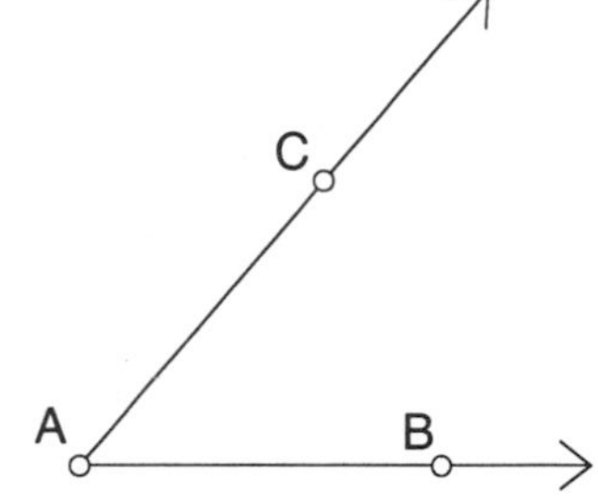

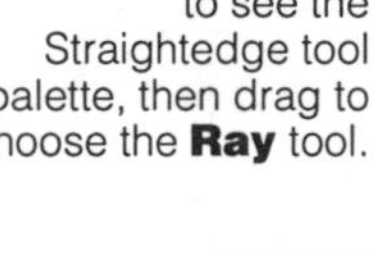

To display or hide a label, choose the **Text** tool, then click on the point. To change the label, double-click the label itself.

5. If necessary, use the **Text** tool to display the point labels. Change them to match the figure.

Q1 Two rays with a common endpoint form an angle. The common endpoint of the rays is called the *vertex* of the angle. Name the vertex of the angle you just made.

When you select an angle in Sketchpad, the vertex must be in the middle, just as when you name an angle.

6. Select, in order, points B, A, and C; then, in the Measure menu, choose **Angle**.
7. Drag point B or point C and observe how the angle measure changes.

Q2 Angles are usually named after three points: a point on one side, the vertex, and a point on the other side. What are two possible names for the angle you just made?

$\angle$ ________ and $\angle$ ________

© 2002 Key Curriculum Press

Q3 What's the smallest angle measure you can make by dragging? What's the greatest?

Q4 Drag a point on your angle until the angle's measure is as close to 0° as possible. Describe this angle.

Q5 Drag a point on your angle until the angle's measure is as close to 90° as possible. Describe this angle.

Q6 Drag a point on your angle until the angle's measure is as close to 180° as possible. Describe this angle.

Q7 An *acute angle* has measure between 0° and 90°. Drag a point on your angle to make it acute. Sketch an example of an acute angle in the space at right.

Q8 An *obtuse angle* has measure between 90° and 180°. Drag a point on your angle to make it obtuse. Sketch an example of an obtuse angle in the space at right.

8. Draw a circle centered at point *A* but not attached to any other points in your sketch.

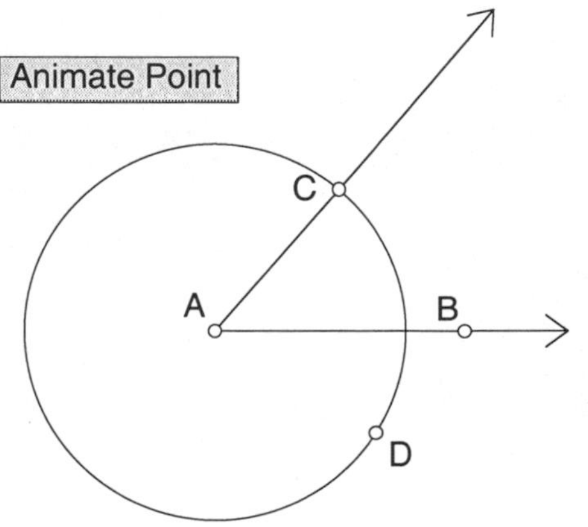

9. Select the circle and point *C*; then, in the Edit menu, choose **Merge Point To Circle**. Point *C* will attach itself to the circle.

Select point *C*. Then choose **Edit | Action Button | Animation**. Choose **slow** from the Speed pop-up menu. Then click OK.

10. Make an action button to animate point *C* around the circle.

© 2002 Key Curriculum Press

11. Press the button (click on it, in other words) to play it. Watch the angle measurement during the animation. (Press the button again to stop the animation.)

Q9 With **Preferences** set to degrees, Sketchpad displays angle measures from 0° to 180°. So when one angle side rotates by more than one-half of a revolution from the other angle side, the angle measure starts to decrease. Suppose the angle measure kept increasing until the angle side had completed one whole revolution. What would be the largest angle measure?

Q10 Draw an angle using the **Segment** tool. Does the measure of the angle depend on the lengths of the sides? Explore this question in Sketchpad, then give your answer and explain your method below.

Explore More

1. Use Sketchpad to model a clock. Choose **Other** in the Speed pop-up menu (see step 10) to set the speeds of the hands properly relative to one another. Once you have a working clock, explain what you did.

© 2002 Key Curriculum Press

Euclid's Proposition 1— An Equilateral Triangle

Name(s): ______________________

Euclid, a Greek mathematician born around 300 B.C., wrote a book called the *Elements,* upon which most school geometry books are still based. All of the geometry in the *Elements* is built up sequentially from a few simple constructions and postulates. Each new property that Euclid presents, or new figure that he constructs, is based on properties he has demonstrated previously. The construction that starts it all is the equilateral triangle. Countless other constructions in the *Elements* depend on being able to construct an equilateral triangle with compass and straightedge. In this activity, you'll construct an equilateral triangle using only Sketchpad's freehand tools—the equivalents of Euclid's compass and straightedge.

Sketch and Investigate

1. Construct $\overline{AB}$.

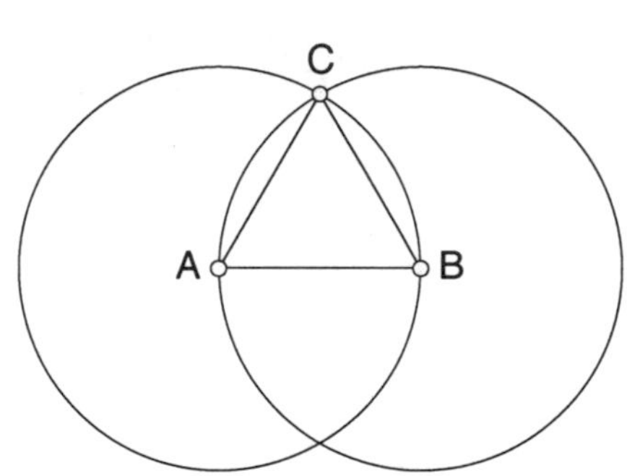

2. Construct circle *AB*. (Make sure you use point *A* for the center and point *B* for the radius-defining point.)
3. Construct circle *BA*. (Use point *B* for the center and point *A* for the radius point this time.)

If you start or finish drawing your segment with the tip of the **Segment** tool directly over the intersection of two objects, both objects will highlight and Sketchpad will construct an endpoint at the intersection.

4. Construct $\overline{AC}$ and $\overline{CB}$, where *C* is a point of intersection of the two circles.

Q1 Drag point *A* or point *B*. What happens to your triangle? Does it appear to stay equilateral?

Q2 Explain why this triangle is always equilateral. (Hints: What roles do the circles play in your construction? How are they related to one another? How are the sides of the triangle related to the circles?)

5. Hide the circles.

To measure an angle, select three points, with the vertex your middle selection. Then, in the Measure menu, choose **Angle**.

6. Measure the three angles.

Q3 Drag point *A* or point *B*. Make a conjecture about the angles in an equilateral triangle.

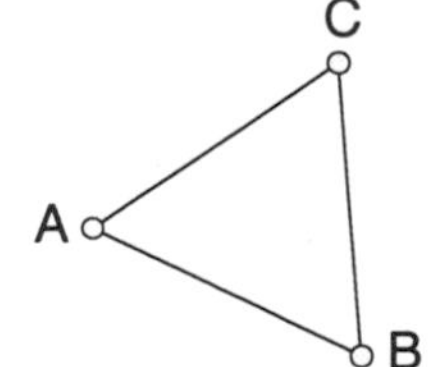

© 2002 Key Curriculum Press

Daisy Designs

Name(s): ______________________

A daisy design is a simple design that you can create using only a compass. From the basic daisy, you can create more complex designs based on the regular hexagon.

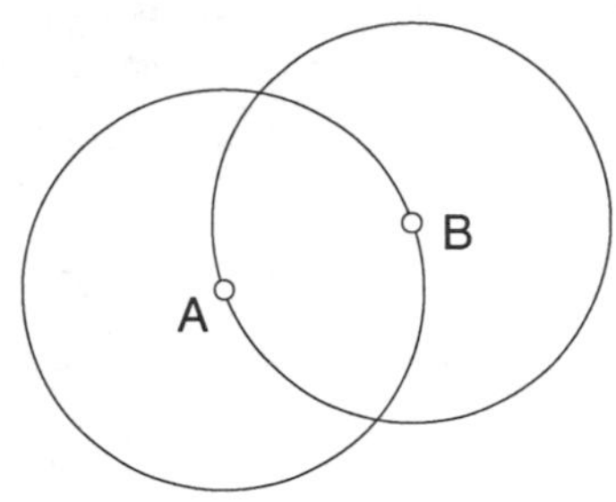

1. Construct circle *AB* (a circle with center *A* and radius point *B*).
2. Construct circle *BA*. Be sure you start your circle with the cursor positioned at point *B* and that you finish your circle with the cursor positioned at point *A*.

If both circles are not controlled by just points *A* and *B*, undo and try again.

3. Drag point *A* and point *B* to confirm that both circles are controlled by these two points.
4. Construct point *C* and point *D*, the two points of intersection of these circles.

Be sure all the circles are connected by constructing them from intersections to existing points in the sketch. Your final daisy should have exactly seven points.

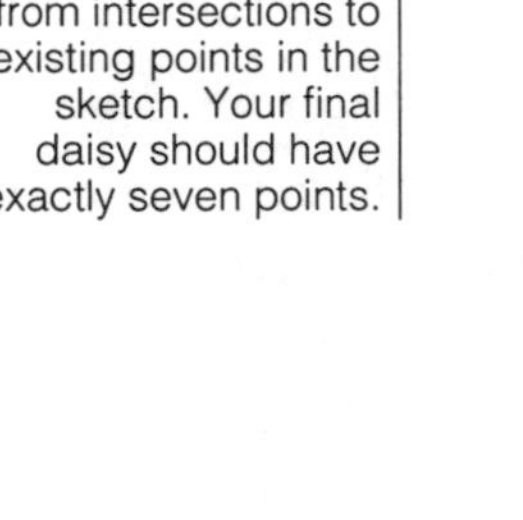

5. Construct a circle from point *C* to point *A*.
6. Continue constructing circles from new intersection points to point *A*. All these circles should have equal radii. The last circle you construct should be centered at point *D*. When you're done, your sketch should look like the figure below right. You should be able to drag it without making it fall apart.

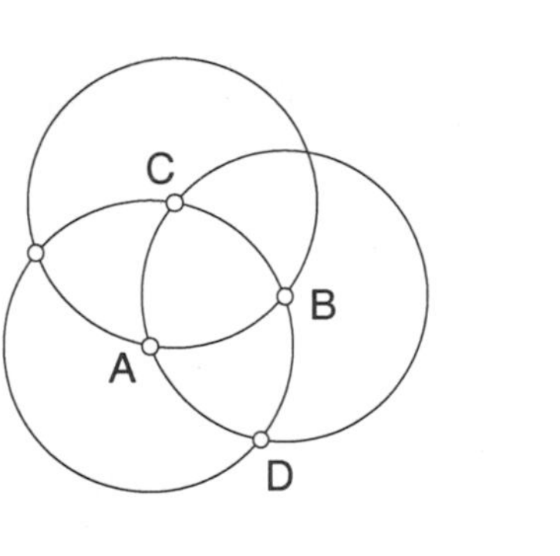

Step 5

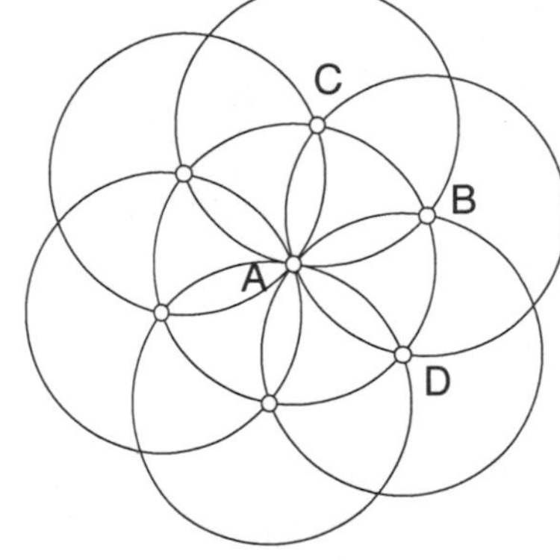

Step 6

7. Use the **Segment** tool to add some lines to your design; then drag point *B* and observe the way your design changes.

The six points of your daisy (besides point *A*) define six vertices of a regular hexagon. You can use these points as the basis for hexagon or star designs like those shown on the next page.

You could construct polygon interiors and experiment with color. You could also construct arcs (select a circle and two points on it) and arc sector and arc segment interiors (select an arc). However, you can

© 2002 Key Curriculum Press

probably get better results by printing out the basic line design and adding color and shading by hand. Once you have all the lines and polygon interiors you want, you can hide unneeded points. Don't hide your original two points, though, because you can use these points to manipulate your figure.

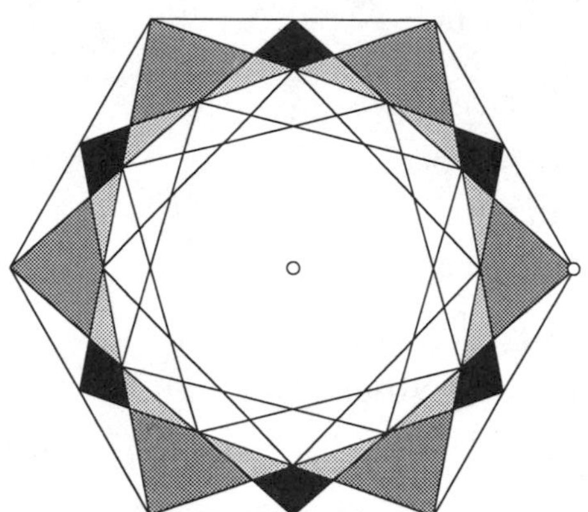

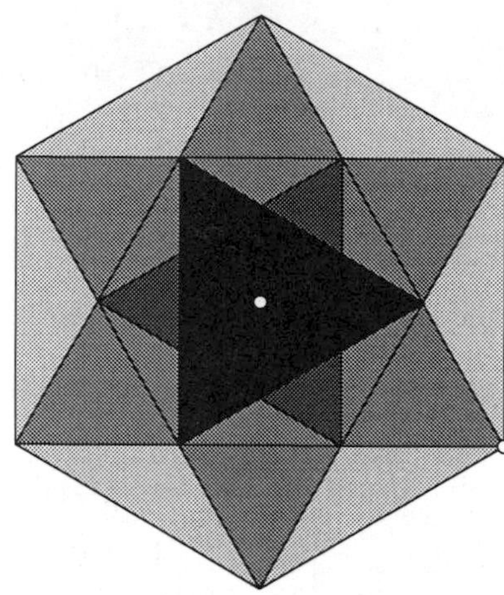

Explore More

For tips on making and using custom tools, choose **Toolbox** from the Help menu, then click on the Custom Tools link.

1. Use the daisy construction to create a custom tool for a regular hexagon. Save the new tool in the Tool Folder (next to the application itself on your hard drive) so it can be used in any open sketch.

© 2002 Key Curriculum Press

Duplicating a Line Segment

Name(s): ____________________

This method for duplicating a line segment with Sketchpad is equivalent to the standard compass-and-straightedge construction. However, Sketchpad's compass (the **Compass** tool) is collapsible, like Euclid's compass, meaning that after you make a circle you can't just pick up the tool, move it somewhere else, and make another circle the same size. As soon as you pick up Euclid's compass (or release the mouse button when you're using Sketchpad's **Compass** tool), you lose your compass setting. Duplicating a segment using only Sketchpad's freehand tools (or Euclid's tools) is more complicated than you'd expect. We'll get around this by using the Construct menu. This construction is the basis for many more complex constructions.

1. Construct $\overline{AB}$. This is your given segment.
2. Construct point *C*. This is one endpoint of your new segment.
3. Select $\overline{AB}$ and point *C*; then, in the Construct menu, choose **Circle By Center+Radius**.
4. Construct $\overline{CD}$, where point *D* is on the circle.
5. Hide the circle.
6. Measure *AB* and *CD*.

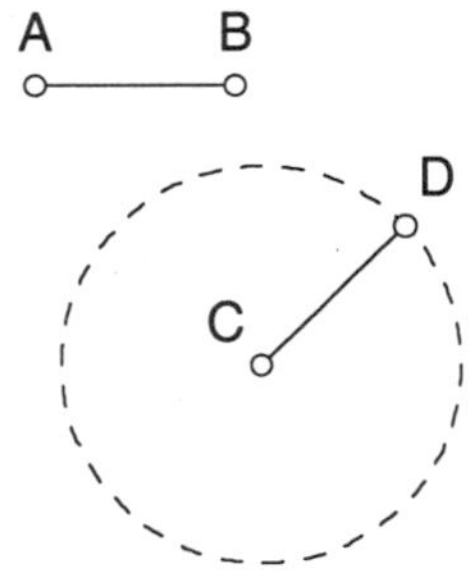

If you start or finish drawing your segment with the tip of the **Segment** tool directly over an object, the object will highlight and Sketchpad will construct an endpoint on that object.

A B D C

Q1 Drag points *C* and *D*. Describe the way each behaves.

Q2 Drag point *A* or point *B*. What effect does changing the length of $\overline{AB}$ have on $\overline{CD}$?

Q3 Write a paragraph describing why this construction works and comparing it to the way you would duplicate a segment using a compass and straightedge. In your paragraph, explain why it is necessary to use the command **Circle By Center+Radius** instead of using Sketchpad's **Compass** tool. (In other words, explain what you can do with an actual compass that you can't do with Sketchpad's compass.) Use a separate sheet, if necessary.

© 2002 Key Curriculum Press

Duplicating an Angle

Name(s): ______________________

In this activity, you'll learn how to duplicate a given angle. The method described is equivalent to the method you would use with a compass and straightedge. You might want to follow the first few steps, then try to figure out the rest on your own.

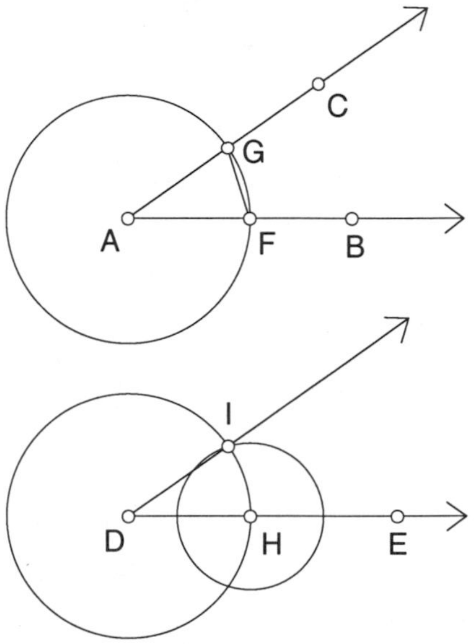

1. Construct $\overrightarrow{AB}$ and $\overrightarrow{AC}$. (This is your given angle.)
2. Below $\angle CAB$, construct $\overrightarrow{DE}$, one side of a new angle.
3. Construct circle *AF*, with point *F* on $\overrightarrow{AB}$.
4. Construct $\overline{AF}$ overlapping $\overrightarrow{AB}$.
5. Construct $\overline{FG}$, where point *G* is the point of intersection of the circle and $\overrightarrow{AC}$.
6. Construct a circle with center *D* and radius equal to *AF*.

Select the point and the segment; then, in the Construct menu, choose **Circle By Center+Radius**.

7. Construct *H*, the point of intersection of this circle with $\overrightarrow{DE}$.
8. Construct a circle with center *H* and radius equal to *FG*.
9. Construct $\overrightarrow{DI}$, where point *I* is the point of intersection of these two circles.
10. If you wish, hide the circles, the segments, and points *H*, *F*, and *G*.
11. Drag point *A*, *B*, *C*, *D*, or *E* and observe how the angles behave. Measure the angles to confirm your observations.

Q1 Explain why this construction works the way it does.

Explore More

1. Here's an easier way to duplicate an angle using the Transform menu instead of Euclidean tools: Construct rays *AB* and *AC* to construct $\angle CAB$. Select, in order, points *B*, *A*, and C; then, in the Transform menu, choose **Mark Angle**. Construct $\overrightarrow{DE}$. Mark point *D* as center and rotate the ray by the marked angle.

© 2002 Key Curriculum Press

Angles Formed by Intersecting Lines

Name(s): ______________________

When two lines intersect, they form four angles. The point of intersection of the lines is the vertex of all four angles. In this activity, you'll investigate relationships between pairs of these angles.

Sketch and Investigate

1. Construct $\overleftrightarrow{AB}$ and $\overleftrightarrow{CD}$ so that they intersect.

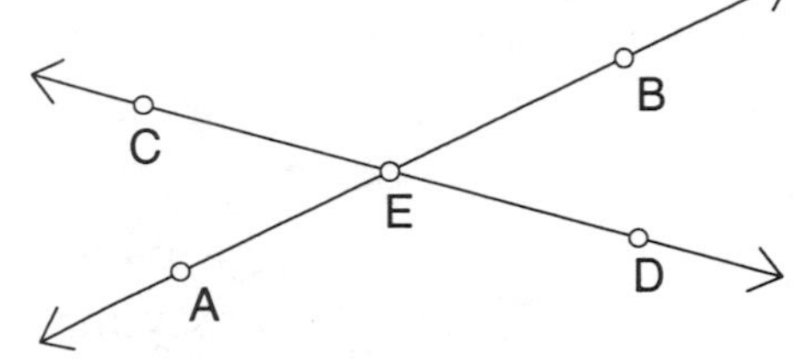

2. Construct point E where the lines intersect.

To measure an angle, select three points, with the vertex your middle selection. Then, in the Measure menu, choose **Angle**.

3. Measure the four angles $\angle DEB$, $\angle BEC$, $\angle CEA$, and $\angle AED$.

4. Drag points B and C and look for relationships among the angle measures. Make sure to keep point E between points A and B and between points C and D.

Q1 In your sketch, $\angle DEB$ and $\angle CEA$ are a pair of *vertical angles.*

a. Name another pair of vertical angles.

b. Write a conjecture about the measures of vertical angles.

Q2 In your sketch, $\angle CEB$ and $\angle DEB$ are a *linear pair* because two of their sides form a line.

a. Find and name all the other linear pairs in your sketch.

Choose **Calculate** from the Measure menu to open the Calculator. Click once on a measurement to enter it into a calculation.

b. Write a conjecture about the relationship between angles in a linear pair. Use the Calculator to test your conjecture.

Q3 Drag a point in your sketch until the angles in a linear pair are congruent. Describe all four angles.

© 2002 Key Curriculum Press

Select three angle measurements; then choose **Edit | Action Button | Hide/Show**.

5. Make a Hide/Show button for three of the four angles.
6. Press the new button (in other words, click on it). It should hide the three angle measures.

Q4 Drag a point so that the one visible angle measure is 63°. Find the measures of the other three angles without looking. Write your guess below, then press the button to check your guess.

7. Test yourself a few more times for practice: Hide the angle measures, drag to change the angles, guess at the hidden angle measures, then check your guess.

Explore More

1. Suppose you had three lines intersecting in a single point to form six angles.
   a. How many angle measures would you need to know in order to find the other angle measures?
   b. Describe any situations in which all the angles are congruent.
2. Suppose you have four lines intersecting in a single point to form eight angles. Answer parts a and b from Explore More 1, above, for this different case.
3. Now generalize your results from the last two questions. Suppose you had n lines intersecting to form $2n$ angles. Answer parts a and b from Explore More 1, above, for this general case.

© 2002 Key Curriculum Press

Properties of Parallel Lines

Name(s): ____________________

In this investigation, you'll discover relationships among the angles formed when parallel lines are intersected by a third line, called a *transversal.*

Sketch and Investigate

1. Construct $\overleftrightarrow{AB}$ and point *C*, not on $\overleftrightarrow{AB}$.

Select the line and the point; then, in the Construct menu, choose **Parallel Line**.

2. Construct a line parallel to $\overleftrightarrow{AB}$ through point *C*.
3. Construct $\overleftrightarrow{CA}$. Drag points *C* and *A* to make sure the three lines are attached at those points.

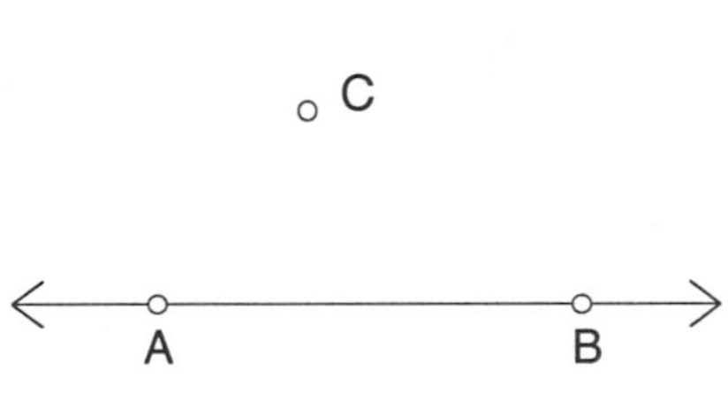

Step 1

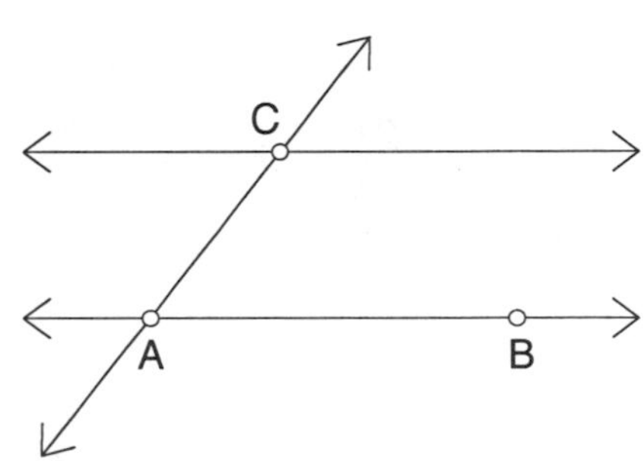

Steps 2 and 3

Using the **Text** tool, click once on a point to show its label. Double-click the label to change it.

4. Construct points *D, E, F, G,* and *H* as shown at right.

To measure an angle, select three points, with the vertex your middle selection. Then, in the Measure menu, choose **Angle**.

5. Measure the eight angles in your figure. Be systematic about your measuring to be sure you don't measure the same angle twice.
6. Drag point *A* or *B* and see which angles stay congruent. Also drag the transversal $\overleftrightarrow{CA}$. (Be careful not to change the point order on your lines. That would change some angles into other angles.) Observe how many of the eight angles you measured appear to be always congruent.

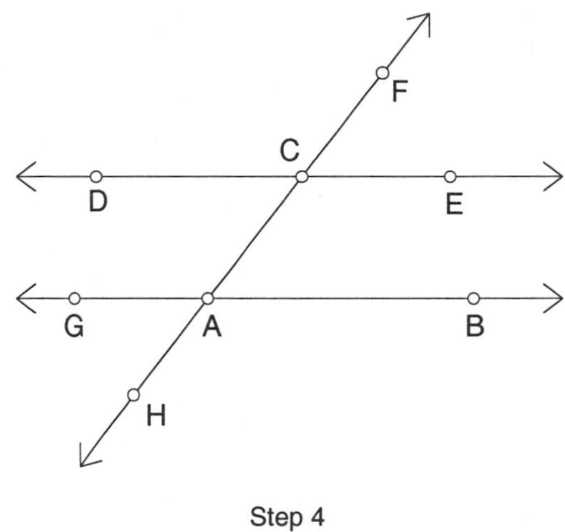

Step 4

Q1 When two parallel lines are crossed by a transversal, the pairs of angles formed have specific names and properties. The chart on the next page shows one example of each type of angle pair. Fill in the chart with a second angle pair of each type, then state what relationship, if any, you observe between the angles in a pair type.

© 2002 Key Curriculum Press

Properties of Parallel Lines (continued)

Angle Type	Pair 1	Pair 2	Relationship
Corresponding	$\angle FCE$ and $\angle CAB$		
Alternate interior	$\angle ECA$ and $\angle CAG$		
Alternate exterior	$\angle FCE$ and $\angle HAG$		
Same-side interior	$\angle ECA$ and $\angle BAC$		
Same-side exterior	$\angle FCD$ and $\angle HAG$		

Q2 One of the angle types has more than one pair. Name that angle type in the chart below, and name the third and fourth pairs of angles of that type.

Angle Type	Pair 3	Pair 4	Relationship

7. Next, you'll investigate the converses of your conjectures. In a new sketch, draw two lines that are not quite parallel. Construct a transversal.

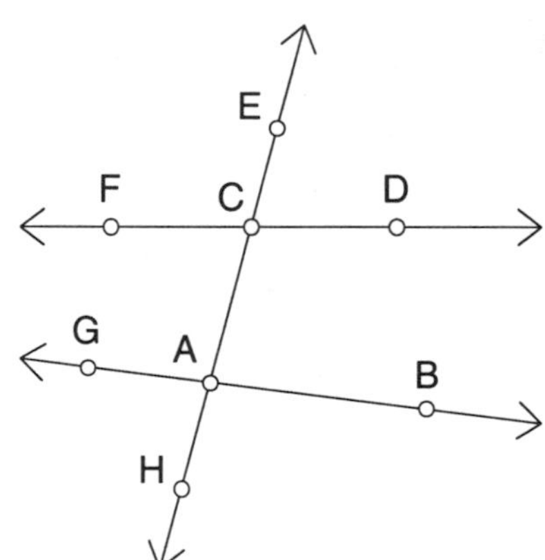

8. Add points as needed, then measure all eight angles formed by the three lines.

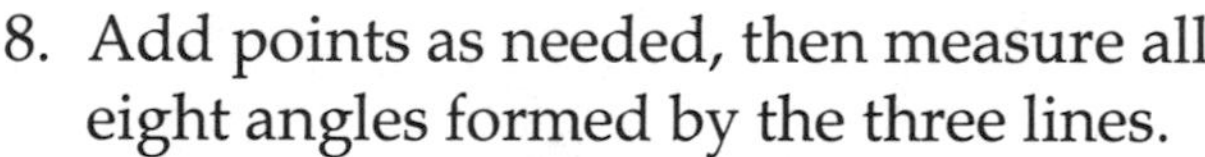

9. Move the lines until you have two sets of four congruent angles.

Q3 If two lines are crossed by a transversal so that corresponding angles, alternate interior angles, and alternate exterior angles are congruent, what can you say about the lines?

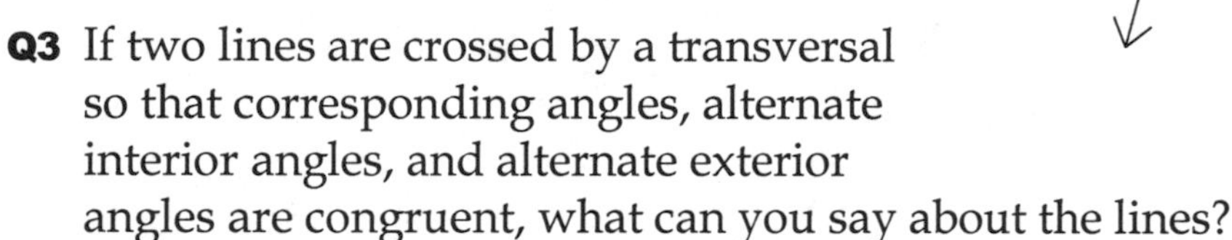

Explore More

1. You can use the converse of the parallel-lines conjecture to construct parallel lines. Construct a pair of intersecting lines $\overleftrightarrow{AB}$ and $\overleftrightarrow{AC}$ as shown. Select, in order, points *C*, *A*, and *B*. Then, in the Transform menu, choose **Mark Angle**. Double-click point *C* to mark it as a center for rotation. You figure out the rest. Explain why this method works.

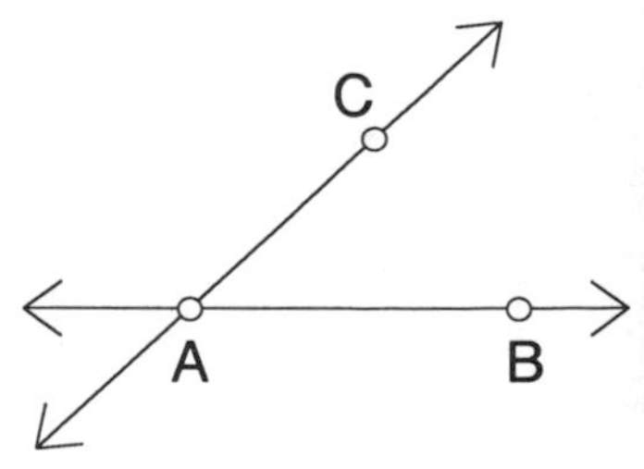

© 2002 Key Curriculum Press

Constructing a Perpendicular Bisector **Name(s):** ____________

In this activity, you'll use only Sketchpad's freehand tools to construct perpendicular bisectors. Then you'll investigate properties of perpendicular bisectors. In Explore More, you'll devise a shortcut for constructing a perpendicular bisector using Sketchpad's Construct menu.

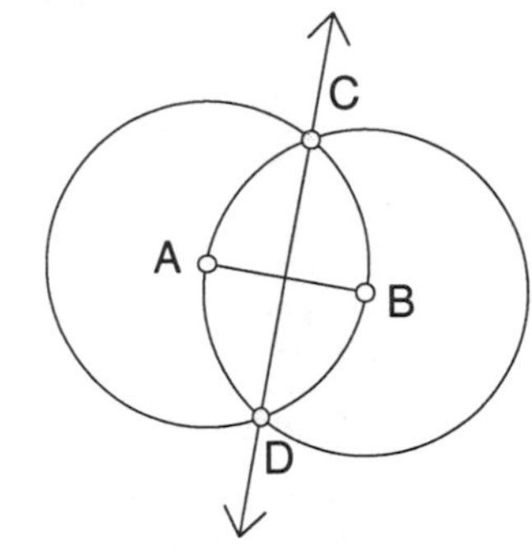

1. Construct $\overline{AB}$.
2. Construct circle *AB*. (Make sure you use point *A* for the center and point *B* for the radius endpoint.)
3. Construct circle *BA*. (Use point *B* for the center and point *A* for the radius point.)

Press and hold down the mouse button on the current **Straightedge** tool, then drag to choose the **Line** tool.

4. Construct $\overleftrightarrow{CD}$, where *C* and *D* are the circles' points of intersection.
5. Drag points *A* and *B* to make sure your construction stays together.

Q1 Line *CD* is the perpendicular bisector of $\overline{AB}$. Without measuring, what can you say about the distances *AC* and *BC* and the distances *AD* and *BD*?

6. Construct *E*, the point of intersection of $\overline{AB}$ and $\overleftrightarrow{CD}$.

Q2 What's special about point *E*? Move points *A* and *B* to confirm your answer.

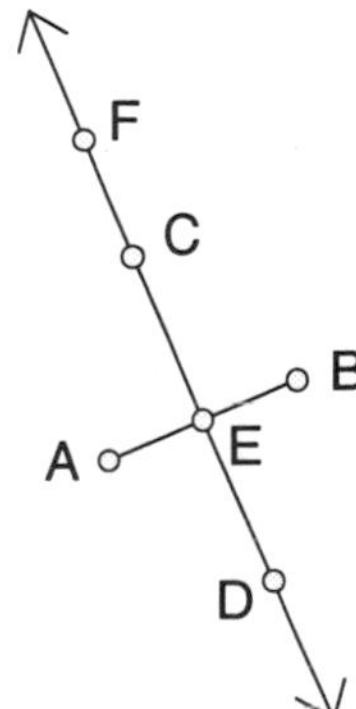

7. Hide the circles.
8. Construct a point *F* on $\overleftrightarrow{CD}$.

To measure a distance, select two points; then, in the Measure menu, choose **Distance**.

9. Measure the distances *FA* and *FB*.

Q3 Drag point *F* up and down the line. Make a conjecture about any point on a segment's perpendicular bisector.

Explore More

For tips on making and using custom tools, choose **Toolbox** from the Help menu, then click on the Custom Tools link.

1. In a new sketch, construct a segment. Figure out how to construct the perpendicular bisector of the segment using the Construct menu. When you've succeeded, make a custom tool and save it in the Tool Folder (next to the application itself on your hard drive). Write a description of the way you did the construction.

© 2002 Key Curriculum Press

The Slope of a Line

Name(s): ______________________

If you are a skier, you might describe the slope of a ski hill. If you are a carpenter, you might describe the slope of a roof you built. An economist might describe the slope of a graph. In this activity, you'll discover how to recognize the slopes of various lines. You will also play a game, with a partner, that challenges you to recognize various slopes.

Sketch and Investigate

Hold the mouse button down on the **Segment** tool to show the **Straightedge** tool palette. Drag right to choose the **Line** tool.

Select the line; then, in the Measure menu, choose **Slope**.

Slope $\overleftrightarrow{AB}$ = -1.82

1. In Preferences, set Distance Units to **cm**.
2. In the Graph menu, choose **Show Grid**.
3. Draw any line.
4. Measure its slope.
5. Drag one of the line's control points and observe the effect on the line's slope.
6. Drag the line itself and observe the effect on its slope.

Q1 Continue to change the slope of your line. Investigate the following questions to prepare yourself for the Slope Game:

a. Which lines have a positive slope and which have a negative slope?

b. What is the slope of a horizontal line?

c. How can you tell a steeper slope from a shallower slope?

d. What is the slope of a vertical line?

© 2002 Key Curriculum Press

Playing the Slope Game

Play this game with a partner.

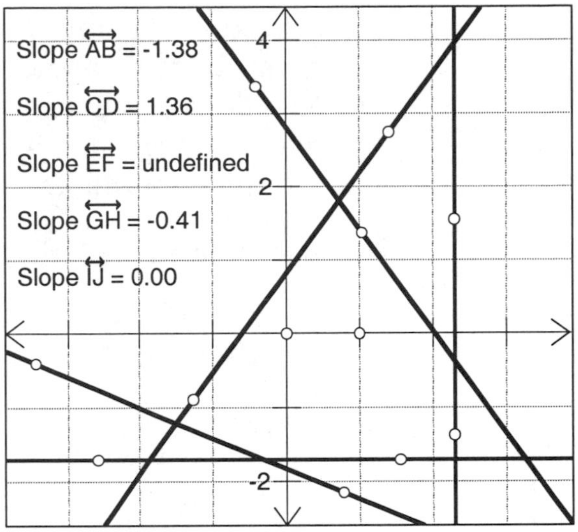

7. Draw five different random lines in your sketch. Make sure their labels are not showing.

Choose the **Line** tool. In the Edit menu, choose **Select All Lines**. Now you can measure all the slopes at once.

8. Measure the slopes of the five lines.

9. Challenge your partner to match each measured slope with a line. Your partner is allowed to drag only measurements, to move them next to the lines they match. The lines and the points are off limits until all the measurements have been matched up with lines.

Click in a blank area to make sure nothing is selected, then choose the **Point** tool. In the Edit menu, choose **Select All Points**. Then, in the Display menu, choose **Show Labels**.

10. To check how you scored, show all the point labels. Award one point for each correctly matched slope.

11. Switch roles, scramble the lines, and play the game again. Add a few more lines to make the game more challenging. Measure the slopes of the new lines.

Q2 Record your scores on a separate sheet.

Explore More

1. The *rise* of a sloped roof is the vertical distance between its lowest point and its highest point. The *run* is the horizontal distance between the lowest and highest points. Carpenters describe the slope of a roof by comparing the rise and the run. Sketch a scale drawing of a two-sided slanted roof that has a rise of 2 and a run of 3. Calculate the slopes of the two sides of the roof.

2. You will not always need to rely on a computer to measure slopes. Experiment with the sketch **Slope of a Line.gsp**. Calculate the slope of the line using the x- and y-coordinates shown in the sketch. Drag points in the sketch to see how they affect your calculation. Check your calculation by measuring the slope of the line. Explain how you calculated the slope.

© 2002 Key Curriculum Press

Equations of Lines

Name(s): ______________________

There are many ways of describing a line. You can describe a line as a straight path that extends forever. You can also describe a line as a collection of points that follow a certain rule. Since you often designate points by their *x*- and *y*-coordinates, your rule for a line can be an equation containing the variables *x* and *y*. Equations like these—called *linear equations* because they represent lines—have many forms. In this activity, you will investigate linear equations.

Sketch and Investigate

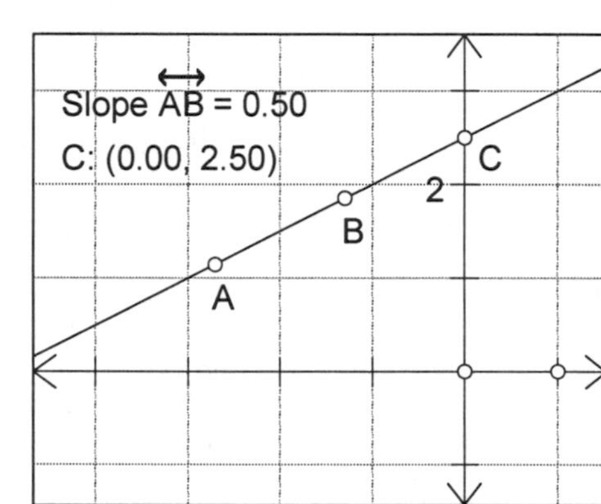

1. In the Graph menu, choose **Show Grid**.
2. Draw a line (not a segment) *AB* so that neither point *A* nor point *B* lies on an axis.
3. Construct point *C* where $\overleftrightarrow{AB}$ intersects the *y*-axis.
4. Measure the slope of the line.

   > Select the line; then, in the Measure menu, choose **Slope**.

5. Drag point *A* or point *B* and observe how this changes the line's slope.
6. Measure the coordinates of point *C* on the *y*-axis. The *y*-coordinate of this point is called the *y-intercept* of the line.

   > Select point *C*; then, in the Measure menu, choose **Coordinates**.

7. Measure the line's equation.

   > Select the line; then, in the Measure menu, choose **Equation**.

8. Drag points *A* and *B* and the line itself, and observe your three measurements.

Q1 A linear equation is in slope-intercept form if it looks like this:

$$y = mx + b$$

where *m* and *b* are specific values. Describe what *m* and *b* represent, using observations from your sketch.

9. Select the equation and make a Hide/Show action button.

   > With the equation selected, choose **Edit | Action Buttons | Hide/Show**.

   Hide Linear Equation

10. Press the button several times to see how it works. Leave the equation hidden when you're done.

© 2002 Key Curriculum Press

Equations of Lines (continued)

Q2 Drag your line into a new position and predict its new equation. Write your prediction in the chart below. Press the *Show linear equation* button to test your prediction. Check the Correct Equation box in the chart if your prediction was correct. If your prediction was off, write the correct equation in the box. Do this at least two more times.

Prediction	Correct Equation (or √)

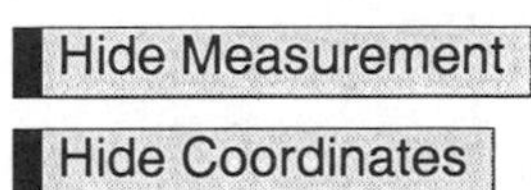

11. Make a Hide/Show button for the slope measurement and another Hide/Show button for the coordinates of point *C*. Make sure point *C* is on the y-axis. Drag the line into a new position and predict its new equation with all three measurements hidden. If you're stuck, give yourself hints by showing only one measurement at a time. Continue this process with new lines until you can figure out the equation of a line when no measurements at all are showing.

Q3 Describe how you can estimate the equation of a line when you're not given any measurements.

Explore More

1. Suppose a pair of parallel lines have y-intercepts that are two units apart. Does this mean that the lines are two units apart from each other? Construct such a pair of lines to investigate this question. Explain how the distance between these parallel lines depends on their slopes.

© 2002 Key Curriculum Press

Slopes of Parallel and Perpendicular Lines

Name(s): ____________________

In this investigation, you'll learn how you can use slope to tell whether lines are parallel or perpendicular.

Sketch and Investigate

Choose **Preferences** from the Edit menu and go to the Units panel.

1. In Preferences, set Angle Precision to **tenths** and Scalar Precision to **hundredths**.

2. Construct $\overleftrightarrow{AB}$ and $\overleftrightarrow{CD}$ and their point of intersection, E.

Select, in order, points *A*, *E*, and *C*; then, in the Measure menu, choose **Angle**.

3. Measure $\angle AEC$.
4. Measure the slopes of $\overleftrightarrow{AB}$ and $\overleftrightarrow{CD}$.

While holding down the Shift key, choose **Hide Coordinate System** from the Graph menu.

5. Hide the coordinate system that appeared when measuring the slopes.
6. Drag point A and observe the slope measures.

Q1 Make the slopes as close to equal as you can. What do you observe about the measure of the angle between the lines?

Q2 If you get the slopes close enough to equal, the angle measure will actually disappear. Why do you think that happens? (*Hint:* The vertex of this angle is the point of intersection of the two lines.)

Q3 Write a conjecture about lines with equal slopes.

Choose **Calculate** from the Measure menu to open the Calculator. Click on a measurement to enter it into a calculation.

7. Calculate the product of the slopes of $\overleftrightarrow{AB}$ and $\overleftrightarrow{CD}$.
8. Make sure that neither line is horizontal. Drag points to make $m\angle AEC$ as close to 90° as you can.

Q4 What is the product of the slopes of perpendicular lines? ____________

Q5 Why is this product always negative?

Q6 The product of the slopes of two lines is undefined if one of the lines is vertical. Why?

© 2002 Key Curriculum Press

Distance from a Point to a Line

Name(s): ______________

Measuring the distance between two points is easy, but how do you measure the distance between a point and a line? There are many different distances, depending on what point you measure to on the line. What's the shortest distance? That's what you'll investigate in this activity.

1. Construct $\overleftrightarrow{AB}$.
2. Construct point C not on $\overleftrightarrow{AB}$.
3. Construct $\overline{CD}$, where point D is on $\overleftrightarrow{AB}$.

Select $\overline{CD}$; then, in the Measure menu, choose **Length**.

4. Measure CD.
5. Drag point D back and forth along the line and observe where CD becomes great and where it becomes small.
6. Locate point D to make CD as small as you can.

Select point C and $\overleftrightarrow{AB}$; then, in the Measure menu, choose **Distance**.

7. Measure the distance from point C to $\overleftrightarrow{AB}$.

Q1 How does CD compare to the distance from C to $\overleftrightarrow{AB}$?

Q2 How does $\overline{CD}$ seem to be related to $\overleftrightarrow{AB}$?

Select, in order, points C, D, and B. Then, in the Measure menu, choose **Angle**.

8. Measure $\angle CDB$ to confirm your conjecture in question Q2.

Q3 How would you define the distance from a point to a line?

Explore More

1. Model this problem in Sketchpad:

   There's a sewage treatment plant at the point where two rivers meet. You want to build a house near the two rivers (upstream from the sewage plant, naturally), but you want the house to be at least 5 miles from the sewage plant. You visit each of the rivers to go fishing about the same number of times, but, being lazy, you want to minimize the amount of walking you do. (You want the sum of the distances from your house to the two rivers to be minimal.) Where should you build your house?

© 2002 Key Curriculum Press

Angle Bisectors

Name(s): ____________________

An *angle bisector* is a ray that has its endpoint at the vertex of the angle and that divides the angle into two angles of equal measure. In this investigation, you'll investigate a special property of points on an angle bisector.

Press and hold down the mouse button on the current **Straightedge** tool. Drag to choose the **Ray** tool.

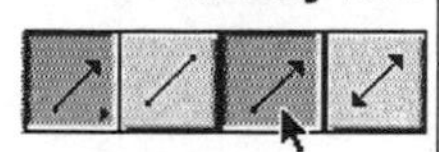

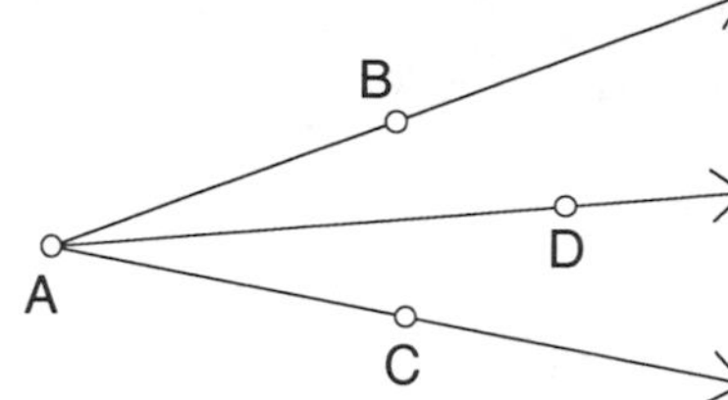

1. Construct $\overrightarrow{AB}$ and $\overrightarrow{AC}$ to form $\angle BAC$.
2. Construct the bisector of $\angle BAC$.
3. Drag point B and observe the angle bisector.
4. Construct point D on the angle bisector.

Select, in order, points *B*, *A*, and *C*; then, in the Construct menu, choose **Angle Bisector**.

Q1 Drag point D. Without measuring, make a guess about the distances from point D to each of the angle's two sides.

Select point *D* and $\overrightarrow{AB}$; then, in the Measure menu, choose **Distance**.

5. Measure the distance from point D to $\overrightarrow{AB}$.
6. Measure the distance from point D to $\overrightarrow{AC}$.
7. Measure angles BAD and DAC.

Select three points that name the angle, with the vertex your second selection; then, in the Measure menu, choose **Angle**.

Q2 Drag point A, B, or C to change $\angle BAC$. How do the measures of angles BAD and DAC compare?

Q3 Drag point D and observe the distances from point D to the two sides of the angle. Write a conjecture about any point on an angle bisector.

Explore More

1. In a new sketch, draw rays AB and AC. Mark $\overrightarrow{AC}$ as a mirror. Reflect $\overrightarrow{AB}$. Drag different points in your sketch. How are $\overrightarrow{AB}$ and $\overrightarrow{AC}$ related?
2. In a new sketch, see if you can construct an angle bisector using only Sketchpad's freehand tools—not the menus. Make a custom tool for this construction and save it in the Tool Folder (next to the application itself on your hard drive).
3. Write the converse of your conjecture in Q3. Is the converse true? Demonstrate the converse with Sketchpad and explain what you did.

For tips on making and using custom tools, choose **Toolbox** from the Help menu, then click on the Custom Tools link.

© 2002 Key Curriculum Press

Trisecting an Angle

Name(s): ______________________

Trisecting an angle with a compass and straightedge is a construction problem that has occupied professional and amateur mathematicians for centuries. Even though it has been proven that the construction can't be done, countless people still think they've found a solution. Others enjoy slightly bending the rules that govern compass-and-straightedge constructions to devise simple angle-trisection methods. It is possible to trisect an angle using Sketchpad, because you can rotate by marked measures and calculations.

Sketch and Investigate

Choose **Preferences** from the Edit menu and go to the Units panel.

1. In Preferences, set Angle Units to **directed degrees**.

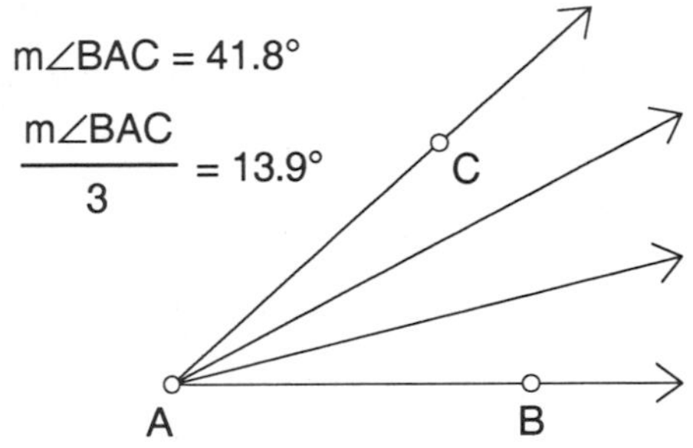

2. Construct $\overrightarrow{AB}$ and $\overrightarrow{AC}$ as shown to form the angle you will trisect.

Select, in order, points *B*, *A*, and *C*; then, in the Measure menu, choose **Angle**.

3. Measure $\angle BAC$.

Choose **Calculate** from the Measure menu to open the Calculator. Click on a measurement to enter it into a calculation.

4. Calculate $m\angle BAC/3$.

m∠BAC = 41.8°

$\frac{m\angle BAC}{3} = 13.9°$

C

A

B

5. Select the calculation; then, in the Transform menu, choose **Mark Angle**.

6. Double-click point *A* to mark it as a center of rotation.

Select $\overrightarrow{AB}$; then, in the Transform menu, choose **Rotate**.

7. Rotate $\overrightarrow{AB}$ by the marked angle.

8. Rotate this new ray again by the marked angle.

Q1 Drag points on the angle and observe the behavior of the trisectors. Explain why they remain trisectors.

Your construction method was similar to what you could do with a protractor. Because you used the angle's measure to trisect it, this method doesn't qualify as a compass-and-straightedge construction. Constructions using only the freehand tools and the Construct menu would be equivalent to compass-and-straightedge constructions.

Explore More

1. Draw a triangle with extended sides using the **Line** tool. Trisect the three interior angles. Find an interesting shape formed by intersecting trisectors.

© 2002 Key Curriculum Press

Drawing a Box with Two-Point Perspective

Name(s): ______________________

Even though a piece of paper or a computer screen is flat, you can draw figures that appear three-dimensional on these two-dimensional surfaces by using perspective drawing. In three dimensions, objects that are farther away appear smaller. Perspective drawing takes advantage of this principle to make flat drawings appear to have depth.

Follow these steps to draw a box with two-point perspective. Labels are shown to clarify these directions, but you probably won't want labels on your drawing.

It's easier to draw a horizontal or vertical line if you hold down the Shift key while you draw.

1. Draw a long horizontal line segment *AB*. This will be your *horizon line*, and its endpoints will be the *vanishing points* of your perspective box.

Line Width is in the Display menu.

2. Draw a short vertical segment *CD* below your horizon line. This will be the front edge of your box. Change its line width to dashed.
3. Construct $\overline{CA}$, $\overline{DA}$, $\overline{CB}$, and $\overline{DB}$.

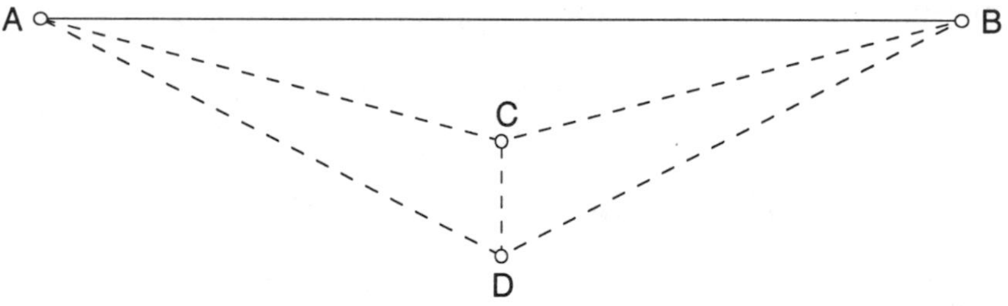

4. Construct point *E* on $\overline{DA}$ and point *F* on $\overline{DB}$.

Select $\overline{CD}$ and points *E* and *F*; then, in the Construct menu, choose **Parallel Lines**. You should get both parallel lines at once.

5. Through points *E* and *F*, construct lines parallel to $\overline{CD}$.
6. Construct $\overline{GB}$ and $\overline{HA}$, where points *G* and *H* are the points where the parallel lines intersect $\overline{CA}$ and $\overline{CB}$.
7. Construct point *I* at the point of intersection of $\overline{GB}$ and $\overline{HA}$.

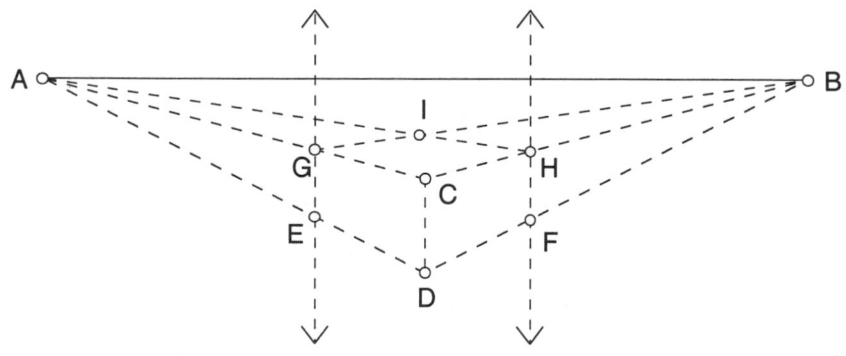

© 2002 Key Curriculum Press

8. Change the line width of $\overline{CD}$ to thick, then complete the box by constructing $\overline{GI}$, $\overline{IH}$, $\overline{HF}$, $\overline{FD}$, $\overline{DE}$, $\overline{EG}$, $\overline{GC}$, and $\overline{CH}$.

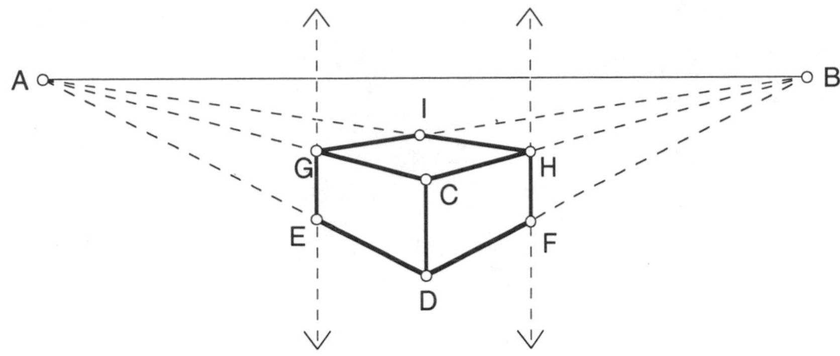

9. Hide all the dashed lines and segments to leave just your box and the horizon line.

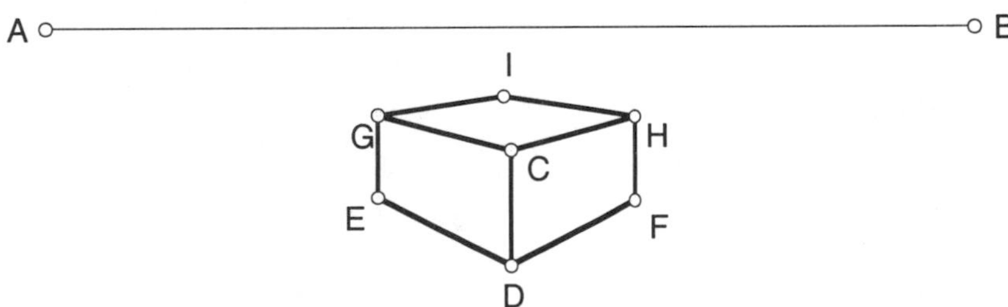

10. Try moving various parts of your box, your horizon segment, and the vanishing points. If you move the front edge of your box above the horizon segment, you'll discover that you haven't created the bottom of your box. Continue sketching to construct the missing edges as shown. (*Hint:* Start by constructing a dashed segment from point *E* to point *B*.)

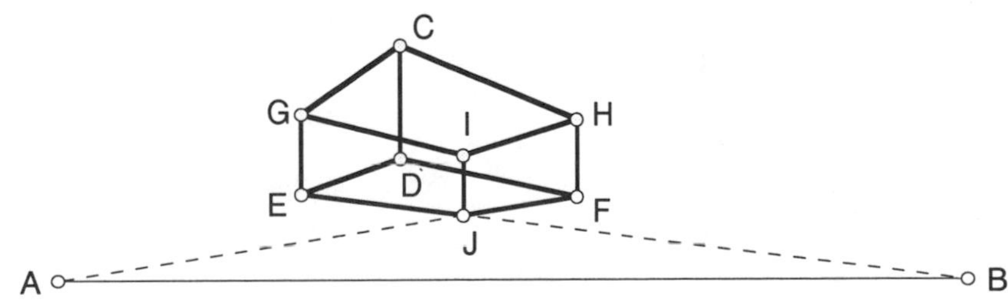

11. Hide unwanted points and segments.

© 2002 Key Curriculum Press

2

Transformations, Symmetry, and Tessellations

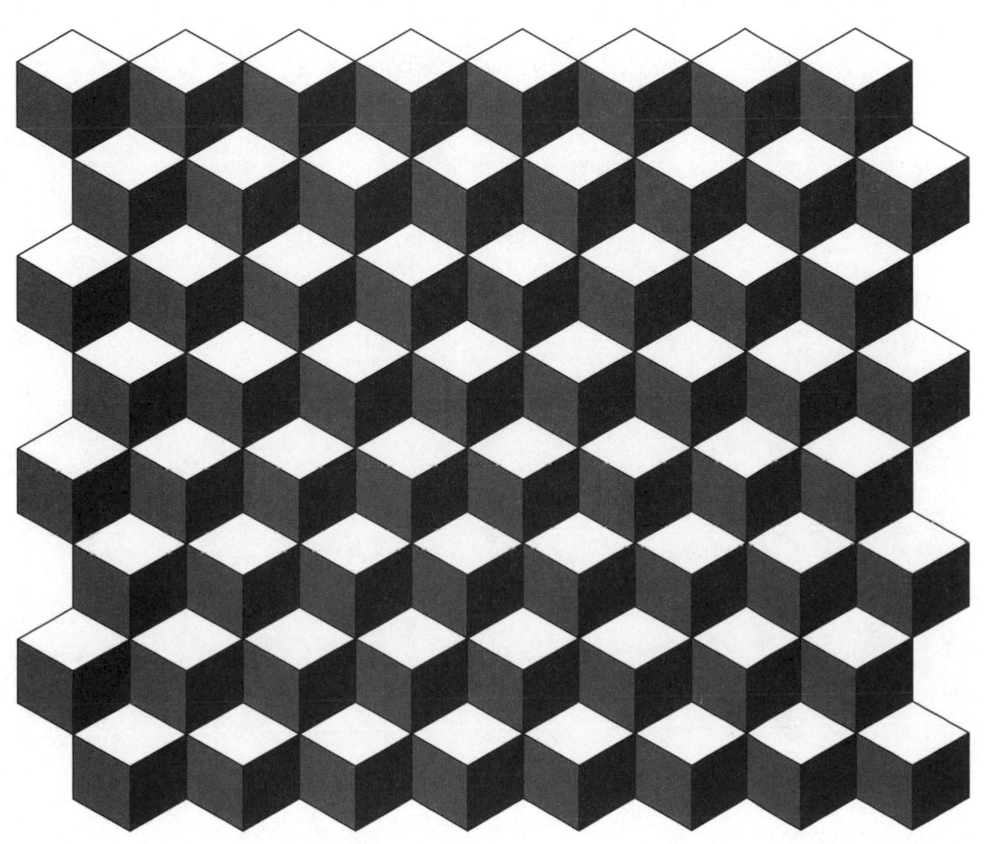

Introducing Transformations

Name(s): ____________________

A *transformation* is a way of moving or changing a figure. There are three types of basic transformations that preserve the size and shape of the figure. These three, *reflections, rotations,* and *translations,* are called *isometries.* Isometries flip, turn, or slide a figure but never bend or distort it. In this activity, you'll experiment with basic isometries by transforming a flag-shaped polygon. (You'll use this shape because it's easy to keep track of where it's pointing.)

Hold down the Shift key as you create points so they'll stay selected as you create new ones. Then choose **Pentagon Interior** from the Construct menu.

Sketch and Investigate: Translations

1. Construct the vertices of a flag shape and construct its interior.

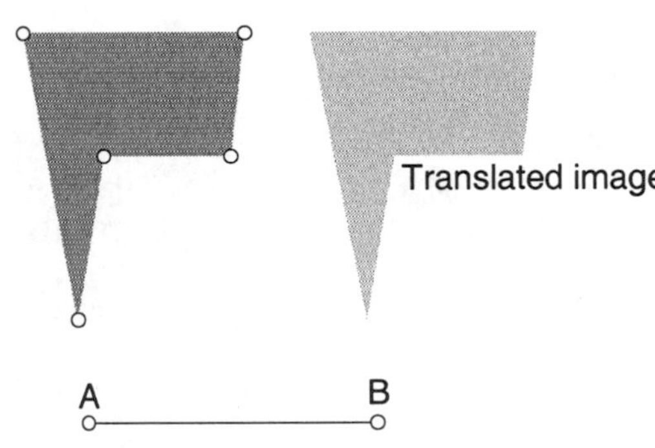

A brief animation indicates that you've marked a vector. Nothing else will happen in your sketch yet.

2. In order to translate a shape, you need to indicate a direction and a distance. To do this, construct segment *AB*. Then select, in order, point *A* and point *B*. In the Transform menu, choose **Mark Vector**.
3. Select the interior of the flag; then, in the Transform menu, choose **Translate**. Make sure By Marked Vector is checked in the Translate dialog box, then click Translate.

With the interior selected, choose a color from the Color submenu of the Display menu.

4. Change the color of the translated image.

Double-click the polygon interior with the **Text** tool to edit its label.

5. Label the translated polygon *Translated image*.
6. Drag point *B* to change your vector, and observe the relationship between the translated image and the original figure.

Q1 Compare the translated image to the original figure. How are they different and how are they the same?

© 2002 Key Curriculum Press

Sketch and Investigate: Rotations

7. In order to rotate a shape, you need to indicate a center of rotation and an angle of rotation. Start by creating angle *ECD* using two attached segments, as indicated at right.

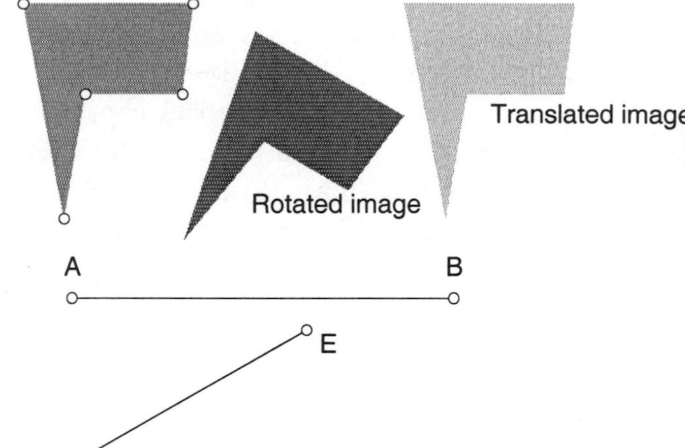

Double-click the point to mark it as a center. → 8. Mark point *C* as a center of rotation.

Select, in order, points *E*, *C*, and *D*. Then choose **Mark Angle** from the Transform menu. → 9. Mark ∠*ECD* as an angle of rotation.

Select the interior. Then choose **Rotate** from the Transform menu. → 10. Rotate the original flag-shaped interior by the marked angle.

11. Change the color of the rotated image and label it *Rotated image*.

12. Drag point *D* to change your angle, and observe the relationship between the rotated image and the original figure.

Q2 Compare the rotated image to the original figure. How are they different and how are they the same?

Sketch and Investigate: Reflections

13. To reflect a shape, you need a *mirror line* (also called a *line of reflection*). Draw a line and label it *Mirror line*.

Double-click the line to mark it as a mirror. → 14. Mark the line as a mirror.

Select the interior and choose **Reflect** from—you guessed it—the Transform menu. → 15. Reflect the original flag-shaped interior. Your image may end up off the screen. If so, move the original figure closer to the mirror line.

16. Change the color of the reflected image. Label it *Reflected image*.

17. Drag your mirror line, and observe the relationship between the reflected image and the original figure.

© 2002 Key Curriculum Press

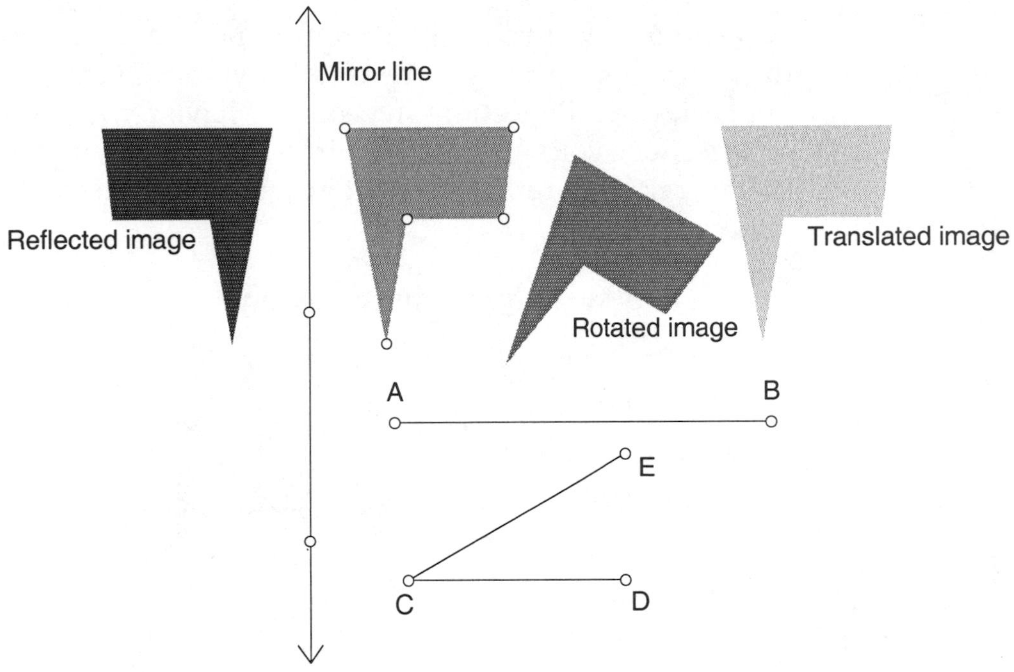

Q3 Compare the reflected image to the original figure. How are they different and how are they the same?

Q4 Explain whether it is possible for any of the three images in your sketch to lie directly on top of one another. Experiment by dragging different parts of your sketch.

Explore More

1. Use reflections, rotations, translations, or combinations of these transformations to make a design.
2. Reflect a figure over a line, then reflect the image over a second line that intersects the first. What single transformation would take your original figure to the second reflected image?
3. Reflect a figure over a line, then reflect the image over a second line that is parallel to the first. What single transformation is the same as this combination of two reflections?

© 2002 Key Curriculum Press

Properties of Reflection

Name(s): ______________________

When you look at yourself in a mirror, how far away does your image in the mirror appear to be? Why is it that your reflection looks just like you, but backward? Reflections in geometry have some of the same properties of reflections you observe in a mirror. In this activity, you'll investigate the properties of reflections that make a reflection the "mirror image" of the original.

Sketch and Investigate: Mirror Writing

1. Construct vertical line *AB*.

2. Construct point *C* to the right of the line.

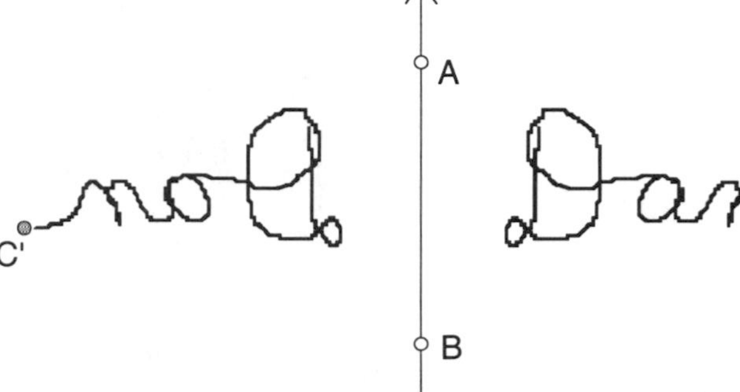

Double-click on the line.

3. Mark $\overleftrightarrow{AB}$ as a mirror.

4. Reflect point *C* to construct point *C*′.

Select the two points; then, in the Display menu, choose **Trace Points**. A check mark indicates that the command is turned on. Choose **Erase Traces** when you wish to erase your traces.

5. Turn on **Trace Points** for points *C* and *C*′.

6. Drag point *C* so that it traces out your name.

Q1 What does point *C*′ trace?

7. For a real challenge, try dragging point *C*′ so that point *C* traces out your name.

Sketch and Investigate: Reflecting Geometric Figures

Select points *C* and *C*′. In the Display menu, you'll see **Trace Points** checked. Choose it to uncheck it.

8. Turn off **Trace Points** for points *C* and *C*′.

9. In the Display menu, choose **Erase Traces**.

10. Construct $\triangle CDE$.

Select the entire figure; then, in the Transform menu, choose **Reflect**.

11. Reflect $\triangle CDE$ (sides and vertices) over $\overleftrightarrow{AB}$.

12. Drag different parts of either triangle and observe how the triangles are related. Also drag the mirror line.

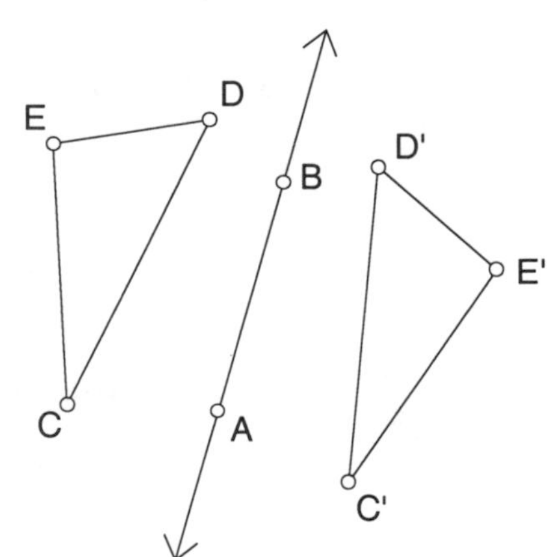

© 2002 Key Curriculum Press

13. Measure the lengths of the sides of triangles *CDE* and *C′D′E′*.

Select three points that name the angle, with the vertex your middle selection. Then, in the Measure menu, choose **Angle**.

14. Measure one angle in Δ*CDE* and measure the corresponding angle in Δ*C′D′E′*.

Q2 What effect does reflection have on lengths and angle measures?

Q3 Are a figure and its mirror image always congruent? State your answer as a conjecture.

Your answer to Q4 demonstrates that a reflection reverses the *orientation* of a figure.

Q4 Going alphabetically from *C* to *D* to *E* in Δ*CDE,* are the vertices oriented in a clockwise or counter-clockwise direction? In what direction (clockwise or counter-clockwise) are vertices *C′*, *D′*, and *E′* oriented in the reflected triangle?

Line Width is in the Display menu.

15. Construct segments connecting each point and its image: *C* to *C′*, *D* to *D′*, and *E* to *E′*. Make these segments dashed.

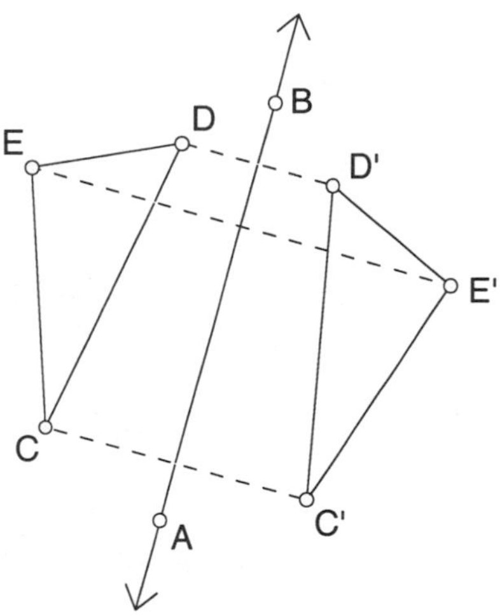

You may wish to construct points of intersection and measure distances to look for relationships between the mirror line and the dashed segments.

16. Drag different parts of the sketch around and observe relationships between the dashed segments and the mirror line.

Q5 How is the mirror line related to a segment connecting a point and its reflected image?

Explore More

1. Suppose Sketchpad didn't have a Transform menu. How could you construct a given point's mirror image over a given line? Try it. Start with a point and a line. Come up with a construction for the reflection of the point over the line using just the tools and the Construct menu. Describe your method.
2. Use a reflection to construct an isosceles triangle. Explain what you did.

© 2002 Key Curriculum Press

Reflections in the Coordinate Plane

Name(s): ______________

In this activity, you'll investigate what happens to the coordinates of points when you reflect them across the x- and y-axes in the coordinate plane.

In the Graph menu, first choose **Show Grid**, then choose **Snap Points**.

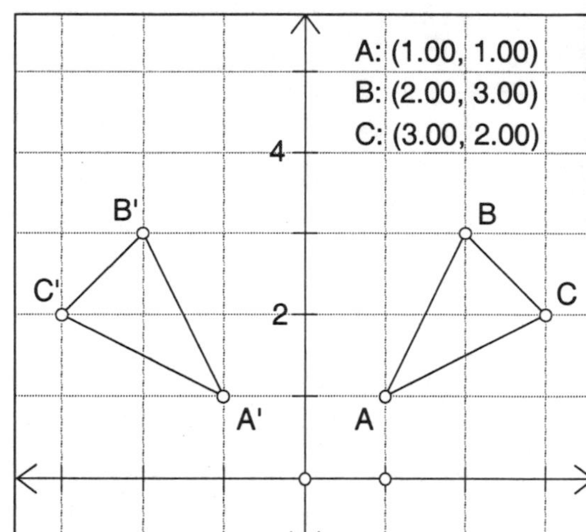

1. Show the grid and turn on point snapping.
2. Draw ΔCDE with vertices on the grid.
3. Measure the coordinates of each vertex.

Double-click the axis to mark it as a mirror.

4. Mark the y-axis as a mirror.

Select the entire figure; then, in the Transform menu, choose **Reflect**.

5. Reflect the triangle.
6. Measure the coordinates of the image's vertices.
7. Drag vertices to different points on the grid and look for a relationship between a point's coordinates and the coordinates of the reflected image across the y-axis.

Q1 Describe any relationship you observe between the coordinates of the vertices of your original triangle and the coordinates of their reflected images across the y-axis.

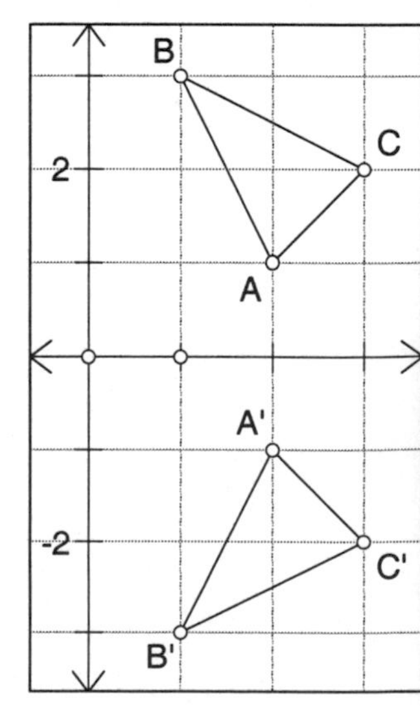

8. Now mark the x-axis as a mirror and reflect your original triangle.
9. Before you measure coordinates, can you guess what they'll be? Measure to confirm.

Q2 Describe any relationship you observe between the coordinates of the original points and the coordinates of their reflected images across the x-axis.

Explore More

1. Draw a line on the grid that passes through the origin and makes a 45° angle with the x-axis (in other words, the line $y = x$). Reflect your triangle across this line. What do you notice about the coordinates of the vertices of this image?

© 2002 Key Curriculum Press

Translations in the Coordinate Plane

Name(s): ______________

In this activity, you'll investigate what happens to the coordinates of points when they're translated in the coordinate plane.

In the Graph menu, first choose **Show Grid**, then choose **Snap Points**.

1. Show the grid and turn on point snapping.

Using the **Text** tool, click on a point to display its label. Double-click the label to change it.

2. Draw a segment from the origin to anywhere on the grid. Label the origin *A* and the other endpoint *B*.

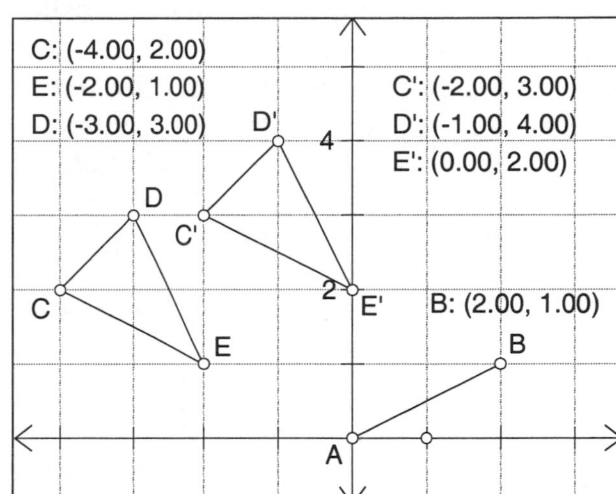

Select point *A* and point *B*, in that order; then, in the Transform menu, choose **Mark Vector**. Watch for the animation indicating the marked vector.

3. Measure the coordinates of point *B*.
4. Mark vector *AB*.
5. Draw $\triangle CDE$ with vertices on the grid.

Select the entire figure; then, in the Transform menu, choose **Translate**.

6. Translate the triangle by the marked vector.
7. Measure the coordinates of the two triangles' six vertices.
8. Experiment by dragging point *B* or any of the triangle vertices. Look for a relationship between a point's coordinates and the coordinates of its image under a translation.

Q1 Where can you drag point *B* so that the original points and the corresponding image points always have the same *y*-coordinates but have different *x*-coordinates?

Q2 Where can you drag point *B* so that the original points and the corresponding image points always have the same *x*-coordinates but have different *y*-coordinates?

Q3 When the vector defined by the origin and point *B* translates your original triangle to the left and up, what must be true of the coordinates of point *B*?

Q4 Suppose point *B* has coordinates (a, b). What are the coordinates of the image of a point (x, y) under a translation by (a, b)?

© 2002 Key Curriculum Press

The Burning Tent Problem

Name(s): ____________________

A camper out for a hike is returning to her campsite. The shortest distance between her and her campsite is along a straight line, but as she approaches her campsite, she sees that her tent is on fire! She must run to the river to fill her canteen, then run to her tent to put out the fire. What's the shortest path she can take? The answer to this question is related to the path a pool ball takes when it bounces off a cushion and the path a ray of light takes when it bounces off a mirror. In this activity, you'll investigate the minimal two-part path that goes from a point to a line and then to another point.

Sketch and Investigate

1. Construct a long horizontal segment *AB* to represent the river.
2. Construct points *C* and *D* on the same side of the segment. Point *C* represents the camper and point *D* represents the tent.
3. Construct $\overline{CE}$ and $\overline{ED}$, where point *E* is any point on $\overline{AB}$. These segments together show a path the camper might take running to the river and then to her tent.
4. Measure the lengths of $\overline{CE}$ and $\overline{ED}$.

Choose **Calculate** from the Measure menu to open the Calculator. Click once on a measurement in your sketch to enter it into a calculation.

5. Use the Calculator to find the sum of these two lengths.

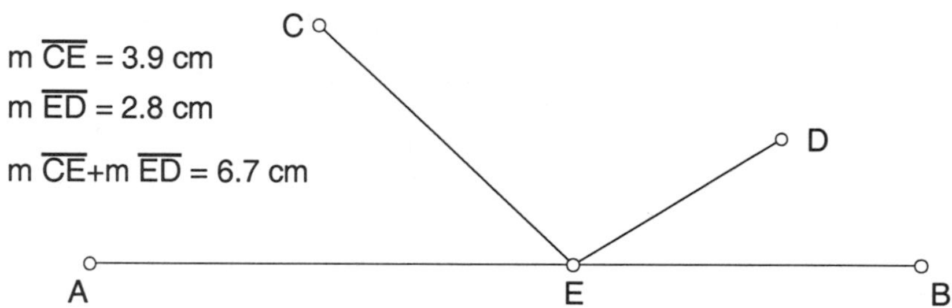

To precisely locate point *E*, you might need to change your precision for calculations to thousandths. To do this, in the Edit menu, choose **Preferences**.

6. Drag point *E* and watch the calculated sum change. Move point *E* to the location on the river to which the camper should run.

Select three points that name the angle, with the vertex your middle selection. Then, in the Measure menu, choose **Angle**.

7. Measure the incoming and outgoing angles the camper's path makes with the river (angles *CEA* and *DEB*).

Q1 Once you've found the minimal path, what appears to be true about the incoming angle and the outgoing angle? (See if you can use the angle measures to make the distance sum even shorter.)

© 2002 Key Curriculum Press

So far, you've dragged point E to find an approximate minimal path. Next, you'll discover how to construct such a path.

Double-click the segment.

8. Mark segment AB as a mirror. (Now that it's marked as a mirror, you can stop thinking of it as a river.)

Select the point; then, in the Transform menu, choose **Reflect**.

9. Reflect point D across this segment to create point D'.
10. Construct $\overline{CD'}$ and change its line width to dashed.

Q2 Why is $\overline{CD'}$ the shortest path from point C to point D'?

Q3 Where should point E be located in relation to $\overline{CD'}$ and $\overline{AB}$ so that the sum $CE + ED$ is minimized? Drag point E to test your conjecture.

Explore More

1. In a new sketch, use a reflection to construct a model of the burning tent problem so that the path from the hiker to the river to the tent is always minimal, no matter where you locate the hiker and the tent.

2. What's the shortest mirror you'd need on a wall in order to see your full reflection from your toes to the top of your head? To explore this question, construct a vertical segment representing you and another vertical segment representing a mirror. Construct a point to represent your eye level just below the top endpoint of the segment representing you. Use a reflection to construct the path a ray of light would take from the top of your head to the mirror and to your eye.

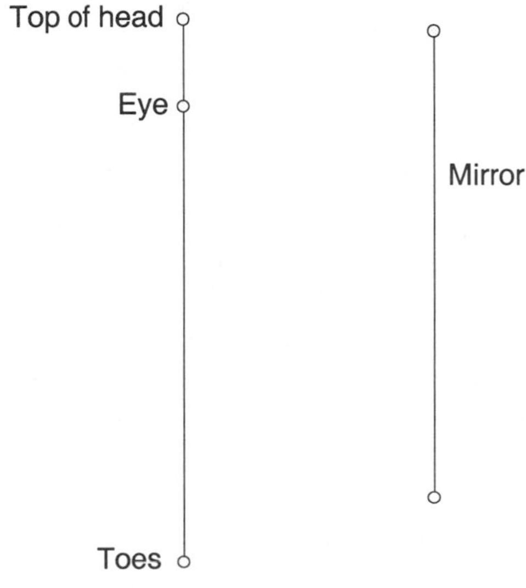

Construct another path that a ray of light would take from your toes to the mirror to your eye. Adjust the mirror length so that it's just long enough for both light rays to reflect off it. How long is the mirror compared to your height?

© 2002 Key Curriculum Press

The Feed and Water Problem

Name(s): ____________________

A rider is traveling from point D to point E between a river and a pasture. Before he gets to E, he wants to stop at the pasture to feed his horse and at the river to water her. What path should he take? Use Sketchpad to model the problem.

Sketch and Investigate

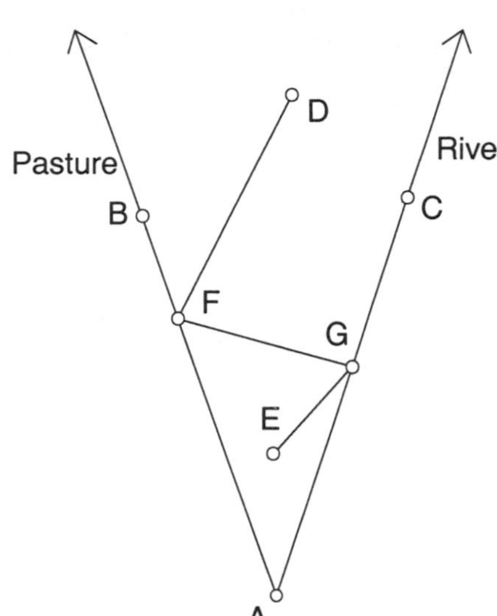

1. Construct $\overrightarrow{AB}$ and $\overrightarrow{AC}$.

Using the **Text** tool, click once on the ray to show its label. Double-click the label to edit it.

2. Label these rays *Pasture* and *River*.
3. Construct points D and E between the rays.
4. Construct $\overline{DF}$ from point D to the pasture, $\overline{FG}$ from the pasture to the river, and $\overline{GE}$ from the river to point E.
5. Measure DF, FG, and GE.

Choose **Preferences** from the Edit menu and go to the Units panel to change precision settings.

6. Set Distance Precision to **thousandths**.

Choose **Calculate** from the Measure menu to open the Calculator. Click once on a measurement in your sketch to enter it into a calculation.

7. Calculate the sum $DF + FG + GE$.
8. Drag points F and G to minimize this sum. (You may have to drag each point several times.)
9. Measure angles DFB, AFG, CGF, and EGA.

Q1 What do you notice about the incoming and outgoing angles the path makes with the pasture and the river when the path is minimized? See if you can use the angle measures, as you drag points F and G, to make the path even shorter.

Explore More

1. Construct your solution so that it works wherever points D and E are located. In a new sketch, construct the rays and points D and E between them. Reflect point D across the pasture. Reflect point E across the river. The distance $D'E'$ is the same as the shortest distance from D to E via the pasture and the river. (Why?) Construct $\overline{D'E'}$ and use it to construct the shortest path from D to E via the pasture and the river. Hide D', E', and $\overline{D'E'}$. You should be able to move D and E and have the path change automatically to minimize the distance.

© 2002 Key Curriculum Press

Planning a Path for a Laser

Name(s): ______________

In this activity, you will use Sketchpad to model the path of a laser beam reflecting off three mirrors and striking a target. If you have a laser and some mirrors, you can test your model on the walls of your classroom.

Sketch and Investigate

1. Make careful measurements of the dimensions of your classroom.
2. Choose one corner of the room to be the origin. This point will have the coordinates (0, 0). Figure out the coordinates of all the other vertices of your room. It will be most convenient to make your measurements in meters.

In the Graph menu, choose **Plot Points**. Enter the coordinates in the Plot Points dialog box and click **Plot**. Click **Done** when you're finished.

3. In Sketchpad, plot the points representing the vertices of your room. You may need to drag the point (1, 0) to scale your axes so you can see all the points.

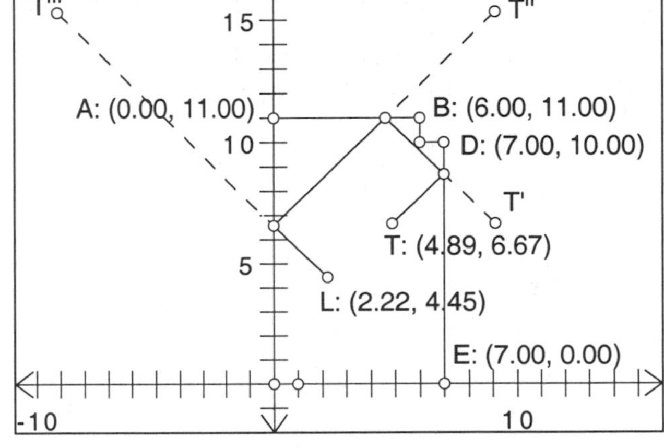

4. Draw segments in your sketch to represent the walls of your room.
5. The laser beam should reflect off three walls of the room and strike a target. Use reflections to construct this path in your sketch. For now, your laser and target point can be anywhere inside the room. You will adjust their positions later.
6. Drag the laser and target points until they are positioned the way you want them. Now figure out where you would locate the mirrors, the actual laser, and the actual target if you were to test your model in your classroom.

Q1 Explain your construction. How did you find the locations for the mirrors?

Explore More

1. Find a laser and some mirrors and give your instructions to another group of students to test your plan. Make sure that the room is dark and that the laser beam is not at anyone's eye level. Report on the success of your plan.

© 2002 Key Curriculum Press

Reflections over Two Parallel Lines

Name(s): ______________________

In this investigation, you'll see what happens when you reflect a figure over a line then reflect the image over a second line parallel to the first.

Sketch and Investigate

Hold down the Shift key while you click with the **Point** tool so that points will stay selected as you construct them. Then, in the Construct menu, choose **Quadrilateral Interior**.

1. Construct any irregular polygon interior.

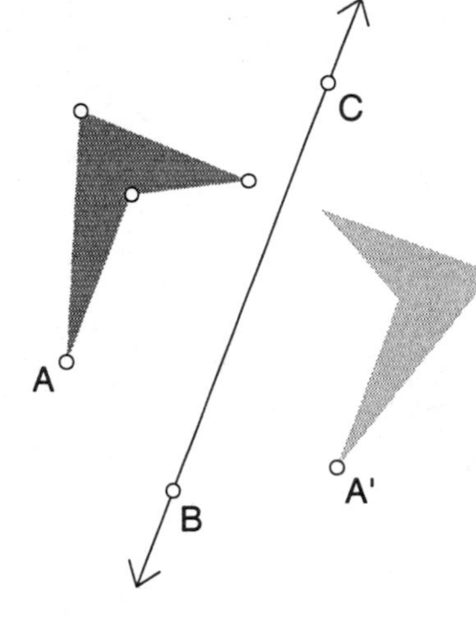

With the **Text** tool, click on a point to display its label. Double-click a label to change it.

2. Show the label of one of the polygon's vertices. Change the label to *A* (if necessary).
3. Construct a line *BC*.

Double-click the line to mark it as a mirror. Select the polygon interior and the point; then, in the Transform menu, choose **Reflect**.

4. Mark the line as a mirror and reflect the polygon and point *A* over it.
5. Construct point *D* and a line through point *D* parallel to $\overleftrightarrow{BC}$.

Select point *D* and $\overleftrightarrow{BC}$; then, in the Construct menu, choose **Parallel Line**.

6. Mark this second line as a mirror and reflect the first reflected image and point *A*′ over it.
7. Drag the original figure and the two lines and observe their relationships to the two images.

Q1 Two reflections move your original figure to its second image. What single transformation do you think will do the same thing? (If you're not sure, go on to the next steps, then come back to this question.)

© 2002 Key Curriculum Press

8. Construct $\overline{AA''}$.

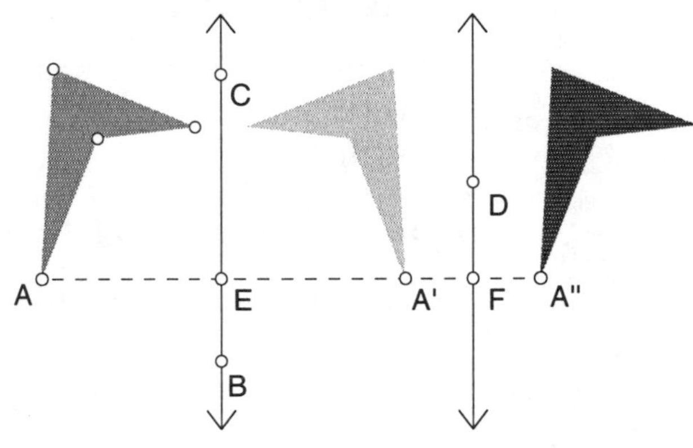

9. Construct points E and F where $\overline{AA''}$ intersects the two lines.

Select points A and A''; then, in the Measure menu, choose **Distance**. Repeat for EF.

10. Measure AA'' and EF.

Q2 Drag one of the lines and compare the two distances. How are they related?

Q3 EF is the distance between the two lines. Why?

Select points A and A'' in order; then, in the Transform menu, choose **Mark Vector**. Select the figure; then, in the Transform menu, choose **Translate**.

11. Mark AA'' as a vector, then translate the original figure by this vector.

Q4 Describe the result of step 11, above. What single transformation is equivalent to the combination of two reflections over parallel lines?

Q5 Answer the following questions to explain why AA'' and EF are related as they are:

a. How does AE compare to EA'? ____________________

b. How does $A'F$ compare to FA''? ____________________

c. $AA' + A'A'' =$ ______________

d. Complete the rest of the explanation on your own.

Explore More

1. In the same sketch, try reflecting your figure and then its image over the two lines in the opposite order. Describe the result.

© 2002 Key Curriculum Press

Reflections over Two Intersecting Lines

Name(s): ____________________

In this investigation, you'll see what happens when you reflect a figure over a line and then reflect the image over a second line that intersects the first.

Sketch and Investigate

Hold down the Shift key while you click with the **Point** tool so that points will stay selected as you construct them. Then, in the Construct menu, choose **Quadrilateral Interior**.

1. Construct any irregular polygon interior.

With the **Text** tool, click on a point to display its label. Double-click a label to change it.

2. Show the label of one of the polygon's vertices and change it to A (if necessary).

3. Construct two intersecting lines and their point of intersection.

Steps 1–3

Double-click the line to mark it as a mirror. Select the polygon and the point; then, in the Transform menu, choose **Reflect**.

4. Mark the line closest to the polygon as a mirror, then reflect the polygon and the labeled point over this line. Change the color of the reflected image. (See the figure below left. If necessary, move the polygon so that the image falls between the lines.)

5. Mark the other line as a mirror, then reflect the image from the first reflection over this second line. Change the color of this second image. (See the figure below right.)

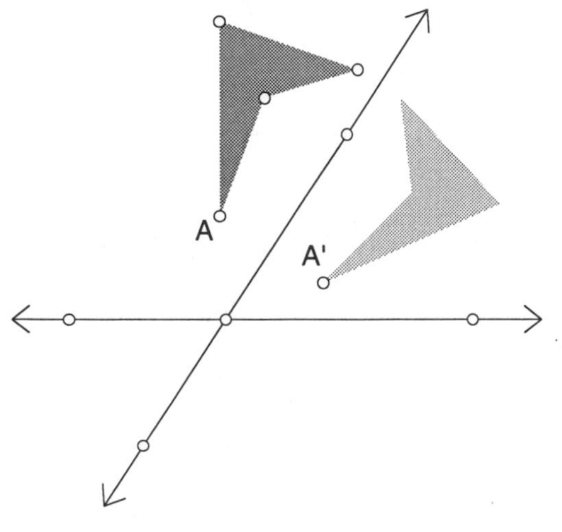

Step 4

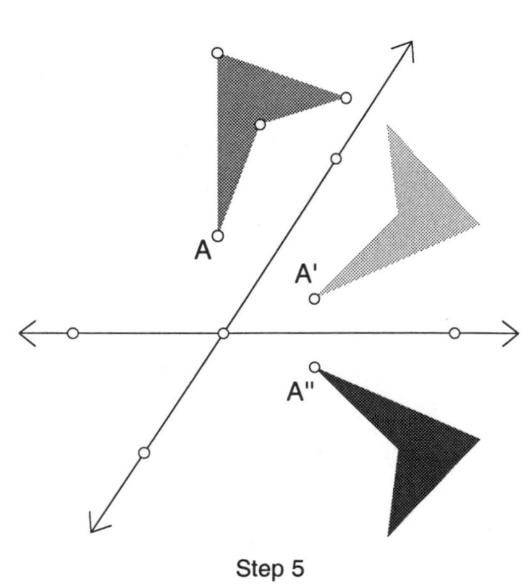

Step 5

© 2002 Key Curriculum Press

6. Drag the original figure and the two lines and observe their relationships to the two images.

Q1 Two reflections move your original figure to its second image. What single transformation do you think will do the same thing? (If you're not sure, go on to the next steps, then come back to this question.)

7. Construct $\overline{AB}$, where point *A* is a point on the original figure and point *B* is the point of intersection of the lines.

8. Construct $\overline{BA'}$ and $\overline{BA''}$.

Select the three points that name the angle, with the vertex your middle selection; then, in the Measure menu, choose **Angle**.

9. Measure $\angle ABA''$.

10. Measure $\angle CBD$, the angle between the lines.

Q2 Compare the two angle measures. How are they related?

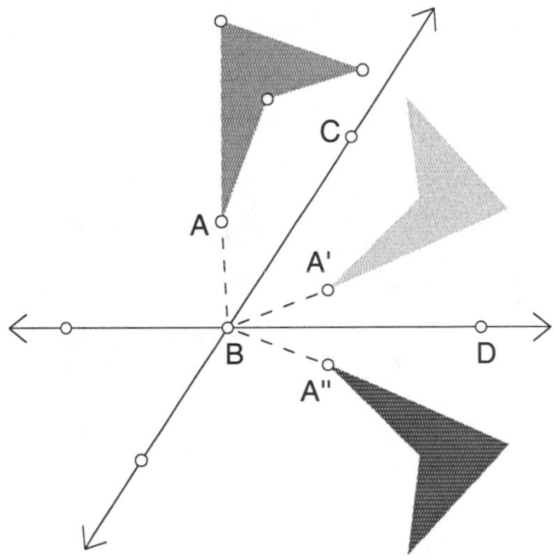

Double-click point *B* to mark it as a center. Select, in order, points *A, B,* and *A''*; then, in the Transform menu, choose **Mark Angle**. Select the figure; then, in the Transform menu, choose **Rotate**.

11. Mark point *B* as a center for rotation and mark $\angle ABA''$, then rotate the original figure by this angle.

Q3 Describe the result of step 11. What single transformation is equivalent to the combination of two reflections over intersecting lines?

Q4 Answer the following questions to explain why m$\angle ABA''$ and m$\angle CBD$ are related the way they are:

a. How does m$\angle ABC$ compare to m$\angle ABA'$? ____________________
(Try to answer without measuring first.)

b. How does m$\angle A'BD$ compare to m$\angle A'BA''$? ____________________

c. m$\angle ABA'$ + m $\angle A'BA''$ = m$\angle$ ________

d. Complete the rest of the explanation on your own. Use a separate sheet, if necessary.

© 2002 Key Curriculum Press

Glide Reflections

Name(s): ______________________

In this activity you will investigate an isometry called a *glide reflection*. Glide reflection is not a transformation found in the Transform menu, but you'll define it as a custom tool, and in the process you'll learn what a glide reflection is and what it does.

Sketch and Investigate

Hold down the Shift key while you click with the **Point** tool so that points will stay selected as you construct them. Then, in the Construct menu, choose **Quadrilateral Interior**.

1. Construct an irregular polygon interior, like polygon *ABCD*, shown at right.

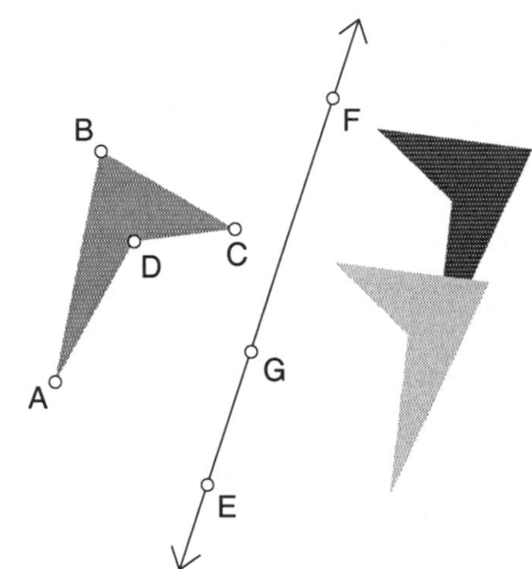

2. Construct line *EF*.

Double-click the line to mark it as a mirror. Select the polygon interior; then, in the Transform menu, choose **Reflect**.

3. Mark $\overleftrightarrow{EF}$ as a mirror and reflect the polygon interior across $\overleftrightarrow{EF}$.
4. Construct a point *G* on the line so that *E* and *G* are about an inch apart.

Select, in order, points *E* and *G*; then, in the Transform menu, choose **Mark Vector**. A brief animation indicates the mark. Select the reflected polygon interior; then, in the Transform menu, choose **Translate**.

5. Mark *EG* as a vector and translate the reflected image by the marked vector. This second image is a glide reflection of your original figure.
6. Drag point *G* to see how it affects the glide-reflected image.
7. Hide the intermediate image (the first reflection).

Line *EF* and vector *EG* will remain marked; you don't have to mark them over and over again.

8. Use the techniques you've learned so far to create two more glide-reflected images, as shown at right.

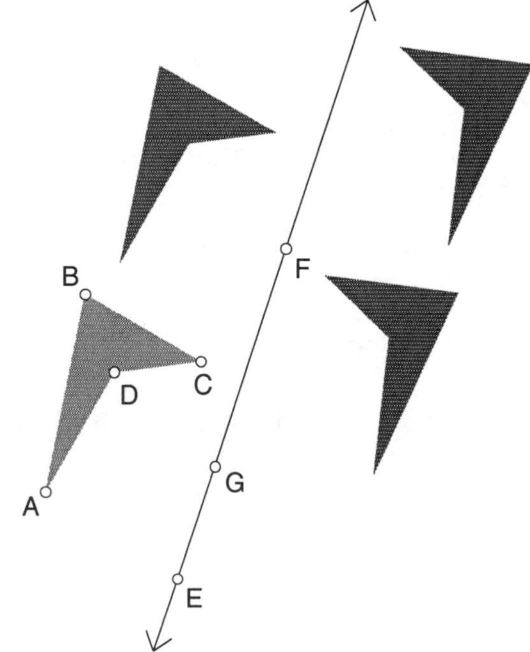

9. Drag parts of your sketch (vertices of the original polygon, point *G*, points *E* and *F*, the line) and observe the effects.

Q1 A glide reflection is the product of two transformations. What are they?

© 2002 Key Curriculum Press

Q2 A translation is also the product of two transformations. What are they?

Q3 A glide reflection can be thought of as a product of what three transformations?

Explore More

For tips on making and using custom tools, choose **Toolbox** from the Help menu, then click on the Custom Tools link.

1. Turn your glide reflection into a custom tool to save yourself time when doing glide reflections. Save the tool in the Tool Folder (next to the application itself on your hard drive) for future use.

2. Create a polygon that looks like a foot, then use glide reflections to make a sketch that looks like footprints in sand. To make the footprints appear sequentially, as if made by a walking invisible person, follow these steps:

   a. Make a Hide/Show action button for each footprint.

   b. Make a Presentation button with the Hide/Show buttons. Choose Sequentially in the Presentation dialog box that appears, and add a one-second Pause Between Actions.

   c. Hide all of the footprints, then press the Presentation button.

3. Experiment with reflections across three random lines. Does this produce a glide reflection?

4. What's the product of a rotation and a reflection? What's the product of a rotation and a translation?

© 2002 Key Curriculum Press

Symmetry in Regular Polygons

Name(s): ____________________

A figure has *reflection symmetry* if you can reflect the figure over a line so that the image will coincide with the original figure. The line you reflect over is called a *line of symmetry* or a *mirror line*. A figure has *rotational symmetry* if you can rotate it some number of degrees about some point so that the rotated image will coincide with the original figure. In this exploration, you'll look for reflection and rotation symmetries of regular polygons.

Sketch and Investigate

Construct your polygon from scratch or use a custom tool. The sketch **Polygons.gsp** includes tools for regular polygons.

1. Construct a regular polygon and its interior. You can use an equilateral triangle, a square, a regular pentagon, or a regular hexagon. You may want to have different groups in your class investigate different shapes.

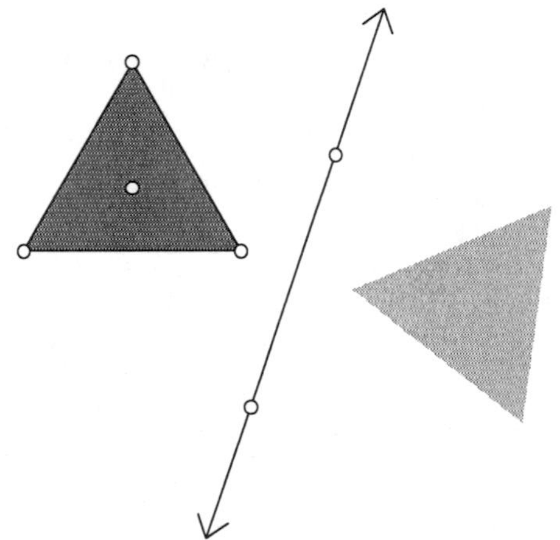

2. Construct a line.

Double-click the line to mark it as a mirror. Select the polygon interior; then, in the Transform menu, choose **Reflect**.

3. Mark the line as a mirror and reflect the polygon interior over it.
4. Give the image a different color.
5. Drag the line until the image of your polygon coincides exactly with the original.

Q1 When a reflection image coincides with the original figure, the reflection line is a line of symmetry. Describe how the line of symmetry is positioned relative to the figure.

6. Drag the line so that it is a different line of symmetry. Repeat until you have found all the reflection symmetries of your polygon.

Q2 Fill in one entry in the table below: the number of reflection symmetries for your polygon. (*Note:* Be careful not to count the same line twice!) You'll come back to fill in other entries as you gather more information.

Number of sides of regular polygon	3	4	5	6	. . .	n
Number of reflection symmetries					. . .	
Number of rotation symmetries					. . .	

© 2002 Key Curriculum Press

Next, you'll look for rotation symmetries.

7. Move the line so that the reflected image is out of the way.
8. If the polygon's center doesn't already exist, construct it.
9. Use the **Segment** tool to construct an angle.

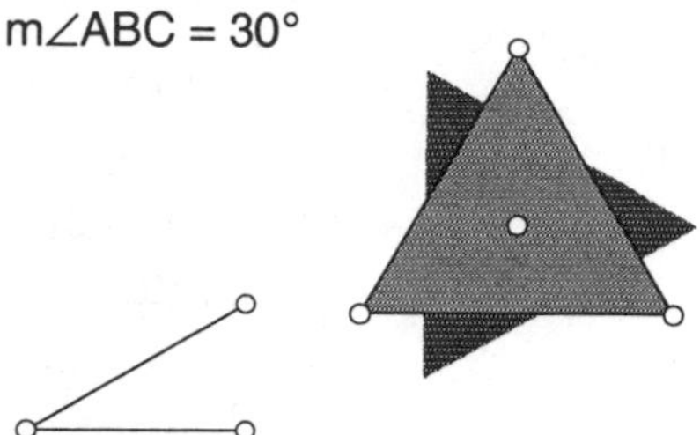

Select the three points, with the vertex your middle selection. Then, in the Measure menu, choose **Angle**.

10. Measure the angle.

Choose **Preferences** from the Edit menu and go to the Units panel.

11. In Preferences, set Angle Units to **directed degrees**.
12. Mark the center of the polygon as a center for rotation and mark the angle measurement. Rotate the polygon interior by this marked angle measurement.

Double-click the point to mark it. Select the angle measurement; then, in the Transform menu, choose **Mark Angle**. Select the interior; then, in the Transform menu, choose **Rotate**.

13. Give the rotated image a different color.
14. Change the angle so that the rotated image fits exactly over the original figure.

Q3 What angle measure causes the figures to coincide?

Polygon: ______________ Rotation angle: ______________

15. Continue changing your angle to find all possible rotation symmetries of your polygon.

Q4 Count the number of times the rotated image coincides with the original when rotating from 0° to 180° and from –180° back to 0°. In your chart on the preceding page, record the total number of rotation symmetries you found. (*Note:* Count no revolutions, or 0°, as one of your rotation symmetries.)

Q5 Combine the results from other members of your class to complete your chart with the reflection and rotation symmetries of other regular polygons.

Q6 Use your findings to write a conjecture about the reflection and rotation symmetries of a regular *n*-gon. Include in your conjecture a statement about the smallest angle of rotational symmetry greater than 0.

© 2002 Key Curriculum Press

Tessellating with Regular Polygons

Name(s): ____________

You've probably seen a floor tiled with square tiles. Squares make good tiles because they can cover a surface without any gaps or overlapping. This kind of tiling is sometimes called a *tessellation*. Are there other shapes that would make good tiles? In this investigation, you'll discover which regular polygons tessellate. You'll need custom tools for creating equilateral triangles, squares, regular pentagons, regular hexagons, and regular octagons. Each custom tool must create its figure from the endpoints of one side of the polygon—not from the center. Such custom tools come with the book, but you may want to create them yourself.

Sketch and Investigate

This step is unnecessary if you've previously placed this sketch in your Tool Folder.

1. Open the sketch **Polygons.gsp**.

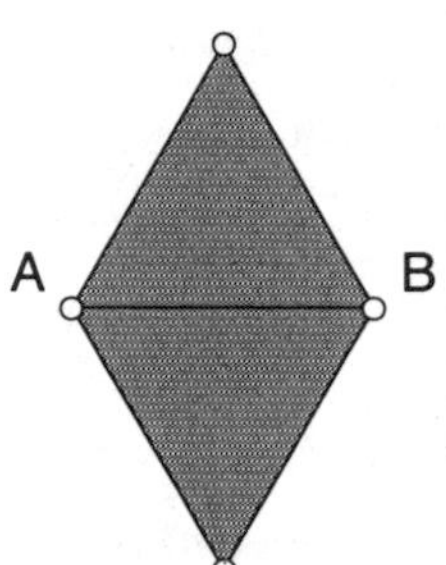

Click on the **Custom** tools icon (the bottom tool in the Toolbox) and choose the desired tool from the menu that appears (in the Polygons submenu). Click twice in the sketch to use the tool.

2. In a blank sketch, use a custom tool to construct an equilateral triangle. Pay attention to the direction in which the triangle is created as you use the tool.

3. Use the custom tool again, this time clicking in the opposite direction, to construct a second equilateral triangle attached to the first.

If your triangles don't stay attached, undo until the second triangle goes away, then try again. You must always start and end your dragging with the cursor positioned on an existing point.

4. Drag several points on the triangles to make sure they're really attached.

5. Keep attaching triangles to edges of existing triangles until you have triangles completely surrounding at least two points.

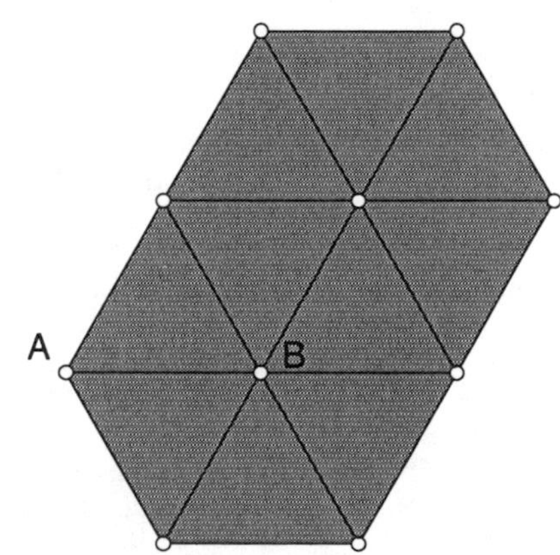

Q1 So far, you've demonstrated that equilateral triangles can tessellate. You can tile the plane with them without gaps or overlapping. Why do equilateral triangles work? (*Hint:* It has to do with their angles.)

6. Repeat the investigation with squares, regular pentagons, regular hexagons, and regular octagons.

Q2 Which of the regular polygons you tried will tessellate and which won't? Why? Answer on a separate sheet.

Q3 Do you think a regular heptagon (seven sides) would tessellate? Explain.

© 2002 Key Curriculum Press

A Tumbling-Block Design

Name(s): ______________________

A tumbling-block design is commonly found in Amish quilt patterns. We can call it an example of "op art" because of its interesting optical effect, which is suggested by its name. A tumbling-block design can be created efficiently with Sketchpad using *translations*.

Sketch and Investigate

Use your own method or a custom tool like **6/Hexagon (Inscribed)** from the sketch **Polygons.gsp**.

1. Construct a regular hexagon.
2. Delete the polygon's interior, if necessary.
3. If the center of the hexagon doesn't already exist, construct it.

To construct a polygon interior, select the vertices in consecutive order; then, in the Construct menu, choose **Quadrilateral Interior**. **Color** is in the Display menu.

4. Construct segments and polygon interiors, and color regions of the hexagon as shown at right.

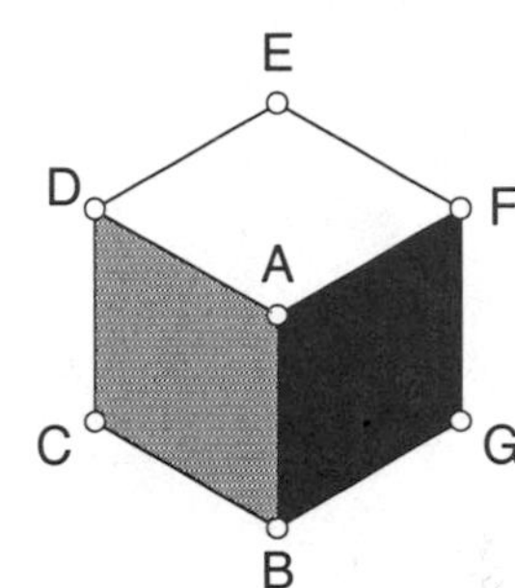

In the next few steps, you'll translate this figure to create a row of blocks.

Select, in order, point *D* and point *F*; then, in the Transform menu, choose **Mark Vector**.

5. Mark the vector *DF*.
6. Select the nine segments and two interiors (in other words, everything but the points).
7. Translate the selection.
8. Translate again two more times so that you have a row of four blocks.
9. Mark *EG* as a vector and translate the entire row of blocks (except the points) by this vector to create a second row of blocks.

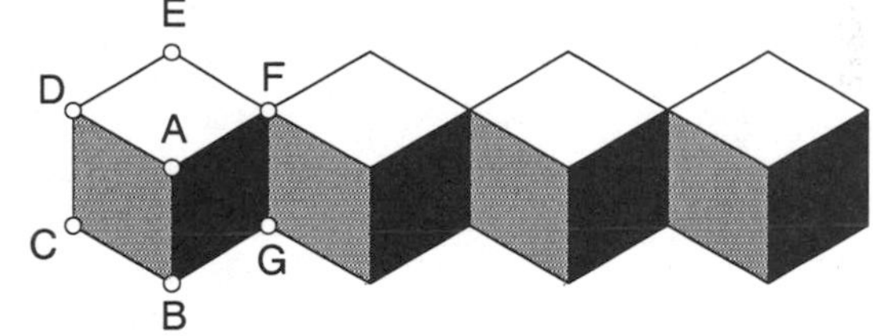

10. Translate again two more times so that you have four rows of blocks.
11. Drag points on your original hexagon to scale and turn the design.
12. Experiment with different color patterns to enhance your design.

© 2002 Key Curriculum Press

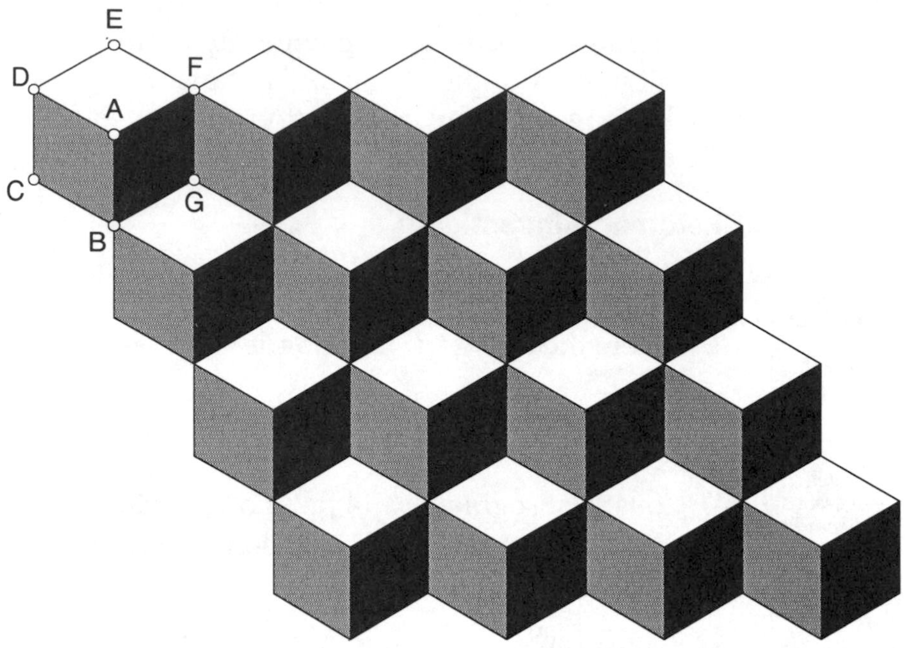

Q1 Describe different shapes in this design. What's the shape of the smallest pieces quilters use in this design?

Q2 Describe the optical effect of the design.

Q3 Describe any places where you have seen this design before.

© 2002 Key Curriculum Press

Tessellating with Triangles

Name(s): ______________________

In this investigation, you'll learn a method for tessellating with any triangle. You'll also discover why all triangles tessellate.

Sketch and Investigate

Select the three vertices; then, in the Construct menu, choose **Triangle Interior**.

1. In the lower left corner of your screen, construct triangle *ABC*.

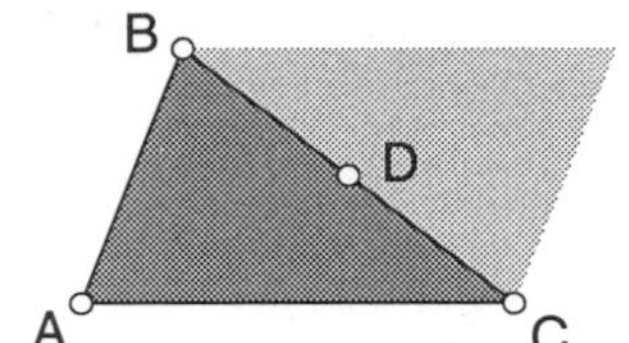

2. Construct its interior.
3. Construct midpoint *D* of side *BC*.

Double-click the point to mark it as a center. Select the triangle interior; then, in the Transform menu, choose **Rotate**.

4. Mark point *D* as a center and rotate the triangle interior by 180°.
5. Give the rotated image a different color.

Color is in the Display menu.

Q1 Drag points and observe the shape formed by the two triangles (the original together with its rotated image). What shape is this? ______________________

Select, in order, point *A* and point *C*; then, in the Transform menu, choose **Mark Vector**. A brief animation indicates the mark. Select the two interiors; then, in the Transform menu, choose **Translate**.

6. Mark *AC* as a vector and translate the two interiors by the marked vector. Translate two more times to make a total of eight triangles.

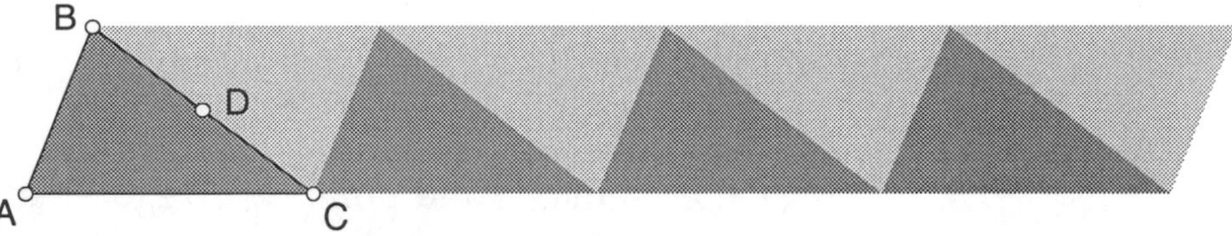

Q2 Drag to confirm that the top and bottom edges of this row of triangles are always straight lines. What does that demonstrate about the sum of the angle measures in the original triangle? Explain. (Write your explanation on a separate sheet.)

7. Mark vector *AB* and translate the entire row by this vector. Repeat until triangles begin to fill your screen.
8. Drag to confirm that no matter what shape your original triangle has, it will always tessellate.

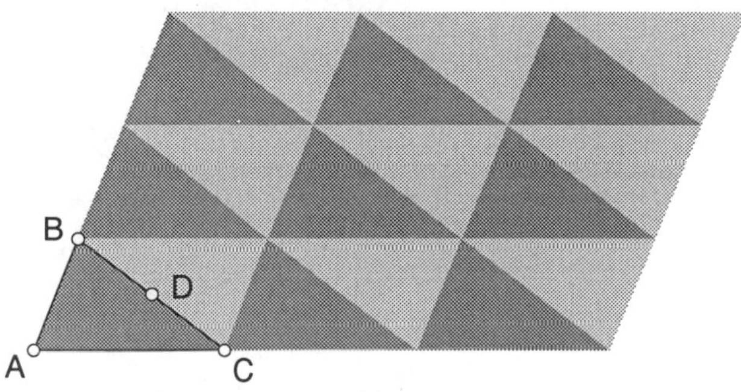

Q3 Look at a point in the tessellation that is completely surrounded by triangles. What is the sum of the angles surrounding this point? Why? (Write your explanation on a separate sheet.)

© 2002 Key Curriculum Press

Tessellations Using Only Translations

Name(s): ______________________

In this activity, you'll learn how to construct an irregularly shaped tile based on a parallelogram. Then you'll use translations to tessellate your screen with this tile.

Sketch

1. Construct $\overline{AB}$ in the lower-left corner of your sketch, then construct point *C* just above $\overline{AB}$.

Select, in order, point *A* and point *B*; then, in the Transform menu, choose **Mark Vector**. Select point *C*; then, in the Transform menu, choose **Translate**.

2. Mark the vector from point *A* to point *B* and translate point *C* by this vector.
3. Construct the remaining sides of your parallelogram.

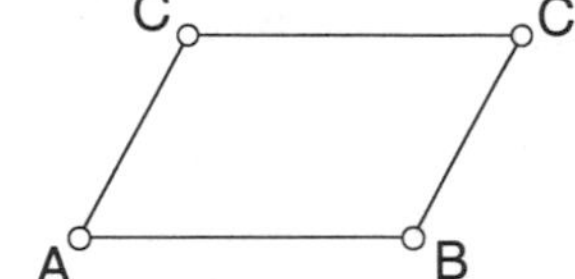

Steps 1–3

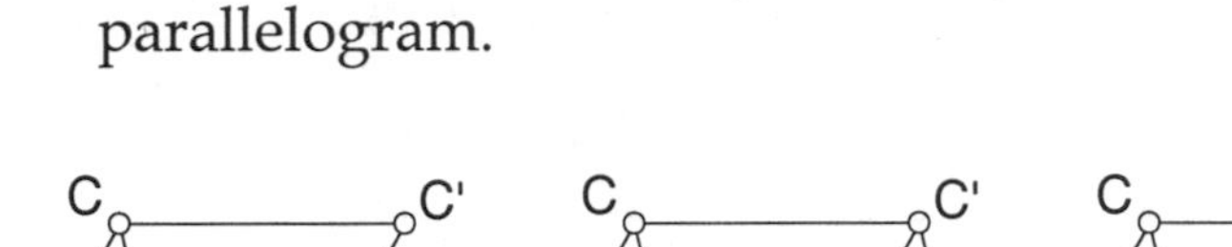

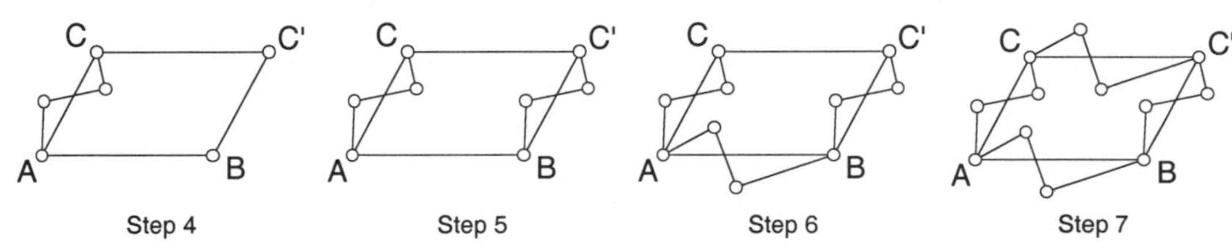

Step 4 Step 5 Step 6 Step 7

4. Construct two or three connected segments from point *A* to point *C*. We'll call this *irregular edge AC*.
5. Select all the segments and points of irregular edge *AC* and translate them by the marked vector. (Vector *AB* should still be marked.)
6. Make an irregular edge from *A* to *B*.
7. Mark the vector from point *A* to point *C* and translate all the parts of irregular edge *AB* by the marked vector.

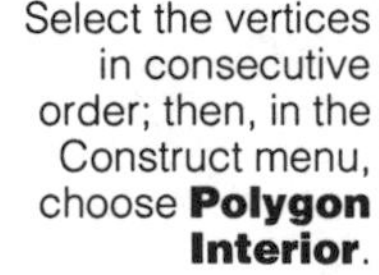

Select the vertices in consecutive order; then, in the Construct menu, choose **Polygon Interior**.

8. Construct the polygon interior of the irregular figure. This is the tile you will translate.
9. Translate the polygon interior by the marked vector. (You probably still have vector *AC* marked.)
10. Repeat this process until you have a column of tiles all the way up your sketch. Change the color of every other tile to create a pattern.

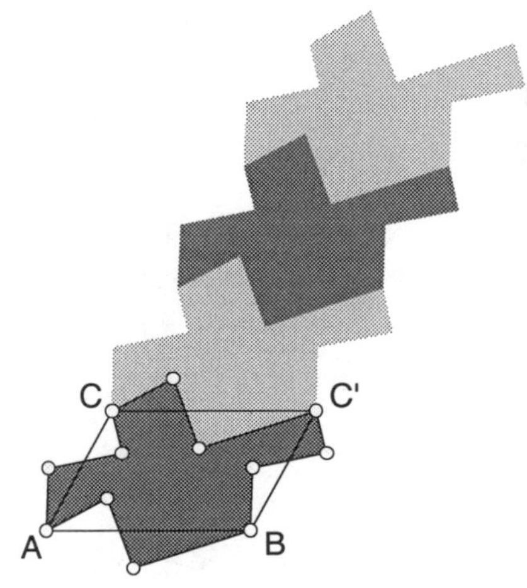

Steps 8–10

© 2002 Key Curriculum Press

11. Mark vector *AB*. Then select all the polygon interiors in your column of tiles and translate them by this marked vector.

12. Continue translating columns of tiles until you fill your screen. Change colors of alternating tiles so you can see your tessellation.

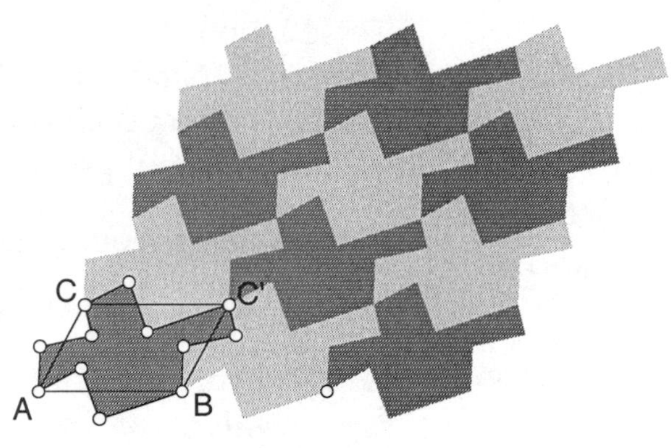

Steps 11 and 12

13. Drag vertices of your original tile until you get a shape that you like or that is recognizable as some interesting form.

Explore More

1. Animate your tessellation. To do this, select the original polygon (or any combination of its vertex points) and choose **Animate** from the Display menu. You can also have your points move along paths you construct. To do this, construct the paths (segments, circles, polygon interiors—anything you can construct a point on) and then merge vertices to paths. (To merge a point to a path, select both and choose **Merge Point to Path** from the Edit menu.) Select the points you wish to animate and, in the Edit menu, choose **Action Buttons | Animation**. Press the Animation button. Adjust the paths so that the animation works in a way you like, then hide the paths.

2. Use Sketchpad to make a translation tessellation that starts with a regular hexagon as the basic shape instead of a parallelogram. (*Hint:* The process is very similar; it just involves a third pair of sides.)

© 2002 Key Curriculum Press

Tessellations That Use Rotations

Name(s): ____________________

Tessellations that use only translations have tiles that all face in the same direction. Using rotations, you can make a tessellation with tiles facing in different directions. The designs in a rotation tessellation have rotation symmetry about points in the tiling.

Sketch and Investigate

Use a custom tool (such as one in the sketch **Polygons.gsp**) or construct the triangle from scratch. If your custom tool constructs an interior, delete the interior. →

1. Construct equilateral triangle *ABC* as shown below.
2. Construct two or three connected segments from *A* to *B*. We'll call this *irregular edge AB.*

Double-click the point to mark it as a center. Select the segments and points; then, in the Transform menu, choose **Rotate**. →

3. Mark point *A* as a center for rotation. Then rotate all the points and segments of irregular edge *AB* by 60°.

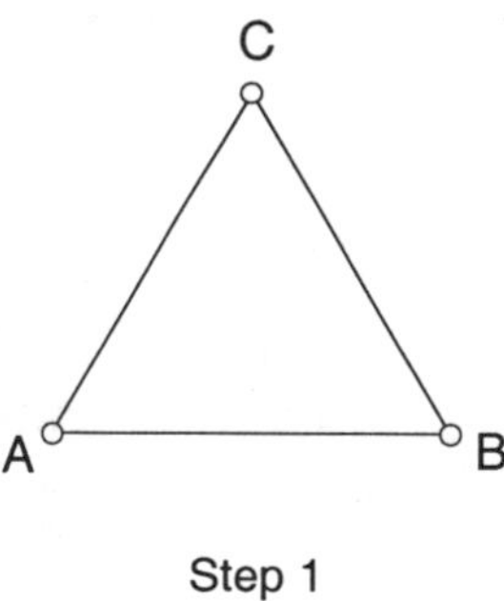

Step 1

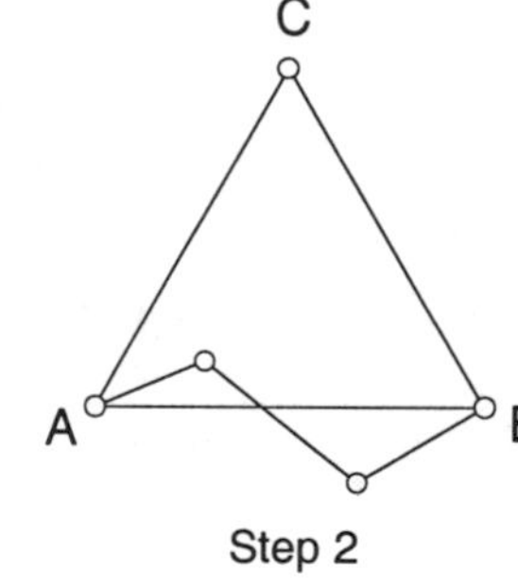

Step 2

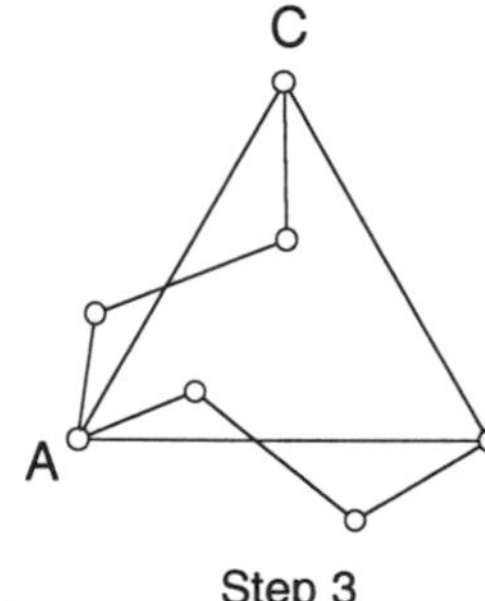

Step 3

4. Construct midpoint *D* of side *CB*.
5. Construct two connected segments from *B* to *D*. We'll call this *irregular edge BD*.
6. Mark point *D* as a center for rotation. Then rotate the point and segments of irregular edge *BD* by 180°.
7. You have finished the edges of your tile. Drag points to see how they behave. When you're done, make sure none of the irregular edges intersect.

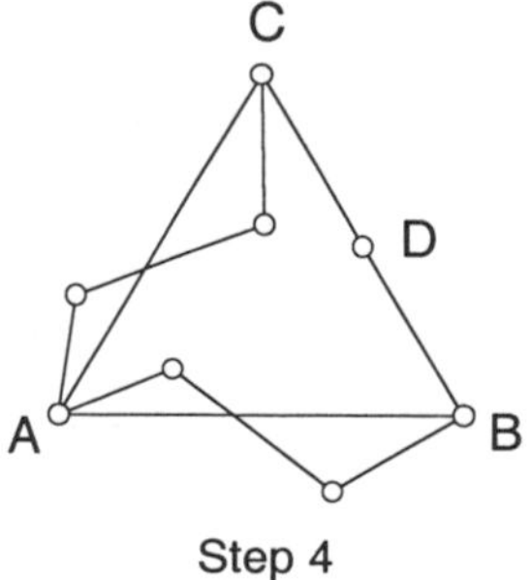

Step 4

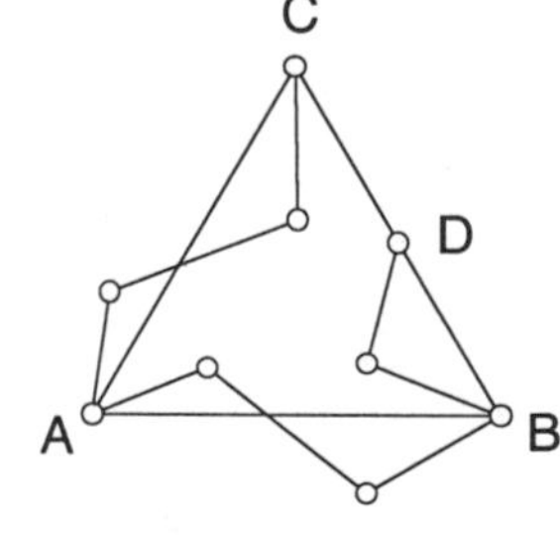

Step 5

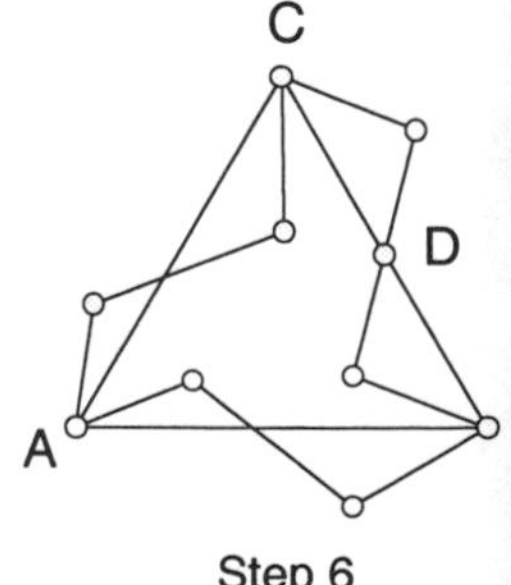

Step 6

© 2002 Key Curriculum Press

Select the vertices in consecutive order; then, in the Construct menu, choose **Polygon Interior**.

8. Construct the polygon interior with vertices along the irregular edges.

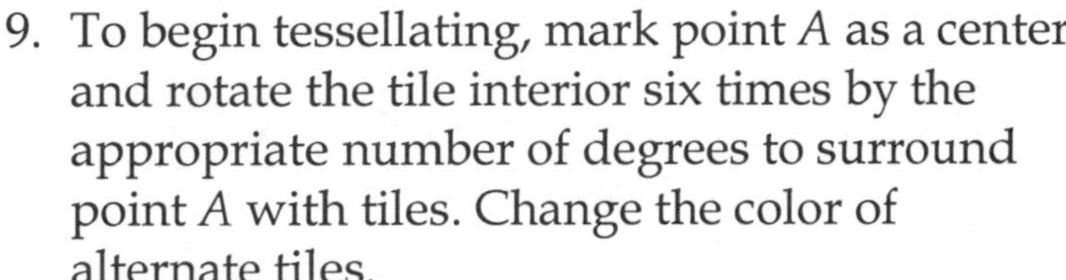

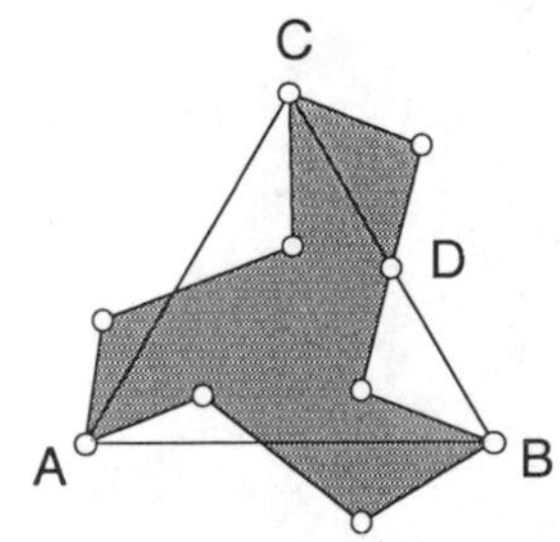

Change the color of your tiles using the Display menu.

9. To begin tessellating, mark point *A* as a center and rotate the tile interior six times by the appropriate number of degrees to surround point *A* with tiles. Change the color of alternate tiles.

10. Mark point *D* as a center and rotate the six tiles by 180°. Reverse their shading as necessary to keep a clear shading pattern.

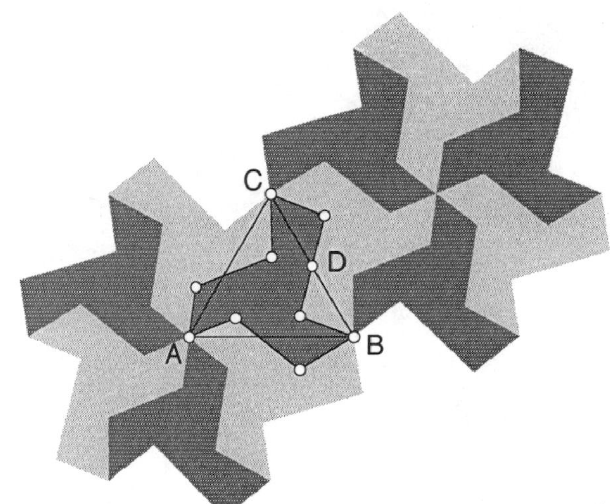

Q1 Look at the tiles surrounding point *A*. What kind of rotation symmetry would the completed tessellation have about this point?

Q2 Look at the tiles surrounding point *D*. What kind of rotation symmetry would the completed tessellation have about this point?

Q3 Look at the tiles surrounding points *B* and *C* so far. What angle of rotation will you have to use to fill in tiles around these points?

11. Use the appropriate rotations to fill in tiles around points *B* and *C*. If you choose an angle that doesn't work right, undo and try a different angle. Change your answer to Q3, if necessary.

12. Drag vertices of your original tile until you get a shape that you like or that is recognizable as some interesting form.

© 2002 Key Curriculum Press

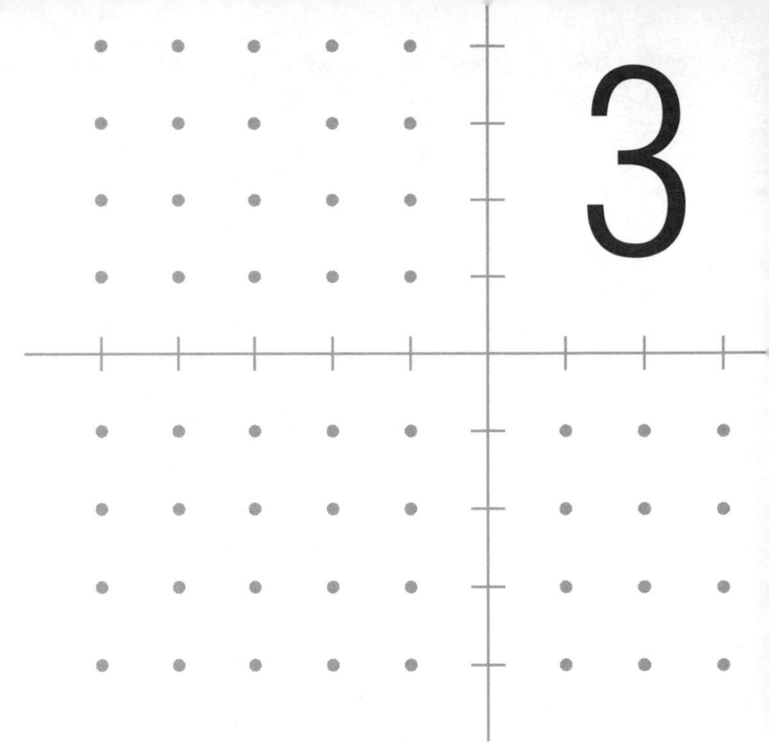

3

Triangles

Defining Triangles

Name(s): ____________________

In this lesson, you'll experiment with an ordinary triangle and with special triangles that were constructed with constraints. The constraints limit what you can change in the triangle when you drag so that certain relationships among angles and sides always hold. By observing these relationships, you will classify the triangles.

1. Open the sketch **Classify Triangles.gsp**.
2. Drag different vertices of each of the four triangles to observe and compare how the triangles behave.

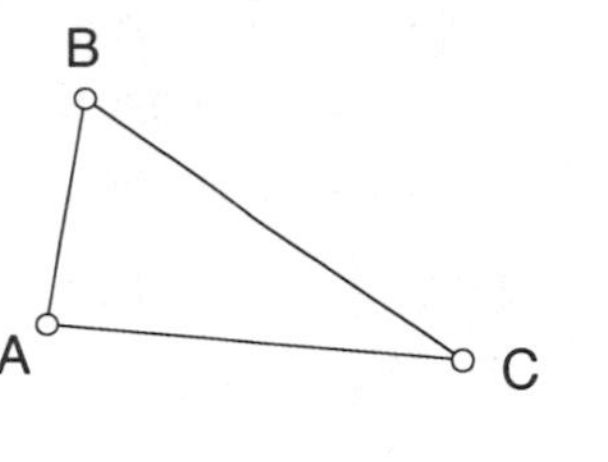

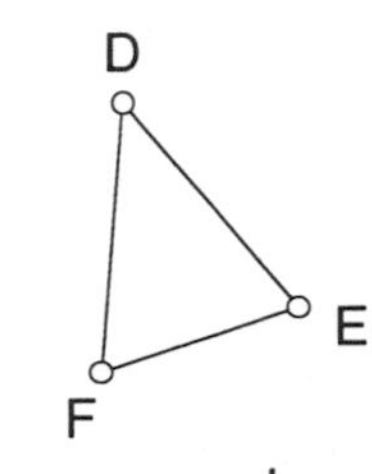

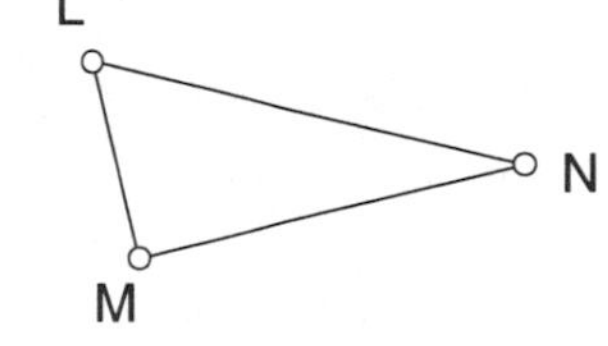

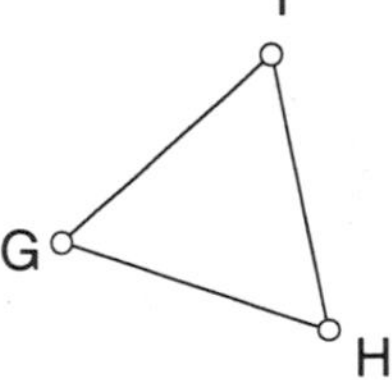

Q1 Which of the triangles seems the most flexible? Explain.

Q2 Which of the triangles seems the least flexible? Explain.

To measure each angle, select three points, with the vertex your middle selection. Then, in the Measure menu, choose **Angle**.

3. Measure the three angles in $\triangle ABC$.
4. Drag a vertex of $\triangle ABC$ and observe the changing angle measures. To answer the following questions, note how each angle can change from being acute to being right or obtuse.

Q3 How many acute angles can a triangle have? ____________________

Q4 How many obtuse angles can a triangle have? ____________________

Acute, right, and *obtuse* are terms used to classify angles. These terms can also be used to classify triangles according to their angles.

Q5 $\triangle ABC$ can be an obtuse triangle or an acute triangle. One other triangle in the sketch can also be either acute or obtuse. Which triangle is it? ______________

Q6 Which triangle is always a right triangle, no matter what you drag? ______________

Q7 Which triangle is always an equiangular triangle? ______________

To measure a length, select a segment. Then, in the Measure menu, choose **Length**.

5. Measure the lengths of the three sides of $\triangle ABC$.
6. Drag a vertex of $\triangle ABC$ and observe the changing side lengths.

© 2002 Key Curriculum Press

Scalene, *isosceles*, and *equilateral* are terms used to classify triangles by relationships among their sides. Because $\triangle ABC$ has no constraints, it can be any type of triangle.

Q8 If none of the side lengths are equal, the triangle is a *scalene* triangle. If two or more of the sides are equal in length, the triangle is *isosceles*. If all three sides are equal in length, it is *equilateral*. Which type of triangle is $\triangle ABC$ most of the time? ______________

Q9 Name a triangle besides $\triangle ABC$ that is scalene most of the time. (Measure if you like, but if you drag things around, you should be able to tell without measuring, just by looking.) ______________

Q10 Which triangle (or triangles) is (are) always isosceles? ______________

Q11 Which triangle is always equilateral? ______________

Q12 For items a–e below, state whether the triangle described is possible or not possible. To check whether each is possible, try manipulating the triangles in the sketch to make one that fits the description. If it's possible to make the triangle, sketch an example on a piece of paper.

a. An obtuse isosceles triangle

b. An acute right triangle

c. An obtuse equiangular triangle

d. An isosceles right triangle

e. An acute scalene triangle

Q13 Write a definition for each of these six terms: *acute triangle, obtuse triangle, right triangle, scalene triangle, isosceles triangle,* and *equilateral triangle*. Use a separate sheet if necessary.

In the Display menu, choose **Show All Hidden** to get an idea of how the triangles in the **Classify Triangles.gsp** sketch were constructed.

Explore More

1. Open a new sketch and see if you can come up with ways to construct a right triangle, an isosceles triangle, and an equilateral triangle. Describe your methods.

© 2002 Key Curriculum Press

Triangle Sum

Name(s): ____________________

This is a two-part investigation. First you'll investigate and make a conjecture about the sum of the measures of the angles in a triangle, then you'll continue sketching to demonstrate why your conjecture is true.

Sketch and Investigate

1. Construct $\triangle ABC$.

> To measure an angle, select three points, with the vertex your middle selection. Then, in the Measure menu, choose **Angle**.

2. Measure its three angles.

m∠CAB = 43.3°
m∠ABC = 87.2°
m∠BCA = 49.5°

B
A
C

> Choose **Calculate** from the Measure menu to open the Calculator. Click once on a measurement to enter it into a calculation.

3. Calculate the sum of the angle measures.
4. Drag a vertex of the triangle and observe the angle sum.

Q1 What is the sum of the angles in any triangle? ____________

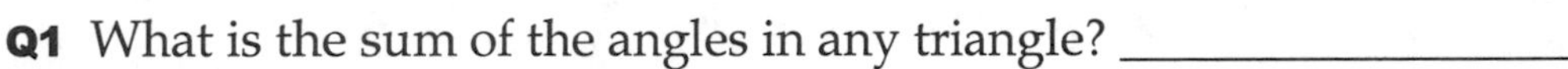

Follow these steps to investigate why your conjecture is true.

> Select point *B* and $\overline{AC}$; then, in the Construct menu, choose **Parallel Line**.

5. Construct a line through point *B* parallel to $\overline{AC}$.
6. Construct the midpoints of $\overline{AB}$ and $\overline{CB}$.

> Select the three vertices; then, in the Construct menu, choose **Triangle Interior**.

7. Construct the interior of $\triangle ABC$.

> Double-click the point to mark it as a center. Select the interior; then, in the Transform menu, choose **Rotate**.

8. Mark one of the midpoints as a center for rotation and rotate the interior by 180° about this point.

> **Color** is in the Display menu.

9. Give the new triangle interior a different color.
10. Mark the other midpoint as a center and rotate the interior by 180° about this point.
11. Give this new triangle interior a different color.

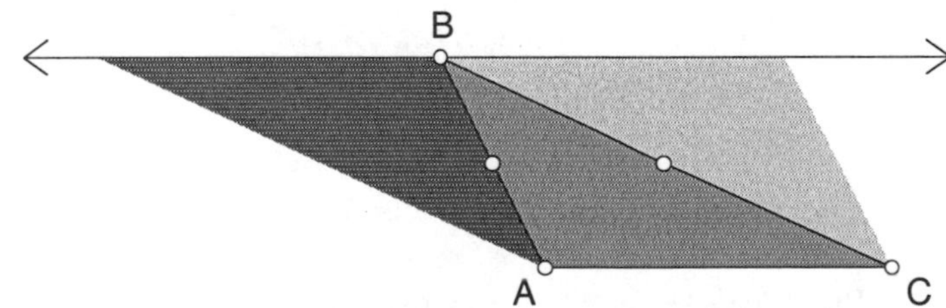

12. Drag point *B* and observe how the three triangles are related to each other and to the parallel line.

Q2 Explain how each of the three angles at point *B* is related to one of the three angles in the triangle. Explain how this demonstrates your conjecture from Q1.

© 2002 Key Curriculum Press

Exterior Angles in a Triangle

Name(s): ________________

An *exterior angle* of a triangle is formed when one of the sides is extended. An exterior angle lies outside the triangle. In this investigation, you'll discover a relationship between an exterior angle and the sum of the measures of the two remote interior angles.

Sketch and Investigate

m∠CAB = 45.5°
m∠ABC = 67.2°
m∠BCD = 112.7°
B
A C D

1. Construct $\triangle ABC$.

> Hold down the mouse button on the **Segment** tool and drag right to choose the **Ray** tool.

2. Construct $\overrightarrow{AC}$ to extend side AC.
3. Construct point D on $\overrightarrow{AC}$, outside of the triangle.

> Select, in order, points *B*, *C*, and *D*. Then, in the Measure menu, choose **Angle**.

4. Measure exterior angle BCD.
5. Measure the remote interior angles $\angle ABC$ and $\angle CAB$.
6. Drag parts of the triangle and look for a relationship between the measures of the remote interior angles and the exterior angle.

> Choose **Calculate** from the Measure menu to open the Calculator. Click once on a measurement to enter it into a calculation.

Q1 How are the measures of the remote interior angles related to the measure of the exterior angle? Use the Calculator to create an expression that confirms your conjecture.

Follow these steps to see why your conjecture is true.

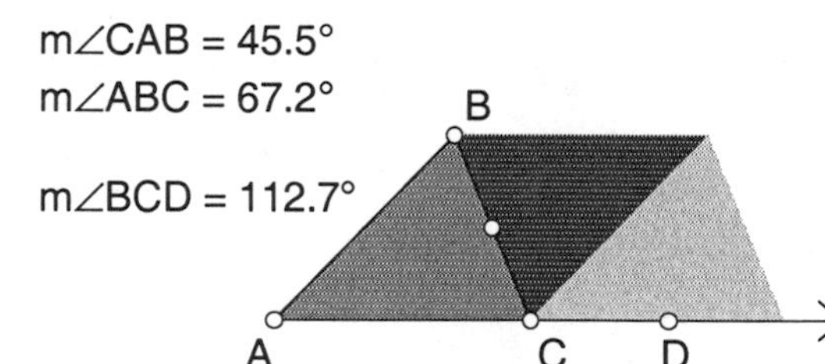

> Select the vertices; then, in the Construct menu, choose **Triangle Interior**.

7. Construct the interior of $\triangle ABC$.

> Select point *A* and point *C* in order; then, in the Transform menu, choose **Mark Vector**.

8. Mark AC as a vector.

> Select the interior; then, in the Transform menu, choose **Translate**.

9. Translate the interior by the marked vector.
10. Give the new triangle interior a different color.
11. Construct the midpoint of $\overline{BC}$.

> Double-click the point to mark it as a center. Select the interior; then, in the Transfrom menu, choose **Rotate**.

12. Mark the midpoint as a center for rotation and rotate the triangle interior about this point by 180°.
13. Give this new triangle interior a different color.

Q2 Explain how the two angles that fill the exterior angle are related to the remote interior angles in the triangle. Explain how this demonstrates your conjecture from Q1. Use the back of this sheet.

© 2002 Key Curriculum Press

Triangle Inequalities

Name(s): ____________________

In this investigation, you'll discover relationships among the measures of the sides and angles in a triangle.

Sketch and Investigate

1. Construct a triangle.

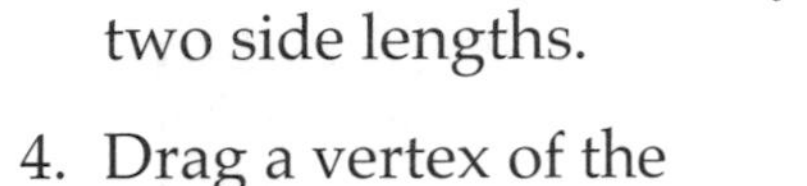
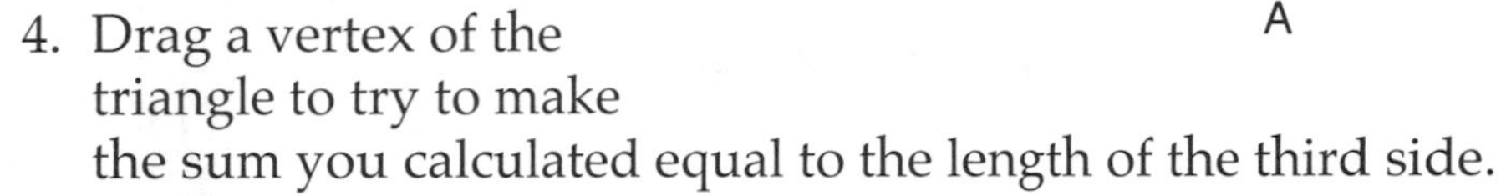

To measure a side, select it; then, in the Measure menu, choose **Length**.

2. Measure the lengths of the three sides.

Choose **Calculate** from the Measure menu to open the Calculator. Click once on a measurement to enter it into a calculation.

3. Calculate the sum of any two side lengths.
4. Drag a vertex of the triangle to try to make the sum you calculated equal to the length of the third side.

Q1 Is it possible for the sum of two side lengths in a triangle to be equal to the third side length? Explain.

Q2 Do you think it's possible for the sum of the lengths of any two sides of a triangle to be less than the length of the third side? Explain.

Q3 Summarize your findings as a conjecture about the sum of the lengths of any two sides of a triangle.

To measure an angle, select three points, with the vertex your middle selection. Then, in the Measure menu, choose **Angle**.

5. Measure $\angle ABC$, $\angle BAC$, and $\angle ACB$.
6. Drag the vertices of your triangle and look for relationships between side lengths and angle measures.

Q4 In each area of the chart below, a longest or shortest side is given. Fill in the chart with the name of the angle with the greatest or least measure, given that longest or shortest side.

$\overline{AB}$ longest side	Largest angle? _____	$\overline{AC}$ longest side	Largest angle? _____	$\overline{BC}$ longest side	Largest angle? _____
$\overline{AB}$ shortest side	Smallest angle? _____	$\overline{AC}$ shortest side	Smallest angle? _____	$\overline{BC}$ shortest side	Smallest angle? _____

Q5 Summarize your findings from the chart as a conjecture.

© 2002 Key Curriculum Press

Triangle Congruence

Name(s): ______________________

If the three sides of one triangle are congruent to three sides of another triangle (SSS), must the two triangles be congruent? What if two sides and the angle between them in one triangle are congruent to two sides and the angle between them in another triangle (SAS)? Which combinations of parts guarantee congruence and which don't? In this activity, you'll investigate that question.

Sketch and Investigate

1. Open the sketch **Triangle Congruence.gsp**. You'll see a figure like the one shown below, along with some text.

Side-Side-Side

C

A B

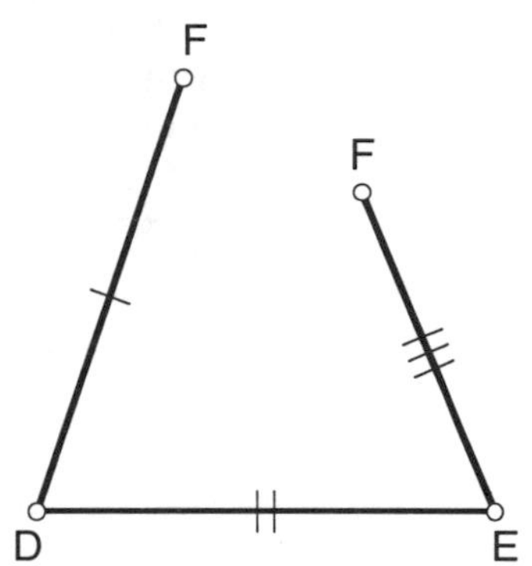

2. Read the text in the sketch and follow the instructions to try to make a triangle *DEF* that is not congruent to ΔABC.

Q1 Could you form a triangle with a different size or shape given the three sides? ______________

Q2 If three sides of one triangle are congruent to three sides of another (SSS), what can you say about the triangles? Write a conjecture that summarizes your findings.

Click on the page tabs at the bottom of the sketch window to switch pages.

3. Go to the SAS page and make a triangle *DEF* with those given parts. Try to make a triangle that is not congruent to ΔABC.

4. Experiment on each of the other pages.

Q3 Of SSS, SAS, SSA, ASA, AAS, and AAA, which combinations of corresponding parts guarantee congruence in a pair of triangles? Which do not?

© 2002 Key Curriculum Press

Properties of Isosceles Triangles

Name(s): ______________

In this activity, you'll learn how to construct an *isosceles triangle* (a triangle with at least two sides the same length). Then you'll discover properties of isosceles triangles.

Sketch and Investigate

1. Construct a circle with center *A* and radius point *B*.
2. Construct radius *AB*.
3. Construct radius *AC*. Drag point *C* to make sure the radius is attached to the circle.
4. Construct $\overline{BC}$.
5. Drag each vertex of your triangle to see how it behaves.

A
C
B

Q1 Explain why the triangle is always isosceles.

6. Hide circle *AB*.
7. Measure the three angles in the triangle.
8. Drag the vertices of your triangle and observe the angle measures.

To measure an angle, select three points, with the vertex your middle selection. Then, in the Measure menu, choose **Angle**.

Q2 Angles *ACB* and *ABC* are the *base angles* of the isosceles triangle. Angle *CAB* is the *vertex angle*. What do you observe about the angle measures?

Explore More

1. Investigate the converse of the conjecture you made in Q2: Draw any triangle and measure two angles. Drag a vertex until the two angle measures are equal. Now measure the side lengths. Is the triangle isosceles?
2. Investigate the statement *if a triangle is equiangular, then it is equilateral* and its converse, *if a triangle is equilateral, then it is equiangular.* Can you construct an equiangular triangle that is not equilateral? Can you construct an equilateral triangle that is not equiangular? Write a conjecture based on your investigation.

© 2002 Key Curriculum Press

Constructing Isosceles Triangles

Name(s): ________________

How many ways can you come up with to construct an isosceles triangle? Try methods that use just the freehand tools (those in the Toolbox) and also methods that use the Construct and Transform menus. Write a brief description of each construction method along with the properties of isosceles triangles that make that method work.

I

S O

Method 1:

Properties:

Method 2:

Properties:

Method 3:

Properties:

Method 4:

Properties:

© 2002 Key Curriculum Press

Medians in a Triangle

Name(s): ______________________

A median in a triangle connects a vertex with the midpoint of the opposite side. In previous investigations, you may have discovered properties of angle bisectors, perpendicular bisectors, and altitudes in a triangle. Would you care to make a guess about medians? You may see what's coming, but there are new things to discover about medians, too.

Sketch and Investigate

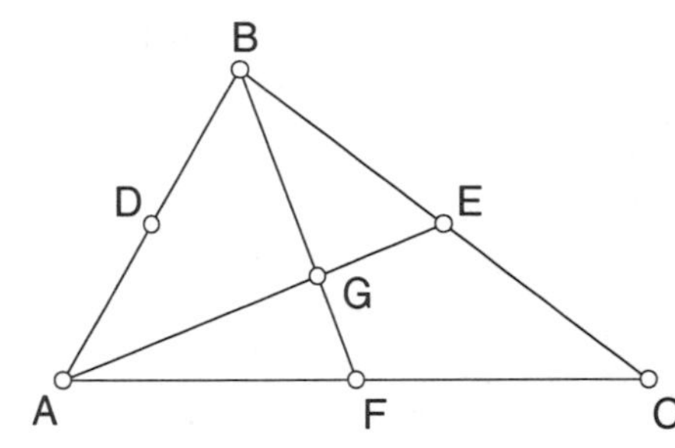

1. Construct triangle *ABC*.
2. Construct the midpoints of the three sides.
3. Construct two of the three medians, each connecting a vertex with the midpoint of its opposite side.

If you've already constructed three medians, select two of them. Then, in the Construct menu, choose **Intersection**.

4. Construct the point of intersection of the two medians.
5. Construct the third median.

Q1 What do you notice about this third median? Drag a vertex of the triangle to confirm that this conjecture holds for any triangle.

Using the **Text** tool, click once on the point to show its label. Double-click the label to change it.

6. The point where the medians intersect is called the *centroid*. Show its label and change it to *Ce* for centroid.

To measure the distance between two points, select them; then, in the Measure menu, choose **Distance**.

7. Measure the distance from *B* to *Ce* and the distance from *Ce* to the midpoint *F*.
8. Drag vertices of ΔABC and look for a relationship between *BCe* and *CeF*.

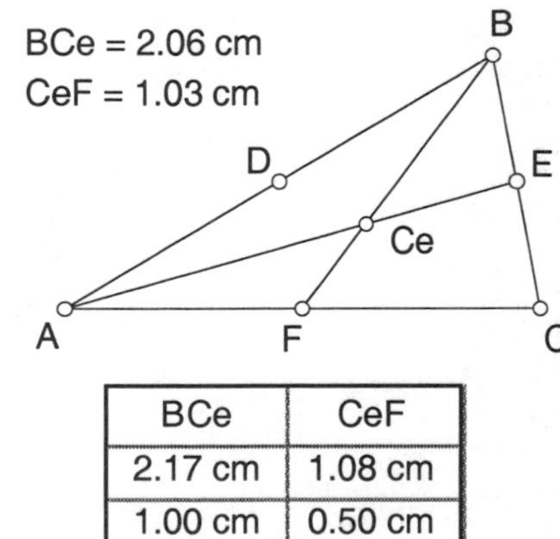

BCe	CeF
2.17 cm	1.08 cm
1.00 cm	0.50 cm
3.24 cm	1.62 cm
2.06 cm	1.03 cm

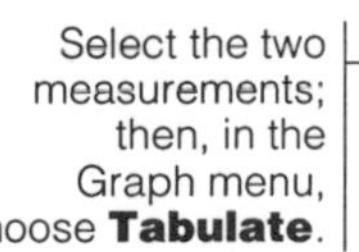

Select the two measurements; then, in the Graph menu, choose **Tabulate**.

9. Make a table with these two measures.
10. Change the triangle and double-click the table values to add another entry.
11. Keep changing the triangle and adding entries to your table until you can see a relationship between the distances *BCe* and *CeF*.

© 2002 Key Curriculum Press

Choose **Calculate** from the Measure menu to open the Calculator. Click once on a measurement to enter it into a calculation.

12. Based on what you notice about the table entries, use the Calculator to make an expression with the measures that will remain constant even as the measures change.

Q2 Write the expression you calculated in step 12.

Q3 Write a conjecture about the way the centroid divides each median in a triangle.

13. Plot the table data on a piece of graph paper or using the **Plot Points** command in the Graph menu. You should get a graph with several collinear points.

14. Draw or construct a line through any two of the data points and measure its slope.

Q4 Explain the significance of the slope of the line through the data points.

Explore More

1. Make a custom tool that constructs the centroid of a triangle. Save your sketch in the **Tool Folder** (next to the Sketchpad application itself on your hard drive) so that the tool will be available for future investigations of triangle centers.

© 2002 Key Curriculum Press

Perpendicular Bisectors in a Triangle

Name(s): ______________________

In this investigation, you'll discover properties of perpendicular bisectors in a triangle. You'll also learn how to construct a circle that passes through each vertex of a triangle.

Sketch and Investigate

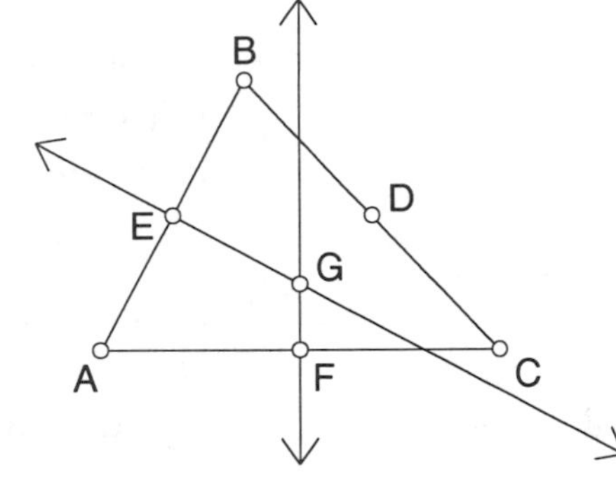

1. Construct triangle *ABC*.
2. Construct the midpoints of the sides.

Select a side and its midpoint; then, in the Construct menu, choose **Perpendicular Line**.

3. Construct two of the three perpendicular bisectors in the triangle.

Click at the intersection with the **Selection Arrow** tool or with the **Point** tool.

4. Construct point *G*, the point of intersection of these lines.
5. Construct the third perpendicular bisector.

Q1 What do you notice about this third perpendicular bisector (not shown)? Drag a vertex of the triangle to confirm that this conjecture holds for any triangle.

6. Drag a vertex around so that point *G* moves into and out of the triangle. Observe the angles of the triangle as you do this.

Q2 In what type of triangle is point *G* outside the triangle? inside the triangle?

Q3 Drag a vertex until point *G* falls on a side of the triangle. What kind of triangle is this? Where exactly does point *G* lie?

Select point *G* and a vertex; then, in the Measure menu, choose **Distance**. Repeat for the other two vertices.

7. Measure the distances from point *G* to each of the three vertices.
8. Drag a vertex of the triangle and observe the distances.

Q4 The point of intersection of the three perpendicular bisectors is called the *circumcenter* of the triangle. What do you notice about the distances from the circumcenter to the three vertices of the triangle?

© 2002 Key Curriculum Press

Make sure you start your circle at point *G* and finish it with the cursor directly over point *A*. Otherwise, the circle may not stay circumscribed when you drag. (If it doesn't, undo and try again.)

9. Construct a circle with center *G* and radius endpoint *A*. This is the circumscribed circle of ΔABC.

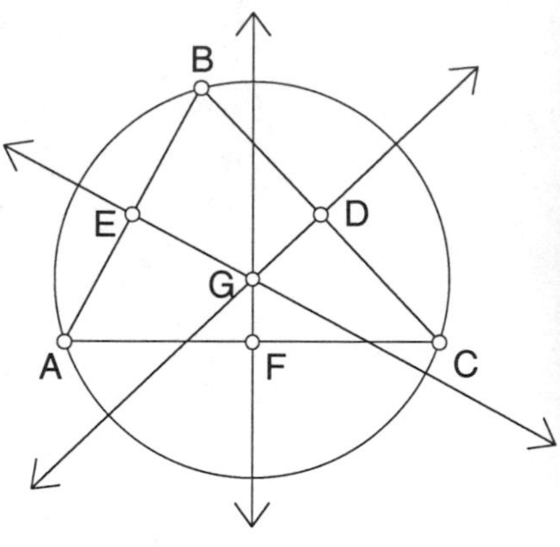

Explore More

1. Make a custom tool that constructs the circumcenter of a triangle. Save your sketch in the **Tool Folder** (next to the Sketchpad application itself on your hard drive) so that the tool will be available for future investigations of triangle centers.
2. Explain why the circumcenter is the center of the circumscribed circle. *Hint:* Recall that any point on a segment's perpendicular bisector is equidistant from the endpoints of the segment. Why would the circumcenter be equidistant from the three vertices of the triangle?
3. See if you can circumscribe other shapes besides triangles. Describe what you try and include below any additional conjectures you come up with.

© 2002 Key Curriculum Press

Altitudes in a Triangle

Name(s): ____________________

In this activity, you'll discover some properties of altitudes in a triangle. An *altitude* is a perpendicular segment from a vertex of a triangle to the opposite side (or to a line containing the side). The side where the altitude ends is the *base* for that altitude, and the length of the altitude is the *height* of the triangle from that base. Because a triangle has three sides, it also has three altitudes. You'll construct one altitude and make a custom tool for the construction. Then you'll use your tool to construct the other two.

Sketch and Investigate

1. Construct triangle *ABC*.

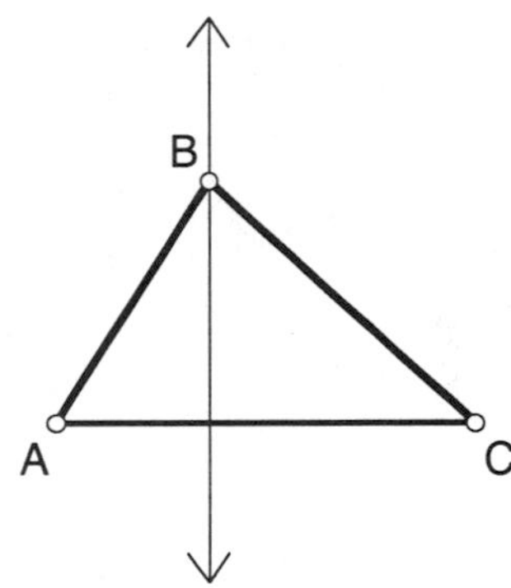

Select point *B* and $\overline{AC}$; then, in the Construct menu, choose **Perpendicular Line**.

2. Construct a line perpendicular to $\overline{AC}$ through point *B*.

Q1 As long as your triangle is acute, this perpendicular line should intersect a side of the triangle. Drag point *B* so that the line falls outside the triangle. Now what kind of triangle is it?

Hold down the mouse button on the **Segment** tool and drag right to choose the **Line** tool. Construct your line through the endpoints of the triangle side.

3. With the perpendicular line outside the triangle, use a line to extend side *AC* so that it intersects the perpendicular line.
4. Construct point *D*, the point of intersection of the extended side and the perpendicular line.
5. Hide the lines.
6. Construct $\overline{BD}$. Segment *BD* is an altitude.

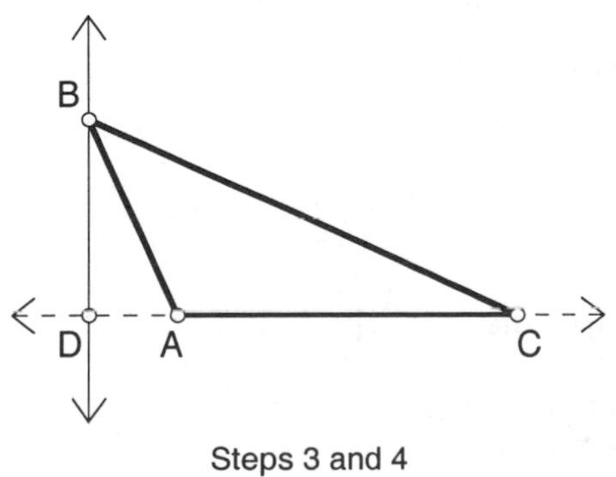

Steps 3 and 4

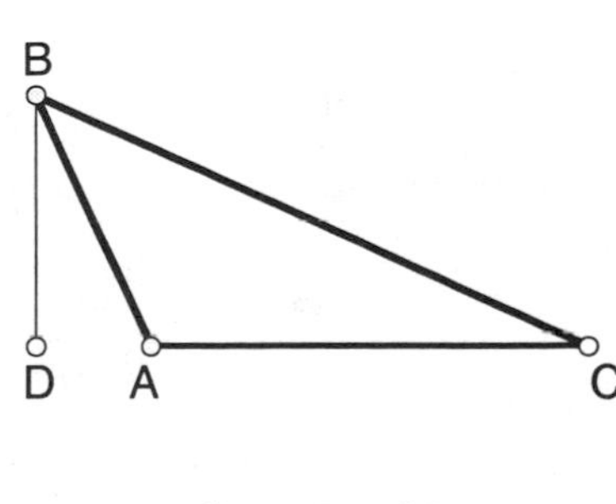

Steps 5 and 6

7. Drag vertices of the triangle and observe how your altitude behaves.

Q2 Where is your altitude when $\angle A$ is a right angle?

© 2002 Key Curriculum Press

8. Drag your triangle so that it is acute again (with the altitude falling inside the triangle).

Select everything in your sketch. Then, press the **Custom** tools icon (the bottom tool in the Toolbox) and choose **Create New Tool** from the menu that appears.

9. Make a custom tool for this construction. Name the tool "Altitude."

Starting with three points (the tool's "givens"), the Altitude tool will construct a triangle and an altitude from one of the vertices. To use the tool, click on the **Custom** tools icon to select the most recently created tool, then click on the three triangle vertices.

10. Use your custom tool on the triangle's vertices to construct a second altitude. Don't worry if you accidentally construct the altitude that already exists. Just use the tool on the vertices again in a different order until you get another altitude.

11. Use your Altitude tool to construct the third altitude in the triangle.

12. Drag the triangle and observe how the three altitudes behave.

Q3 What do you notice about the three altitudes when the triangle is acute?

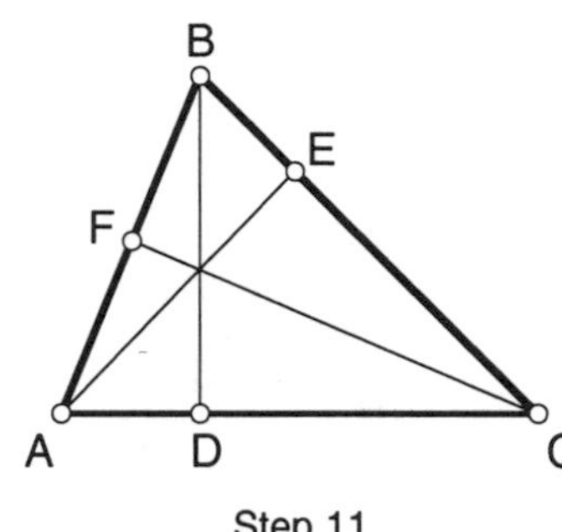

Step 11

Q4 What do you notice about the altitudes when the triangle is obtuse?

When the triangle is obtuse, the three altitudes don't intersect. But do you think they would if they were long enough? Follow the steps below to investigate that question.

13. Make sure the triangle is obtuse. Construct two lines that each contain an altitude.

If you've already constructed three lines, select two of them; then, in the Construct menu, choose **Intersection**.

14. Construct their point of intersection. This point is called the *orthocenter* of the triangle.

15. Construct a line containing the third altitude.

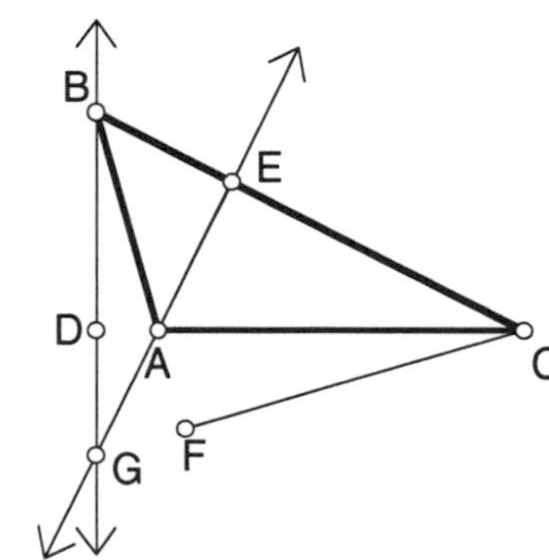

Steps 13 and 14

16. Drag the triangle and observe the lines.

Q5 What do you notice about the lines containing the altitudes?

Explore More

1. Hide everything in your sketch except the triangle and the orthocenter. Make and save a custom tool called "Orthocenter." You can use this tool in other investigations of triangle centers.

© 2002 Key Curriculum Press

Angle Bisectors in a Triangle

Name(s): ____________________

In this investigation, you'll discover some properties of angle bisectors in a triangle.

Sketch and Investigate

1. Construct triangle ABC.

Select three points, with the vertex your middle selection. Then, in the Construct menu, choose **Angle Bisector**.

2. Construct the bisectors of two of the three angles: $\angle A$ and $\angle B$.

Click at the intersection with the **Arrow** or the **Point** tool. Or select the two bisectors, then, in the Construct menu, choose **Intersection**.

3. Construct point D, the point of intersection of the two angle bisectors.

4. Construct the bisector of $\angle C$.

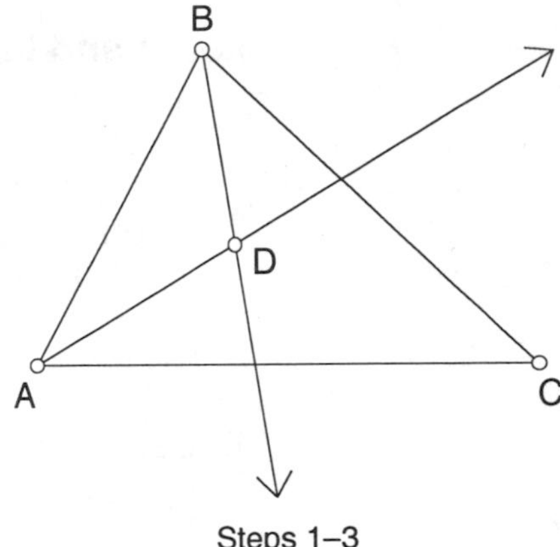

Steps 1–3

Q1 What do you notice about this third angle bisector (not shown)? Drag each vertex of the triangle to confirm that this observation holds for any triangle.

Select point *D* and one side of the triangle. Then, in the Measure menu, choose **Distance**. Repeat for the other two sides.

5. Measure the distances from D to each of the three sides.

6. Drag each vertex of the triangle and observe the distances.

Q2 The point of intersection of the angle bisectors in a triangle is called the *incenter*. Write a conjecture about the distances from the incenter of a triangle to the three sides.

Explore More

1. An inscribed circle is a circle inside a triangle that touches each of the three sides at one point. Construct an inscribed circle that stays inscribed no matter how you drag the triangle. (*Hint:* You'll need to construct a perpendicular line.)

2. Make and save a custom tool for constructing the incenter of a triangle (with or without the inscribed circle). You can use this tool when you investigate properties of other triangle centers.

3. Explain why the intersection of the angle bisectors would be the center of the inscribed circle. *Hint:* Recall that any point on an angle bisector is equidistant from the two sides of the angle. Why would the incenter be equidistant from the three sides of the triangle?

© 2002 Key Curriculum Press

The Euler Segment

Name(s): ____________________

In this investigation, you'll look for a relationship among four points of concurrency: the incenter, the circumcenter, the orthocenter, and the centroid. You'll use custom tools to construct these triangle centers, either those you made in previous investigations or pre-made tools.

Sketch and Investigate

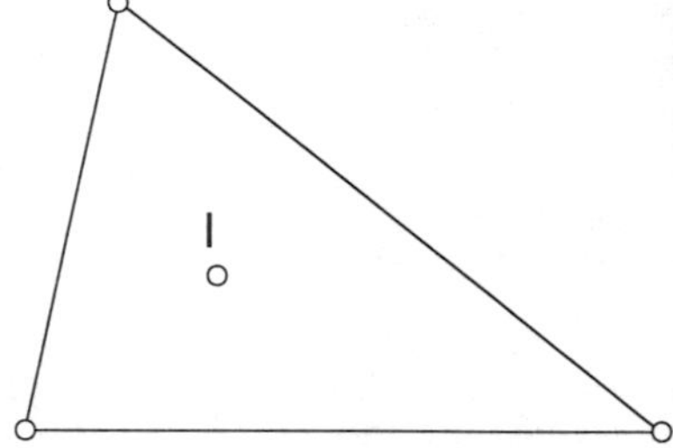

1. Open a sketch (or sketches) of yours that contains tools for the triangle centers: incenter, circumcenter, orthocenter, and centroid. Or open **Triangle Centers.gsp**.
2. Construct a triangle.
3. Use the **Incenter** tool on the triangle's vertices to construct its incenter.
4. If necessary, give the incenter a label that identifies it, such as *I* for incenter.
5. You need only the triangle and the incenter for now, so hide anything extra that your custom tool may have constructed (such as angle bisectors or the incircle).

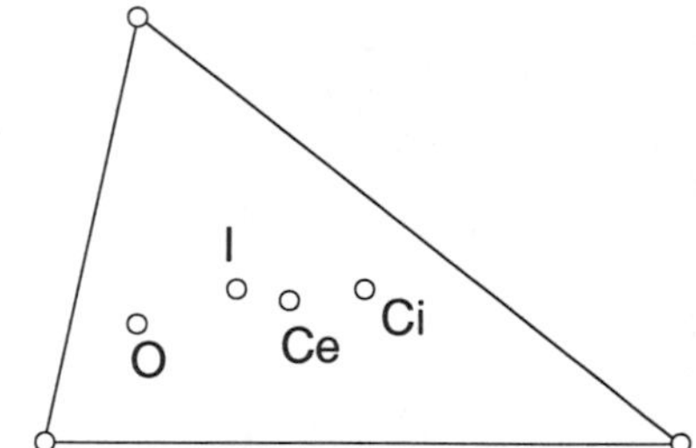

6. Use the **Circumcenter** tool on the same triangle. Hide any extras so that you have just the triangle, its incenter, and its circumcenter. If necessary, give the circumcenter a label that identifies it.
7. Use the **Orthocenter** tool on the same triangle, hide any extras, and label the orthocenter.
8. Use the **Centroid** tool on the same triangle, hide extras, and label the centroid. You should now have a triangle and the four triangle centers.

Q1 Drag your triangle around and observe how the points behave. Three of the four points are always collinear. Which three?

9. Construct a segment that contains the three collinear points. This is called the *Euler segment.*

© 2002 Key Curriculum Press

Q2 Drag the triangle again and look for interesting relationships on the Euler segment. Be sure to check special triangles, such as isosceles and right triangles. Describe any special triangles in which the triangle centers are related in interesting ways or located in interesting places.

Q3 Which of the three points are always endpoints of the Euler segment and which point is always between them?

To measure the distance between two points, select the two points. Then, in the Measure menu, choose **Distance**. (Measuring the distance between points is an easy way to measure the length of part of a segment.)

10. Measure the distances along the two parts of the Euler segment.

Q4 Drag the triangle and look for a relationship between these lengths. How are the lengths of the two parts of the Euler segment related? Test your conjecture using the Calculator.

Explore More

1. Construct a circle centered at the midpoint of the Euler segment and passing through the midpoint of one of the sides of the triangle. This circle is called the *nine-point circle*. The midpoint it passes through is one of the nine points. What are the other eight? (*Hint:* Six of them have to do with the altitudes and the orthocenter.)
2. Once you've constructed the nine-point circle, drag your triangle around and investigate special triangles. Describe any triangles in which some of the nine points coincide.

© 2002 Key Curriculum Press

Excircles of a Triangle

Name(s): ____________________

You may have learned previously to inscribe a circle inside a triangle: Find the intersection of the angle bisectors and use that point as the center of the circle. In this demonstration, you'll define an *excircle* and investigate its properties.

Sketch and Investigate

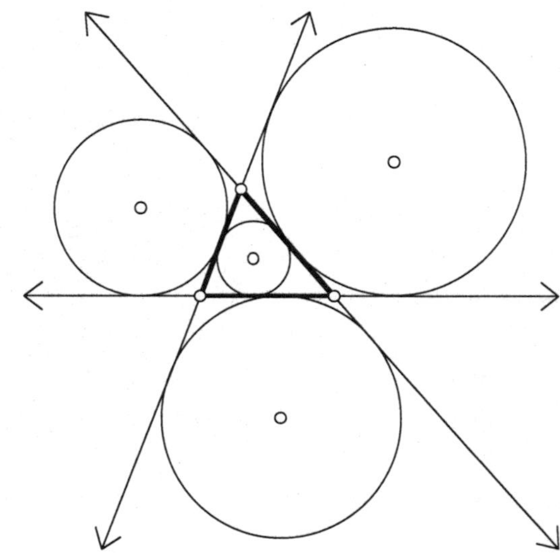

1. Open the sketch **Excircles.gsp**. You'll see a small triangle with a small circle inside it (the incircle) and three larger circles outside of it (excircles).
2. Drag any vertex of the small triangle.

Q1 What do you notice about the incircle?

Q2 What do you notice about each excircle?

To better understand what an excircle is, you should experiment with constructing circles inside angles. Follow the steps below.

3. Open a new sketch, but leave the excircles sketch open.

Press and hold down the mouse button on the **Segment** tool to show the **Straightedge** palette. Drag right to choose the **Ray** tool.

4. Use the **Ray** tool to construct an angle *BAC*, as shown.
5. Experiment to discover a way to construct a circle that is tangent to both sides of the angle.

Q3 Where must the center of the circle be located?

© 2002 Key Curriculum Press

6. Return to the excircles sketch and drag things around, keeping in mind what you may have just discovered about circles and angles.
7. Draw a ray from one vertex of the triangle through the center of any of the excircles.

Q4 What is special about this ray? How do you know?

8. Draw rays from each vertex of the triangle through each excircle center.
9. Drag the triangle vertices and observe relationships in the figure.

Q5 Write as many conjectures as you can about relationships in this sketch.

Explore More

1. See if you can re-create this sketch from scratch. For hints, try showing everything that is hidden.

© 2002 Key Curriculum Press

The Surfer and the Spotter

Name(s): ____________________

Two shipwreck survivors manage to swim to a desert island. As it happens, the shape of the island is a perfect equilateral triangle. The survivors have very different dispositions. Sarah soon discovers that the surfing is outstanding on all three of the island's coasts, so she crafts a surfboard from a fallen tree. Because there is plenty of food on the island, she's content to stay on the island and surf for the rest of her days. Spencer, on the other hand, is more a social animal and sorely misses civilization. Every day he goes to a different corner of the island and searches the waters for passing ships. Each castaway wants to locate a home in the place that best suits his or her needs. They have no interest in living in the same place, though if it turns out to be advantageous, neither is against the idea either. Sarah wants to visit each beach with equal frequency, so she wants to find the spot that minimizes the total length of the three paths from home to the three sides of the island. Spencer wants his house to be situated so that the total length of the three paths from his home to the three corners of the island is minimized. Where should they locate their huts?

Sketch and Investigate

Use a custom tool or construct the triangle from scratch.

1. Construct an equilateral triangle *ABC*.

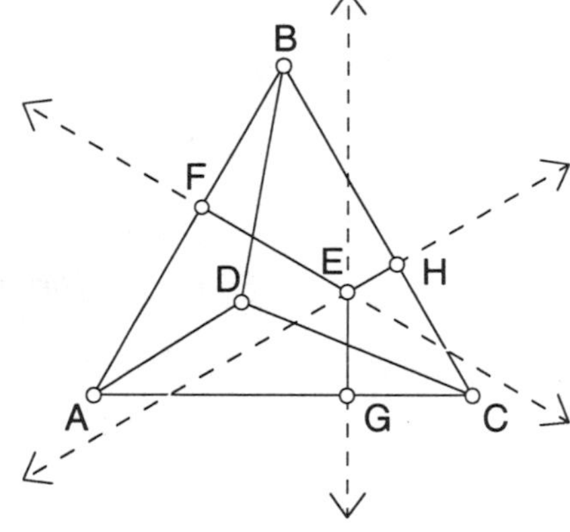

2. Construct $\overline{DA}$, $\overline{DB}$, and $\overline{DC}$, where *D* is any point inside the triangle. Point *D* represents Spencer's hut and the segments represent paths to the corners of the island.

3. Construct point *E* anywhere inside the triangle.

Select point *E* and the three sides. Then, in the Construct menu, choose **Perpendicular Lines**. You'll get all three perpendicular lines.

4. Construct lines through point *E* perpendicular to each of the three sides of the triangle.

5. Construct $\overline{EF}$, $\overline{EG}$, and $\overline{EH}$, where *F*, *G*, and *H* are the points where the perpendiculars intersect the sides of the triangle.

6. Hide the perpendicular lines. Point *E* represents Sarah's hut and the segments from it represent the paths from her hut to the beaches.

Choose **Calculate** from the Measure menu to open the Calculator. Click once on a measurement to enter it into a calculation.

7. Measure *DA*, *DB*, and *DC* and calculate *DA* + *DB* + *DC*.

8. Measure *EF*, *EG*, and *EH* and calculate *EF* + *EG* + *EH*.

9. Move points *D* and *E* (Spencer and Sarah) around inside your triangle. See if you can find the best location for each castaway.

Q1 What are the best locations for Spencer's and Sarah's huts? On a separate sheet, explain why these are the best locations.

© 2002 Key Curriculum Press

Morley's Theorem

Name(s): ______________________

You may know that it's impossible to trisect an angle with compass and straightedge. Sketchpad, however, makes it easy to trisect an angle. In this investigation, you'll trisect the three angles in a triangle and discover a surprising fact about the intersections of these angle trisections.

Sketch and Investigate

1. Use the **Ray** tool to construct triangle *ABC*, drawing your rays in counter-clockwise order as shown.

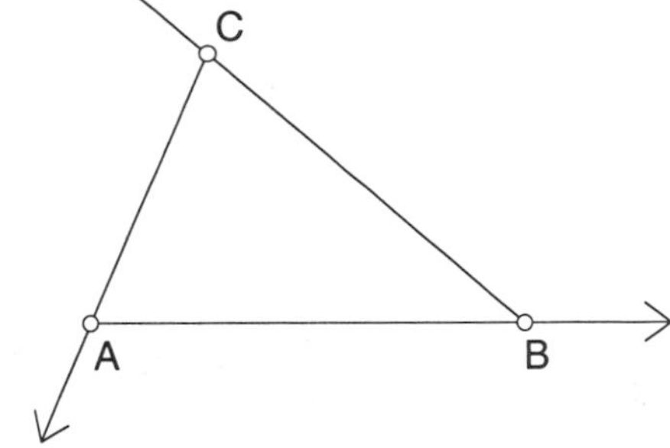

Step 1

2. Measure $\angle BAC$.

Choose **Calculate** from the Measure menu to open the Calculator. Click once on a measurement to enter it into a calculation.

3. Use the Calculator to create an expression for $m\angle BAC/3$.

Double-click point *A* to mark it as a center.

4. Mark point *A* as a center for rotation.

Select the calculation; then, in the Transform menu, choose **Mark Angle Measurement**.

5. Mark the angle measurement $m\angle BAC/3$.
6. Rotate ray *AB* by the marked angle. Rotate it again to trisect $\angle CAB$.

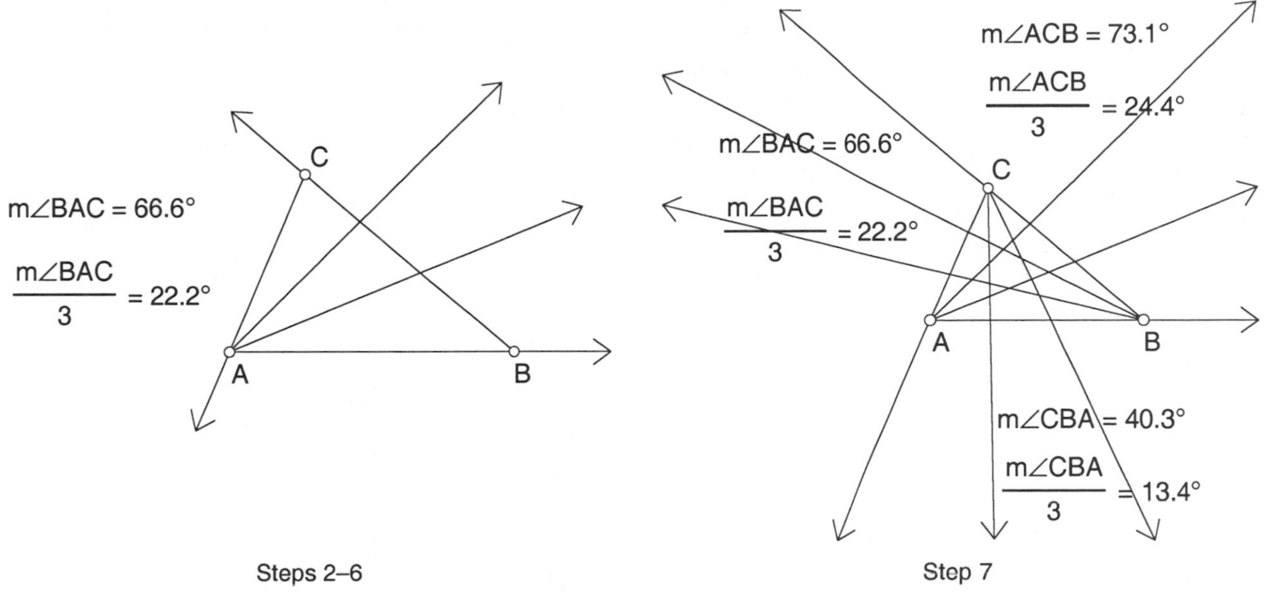

Steps 2–6

Step 7

7. Measure the other two angles and repeat steps 3 through 6 on those angles to trisect them.
8. Morley's theorem states that certain intersections of these angle trisectors form an equilateral triangle. Can you find it? Drag vertices of the triangle and watch the intersections of the trisectors.

© 2002 Key Curriculum Press

Construct the intersection points and select them. Then, in the Construct menu, choose **Triangle Interior**.

9. When you think you know which intersections form an equilateral triangle, construct those intersection points and the equilateral triangle's interior.
10. Drag to confirm that you've constructed the triangle at the correct intersections. If you can't tell for sure by looking, make the measurements necessary to confirm that the triangle is equilateral.

Q1 State Morley's theorem.

Explore More

1. See if you can find other relationships or special triangles in your figure.
2. Construct rays from the vertices of your original triangle through the opposite vertices of the equilateral triangle. What do you notice?
3. Construct a triangle using lines instead of rays. Trisect one set of exterior angles. Can you find an equilateral triangle among the intersections of these trisectors?

© 2002 Key Curriculum Press

Napoleon's Theorem

Name(s): ______________________________

French emperor Napoleon Bonaparte fancied himself as something of an amateur geometer and liked to hang out with mathematicians. The theorem you'll investigate in this activity is attributed to him.

Sketch and Investigate

1. Construct an equilateral triangle. You can use a pre-made custom tool or construct the triangle from scratch.

One way to construct the center is to construct two medians and their point of intersection.

2. Construct the center of the triangle.

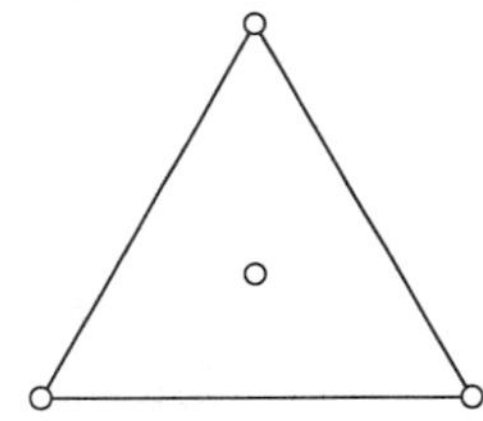

3. Hide anything extra you may have constructed to construct the triangle and its center so that you're left with a figure like the one shown at right.

Select the entire figure; then choose **Create New Tool** from the Custom Tools menu in the Toolbox (the bottom tool).

4. Make a custom tool for this construction.

Next, you'll use your custom tool to construct equilateral triangles on the sides of an arbitrary triangle.

5. Open a new sketch.

6. Construct ΔABC.

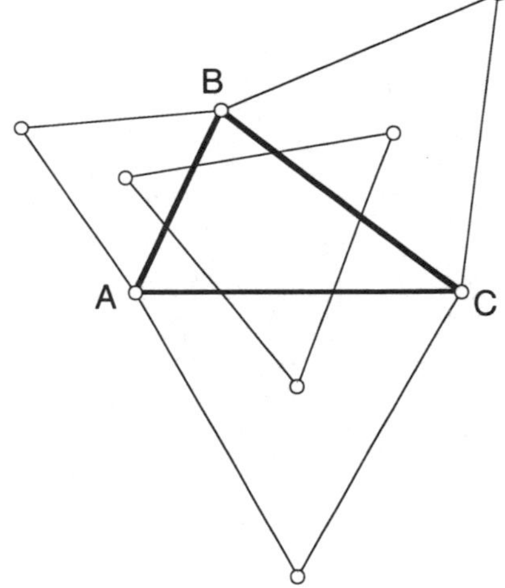

Be sure to attach each equilateral triangle to a pair of triangle *ABC*'s vertices. If your equilateral triangle goes the wrong way (overlaps the interior of ΔABC) or is not attached properly, undo and try attaching it again.

7. Use the custom tool to construct equilateral triangles on each side of ΔABC.

8. Drag to make sure each equilateral triangle is stuck to a side.

9. Construct segments connecting the centers of the equilateral triangles.

10. Drag the vertices of the original triangle and observe the triangle formed by the centers of the equilateral triangles. This triangle is called the outer Napoleon triangle of ΔABC.

Q1 State what you think Napoleon's theorem might be.

Explore More

1. Construct segments connecting each vertex of your original triangle with the most remote vertex of the equilateral triangle on the opposite side. What can you say about these three segments?

© 2002 Key Curriculum Press

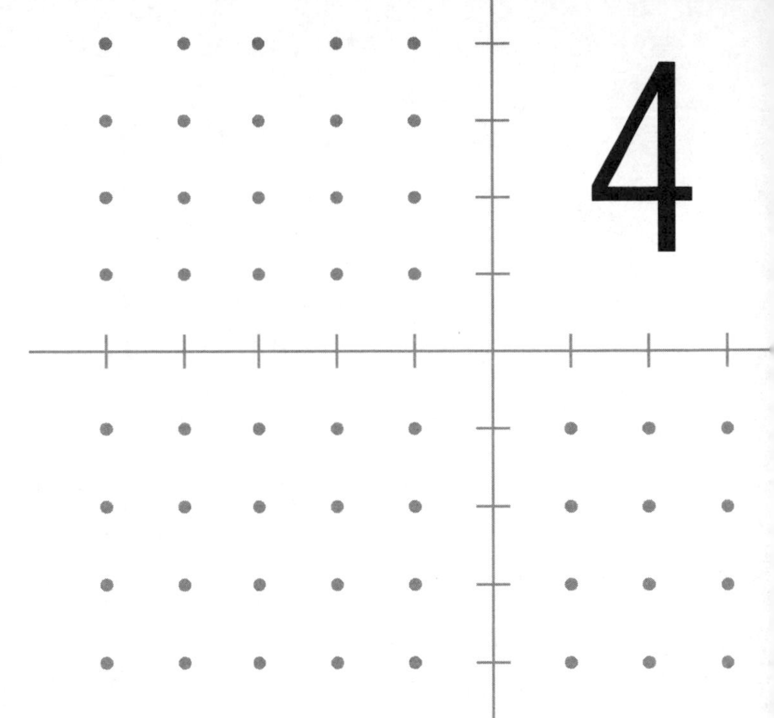

4

Quadrilaterals

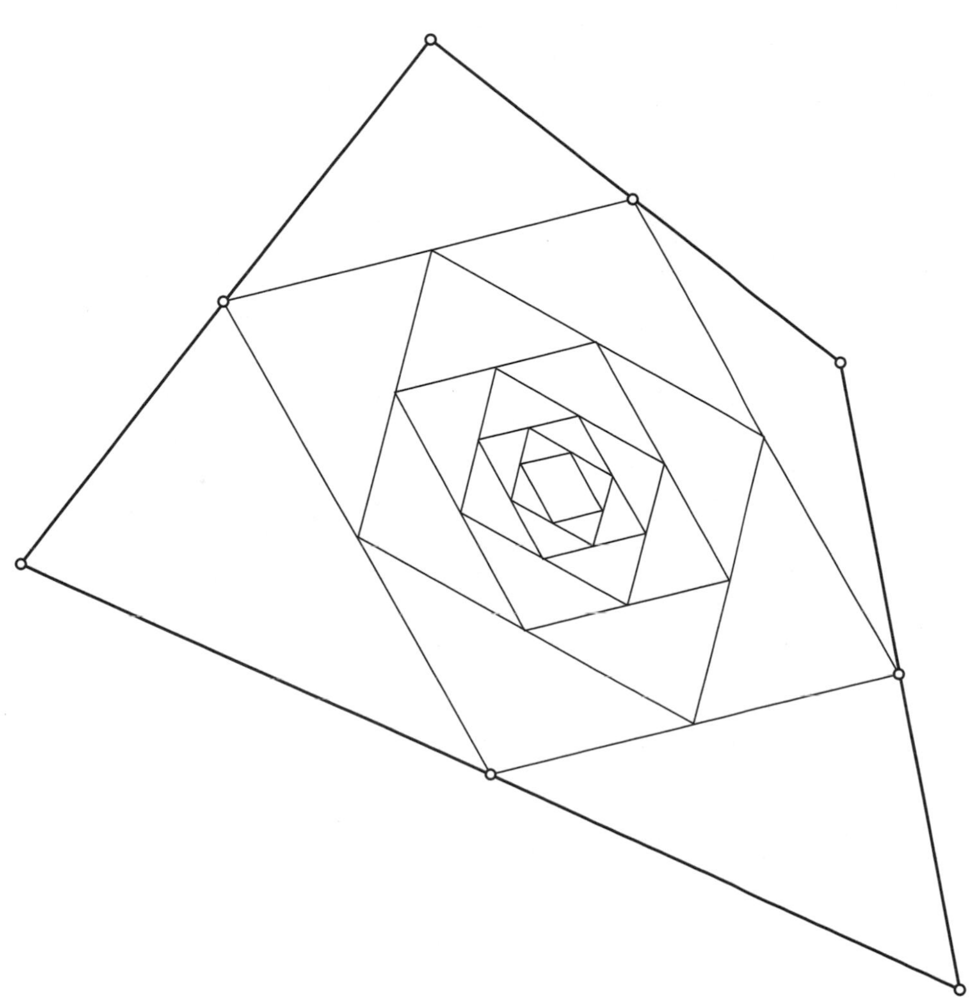

Defining Special Quadrilaterals

Name(s): ____________________

Trapezoids, kites, parallelograms, rectangles, rhombuses, and squares have special properties that distinguish them from other quadrilaterals. In this investigation, you'll experiment with these shapes to discover what makes them different from "ordinary" quadrilaterals.

Trapezoids and Kites

1. Open the document **Special Quads.gsp**.

2. Drag various parts of these quadrilaterals. Each quadrilateral has a different set of constraints in its construction that keeps it what it is.

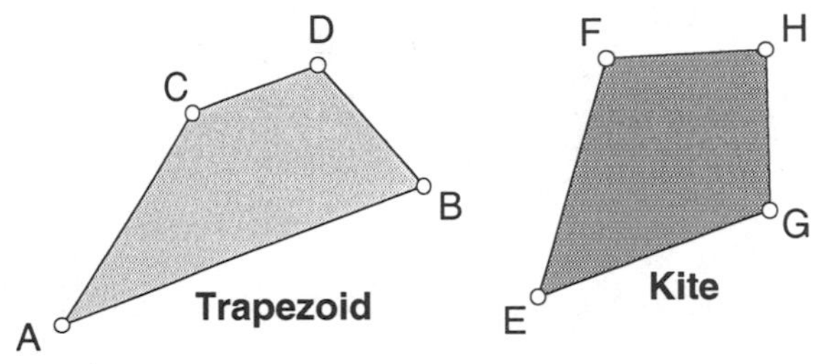

3. Measure the slopes of the four sides of the trapezoid.

If lines (or segments) have the same slope, they are parallel.

Q1 How many pairs of sides in the trapezoid are always parallel? Use your observations to define *trapezoid*.

4. Measure the lengths of the four sides of the kite.

Q2 Which sides are always equal in length? Use your observations to define *kite*.

Parallelograms

Each quadrilateral has a different set of constraints in its construction that keeps it what it is. For example, you can drag vertices of the rhombus to make different shapes, but you'll still have a rhombus.

5. Go to page 2 of **Special Quads.gsp**.

6. Drag various parts of these quadrilaterals.

7. Measure the slopes of the sides of the parallelogram.

Q3 Drag parts of the parallelogram. How many pairs of sides are parallel? Use your observations to define *parallelogram*.

© 2002 Key Curriculum Press

To measure an angle, select three points, with the vertex your middle selection. Then, in the Measure menu, choose **Angle**.

8. Measure the angles in the rectangle.

Q4 Drag parts of the rectangle. Use your observations to define *rectangle.*

9. Measure the side lengths in the rhombus.

Q5 Drag parts of the rhombus. Use your observations to define *rhombus.*

10. Measure the side lengths and angles of the square.

Q6 Drag parts of the square. Use your observations to define *square.*

Q7 Drag the rhombus so that it's also a rectangle (or at least close to it). What's the best name for this shape? ______________

Q8 Drag the rectangle so that it's also a rhombus (or at least close to it). What's the best name for this shape? ______________

Q9 Based on your observations in Q7 and Q8, write a definition of *square* different from your definition in Q6.

Q10 In a–e below, circle the word—*always, sometimes,* or *never*—that makes the sentence true.

a. A parallelogram is (always/sometimes/never) a square.

b. A rectangle is (always/sometimes/never) a rhombus.

c. A square is (always/sometimes/never) a rhombus.

d. A rectangle is (always/sometimes/never) a parallelogram.

e. A parallelogram that is not a rectangle is (always/sometimes/never) a square.

Explore More

In the Display menu, choose **Show All Hidden** to get an idea of how the quadrilaterals in the **Special Quads** sketch were constructed.

1. In a new sketch, try to construct one or more of the special quadrilaterals that you defined in this activity. Make sure your quadrilateral keeps its defining properties when you drag. Describe your construction method.

© 2002 Key Curriculum Press

Properties of Parallelograms

Name(s): ______________________

A *parallelogram* is a quadrilateral whose opposite sides are parallel. In this activity, you will construct a parallelogram using the definition, then investigate properties of parallelograms.

Sketch and Investigate

Select $\overline{AB}$ and point *C*; then, in the Construct menu, choose **Parallel Line**.

1. Construct $\overline{AB}$ and point *C* above the segment.
2. Construct a line through *C* parallel to $\overline{AB}$.

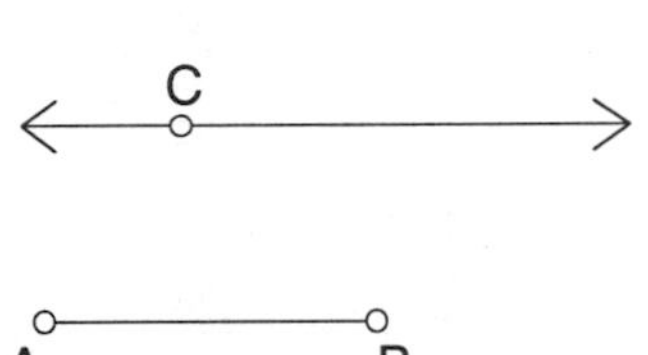

Steps 1 and 2

Steps 3–5

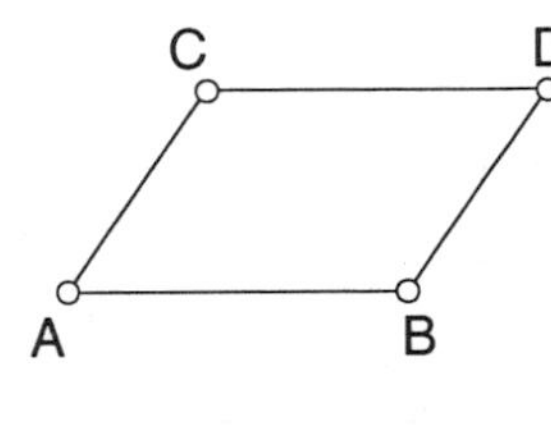

Step 6

3. Construct $\overline{AC}$.
4. Construct a line through *B* parallel to $\overline{AC}$.
5. Construct point *D*, the point of intersection of the two lines.
6. Hide both lines, then finish your parallelogram by constructing the missing segments.
7. Drag different vertices of your parallelogram to make sure it's constructed properly.

To measure an angle, select three points, with the vertex your middle selection. Then, in the Measure menu, choose **Angle**.

8. Measure the sides and angles of the parallelogram.
9. Drag different parts of the parallelogram and observe the measurements.

Q1 Write at least three conjectures about the sides and angles of a parallelogram. Use a separate sheet.

10. Construct the diagonals and their point of intersection.

Select a segment; then, in the Measure menu, choose **Length**. Or select two points and choose **Distance**.

11. Drag parts of the parallelogram and observe the diagonals. Measure lengths that look as if they might be related.

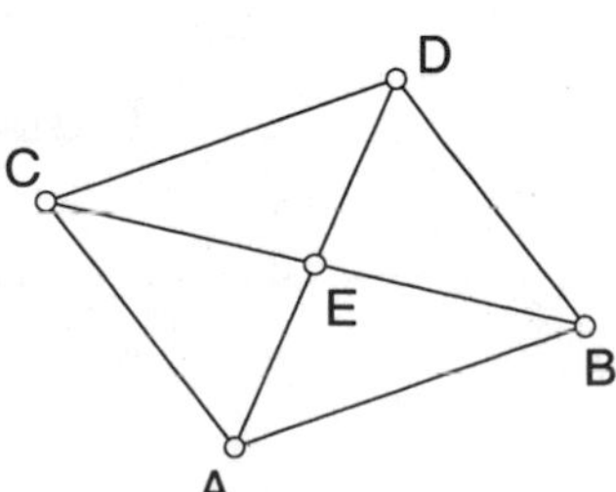

Q2 Write a conjecture about the diagonals of a parallelogram. Use a separate sheet if necessary.

© 2002 Key Curriculum Press

Constructing Parallelograms

Name(s): ____________________

How many ways can you come up with to construct a parallelogram? Try methods that use the Construct menu, the Transform menu, or combinations of both. Consider how you might use diagonals. Write a brief description of each construction method along with the properties of parallelograms that make that method work.

Method 1:

Properties:

Method 2:

Properties:

Method 3:

Properties:

Method 4:

Properties:

© 2002 Key Curriculum Press

Properties of Rectangles

Name(s): ____________________

A *rectangle* is a quadrilateral with four right angles. In this investigation, you'll construct a rectangle using its definition and discover that a rectangle has many special properties besides its equal angles.

Sketch and Investigate

1. Construct $\overline{AB}$.

Select points *A* and *B* and $\overline{AB}$; then, in the Construct menu, choose **Perpendicular Lines**. You'll get both perpendicular lines at once.

2. Construct lines perpendicular to $\overline{AB}$ through points *A* and *B*.

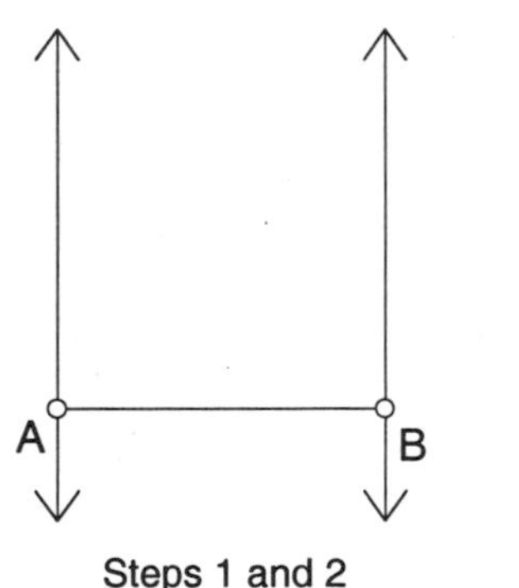

Steps 1 and 2

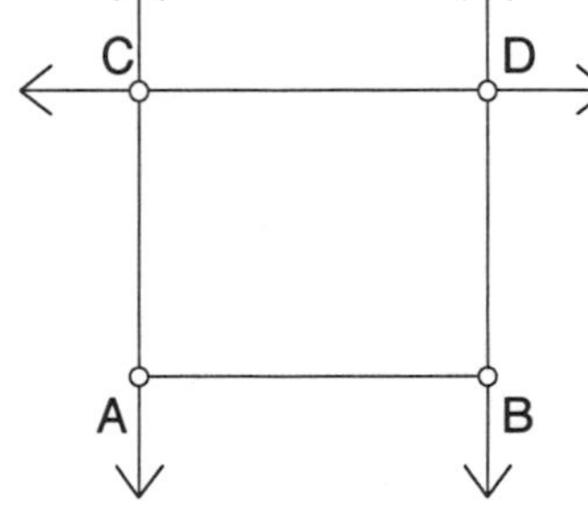

Steps 3–5

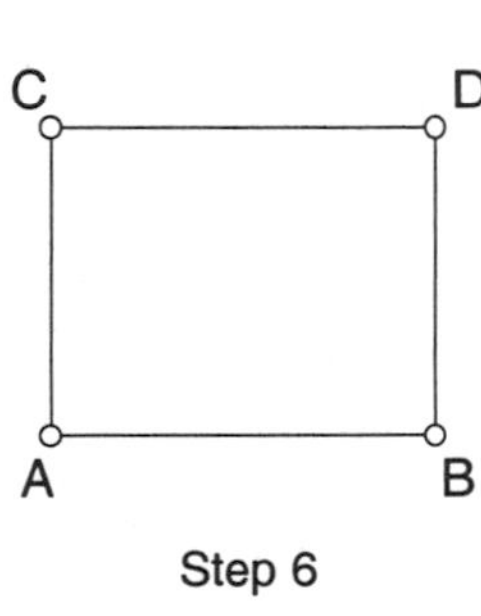

Step 6

3. Construct point *C* on the line through point *A*.
4. Construct a line through point *C* perpendicular to $\overleftrightarrow{AC}$.
5. Construct the fourth vertex, point *D*, at the intersection of this line and the line through point *B*.
6. Hide the lines, then construct segments to complete the rectangle.
7. Measure the sides of the rectangle.
8. Drag different vertices of your rectangle to make sure it's constructed properly. Observe the side lengths as you drag.

Q1 Make a conjecture about the sides of a rectangle.

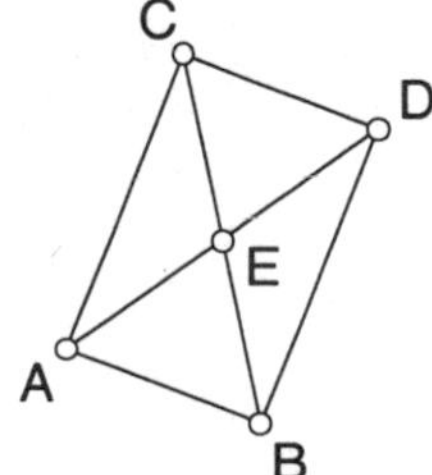

9. Construct the diagonals and their point of intersection.

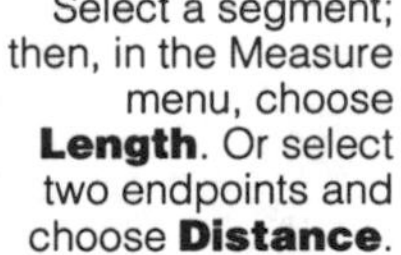
Select a segment; then, in the Measure menu, choose **Length**. Or select two endpoints and choose **Distance**.

10. Drag parts of the rectangle and observe the diagonals. Measure lengths that look as if they might be related.

Q2 Write at least two conjectures about the diagonals of a rectangle. Use another sheet of paper if necessary.

© 2002 Key Curriculum Press

Constructing Rectangles

Name(s): ______________

How many ways can you come up with to construct a rectangle? Try methods that use the Construct menu, the Transform menu, or combinations of both. Consider how you might use diagonals. Write a brief description of each construction method along with the properties of rectangles that make that method work.

C D
A B

Method 1:

Properties:

Method 2:

Properties:

Method 3:

Properties:

Method 4:

Properties:

© 2002 Key Curriculum Press

Properties of Rhombuses

Name(s): ______________________

A rhombus is an equilateral quadrilateral. In this investigation, you'll discover many other properties of rhombuses.

Sketch and Investigate

1. Construct circle AB.

Be sure to use the circle's points as endpoints for $\overline{AB}$.

2. Construct $\overline{AB}$.
3. Construct $\overline{AC}$, where point C is a point on the circle.

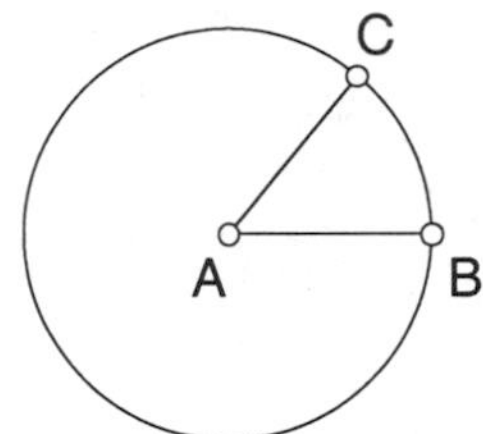

Steps 1–3

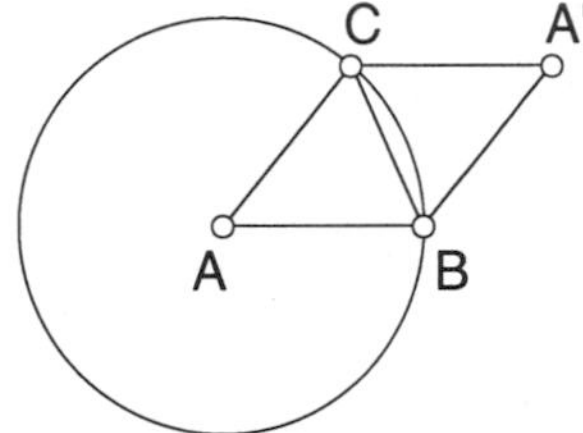

Steps 4 and 5

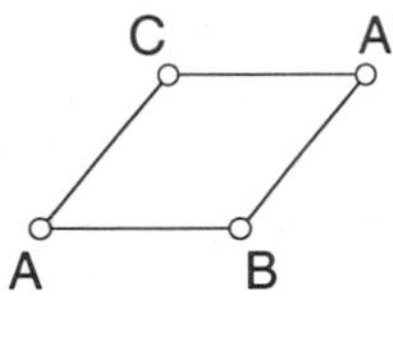

Step 6

4. Construct $\overline{BC}$.

Double-click $\overline{BC}$ to mark it as a mirror. Select point A, $\overline{AC}$, and $\overline{AB}$; then, in the Transform menu, choose **Reflect**.

5. Mark $\overline{BC}$ as a mirror and reflect point A, $\overline{AC}$, and $\overline{AB}$ over it.
6. Hide the circle and $\overline{BC}$.
7. Drag different vertices of your rhombus to make sure it's constructed properly.

To measure slope, first select a segment. Then, in the Measure menu, choose **Slope**. To measure an angle, first select three points, with the vertex your middle selection.

8. Measure the slopes of the rhombus's sides and measure the angles.
9. Drag different vertices and observe these measures.

Q1 Write at least three conjectures about the sides and angles of a rhombus.

10. Construct the diagonals and their point of intersection.

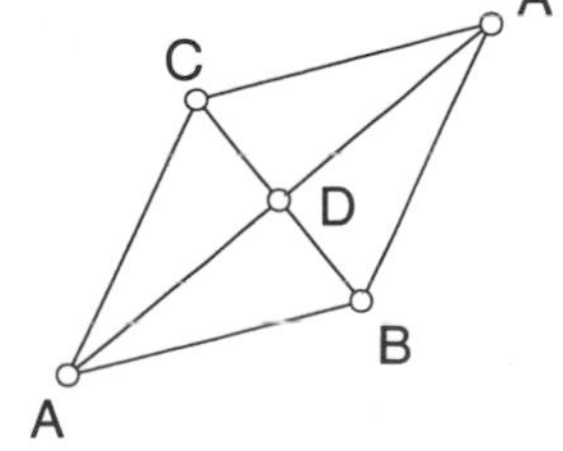

To measure a length, select a segment. Then, in the Measure menu, choose **Length**. Or select two endpoints and choose **Distance**.

11. Drag parts of the rhombus and observe how the diagonals are related to each other and to the angles in the rhombus. Measure lengths and angles that look as if they might be related.

Q2 Write at least three conjectures about the diagonals of a rhombus. Use another sheet of paper if necessary.

© 2002 Key Curriculum Press

Constructing Rhombuses

Name(s): ____________________

How many ways can you come up with to construct a rhombus? Try methods that use the Construct menu, the Transform menu, or combinations of both. Consider how you might use diagonals. Write a brief description of each construction method along with the properties of rhombuses that make that method work.

D
B
C
A

Method 1:

Properties:

Method 2:

Properties:

Method 3:

Properties:

Method 4:

Properties:

© 2002 Key Curriculum Press

Properties of Isosceles Trapezoids

Name(s): ____________________

A *trapezoid* is a quadrilateral with exactly one pair of parallel sides. An isosceles trapezoid is just what you'd expect: its legs (the nonparallel sides) have equal length. In this activity, you'll construct an isosceles trapezoid and investigate its properties.

Sketch and Investigate

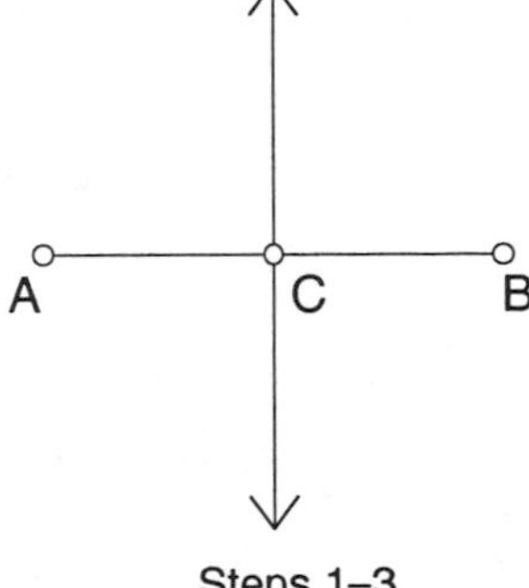

Steps 1–3

1. Construct $\overline{AB}$.
2. Construct the midpoint C of $\overline{AB}$.
3. Construct a line through point C perpendicular to $\overline{AB}$.
4. Construct $\overline{AD}$.

> Select Point C and $\overline{AB}$; then, in the Construct menu, choose **Perpendicular Line**.

5. Mark the perpendicular line as a mirror, then reflect $\overline{AD}$ and point D.

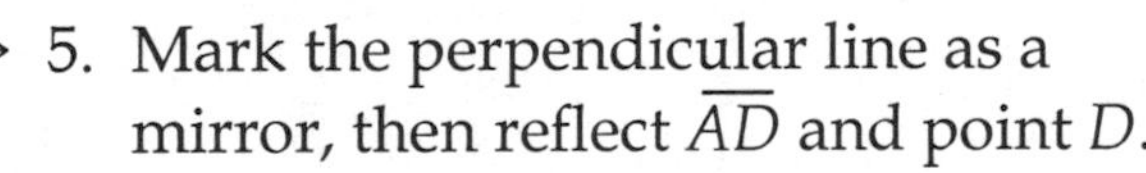

> Double-click the line to mark it as a mirror. Select $\overline{AD}$ and point D; then, in the Transform menu, choose **Reflect**.

6. Construct $\overline{DD'}$.

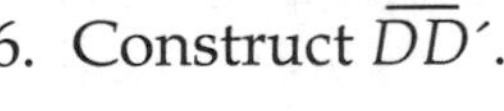

7. Hide the perpendicular line and midpoint C.

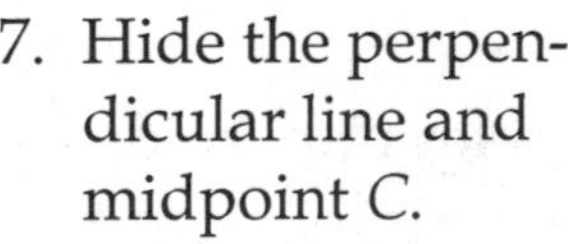

8. Drag points A, B, and D to make trapezoids of different sizes and shapes. Make sure you note when your trapezoid turns into a rectangle.

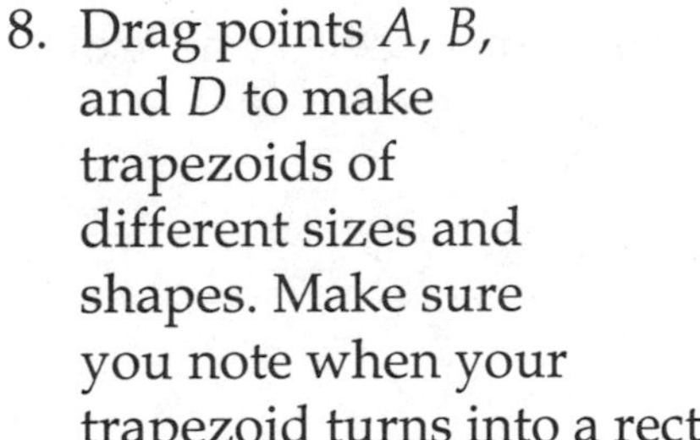

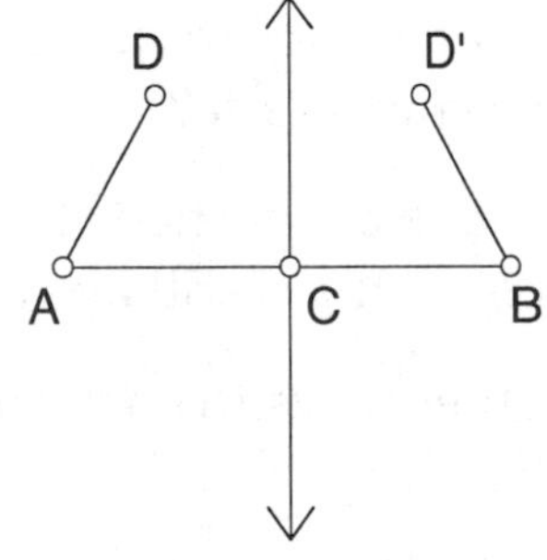

Steps 4 and 5

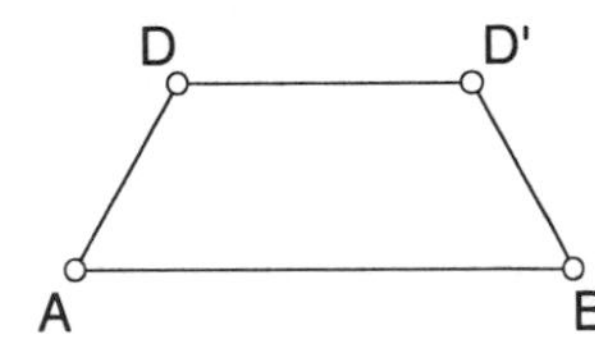

Steps 6 and 7

Q1 Based on your construction, describe the symmetry of an isosceles trapezoid.

9. Measure the four angles in your trapezoid.
10. Drag the vertices of the trapezoid and observe your angle measures.

> To measure an angle, select three points, with the vertex your middle selection. Then, in the Measure menu, choose **Angle**.

Q2 Make a conjecture about the base angles of an isosceles trapezoid. (Both of the parallel sides are considered bases, so a trapezoid has two pairs of base angles.)

© 2002 Key Curriculum Press

Q3 Make a conjecture about angle pairs that aren't at the same base.

11. Draw the diagonals in your trapezoid.
12. Measure the lengths of the two diagonals.
13. Drag the vertices of the trapezoid and observe your measures.

Q4 Write a conjecture about the diagonals in an isosceles trapezoid.

Explore More

1. The vertices in your construction can be dragged so that your figure is no longer a trapezoid. What shape can you make? Do your conjectures apply to this shape?
2. Investigate properties of nonisosceles trapezoids. Which, if any, of your conjectures still apply?
3. Find other ways to construct an isosceles trapezoid. Explain what you did.

© 2002 Key Curriculum Press

Constructing Isosceles Trapezoids

Name(s): ____________

How many ways can you come up with to construct an isosceles trapezoid? Try methods that use the Construct menu, the Transform menu, or combinations of both. Consider how you might use diagonals. Write a brief description of each construction method along with the properties of isosceles trapezoids that make that method work.

Method 1:

Properties:

Method 2:

Properties:

Method 3:

Properties:

Method 4:

Properties:

© 2002 Key Curriculum Press

Midsegments of a Trapezoid and a Triangle

Name(s): ____________________

A *midsegment* in a trapezoid connects the midpoints of the two nonparallel sides. In a triangle, the midsegment connects the midpoints of any two sides. In this investigation, you'll construct a trapezoid and its midsegment and discover some properties of the midsegments of a trapezoid. Then you'll apply these properties to the special case of a triangle.

Sketch and Investigate

1. Construct $\overline{AB}$.
2. Construct point *C* not on $\overline{AB}$.

Select point *C* and $\overline{AB}$; then, in the Construct menu, choose **Parallel Line**.

3. Construct a line through point *C* parallel to $\overline{AB}$.
4. Construct $\overline{CD}$, where point *D* is a point on the parallel line.

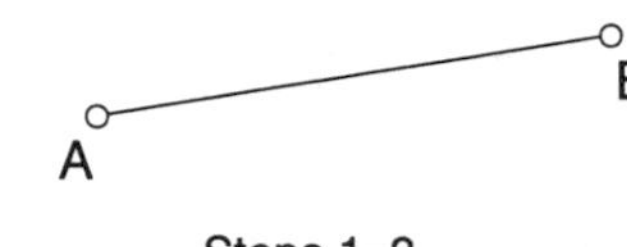

Steps 1–3

5. Construct $\overline{AC}$ and $\overline{DB}$, the legs of your trapezoid.

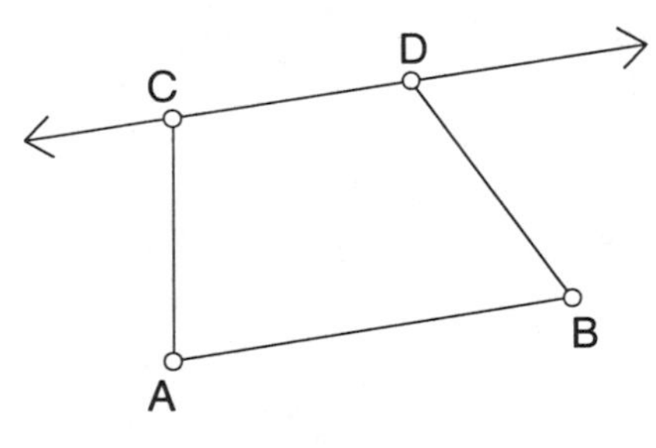

Steps 4 and 5

Steps 6–8

Select the line; then, in the Display menu, choose **Hide**.

6. Hide the parallel line.
7. Construct points *E* and *F*, the midpoints of $\overline{AC}$ and $\overline{DB}$.
8. Construct $\overline{EF}$, the midsegment of trapezoid *ACDB*.

To measure all three lengths at once, select all three segments. Then, in the Measure menu, choose **Length**.

9. Measure *AB*, *EF*, and *CD*.

Notice that *EF* is some number between *AB* and *CD*.

10. Drag various parts of the trapezoid and look for a relationship among the lengths of the midsegment and the bases.

Choose **Calculate** from the Measure menu to open the Calculator. Click once on a measurement to enter it into a calculation.

11. Use the measurements for *AB* and *CD* to calculate an expression equal to *EF*.

Q1 Write a conjecture about the midsegment of a trapezoid.

© 2002 Key Curriculum Press

12. Measure the slopes of $\overline{AB}$, $\overline{EF}$, and $\overline{CD}$.

Q2 Write a conjecture about the slope of the midsegment of a trapezoid.

13. Drag point D until CD is as close to 0 as you can make it. Now you have a triangle.

14. Drag points A and B. Observe the relationship between AB and EF and observe the relationship between the slopes.

Q3 Make a conjecture about a midsegment of a triangle.

Explore More

1. Come up with an area formula for a trapezoid and a triangle that uses the length of a midsegment.
2. In a new sketch, draw ΔABC. Mark point B as a center and dilate points A and C by a scale factor of 1/3 (or some other scale factor). Construct $\overline{A'C'}$. How do the length and direction of $\overline{A'C'}$ compare with those of $\overline{AC}$?
3. In a new sketch, construct a triangle with all three midsegments. This divides the triangle into four smaller triangles. Investigate the properties of these triangles.
4. Create a custom tool for constructing a triangle and the midpoints of its sides. Use this tool on the midpoints of the original triangle, then on the midpoints of the newly constructed triangle, and so on. Make conjectures about the smaller successive midpoint triangles. (You can also do this exploration using **Iterate** in the Transform menu.)

© 2002 Key Curriculum Press

Midpoint Quadrilaterals

Name(s): ____________________________

In this investigation, you'll discover something surprising about the quadrilateral formed by connecting the midpoints of another quadrilateral.

Sketch and Investigate

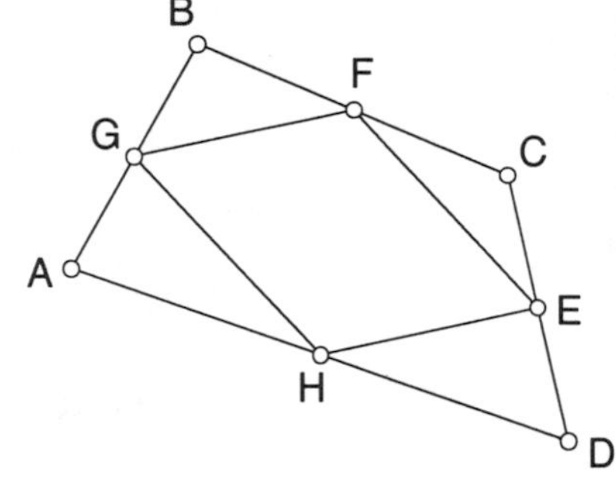

1. Construct quadrilateral *ABCD*.

If you select all four sides, you can construct all four midpoints at once.

2. Construct the midpoints of the sides.
3. Connect the midpoints to construct another quadrilateral, *EFGH*.
4. Drag vertices of your original quadrilateral and observe the midpoint quadrilateral.
5. Measure the four side lengths of this midpoint quadrilateral.

Q1 Measure the slopes of the four sides of the midpoint quadrilateral. What kind of quadrilateral does the midpoint quadrilateral appear to be? How do the measurements support that conjecture?

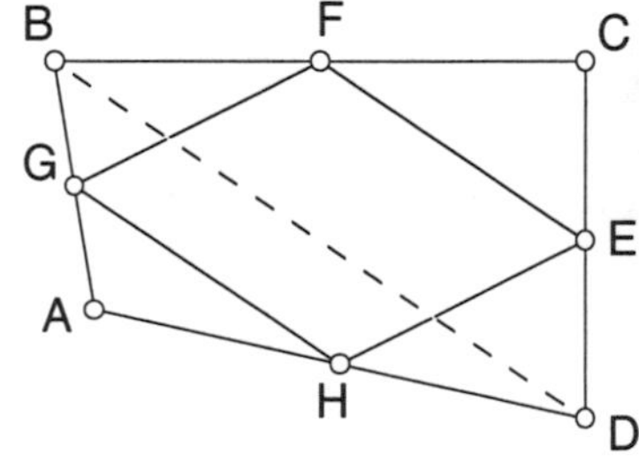

6. Construct a diagonal.
7. Measure the length and slope of the diagonal.
8. Drag vertices of the original quadrilateral and observe how the length and slope of the diagonal are related to the lengths and slopes of the sides of the midpoint quadrilateral.

Q2 The diagonal divides the original quadrilateral into two triangles. Each triangle has as a midsegment one of the sides of the midpoint quadrilateral. Use this fact and what you know about the slope and length of the diagonal to write a paragraph explaining why the conjecture you made in Q1 is true. Use a separate sheet of paper if necessary.

© 2002 Key Curriculum Press

Special Midpoint Quadrilaterals

Name(s): ____________________

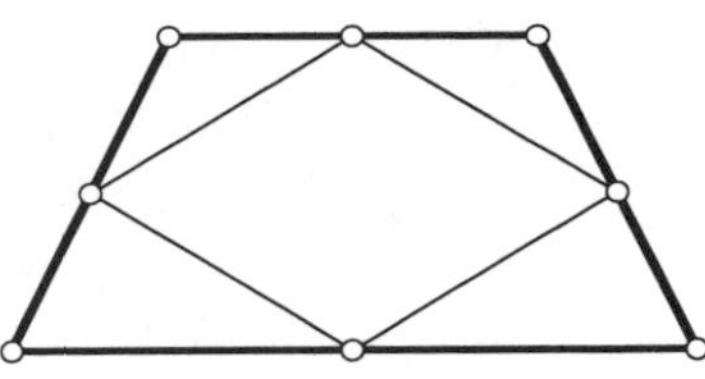

You may already know that if you connect the midpoints of any quadrilateral in consecutive order, you always form a parallelogram. Some quadrilaterals yield special parallelograms. For example, the midpoint quadrilateral of an isosceles trapezoid is a rhombus. What properties of an isosceles trapezoid cause its midpoint quadrilateral to be a rhombus? Are there other quadrilaterals whose midpoint quadrilaterals are always rhombuses? In this activity, you'll discover properties of the most general quadrilaterals whose midpoint quadrilaterals are special parallelograms.

Sketch and Investigate

1. Open the sketch **Special Midpoint Quads.gsp**. Drag vertices of these quadrilaterals and observe how they behave.
2. As you drag vertices of the outside quadrilaterals, observe the midpoint quadrilaterals. Decide which is always a rectangle, which is always a rhombus, and which is always a square. You should be able to tell by looking, without measuring anything.
3. Try to determine what's special about each outside quadrilateral. Add to the constructions and measure things as necessary.

Press the **Show Hint** button if you need help seeing what's special about these quadrilaterals. Once you've shown the hint, drag each quadrilateral again.

Q1 Describe the properties of the following quadrilaterals:

a. A quadrilateral whose midpoint quadrilateral is a rhombus

b. A quadrilateral whose midpoint quadrilateral is a rectangle

c. A quadrilateral whose midpoint quadrilateral is a square

Explore More

1. For each of the quadrilaterals described above, explain why it has a rhombus, a rectangle, or a square for its midpoint quadrilateral.
2. In a new sketch, try each of the constructions described above yourself.

© 2002 Key Curriculum Press

Summarizing Properties of Quadrilaterals

Name(s): ____________________

How much do you know about quadrilaterals? This is your chance to summarize and use what you know and maybe discover some things you didn't know. In this activity, you'll draw an arbitrary quadrilateral and measure just about everything there is to measure on it. Then you'll use those measurements to make it into various special quadrilaterals, positioning its vertices on the coordinate grid.

Preferences is in the Edit menu.

1. On the Units panel of Preferences, set Distance Units to **cm**.

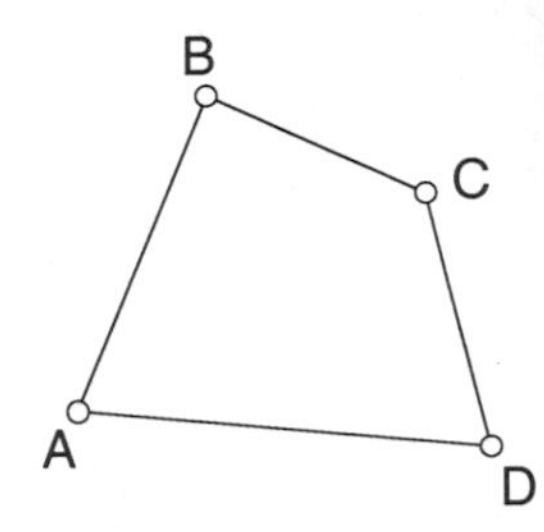

2. Construct quadrilateral *ABCD*.

Use the **Text** tool. Double-click in an empty part of your sketch to open a caption, then begin typing. You can style your text using the Text Palette that appears.

3. In separate captions across the top of your sketch, type the headings Sides, Angles, Diagonals, and Slopes. (See the figure in step 11.)
4. Measure the lengths of the four sides. Arrange these measurements under the Sides heading.

To measure an angle, select three points, with the vertex your middle selection. Then, in the Measure menu, choose **Angle**.

5. Measure each of the four angles. Arrange these measures under the Angles heading.
6. Construct diagonals $\overline{AC}$ and $\overline{BD}$.
7. Construct point *E*, the point of intersection of the diagonals.
8. Measure the length of each diagonal and arrange these measurements under Diagonals.
9. Measure $\angle AEB$. Put this measurement under Diagonals.

Select points *A* and *E*; then, in the Measure menu, choose **Distance**. Repeat for the other distances.

10. Measure *AE*, *EC*, *BE*, and *ED* and arrange these measurements under Diagonals.
11. Measure the slopes of the four sides. Arrange these measures under the Slopes heading.

Sides	**Angles**	**Diagonals**	**Slopes**
m $\overline{AB}$ = 1.91 cm	m∠DAB = 65°	m $\overline{AC}$ = 3.79 cm	Slope $\overline{AB}$ = 1.677
m $\overline{BC}$ = 2.45 cm	m∠ABC = 121°	m $\overline{BD}$ = 3.37 cm	Slope $\overline{BC}$ = -0.003
m $\overline{CD}$ = 2.02 cm	m∠BCD = 98°	m∠AEB = 62°	Slope $\overline{CD}$ = -7.504
m $\overline{DA}$ = 3.71 cm	m∠CDA = 77°	AE = 2.15 cm	Slope $\overline{DA}$ = -0.099
		EC = 1.64 cm	
		BE = 1.20 cm	
		ED = 2.17 cm	

© 2002 Key Curriculum Press

In the Graph menu, choose **Snap Points**.

12. Turn point snapping on.

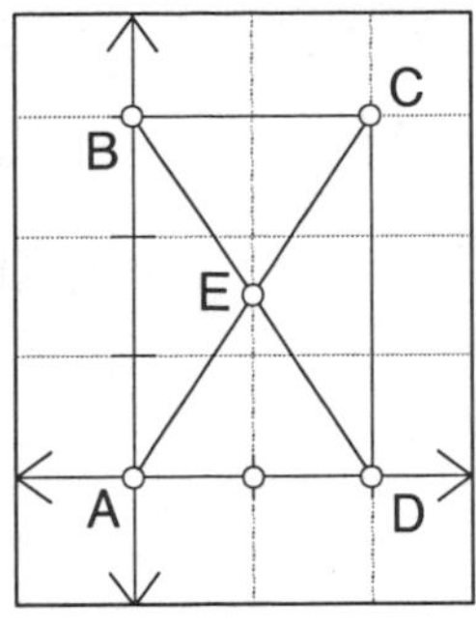

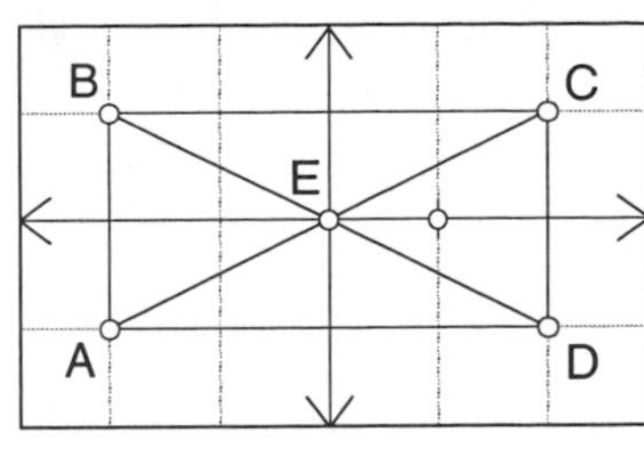

13. Use all the measurements and what you know about rectangles to position the vertices on the grid in such a way that you know the quadrilateral is a rectangle. The slopes can help you: Recall that lines with equal slopes are parallel.

Take advantage of the axes when you position the vertices.

14. Try several different methods of positioning vertices so that the quadrilateral is a rectangle. Observe the measures of the sides, angles, and diagonals of these rectangles.

Q1 Fill in the "Rectangle" column in the chart below. Write "Yes" if the property is true for all rectangles and "No" if it is ever not true.

	Rectangle	Rhombus	Square	P'gram	Kite	Iso. Trap.
Opposite Sides ≅						
Opposite ∠s ≅						
Consecutive ∠'s sum = 180°						
Diagonals ≅						
Diagonals ⊥						
Diagonals bisect each other						

Positioning the rhombus is tricky. Try positioning the diagonals on the axes. Be creative about the ways you position your squares.

Q2 Experiment with positioning vertices to form parallelograms, rhombuses, squares, kites, and isosceles trapezoids. Fill in the boxes in the chart for those shapes. Remember that one counterexample is enough reason to write "No."

Q3 Which shapes named in the chart are parallelograms? How does the information in the chart support your answer? Answer on a separate sheet of paper.

Q4 A square can be defined as a rhombus and a rectangle. How does the information in the chart support this definition? Answer on a separate sheet of paper.

Q5 Is a rectangle a special kind of isosceles trapezoid? Explain.

© 2002 Key Curriculum Press

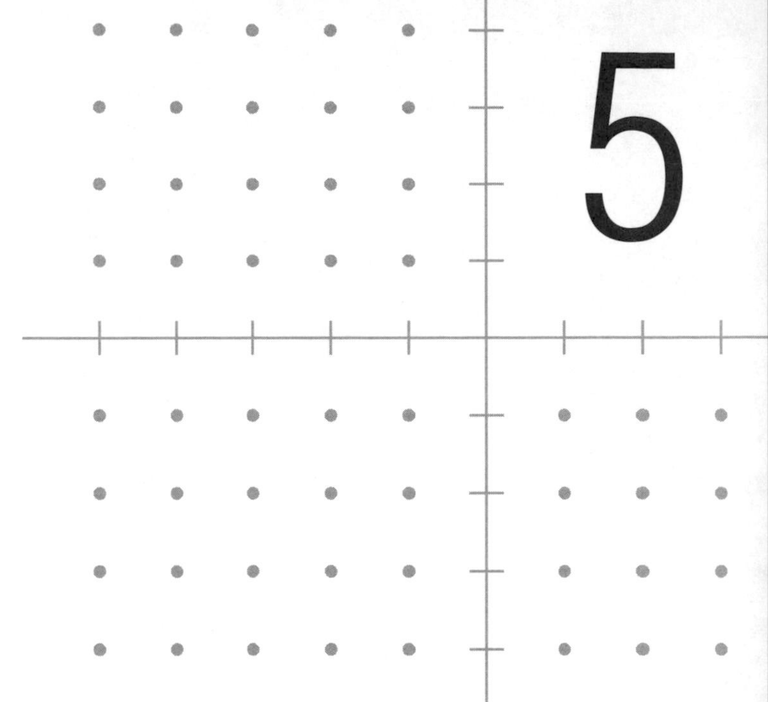

5

Polygons

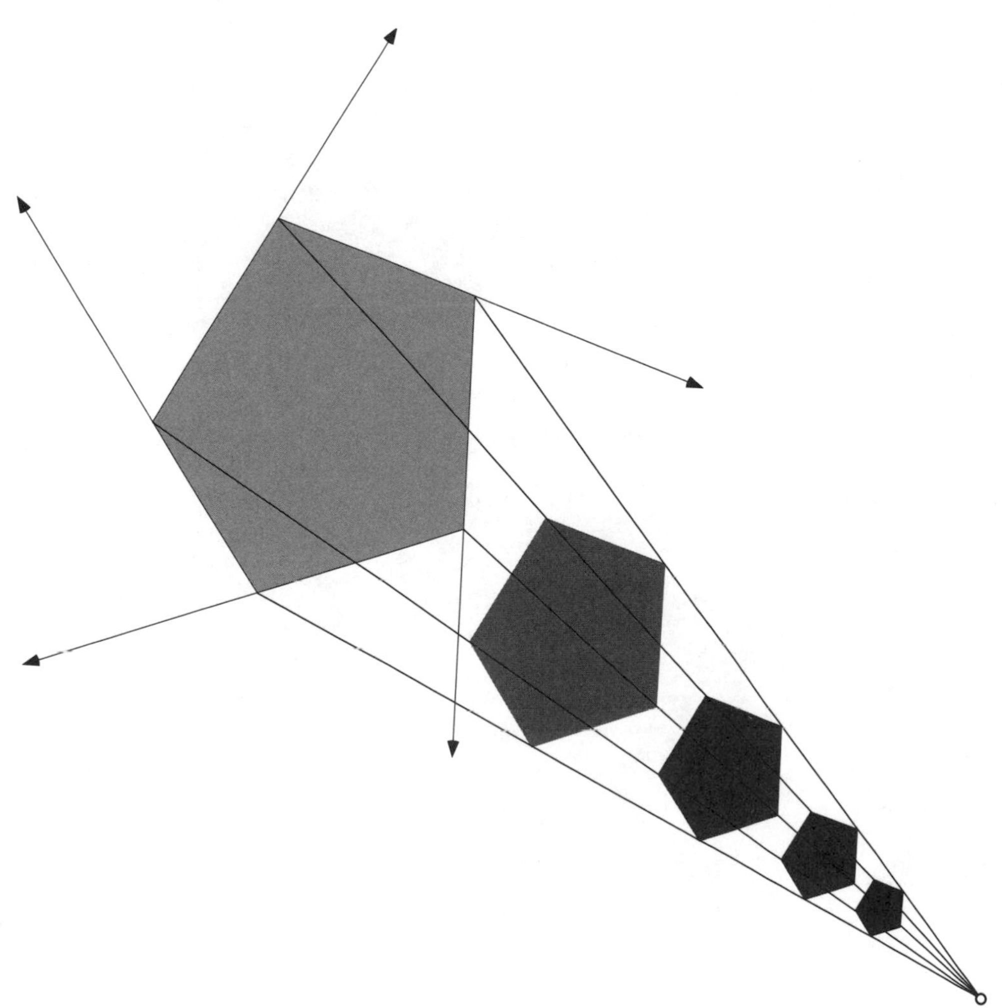

Exterior Angles in a Polygon

Name(s): ____________________

An exterior angle of a polygon is formed when one of the sides is extended. Exterior angles lie outside a convex polygon. In this investigation, you'll discover the sum of the measures of the exterior angles in a convex polygon.

Do this investigation with a triangle, a quadrilateral, or a pentagon. Plan together with classmates at nearby computers to investigate different polygons so that you can compare your results. The activity here shows a pentagon. Don't let that throw you if you're investigating a triangle or a quadrilateral—the basic steps are the same.

Sketch and Investigate

Hold down the mouse button on the **Segment** tool, then drag right to choose the **Ray** tool.

1. Use the **Ray** tool to construct a polygon with each side extended in one direction. Be sure to construct the polygon without creating any extra points. Your initial sketch should have the same number of points (vertices) as sides. If your polygon didn't end up convex, drag a vertex to make it convex.

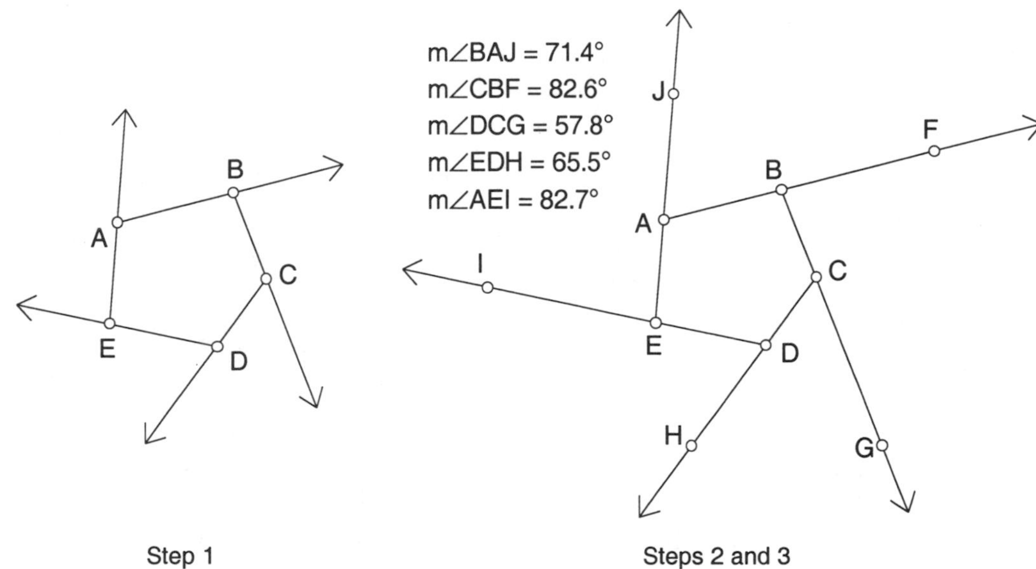

Step 1

Steps 2 and 3

To measure an angle, select three points, with the vertex your middle selection. Then, in the Measure menu, choose **Angle**.

2. Construct a point on each ray outside of the polygon so that you'll be able to measure exterior angles.
3. Measure each exterior angle. Be careful to measure the correct ones!

Choose **Calculate** from the Measure menu to open the Calculator. Click once on a measurement to enter it into a calculation.

4. Calculate the sum of the exterior angles.
5. Drag different vertices of your polygon and observe the angle measures and their sum. Be sure the polygon stays convex.
6. Compare your observations with those of classmates who did this investigation with different polygons.

© 2002 Key Curriculum Press

Q1 Write a conjecture about the sum of the measures of the exterior angles in any polygon.

Follow the steps below for another way to demonstrate this conjecture.

Double-click a point to mark it as a center.

7. Mark any point in the sketch as a center for dilation.

In the Edit menu, choose **Select All**. Then click on each measurement to deselect it.

8. Select everything in the sketch except for the measurements.

Hold down the mouse button on the **Arrow** tool, then drag right to choose the **Dilate Arrow** tool.

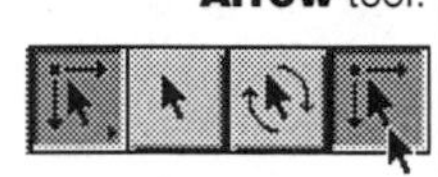

9. Change your **Arrow** tool to the **Dilate Arrow** tool and use it to drag any part of the construction toward the marked center. Keep dragging until the polygon is nearly reduced to a single point.

Q2 Write a paragraph explaining how this demonstrates the conjecture you made in Q1.

Explore More

In the Edit menu, choose **Preferences** and go to the Units panel. In the Angle Units pop-up menu, choose **directed degrees**.

1. Investigate the sum of the exterior angle measures in concave polygons. For this investigation, you may want to measure angles in directed degrees. The sign of an angle measured in directed degrees depends on the order in which you select points.

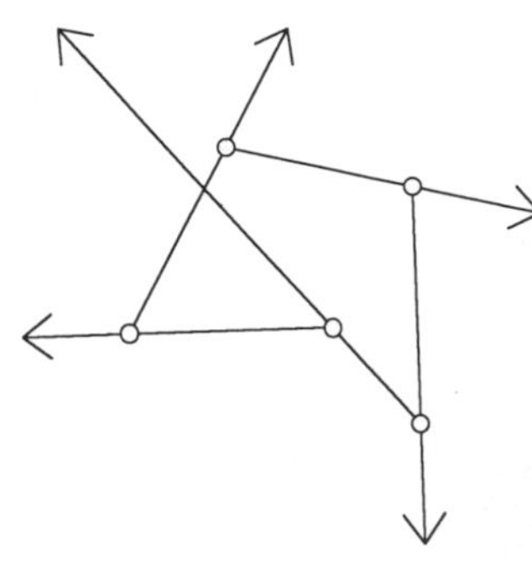

© 2002 Key Curriculum Press

Star Polygons

Name(s): ______________________

If you're a doodler, you probably learned at an early age how to draw a five-pointed star. In this activity, you'll discover a relationship among the angles of such a star. Then you'll investigate angles in other types of star polygons.

1. Construct five points arranged so that they roughly lie on a circle.

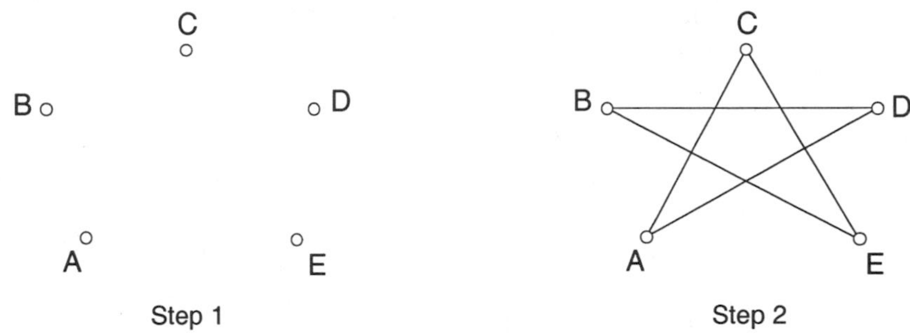

To measure an angle, select three points, with the vertex your middle selection. Then, in the Measure menu, choose **Angle**.

Choose **Calculate** from the Measure menu to open the Calculator. Click once on a measurement to enter it into a calculation.

2. Connect every second point with segments: $\overline{AC}$, $\overline{CE}$, $\overline{EB}$, $\overline{BD}$, and $\overline{DA}$.
3. Measure the five angles A through E at the star points.
4. Calculate the sum of the five angle measures.
5. Drag any star point and observe the angle measures and the sum.

Q1 In the chart below, write the angle measure sum for the five-pointed star in which every second point is connected.

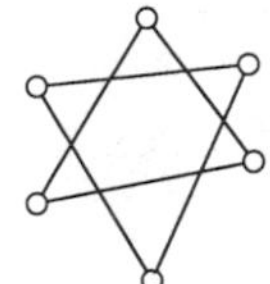

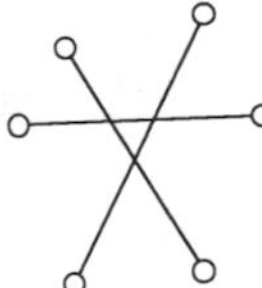

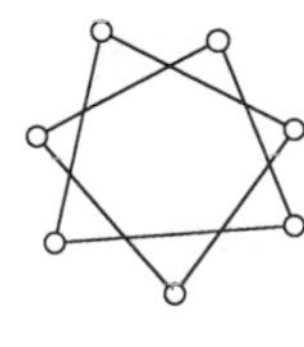

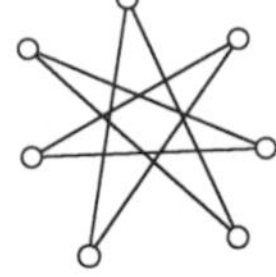

Q2 Investigate other star polygons and complete the rest of the chart. Examples of six- and seven-pointed star polygons formed by connecting every second or third point are shown at left. Plan together with classmates so that you don't have to investigate every case yourself. Also, look for patterns that you can use to fill in the chart without having to construct all the stars. Use the back of this page or a separate sheet of paper to describe any patterns you observe.

	Angle measure sums by the ways points are connected		
# of star points	Every 2nd point	Every 3rd point	Every 4th point
5			
6			
7			
8			
9			

© 2002 Key Curriculum Press

Polygon Angle Measure Sums

Name(s): ____________________

You may already know what the sum of the angle measures is in any triangle. In this activity, you'll see how that sum is related to the sum of the angle measures in other polygons.

Sketch and Investigate

1. Use the **Segment** tool to draw a triangle, a quadrilateral, and a pentagon across the top of your sketch.

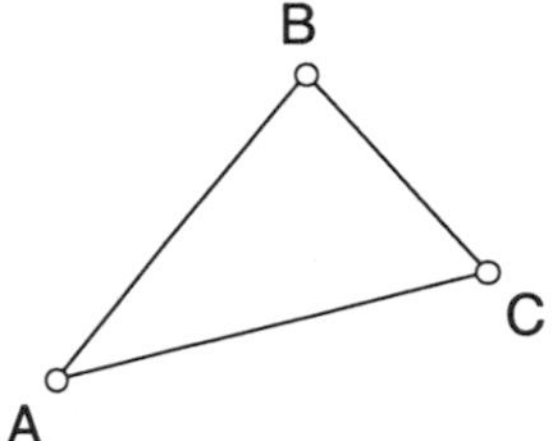

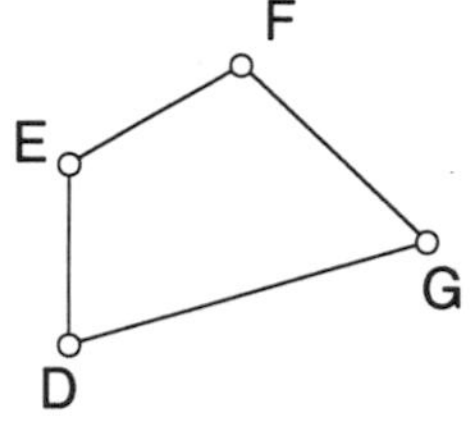

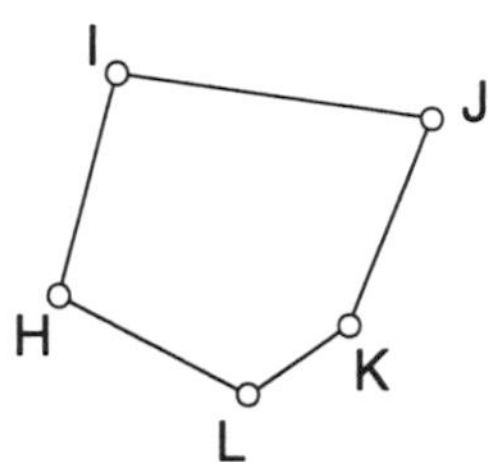

To measure an angle, select three points, with the vertex your middle selection. Then, in the Measure menu, choose **Angle**.

2. Measure each of the three angles in the triangle and arrange the measurements under the triangle.
3. Measure the four angles of the quadrilateral and arrange them under the quadrilateral.
4. Measure the five angles of the pentagon and arrange them under the pentagon.

Choose **Calculate** from the Measure menu to open the Calculator. Click once on a measurement to enter it into a calculation. If the Calculator is in the way of your measurements, move it by dragging the title bar.

5. Calculate the sum of the triangle angle measures.
6. Drag any vertex of the triangle and observe the angle measures and the sum.
7. Calculate the sum of the quadrilateral angle measures.
8. Drag any vertex of the quadrilateral and observe the angle measures and the sum. Be sure to keep the quadrilateral convex.
9. Calculate the sum of the pentagon angle measures.
10. Drag any vertex of the pentagon and observe the angle measures and the sum. Be sure to keep the pentagon convex.

Q1 Did any of the sums change when you dragged (as long as the polygons were convex)?

© 2002 Key Curriculum Press

Q2 Describe the pattern in the angle measure sums as you increased the number of sides in a polygon.

11. Draw a diagonal in the quadrilateral.
12. Draw two diagonals from one vertex in the pentagon.

Q3 Write a paragraph explaining what these diagonals have to do with the pattern you described in Q2.

Q4 Write an expression for the sum of the angle measures in an *n*-gon.

Explore More

1. Sketchpad does not display angle measures greater than 180°, so if you drag your polygon so that it's concave, Sketchpad measures the angle outside the polygon instead of the interior angle. Suppose you were able to measure angles greater than 180°. Do you think a concave polygon would have the same angle measure sum as a convex polygon with the same number of sides? Explain why or why not.

© 2002 Key Curriculum Press

Constructing Regular Polygons

Name(s): ______________

A *regular polygon* is a polygon whose sides all have equal length and whose angles all have equal measure. The easiest way to construct regular polygons with Sketchpad is to use rotations. The figures below show pentagons constructed by two different methods.

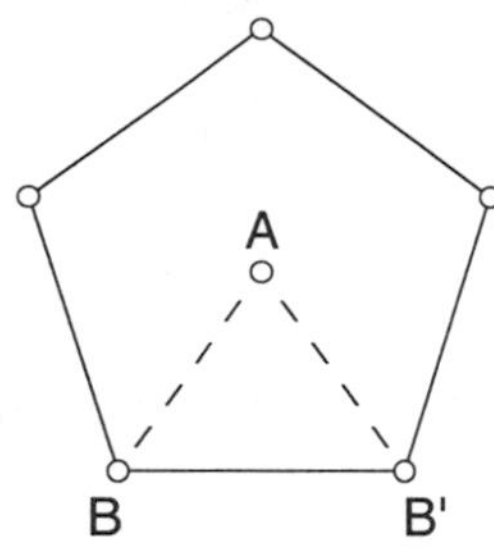

This pentagon was constructed by rotating vertex *B* around center point *A*. ∠*BAB′* is a *central angle* of the polygon.

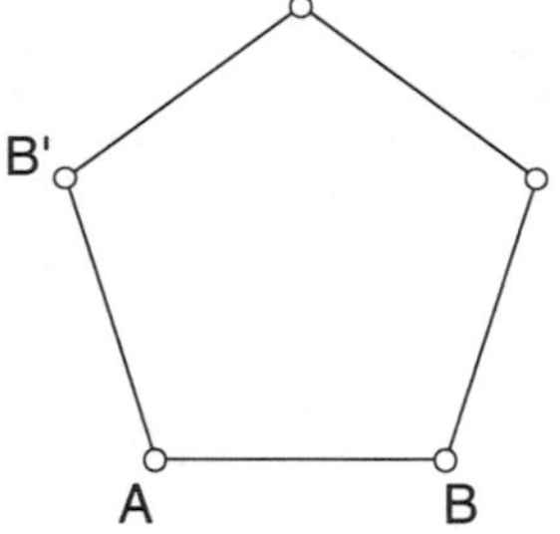

This pentagon was constructed by rotating vertex *B* around vertex *A*. ∠*BAB′* is an *interior angle* of the polygon.

Before you rotate anything, you must mark a center of rotation. Double-click a point to mark it as a center. Select what you want to rotate; then, in the Transform menu, choose **Rotate**.

→ Experiment with using rotations to construct different regular polygons. Figure out central angle measures to rotate by and interior angle measures to rotate by. Each time you make a polygon that seems correct, drag points to make sure it holds together. Make custom tools of your successful constructions to use in later work. Fill in the chart below with the central and interior angle measures for the named regular polygons, whether you have time to construct them all or not. Indicate which constructions you made custom tools for.

To make a custom tool, select the entire figure. Then, click on the **Custom** tools icon (the bottom tool in the Toolbox), and choose **Create New Tool** from the menu that appears.

Polygon	Central angle measure	Interior angle measure	Saved tool? (Y or N)
Equilateral triangle			
Square			
Regular pentagon (5)			
Regular hexagon (6)			
Regular octagon (8)			
Regular nonagon (9)			
Regular decagon (10)			
Regular *n*-gon			

Explore More

1. The regular heptagon (seven sides) doesn't appear on the chart because the angle measures aren't "nice." What are they? To construct the regular heptagon, use the Calculator to calculate an expression for the desired angle, then mark that measurement as an angle for rotation.

© 2002 Key Curriculum Press

Constructing Templates for the Platonic Solids

Name(s): ____________________

You've probably constructed an equilateral triangle. That construction was the first proposition in Euclid's *Elements*. After thirteen books of carefully sequenced constructions and theorems, the grand finale of Euclid's *Elements* is his proof that there are exactly five Platonic solids. A *Platonic solid* is a polyhedron whose faces are all congruent, regular polygons meeting at each vertex in the same way. The five solids are shown below.

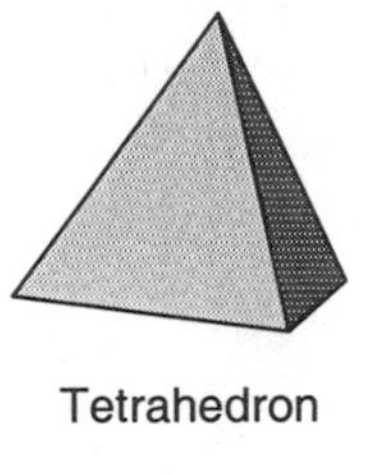
Tetrahedron

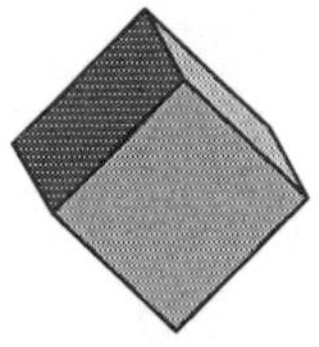
Cube

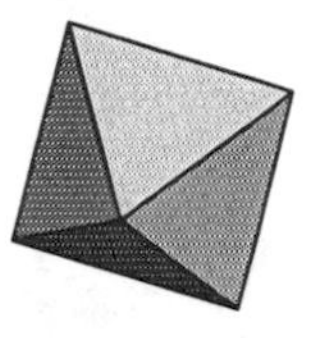
Octahedron

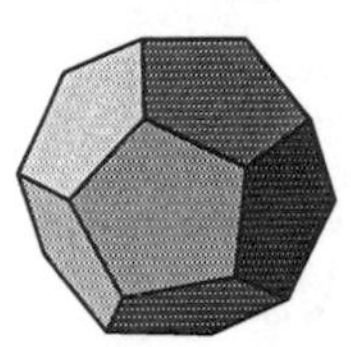
Dodecahedron

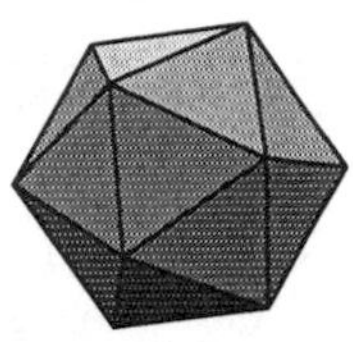
Icosahedron

With Sketchpad, you can construct a template for an unfolded polyhedron and print it on a piece of stiff paper. Then you can cut it out and fold it into the polyhedron, taping together the edges. Each of the solids has more than one possible template. Two examples are shown here.

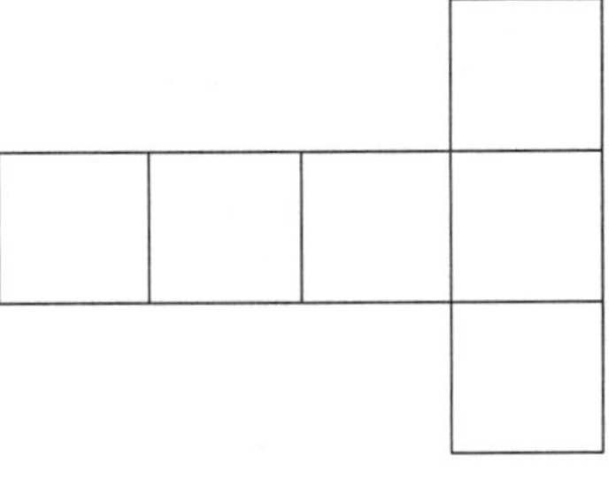
Cube (Hexahedron)

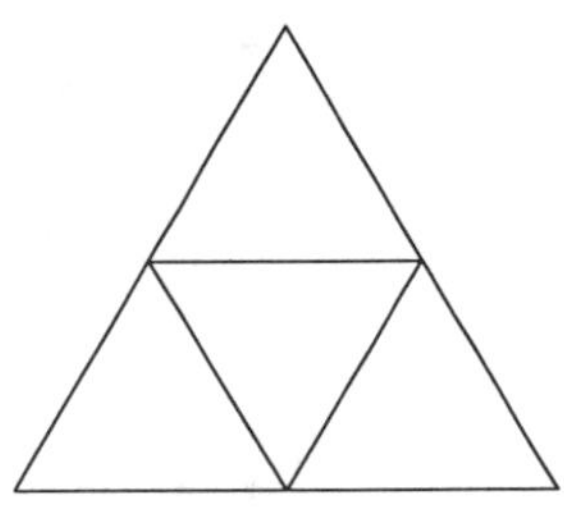
Tetrahedron

As you can see, the cube has six square faces. The four faces of the tetrahedron are equilateral triangles. An octahedron has eight faces, a dodecahedron has twelve faces, and an icosahedron has twenty faces.

Use the Transform menu for reflections and rotations. You'll need to mark mirrors (segments) for reflections and to mark centers (points) for rotations.

→ Use Sketchpad to create templates for one or more of the other Platonic solids. Once you've created a regular polygon, you can use reflections and/or rotations to create an adjacent one on your template. You can also use custom tools for regular polygons to create your templates. Describe the method you used to make each template.

Before you print, in the File menu, choose **Print Preview**. Make sure the template fits on a page. If it doesn't, check the Scale To Fit Page box.

→ If you can, print your templates, cut them out, and fold them to see if they work the way you imagined.

Explore More

1. Make templates for other three-dimensional shapes: cylinders, prisms, and so on.
2. Do some research and make templates for semiregular polyhedra (called *Archimedean solids*).

© 2002 Key Curriculum Press

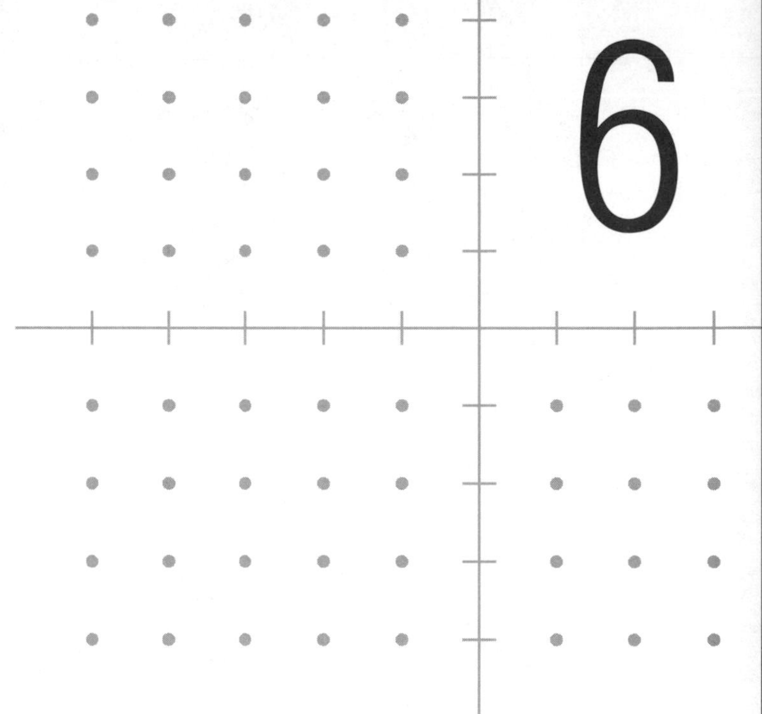

6 Circles

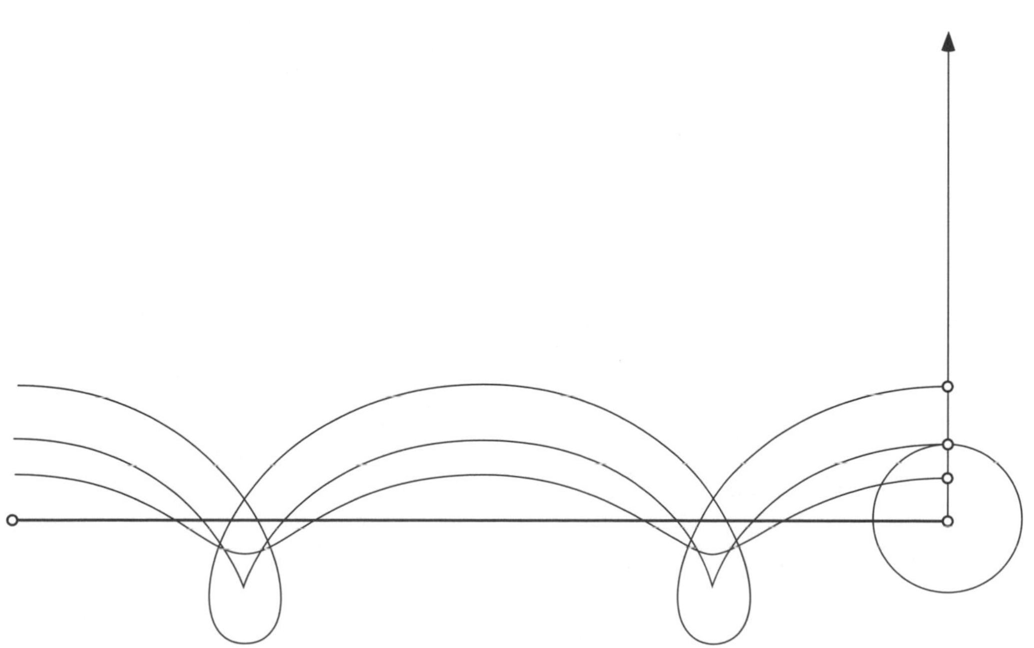

Introducing Circles

Name(s): ______________________

A circle is the set of all points in a plane the same distance from a given point. In this activity, you'll construct circles and investigate the meaning of this definition and other circle definitions.

Sketch and Investigate

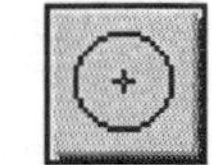

The **Compass** tool

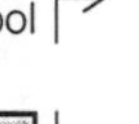

The **Selection Arrow** tool

1. Use the **Compass** tool to construct a circle. Two points define your circle.

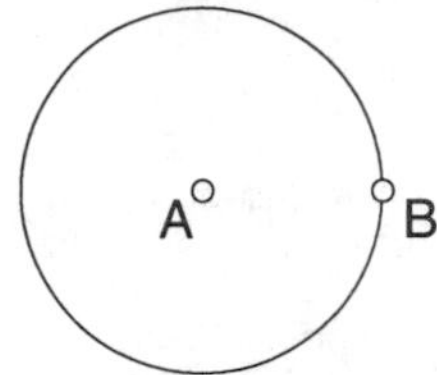

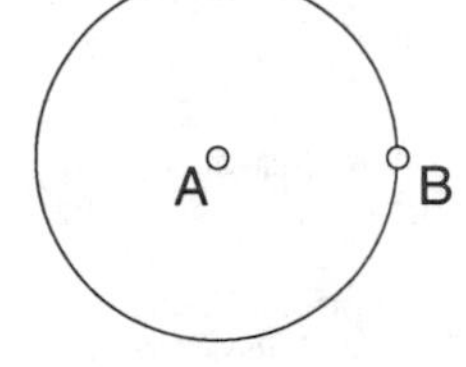

2. Choose the **Selection Arrow** tool and drag each point to see how it affects the circle.

Q1 Describe how each point affects the circle.

The **Text** tool

Click once on an object to show or hide its label. Drag the label to move it. Double-click the label to change it.

3. Choose the **Text** tool. Show the point labels and change them, if necessary, to match the diagram.
4. Choose the **Segment** tool and construct segment *AB*. This segment is called a *radius*.

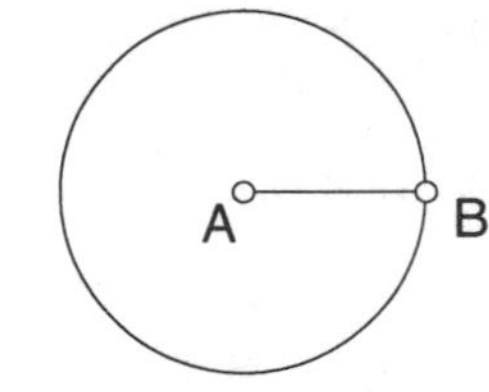

5. Choose the **Selection Arrow** tool. Select the segment and, in the Measure menu, choose **Length**. This length is also called the *radius* of the circle.

In most books, a circle is named after its center point. The circle shown at right would be called circle *A*. However, it's often convenient to name a Sketchpad circle after both points that define it, so you could call the circle at right circle *AB*.

6. Select the circle and, in the Measure menu, choose **Radius**.
7. Drag point *A* or point *B* and observe these measures.
8. Use the **Point** tool to construct point *C* on the circle.

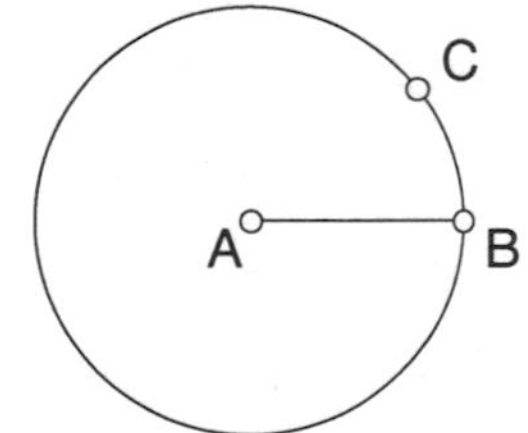

9. Choose the **Selection Arrow** tool. Click in blank space to deselect all objects. Select point *A* and point *C*. In the Measure menu, choose **Distance**.
10. Drag point *C* around the circle and observe the distance *AC*.

Q2 True or false: The radius of a circle is the distance from the center to *any* point on the circle. ______________

11. Construct a circle centered at point *A* with control point *D*, as shown at right.
12. Drag point *D* so that circle *AD* moves inside and outside circle *AB*.

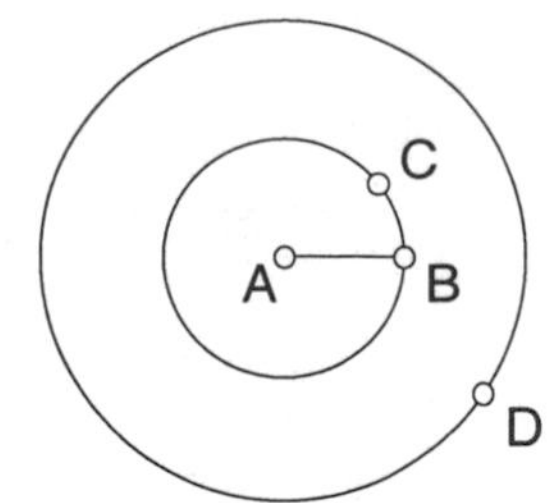

© 2002 Key Curriculum Press

Q3 If two or more coplanar circles share the same center, they are *concentric* circles. How many circles can share the same center? (Why might it be convenient to name circles after two points?)

Select $\overline{AB}$ and point *E*; then, in the Construct menu, choose **Circle By Center+Radius**.

13. Construct a point *E* anywhere in your sketch.
14. Construct a circle with center *E* and radius *AB*.
15. Drag point *B* to see how it affects circle *E*.

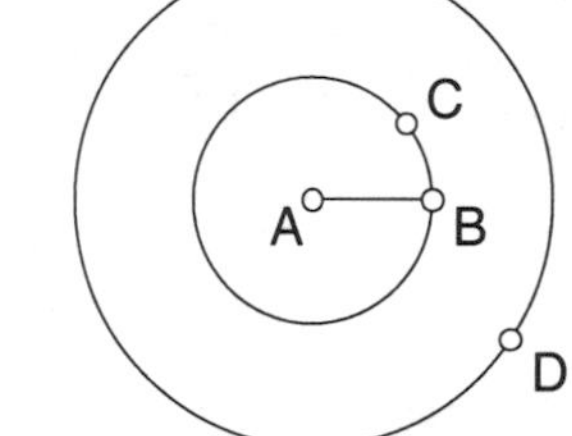

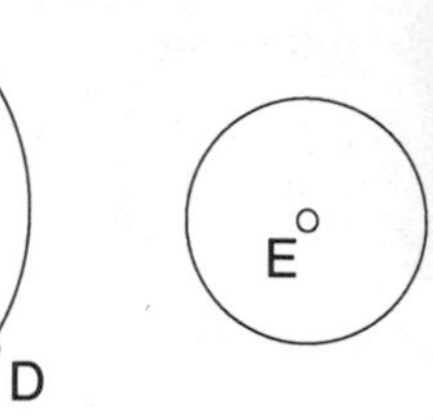

Sketchpad will call the circle something like "circle c1" instead of "circle *E*."

16. Measure the radius of circle *E*.

Q4 Circle *E* and circle *AB* are *congruent circles*. Write a definition of congruent circles.

17. Construct $\overline{FG}$, where points *F* and *G* are points on circle *E*. This segment is called a *chord* of the circle.
18. Measure the length of $\overline{FG}$.
19. Drag point *F* around the circle and observe the length measure.

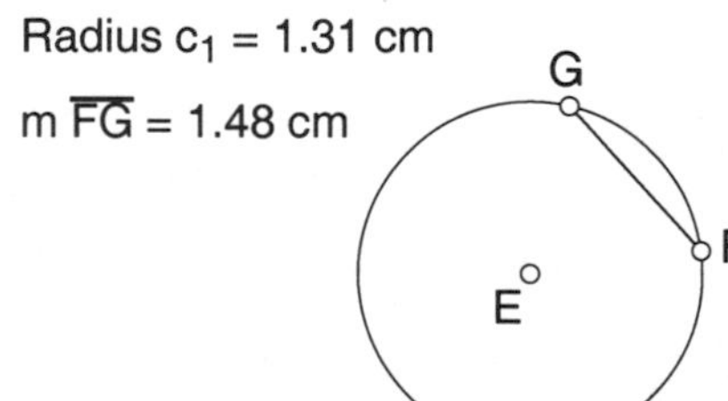

Q5 Make the length of $\overline{FG}$ as great as you can. When a chord in a circle is as long as it can possibly be, it is called a *diameter*. Describe a diameter.

Q6 The length of a diameter segment is also called the diameter of the circle. How does the diameter of a circle compare to the radius?

Explore More

1. In the activity, you constructed a chord that you could make into a diameter by dragging one of its endpoints. But this chord won't stay a diameter if you change the circle. Figure out a way to construct a circle and a diameter that will always stay a diameter when you drag. (*Hint:* There are many ways to do this. One way uses a ray.) Describe your method.

© 2002 Key Curriculum Press

Chords in a Circle

Name(s): ____________________

A chord in a circle is a segment with endpoints on the circle. In this activity, you'll investigate properties of chords.

Sketch and Investigate

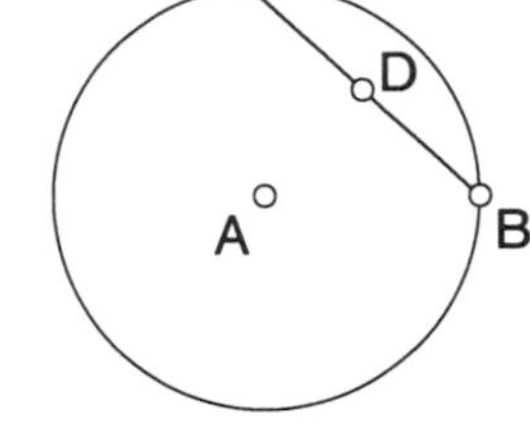

1. Construct circle AB.
2. Construct chord BC.
3. Construct the midpoint D of the chord.

Select point D and $\overline{BC}$; then, in the Construct menu, choose **Perpendicular Line**.

4. Construct a line through point D perpendicular to $\overline{BC}$. This line is the perpendicular bisector of the chord. (It's not shown in the figure.)
5. Drag point C around the circle and observe the perpendicular line.

Q1 Write a conjecture about the perpendicular bisector of any chord in a circle.

Select the line; then, in the Display menu, choose **Hide Line**.

6. Hide the perpendicular bisector and construct $\overline{AD}$.
7. Measure the length of $\overline{AD}$. This is the distance from the chord to the center.
8. Measure the length of $\overline{BC}$.
9. Drag point C around the circle and observe the measures.

Q2 How is the length of the chord related to its distance from the center?

If you don't see point G, scale the axes by dragging point F toward point E.

10. You can make a graph that shows this relationship: Select the length of $\overline{BC}$ and the length of $\overline{AD}$, in that order; then, in the Graph menu, choose **Plot As (x, y)**. You should get axes and a point G whose coordinates are the measures you selected.

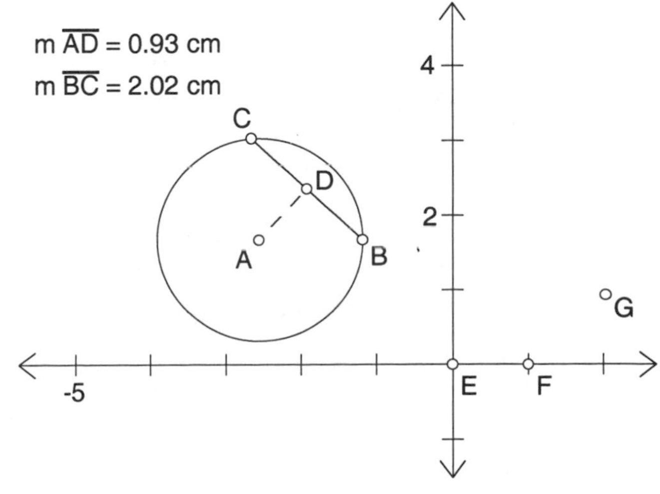

© 2002 Key Curriculum Press

11. Drag point C to see how it controls point G.
12. To graph all the possible locations for point G, select it and point C; then, in the Construct menu, choose **Locus**.
13. Drag point C to see point G travel along the locus.
14. Drag point A or point B to see what effect changing the circle's radius has on the graph.

Q3 Write a paragraph describing the graph. Answer these questions in your paragraph: Look at the value of y where the locus intersects the y-axis. What does this value represent in the circle? Look at the value of x where the locus intersects the x-axis. What does this value represent in the circle? As point G moves from left to right, what happens to the value of its y-coordinate? What does this have to do with what's happening to the chord? Use a separate sheet of paper.

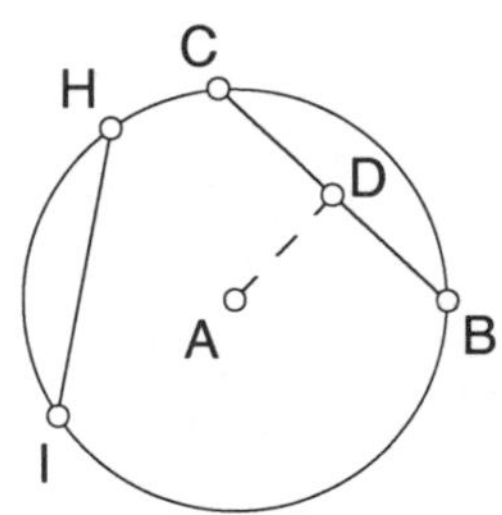

15. Construct $\overline{HI}$, another chord on the circle.
16. Measure HI.

Select $\overline{HI}$ and point A; then, in the Measure menu, choose **Distance**.

17. Measure the distance from $\overline{HI}$ to the center of the circle.
18. Drag point H or point I and watch the length measure. Try to make this length as close to the length of $\overline{BC}$ as you can.

Q4 Write a conjecture about congruent chords in a circle.

Explore More

1. Plot as (x, y) the length of $\overline{HI}$ and the distance from $\overline{HI}$ to the center. How does this plotted point compare to point G when $HI = BC$?
2. An arc is part of a circle. You can construct an arc from any three points. In a new sketch, construct a three-point arc. Now use your conjecture from Q1 to construct the center of the circle containing the arc. Construct the circle to confirm that you found the correct point. Explain what you did.

© 2002 Key Curriculum Press

Tangents to a Circle

Name(s): ____________________

A line can intersect a circle in zero, one, or two points. A line that intersects a circle in exactly one point—that just touches the circle without going into the circle's interior—is called a *tangent*. The point of intersection is called the *point of tangency*. A line that intersects a circle in two points is called a *secant*. In this investigation, you'll construct a secant, then manipulate it until it becomes a tangent to discover an important property of tangents.

Sketch and Investigate

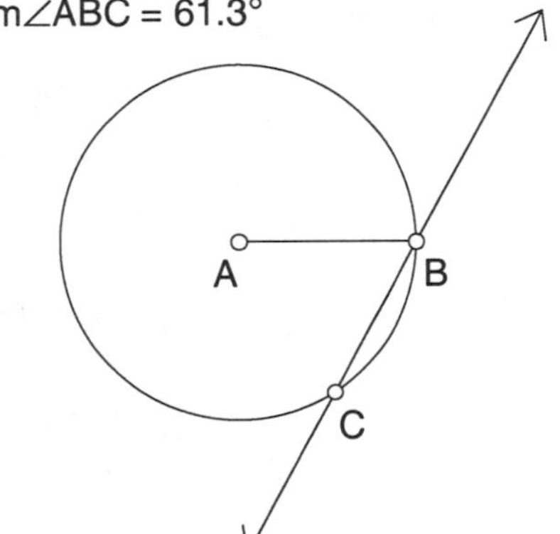

1. Construct circle AB.
2. Construct $\overline{AB}$.
3. Construct secant $\overleftrightarrow{BC}$, making sure point C falls on the circle.

   Hold down the mouse button on the **Segment** tool, then drag right to choose the **Line** tool.

4. Measure $\angle ABC$.

   Select, in order, points *A*, *B*, and *C*. Then, in the Measure menu, choose **Angle**.

5. Drag point C around the circle and observe the angle measure.

Q1 What happens to $m\angle ABC$ as point C gets closer to point B? What's the measure of $\angle ABC$ when point C is right on top of point B?

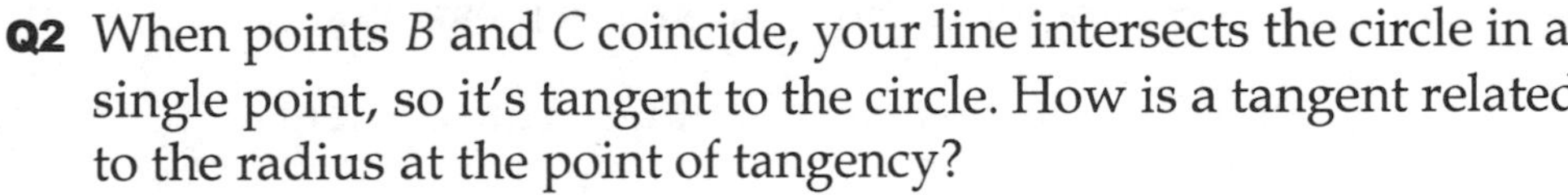

Q2 When points B and C coincide, your line intersects the circle in a single point, so it's tangent to the circle. How is a tangent related to the radius at the point of tangency?

Q3 Use what you observed in Q2 to construct a line in your sketch that is always tangent to the circle. Describe how you did it.

Explore More

1. Come up with methods for constructing two circles that always intersect in one point. The circles could be *internally tangent* (one inside the other) or *externally tangent* (neither inside the other).

© 2002 Key Curriculum Press

Tangent Segments

Name(s): ____________________

In this activity, you'll learn how to construct tangents. Then you'll compare the lengths of two tangent segments from the common intersection point to the points of tangency.

Sketch and Investigate

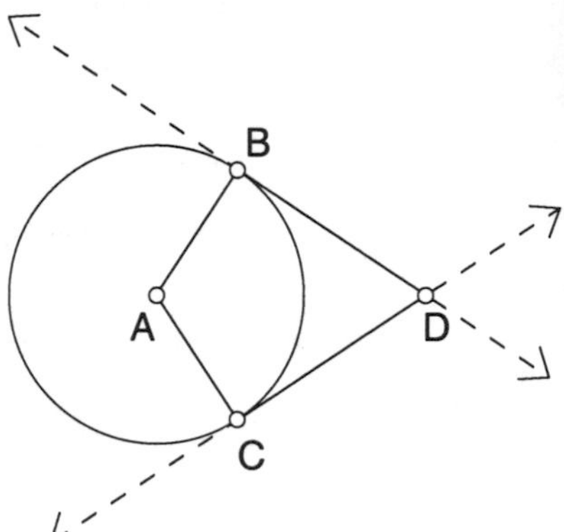

1. Construct circle AB and radius AB.

Select $\overline{AB}$ and point B; then, in the Construct menu, choose **Perpendicular Line**.

2. Construct a line perpendicular to $\overline{AB}$ through point B. This line is tangent to the circle.
3. Drag point B to confirm that the line stays tangent.
4. Construct a second radius AC.
5. Construct a tangent through point C.
6. Drag point C to confirm that this line stays tangent.
7. Construct point D where the tangent lines intersect.

Select the lines; then, in the Display menu, choose **Hide Lines**.

8. Hide the lines.
9. Construct segments BD and CD.
10. Measure BD and CD.
11. Drag point C and observe the measures.

Q1 Write a conjecture about tangent segments.

Explore More

1. Construct $\overline{AD}$. Investigate relationships among the angles and sides of the two triangles formed. Are the triangles congruent? If so, explain why.
2. Construct a circle and a point outside the circle. Come up with a method for constructing two tangents from the given point. Describe your method.
3. Come up with methods for constructing two or more circles with a common tangent (a line tangent to both circles). *Hint:* Construct the second circle after you've constructed the first circle's tangent. Describe your method.

© 2002 Key Curriculum Press

Arcs and Angles

Name(s): ____________________

An angle with its vertex at the center of a circle is called a *central angle*. An angle whose sides are chords of a circle and whose vertex is on the circle is called an *inscribed angle*. In this activity, you'll investigate relationships among central angles, inscribed angles, and the arcs they intercept.

Sketch and Investigate

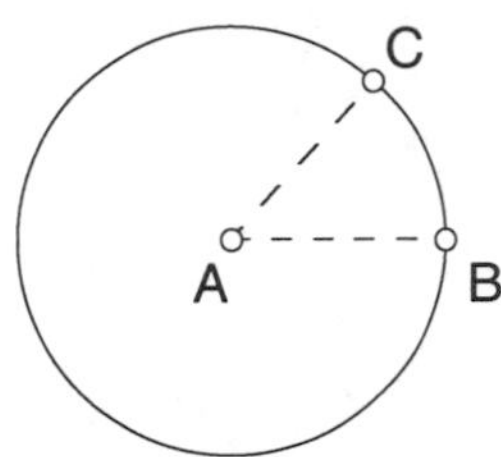

1. Construct circle AB.
2. Construct $\overline{AB}$ and make this segment dashed.
3. Construct $\overline{AC}$, where point C is a point on the circle.

Select the segment and choose **Display | Line Width | Dashed**.

You've just created central angle BAC. Points B and C divide the circle into two arcs. The shorter arc is called a *minor arc* and the longer one is called a *major arc*. A minor arc is named after its endpoints. In the figure above right, the central angle BAC intercepts $\overset{\frown}{BC}$, where $\overset{\frown}{BC}$ is the minor arc.

4. Construct the arc on the circle from point B to point C. While the arc is selected, make it thick.

Select, in order, point B, point C, and the circle. Then, in the Construct menu, choose **Arc On Circle**.

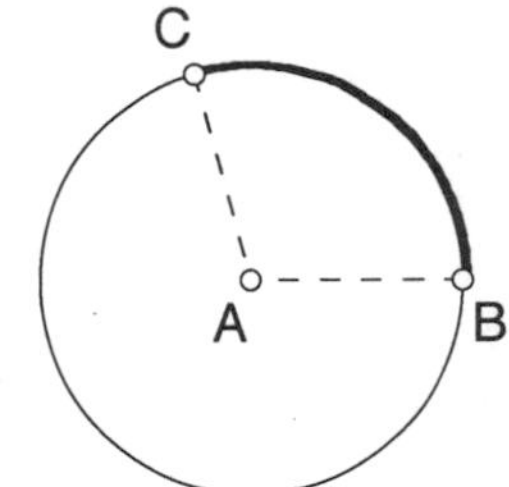

5. Drag point C around the circle to see how it controls the arc. When you're finished experimenting, locate point C so that the thick arc is a minor arc.
6. Measure the arc angle of $\overset{\frown}{BC}$.

Select $\overset{\frown}{BC}$; then, in the Measure menu, choose **Arc Angle**.

7. Measure $\angle BAC$.

Select, in order, points B, A, and C. Then, in the Measure menu, choose **Angle**.

8. Drag point C around the circle again and observe the measures. Pay attention to the differences when the arc is a minor arc and when it is a major arc.

Q1 Write a conjecture about the measure of the central angle and the measure of the minor arc it intercepts.

Q2 Write a conjecture about the measure of the central angle and the measure of the major arc.

© 2002 Key Curriculum Press

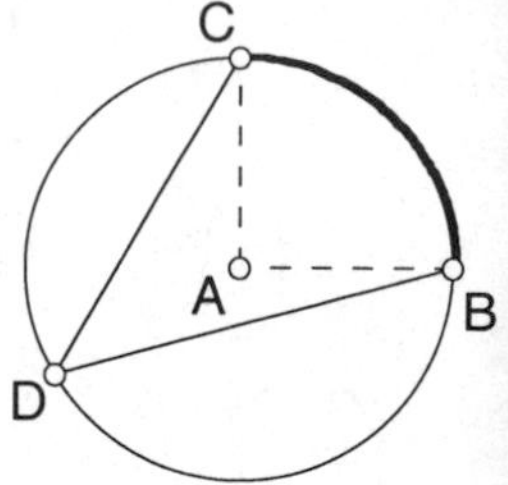

9. Construct $\overline{DC}$ and $\overline{DB}$, where point D is a point on the circle, to create inscribed angle CDB.

10. Measure $\angle CDB$.

11. Drag point C and observe the measures of the arc angle and $\angle CDB$.

Q3 Write a conjecture about the measures of an inscribed angle and the arc it intercepts.

12. Drag point D (but not past point C or point B) and observe the measure of $\angle CDB$.

Q4 Write a conjecture about all the inscribed angles that intercept the same arc.

13. Drag point C so that the thick arc is as close to being a semicircle as you can make it.

14. Drag point D and observe the measure of $\angle CDB$.

Q5 Write a conjecture about angles inscribed in a semicircle.

Explore More

1. In a new sketch, construct a circle and an arc on the circle. Measure the circumference of the circle, the arc angle, and the arc length. Use the circumference and arc angle measurements to calculate an expression equal to the arc length. Explain what you did.

2. Use your conjecture in Q5 to come up with a method for constructing a right triangle. Describe your method.

© 2002 Key Curriculum Press

The Circumference/Diameter Ratio

Name(s): ________________

In this activity, you'll discover a relationship between a circle's circumference and its diameter. Even if that relationship is familiar to you, the investigation may demonstrate it in a different way.

Sketch and Investigate

1. Construct $\overline{AB}$.
2. Construct point C, the midpoint of $\overline{AB}$.
3. Construct circle CB.

> Be sure the cursor is positioned directly on point *B* when you release the mouse button.

A B

Step 1

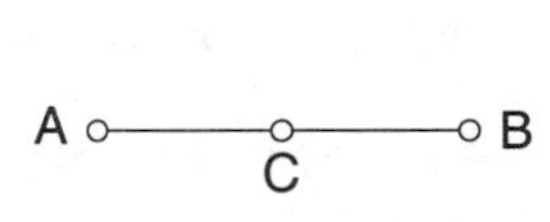

Step 2

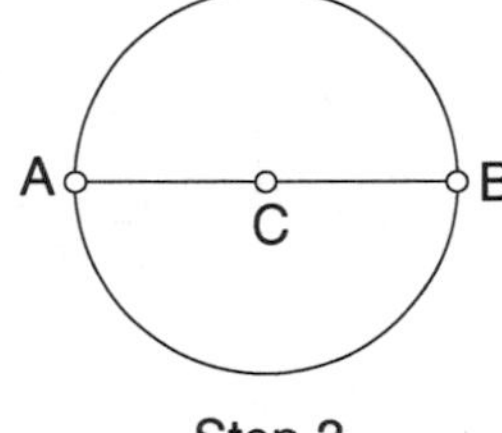

Step 3

> Select the circle; then, in the Measure menu, choose **Circumference**.

4. Measure the circumference of the circle.
5. Measure AB (the diameter of the circle).
6. Make the circle small.

> Select, in order, the length measurement and the circumference measurement. Then, in the Graph menu, choose **Tabulate**.

7. Make a table for the length measurement and the circumference measurement.

> Double-click inside the table to add an entry.

8. Make the circle a little bigger; then add an entry to the table.
9. Repeat step 8 until your table has at least four entries.

> Choose **Plot Points** from the Graph menu and enter the coordinates of the points in your table.

10. Plot the table data. You may need to drag point E toward point D to scale your axes so that you can see the points.

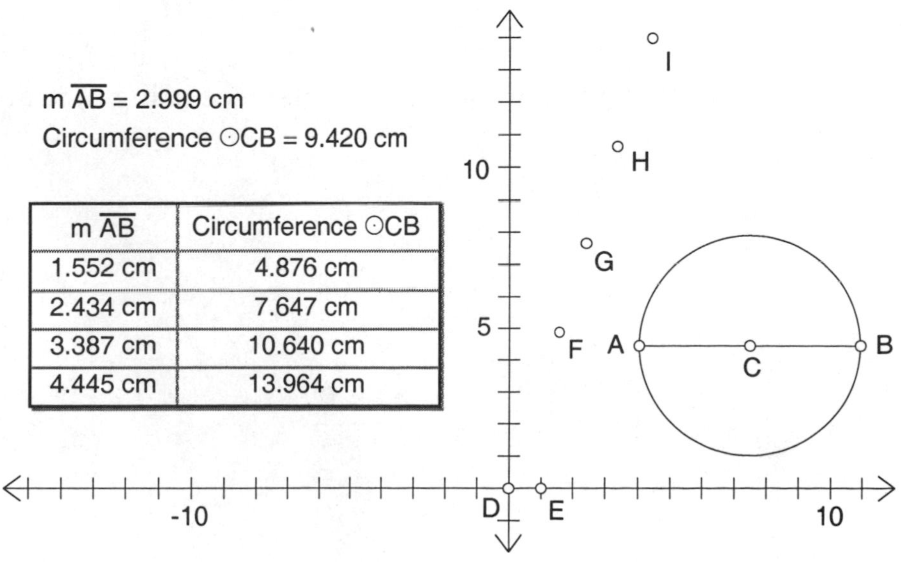

m $\overline{AB}$	Circumference ⊙CB
1.552 cm	4.876 cm
2.434 cm	7.647 cm
3.387 cm	10.640 cm
4.445 cm	13.964 cm

© 2002 Key Curriculum Press

Q1 Describe the points that appear on the graph.

Select, in order, the diameter measurement and the circumference measurement. Then, in the Graph menu, choose **Plot As (x, y)**.

11. Plot the diameter and circumference measurements as (x, y). Change the color of this point so you can tell it from other points on the graph. Also, in the Display menu, choose **Trace Point**.
12. Drag point A or point B to change your circle. Watch the plotted point.
13. Construct a ray from point D (the origin) to any of the plotted points.
14. Measure the slope of the ray.

Q2 How is the slope of the ray related to circumference/diameter ratio for the circles?

Q3 What's the significance of the fact that all the plotted points lie on this ray?

Q4 The circumference/diameter ratio is represented by the Greek letter π (pi). Complete the following formulas using π, C for circumference, and D for diameter:

$\pi =$ ___________

$C =$ ___________

Q5 Write a formula for circumference using C, π, and r (for radius).

© 2002 Key Curriculum Press

The Cycloid

Name(s): ______________________

Imagine that a bug is clinging tightly to a bicycle wheel as the bicycle travels down the road. What path does the bug travel? Is the path the same whether the bug is at the center of the wheel or at its edge? In this activity, you'll investigate those questions.

Sketch and Investigate

You'll start by constructing a stationary circle with a rotating spoke.

1. Draw a point *A* and a short segment *BC*.

Select the point and the segment; then, in the Construct menu, choose **Circle By Center+Radius**.

2. Construct the circle centered at *A* with radius equal to *BC*.

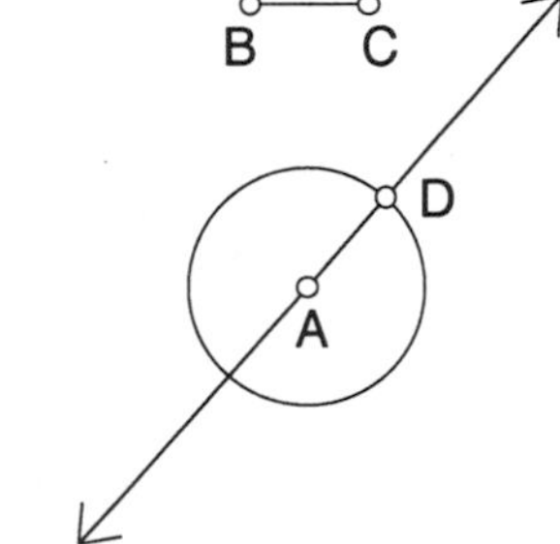

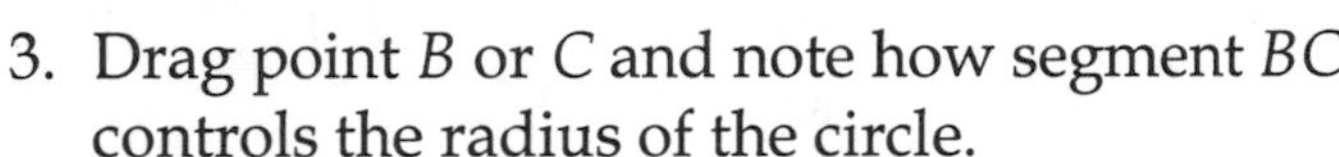

3. Drag point *B* or *C* and note how segment *BC* controls the radius of the circle.

Select point *D;* then, in the Display menu, choose **Animate Point**. To stop the animation, choose **Stop Animation** or press the Stop button on the Motion Controller.

4. Construct line $\overleftrightarrow{AD}$, where *D* is a point on the circle.
5. Animate point *D* around the circle.

Now you'll attach the circle to a straight path and construct a point representing the bug.

To make it easy to draw a horizontal segment, hold down the Shift key while you draw the segment.

6. Construct a long horizontal segment *EF* from right to left.
7. Merge point *A* onto the segment. To do this, select point *A* and $\overline{EF}$ and choose **Merge Point To Segment** from the Edit menu.
8. Construct point *G* on line *AD,* inside the circle. (Point *G* represents the bug.)
9. While point *G* is selected, choose **Trace Point** in the Display menu.
10. Hide line *AD*.

Select, in order, points *A* and *D;* then choose **Edit | Action Buttons | Animation**. Choose **forward** from the Direction pop-up menu, then click OK.

11. Make an action button to animate point *A* forward at medium speed and point *D* counter-clockwise at medium speed.

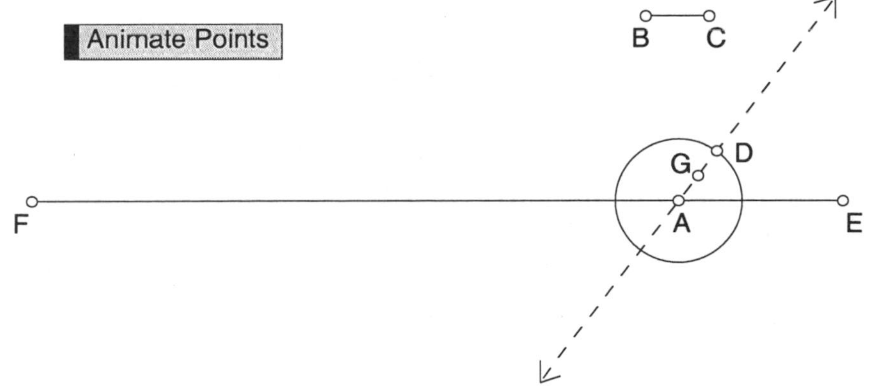

© 2002 Key Curriculum Press

If the traces clutter the screen, choose **Erase Traces** from the Display menu. Or you can choose **Preferences** from the Edit menu, go to the Color panel, and check the Fade Traces Over Time box.

12. Press this new action button to observe the path of point *G*. This path is called a **cycloid**. (Press the button again when you wish to stop the animation.)

13. Try the animation with point *G* on the circle and again with point *G* outside the circle.

Q1 In the space below, sketch what the cycloid looks like when point *G* is inside the circle, on the circle, and outside the circle.

Inside the circle	On the circle	Outside the circle

14. Measure the length of segment *EF* and the circumference of the circle.

15. Adjust your sketch so that point *G* traces exactly two cycles of the curve. Note the two measurements. Then adjust the sketch so that point *G* traces three cycles.

Q2 How are the circumference of the circle and the length of the segment related when point *G* traces two cycles? three cycles?

Q3 Because the cycloid curve repeats itself, it is called *periodic*. The distance from a point on one cycle to the corresponding point on the next cycle (for example, the distance from a peak to a peak) is called the *period* of the curve. What would be the period of the curve if the circle had a radius of 1 cm?

Q4 How does point *G*'s position—inside, outside, or on the circle—affect the period of the cycloid?

© 2002 Key Curriculum Press

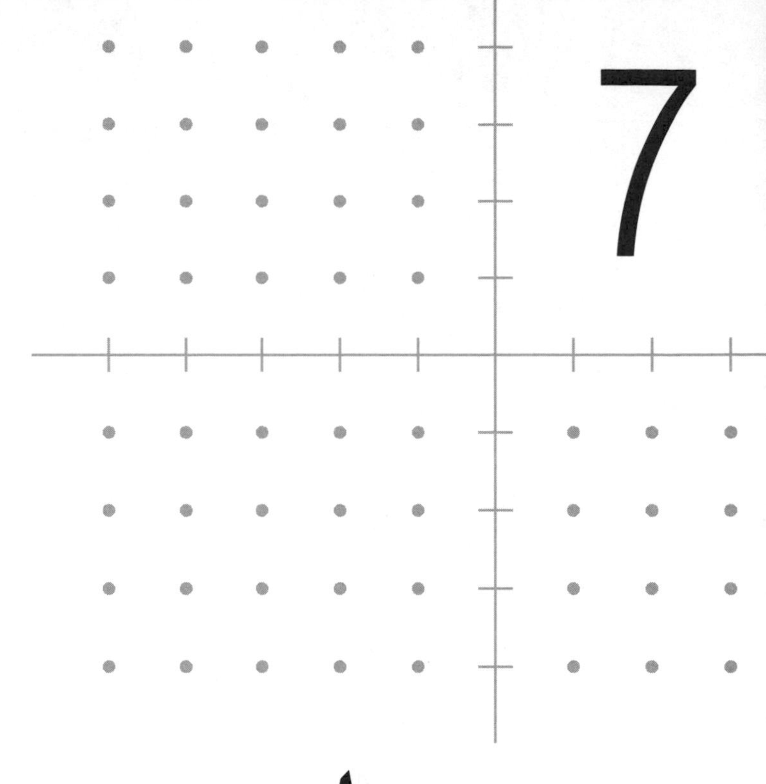

7

Area

Areas of Parallelograms and Triangles

Name(s): ______________________

You'll discover a relationship between the areas of parallelograms and triangles by investigating a process called *shearing*. This will give you a formula for area that you can generalize for all parallelograms.

Sketch and Investigate

1. Construct a horizontal line *AB*.
2. Construct point *C* above $\overleftrightarrow{AB}$.

Select point *C* and $\overleftrightarrow{AB}$; then, in the Construct menu, choose **Parallel Line**.

3. Construct a line parallel to $\overleftrightarrow{AB}$ through point *C*.
4. Hide points *A*, *B*, and *C*.
5. Construct $\overline{DE}$ from the bottom line to the top line.
6. Construct point *F* on the bottom line.
7. Construct a line through point *F* parallel to $\overline{DE}$.
8. Construct point *G* where this line intersects the top line.

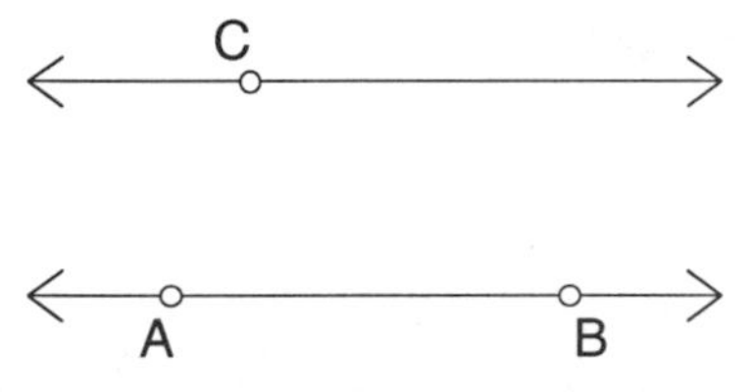

Steps 1–3

Steps 4 and 5

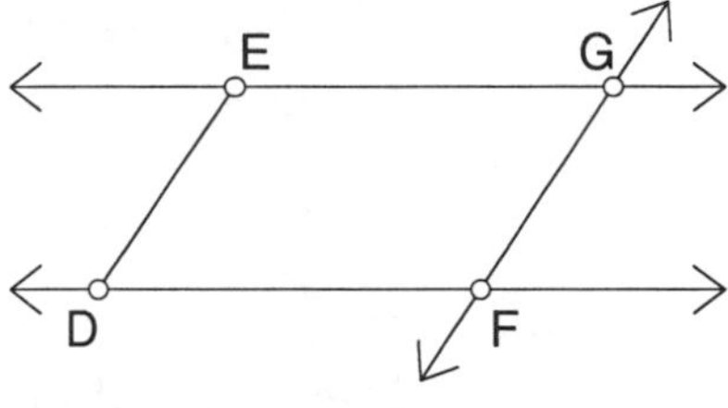

Steps 5–7

Select the vertices in consecutive order; then, in the Construct menu, choose **Quadrilateral Interior**.

9. Construct interior *DEGF*.
10. Hide $\overleftrightarrow{FG}$.
11. Construct $\overline{FG}$.

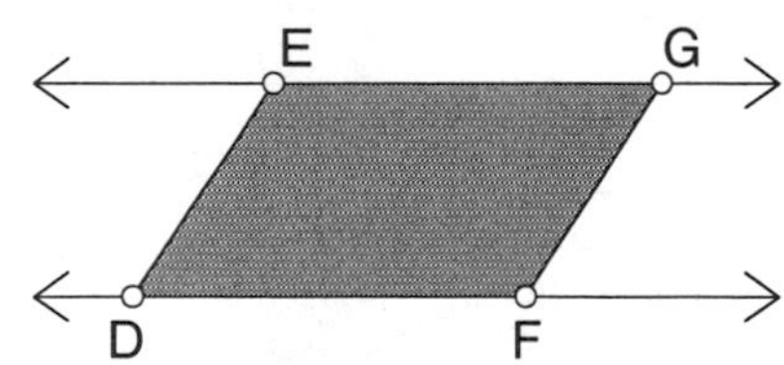

Select the interior by clicking on it; then, in the Measure menu, choose **Area**.

12. Measure the area of parallelogram *DEGF*.
13. Observe the area measurement as you drag in each of these ways:
    - Drag point *E* to shear the parallelogram.
    - Drag point *D* or point *F* to change the base of the parallelogram.
    - Drag either $\overleftrightarrow{EG}$ or $\overleftrightarrow{DF}$ up or down to change the height.

Q1 Which of these actions change the area and which don't? Explain why you think this is so.

© 2002 Key Curriculum Press

The height of the parallelogram is the distance between the two parallel lines. To construct a segment whose length is this height, follow steps 14 and 15.

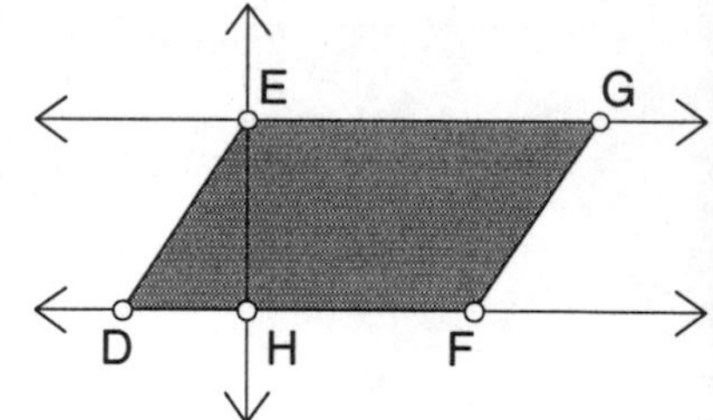

14. Construct a line through point E perpendicular to $\overleftrightarrow{DF}$.
15. Construct $\overline{EH}$, where H is the point of intersection of $\overleftrightarrow{DF}$ and the perpendicular line.
16. Hide the perpendicular line.
17. Measure EH.

Select the two endpoints; then, in the Measure menu, choose **Distance**.

18. Measure DF, the base of the parallelogram.

Choose **Calculate** from the Measure menu to open the Calculator. Click once on a measurement to enter it into a calculation.

Q2 Use these measurements to calculate an expression equal to the area of the parallelogram. Write your expression below.

Q3 Write a formula for the area of the parallelogram using A for area, b for base, and h for height.

Next, you'll investigate how the area of the parallelogram is related to the area of a triangle.

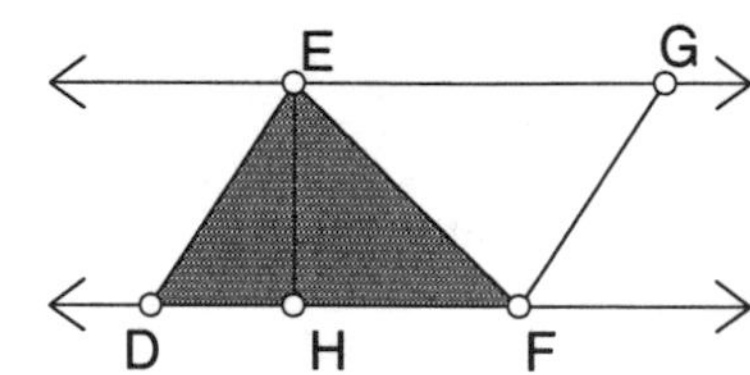

19. Hide the interior of the parallelogram.
20. Construct diagonal EF.
21. Construct polygon interior DEF.
22. Measure the area of triangle DEF.
23. Drag point E and observe the area measurements.

Q4 How is the triangle's area related to the parallelogram's area? Write a formula for the area of the triangle using A for area, b for base, and h for height.

Explore More

1. Make an action button to animate point E along its line. Explain what this animation demonstrates about shearing.

© 2002 Key Curriculum Press

A Triangle Area Problem

Name(s): ____________________

In this investigation, you'll divide a triangle into regions and explore the relationship among these areas.

Sketch and Investigate

1. Construct $\triangle ABC$.

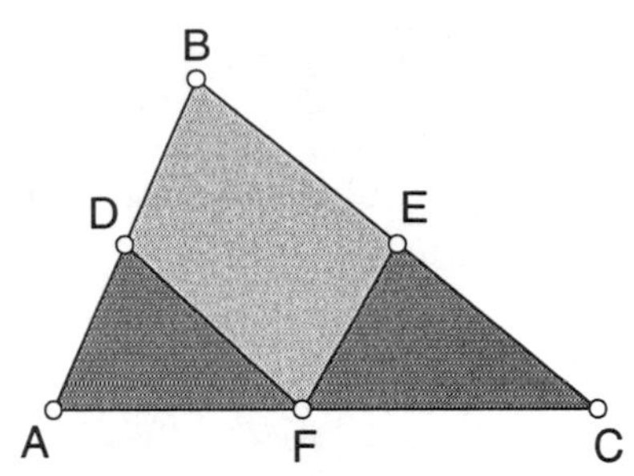

2. Construct points D and E, the midpoints of $\overline{AB}$ and $\overline{BC}$.
3. Construct $\overline{DF}$ and $\overline{EF}$, where point F is any point on $\overline{AC}$.
4. Construct the polygon interiors of triangles ADF and FEC and quadrilateral $BDFE$.

Select the vertices of the polygon in consecutive order; then, in the Construct menu, choose **Triangle Interior** or **Quadrilateral Interior**.

Q1 Move point F back and forth along $\overline{AC}$. Without measuring, guess how the areas of the triangles are related to the area of the quadrilateral. (*Hint:* Look at special cases, such as when F is at the midpoint, point A, and point C.)

5. Measure the areas of the triangles and the quadrilateral to check your guess.

Q2 Write a conjecture about how the areas of the triangles are related to the area of the quadrilateral.

Q3 Explain why you think your conjecture is always true.

Explore More

1. Make an action button to animate point F along $\overline{AC}$.
2. Here's another challenging area problem: Construct a square. Find two segments from one of the vertices that divide the square into three equal areas. Where should the other endpoints of these segments be located?

© 2002 Key Curriculum Press

Triangle Area/Perimeter

Name(s): ______________________

Is it possible to construct two noncongruent triangles that have both equal areas and equal perimeters? Use Sketchpad to investigate this question. Use the space below to describe your findings, or print a sketch with comments that describe your findings.

To measure area and perimeter, you must first construct an interior. To construct an interior, select the vertices in consecutive order. Then, in the Construct menu, choose **Triangle Interior**.

Q1 If possible, draw and label two noncongruent triangles that have equal areas and perimeters in the space below. (Or print your sketch and attach it to this paper.) If you find it's not possible, illustrate why.

Q2 In the space below, write a description of what you did in this investigation. If you created two noncongruent triangles with equal areas and perimeters, describe how you did it.

© 2002 Key Curriculum Press

A Square Within a Square

Name(s): ____________________

In this investigation, you'll construct a square and four segments within it that intersect to form a second square. Then you'll discover an interesting area relationship between these squares.

Sketch and Investigate

You can use the tool **4/Square (Inscribed)** from the sketch **Polygons.gsp**.

1. Construct a square with its center and its interior. Use a custom tool or do the construction from scratch.

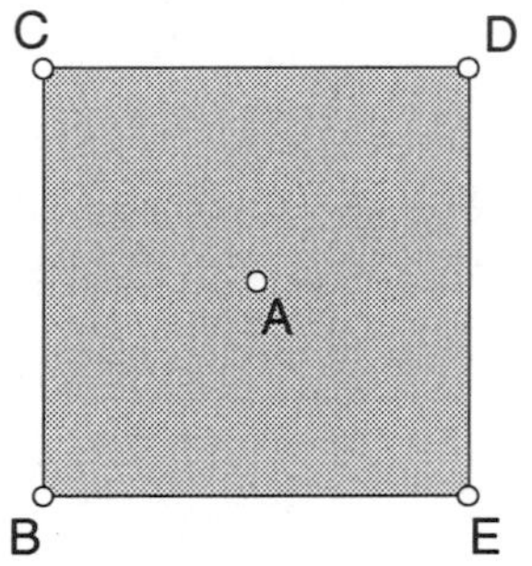

Using the **Text** tool, click once on a point to display its label. Double-click the label to change it.

2. Change the labels, if necessary, to match the figure at right.
3. Construct point F on $\overline{BE}$, closer to point E.

Double-click point A to mark it as a center. Select point F; then, in the Transform menu, choose **Rotate**.

4. Mark point A as a center and rotate point F by 90° to construct point F'.
5. Rotate point F' by 90° to construct point F'', then rotate point F'' by 90° to construct F'''.
6. Construct $\overline{BF''}$, $\overline{CF'}$, $\overline{DF}$, and $\overline{EF'''}$ as shown in the figure at right.

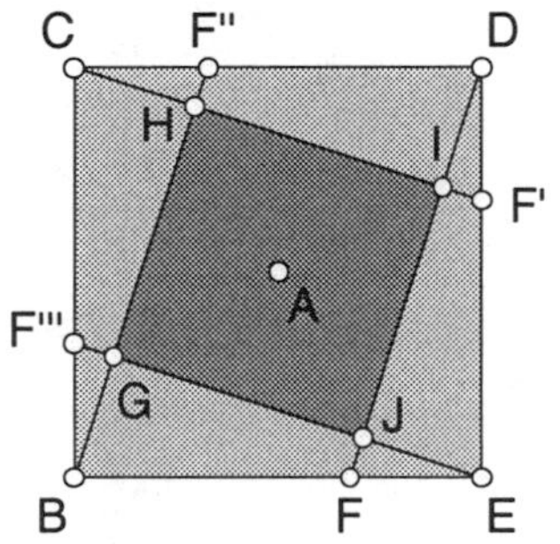

C D A B E

C F'' D H I F' A F''' G J B F E

Select the vertices in consecutive order; then, in the Construct menu, choose **Quadrilateral Interior**.

7. Construct points of intersection G, H, I, and J and interior $GHIJ$. Give it a darker color than the outside square interior.
8. Measure the areas of the outer and inner squares.

Choose **Calculate** from the Measure menu to open the Calculator. Click once on a measurement to enter it into a calculation.

9. Calculate the ratio of the larger area to the smaller area.
10. Drag point F and observe this ratio. Make a guess as to what the ratio would be if point F were at the midpoint.

It's difficult to drag point F exactly to the midpoint. For that reason, you'll construct the midpoint and other interesting points and make Movement buttons to move point F to precise locations.

11. Construct the midpoint of $\overline{BD}$ and change its label to 1/2.

Select, in order, point F and point 1/2. Then choose **Edit | Action Buttons | Movement**.

12. Make a Movement button to move point F to point 1/2.
13. Press the *Move F —> 1/2* button.

Q1 What is the area ratio? Is it what you expected?

© 2002 Key Curriculum Press

After you mark the center, select point *E* and, in the Transform menu, choose **Dilate**. Enter 1 for the numerator of the scale factor and 3 for the denominator.

14. Mark point *B* as a center and dilate point *E* by a scale factor of 1/3. Change the label of the dilated point to 1/3.
15. Construct 1/4 and 1/5 points in the same way.
16. Make buttons to move point *F* to point 1/3, to point 1/4, and to point 1/5.

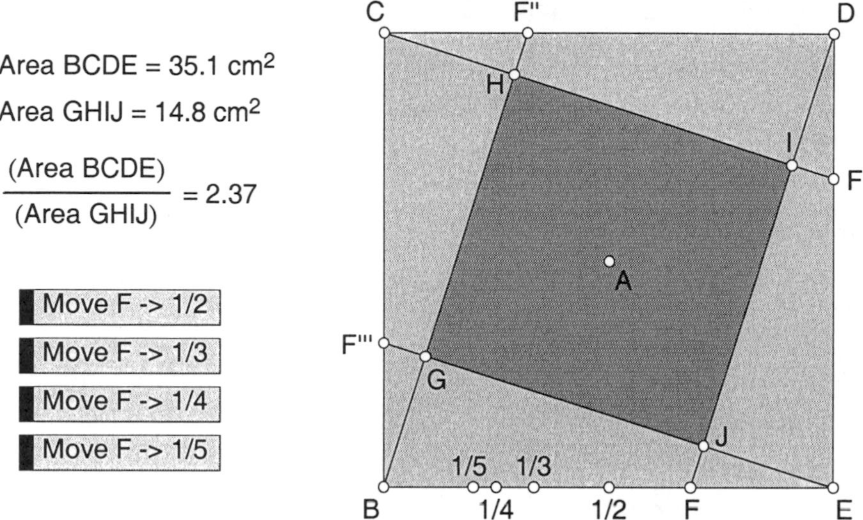

17. Use your Movement buttons to investigate the other ratios.

Q2 Write the area ratios for side-divisions of 1/3, 1/4, and 1/5.

Q3 Look for a pattern in the area ratios and predict the area ratio for a side-division ratio of 1/6.

Explore More

1. Write an expression that gives the area ratio when the side is divided into a ratio of $1/n$.

© 2002 Key Curriculum Press

A Triangle Within a Triangle

Name(s): ____________________

If you connect each vertex of a triangle with a trisection point on the opposite side, you'll form a second triangle within the first. In this activity, you'll investigate a relationship between the two triangles.

Sketch and Investigate

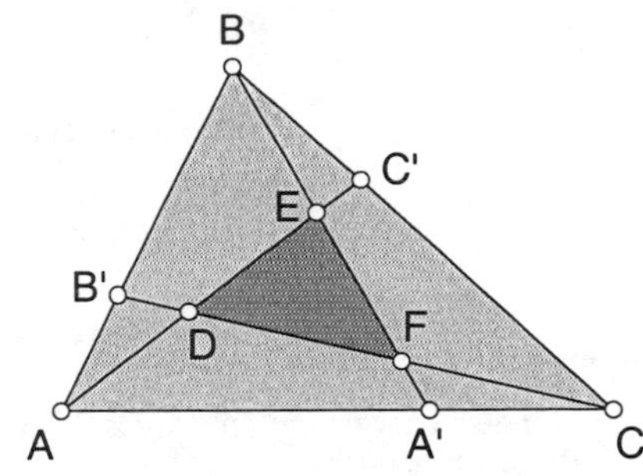

1. Construct ΔABC.

Double-click point *A* to mark it as a center. Select point *B*; then, in the Transform menu, choose **Dilate**. Enter 1 for the numerator of the scale factor and 3 for the denominator.

2. Mark point *A* as a center and dilate point *B* by a scale factor of 1/3.
3. Mark point *B* as a center and dilate point *C* by a scale factor of 1/3.
4. Mark point *C* as a center and dilate point *A* by a scale factor of 1/3.
5. Construct segments from each vertex to the 1/3 point on the opposite side.
6. Construct points of intersection *D*, *E*, and *F*. These points are the vertices of an inner triangle formed by the segments you constructed in step 5.

Select the triangle's vertices; then, in the Construct menu, choose **Triangle Interior**.

7. Construct the interiors of the outer and inner triangles. Make the outer triangle a lighter shade.
8. Drag a vertex of the outer triangle and observe the inner triangle. Before you measure, try to guess the relationship between the larger and smaller areas.

Click on an interior to select it; then, in the Measure menu, choose **Area**.

9. Measure the areas of the outer and inner triangles.

Choose **Calculate** from the Measure menu to open the Calculator. Click once on a measurement to enter it into a calculation.

10. Calculate the ratio of the larger area to the smaller. Surprised?
11. Drag a vertex of the outer triangle and observe the area ratio.

Q1 Write a conjecture about the area ratio.

Explore More

1. Investigate whether or not the large and small triangles are similar.
2. Try this investigation again, subdividing the sides of the triangle into fourths.
3. Try this investigation on a quadrilateral.

© 2002 Key Curriculum Press

A Rectangle with Maximum Area **Name(s):** ____________________

Suppose you had a certain amount of fence and you wanted to use it to enclose the biggest possible rectangular field. What rectangle shape would you choose? In other words, what type of rectangle has the most area for a given perimeter? You'll discover the answer in this investigation. Or, if you have a hunch already, this investigation will help confirm your hunch and give you more insight into it.

Sketch and Investigate

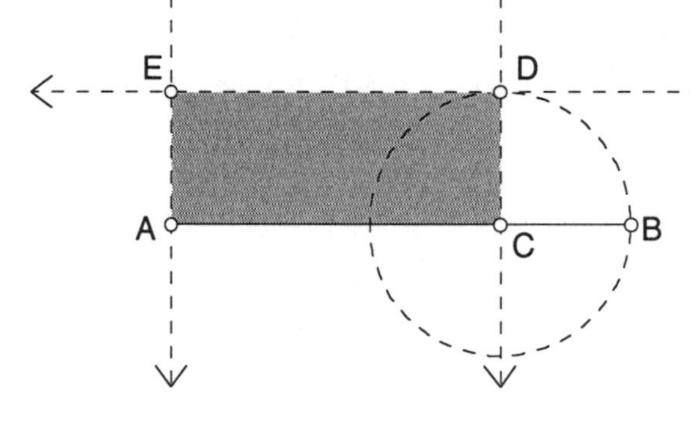

1. Construct $\overline{AB}$.
2. Construct $\overline{AC}$ on $\overline{AB}$.
3. Construct lines perpendicular to $\overline{AB}$ through points *A* and *C*.
4. Construct circle *CB*.
5. Construct point *D* where this circle intersects the perpendicular line.
6. Construct a line through point *D*, parallel to $\overline{AB}$.
7. Construct point *E*, the fourth vertex of rectangle *ACDE*.
8. Construct interior *ACDE*.
9. Measure the area and perimeter of this polygon.
10. Drag point *C* back and forth and observe how this affects the area and perimeter of the rectangle.
11. Measure *AC* and *AE*.

Select $\overline{AB}$, point *A*, and point *C*. Then, in the Construct menu, choose **Perpendicular Line**. (Step 3)

Be sure to release the mouse—or click the second time—with the pointer over point *B*. (Step 4)

Select the vertices of the rectangle in consecutive order. Then, in the Construct menu, choose **Quadrilateral Interior**. (Step 8)

Select point *A* and point *C*. Then, in the Measure menu, choose **Distance**. Repeat to measure *AE*. (Step 11)

Q1 Without measuring, state how *AB* is related to the perimeter of the rectangle. Explain why this rectangle has a fixed perimeter.

Q2 As you drag point *C*, observe what rectangular shape gives the greatest area. What shape do you think that is?

© 2002 Key Curriculum Press

A Rectangle with Maximum Area (continued)

In steps 12–14, you'll explore this relationship graphically.

Select, in order, measurements *AC* and Area *ACDE*. Then choose **Plot As (x, y)** from the Graph menu. If you can't see the plotted point, drag the unit point at (1, 0) to scale the axes.

12. Plot the measurements for the length of $\overline{AC}$ and the area of *ACDE* as (x, y). You should get axes and a plotted point *H*, as shown below.

13. Drag point *C* to see the plotted point move to correspond to different side lengths and areas.

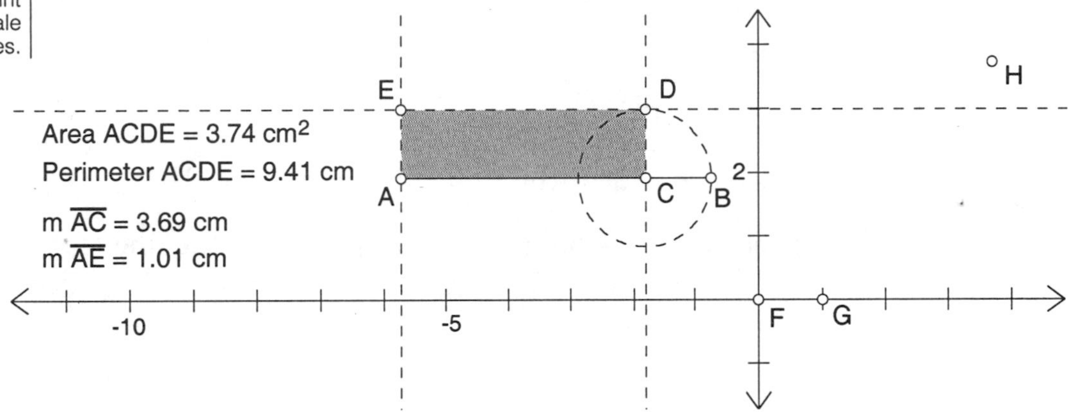

Select point *H* and point *C*; then, in the Construct menu, choose **Locus**.

14. To see a graph of all possible areas for this rectangle, construct the locus of plotted point *H* as defined by point *C*. It should now be easy to position point *C* so that point *H* is at a maximum value for the area of the rectangle.

You may wish to select point *H* and measure its coordinates.

Q3 Explain what the coordinates of the high point on the graph are and how they are related to the side lengths and area of the rectangle.

15. Drag point *C* so that point *H* moves back and forth between the two low points on the graph.

Q4 Explain what the coordinates of the two low points on the graph are and how they are related to the side lengths and area of the rectangle.

Explore More

1. Investigate area/perimeter relationships in other polygons. Make a conjecture about what kinds of polygons yield the greatest area for a given perimeter.
2. What's the equation for the graph you made? Let *AC* be x and let *AB* be $(1/2)P$, where P stands for the perimeter (a constant). Write an equation for area, A, in terms of x and P. What value for x (in terms of P) gives a maximum value for A?

© 2002 Key Curriculum Press

The Area of a Trapezoid

Name(s): ____________________

A trapezoid is a quadrilateral with exactly two parallel sides. In this investigation, you'll construct a trapezoid, then transform it into a shape whose area formula you should be familiar with. From that formula, you'll derive a formula for the area of a trapezoid.

Sketch and Investigate

1. Construct $\overline{AB}$.
2. Construct $\overline{AC}$.

Select point C and $\overline{AB}$; then, in the Construct menu, choose **Parallel Line**.

3. Construct a line through point C parallel to $\overline{AB}$.
4. Construct $\overline{DB}$, where point D is a point on the line.

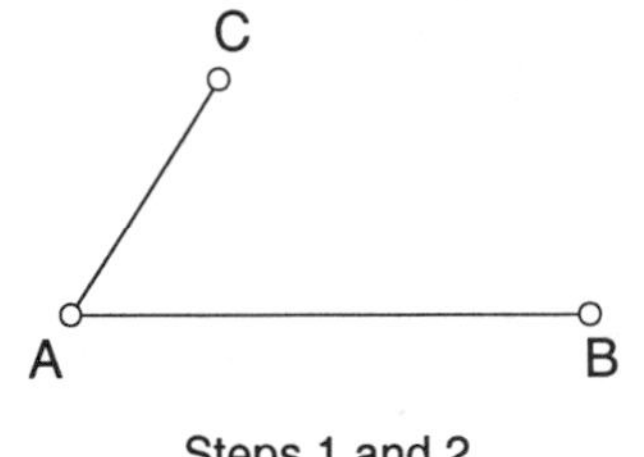

Steps 1 and 2

Step 3

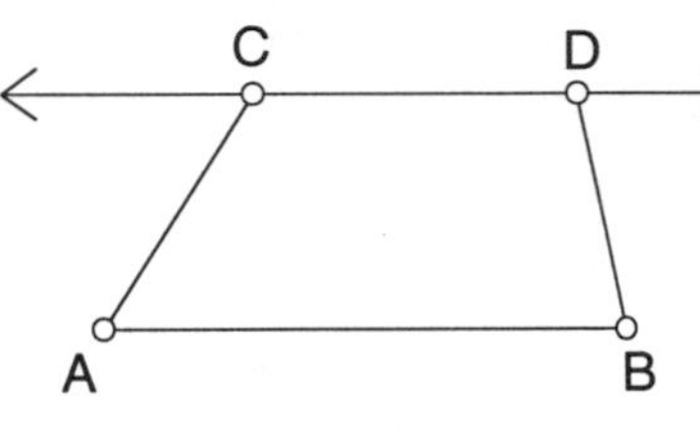

Step 4

Select the line; then, in the Display menu, choose **Hide**.

5. Hide the line.
6. Construct $\overline{CD}$.

Select the vertices in consecutive order; then, in the Construct menu, choose **Quadrilateral Interior**.

7. Construct the interior of trapezoid $ABDC$.
8. Measure the area of $ABDC$.
9. Measure the lengths of the bases of the trapezoid, $\overline{AB}$ and $\overline{CD}$.

Area ABDC = 4.20 cm^2

m $\overline{AB}$ = 3.78 cm

m $\overline{CD}$ = 2.15 cm

Distance C to $\overline{AB}$ = 1.42 cm

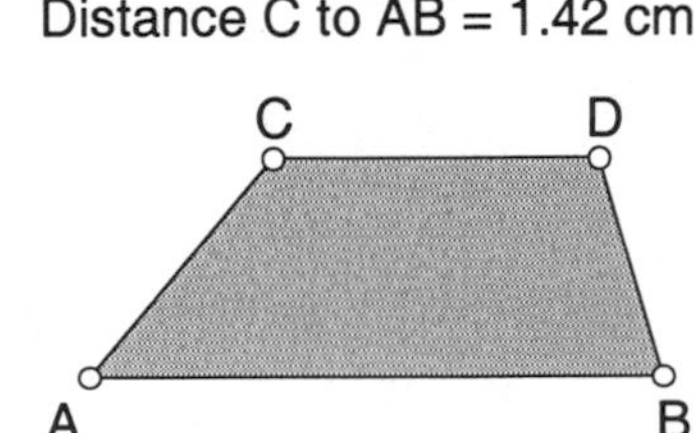

Select point C and $\overline{AB}$; then, in the Measure menu, choose **Distance**.

10. Measure the distance from point C to $\overline{AB}$. This is the height of the trapezoid.
11. Drag different parts of the trapezoid and observe the measures.

At this point, it's probably hard to see any relationships between the area measure and the base and height measurements. Continue sketching to investigate the relationship.

12. Construct the midpoint E of $\overline{DB}$.

Double-click point E to mark it as a center. Select the trapezoid. In the Transform menu, choose **Rotate**.

13. Mark point E as a center and rotate the entire trapezoid by 180°.
14. Drag parts of the figure and observe the shape formed by the trapezoid and its rotated image.

© 2002 Key Curriculum Press

Q1 What shape do the two combined trapezoids form?

Q2 Let b_1 represent the length of base AB and let b_2 represent the length of base CD. What is the length of the base of the shape formed by the combined trapezoids?

Q3 Write a formula for the area of the combined shape in terms of b_1, b_2, and h (for height).

Q4 Write a formula for the area of a single trapezoid in terms of b_1, b_2, and h.

Choose **Calculate** from the Measure menu to open the Calculator. Click once on a measurement to enter it into a calculation. Use parentheses where necessary.

Q5 In your sketch, check that you've derived the correct formula by calculating an expression equal to the area of the trapezoid. Use AB, CD, and the distance from point C to $\overline{AB}$ in your expression. Record your expression below.

Explore More

1. Construct the midpoints of the nonparallel sides of the trapezoid. Connect these midpoints with a segment. Use the length of this midsegment to invent a new area formula.
2. Construct a triangle inside your trapezoid whose area is always half the area of the trapezoid. Explain what you did. Is there more than one way to do it?

© 2002 Key Curriculum Press

Dividing Land

Name(s): ______________________

When farmers Clarence and Myrtle died, they left their two daughters their land with instructions to divide it equally. One daughter, Ella, was considerably more conniving than her sister, Jo. The land, unfortunately, was shaped as an irregular quadrilateral, and it wasn't immediately obvious how to divide it equally. Ella first tried to get Jo to agree to split it down the diagonal *AC* shown, with Ella getting region *ACD* and Jo getting region *ABC*. Jo could see that was a bad deal.

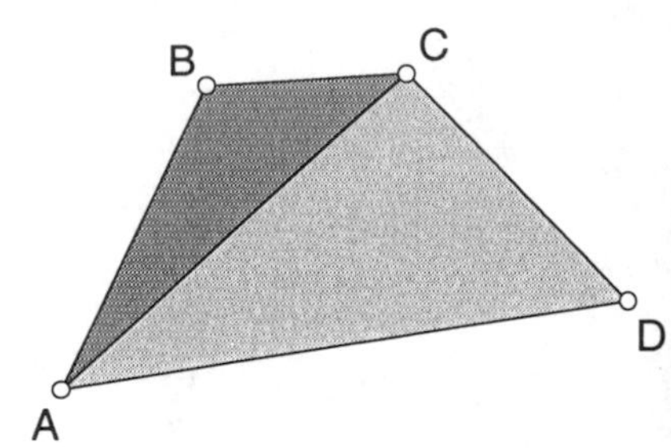

Ella then offered to split the land with both diagonals. Ella would take two regions, *AED* and *BEC*, leaving Jo with regions *ABE* and *CED*. This sounded good to Jo, but when she checked it out, she found that the sums of the areas of the respective regions were still not equal. "Ah," said Ella, "but the *products* of the areas of our regions *are* equal!" This stumped Jo, and she agreed to the deal out of sheer awe for Ella's discovery.

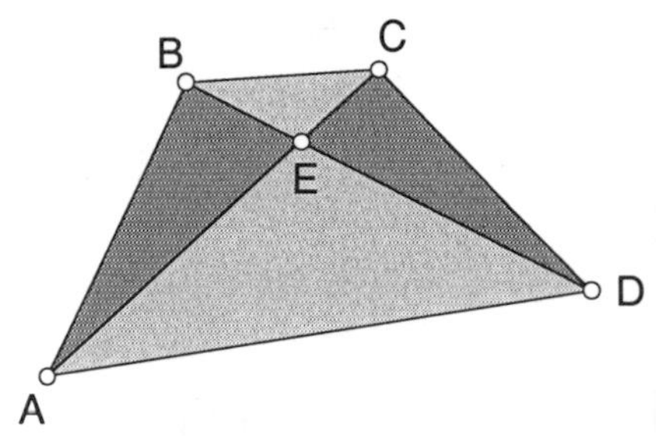

Sketch and Investigate

Model this problem with Sketchpad. Is Ella's claim true for all quadrilaterals? Does that mean that this was a fair way to divide the land? Why or why not? See if you can show why Ella's conjecture is true. Write your findings in the space below.

Explore More

1. Come up with a way to divide an irregular quadrilateral using only two segments so that the four regions can be divided equally between two people.

© 2002 Key Curriculum Press

Areas of Regular Polygons and Circles

Name(s): ____________________

A regular polygon has congruent sides and congruent angles. You can divide any regular polygon into congruent triangles by drawing segments from the center to each vertex. You can then use the area of one of these triangles to find the area of the polygon. This method can be extended to derive a formula for the area of a circle. In this activity, you'll manipulate a sketch in which you can vary the number of sides of a regular polygon to see how that affects the area.

Sketch and Investigate

1. Open the sketch **To a Circle.gsp**.

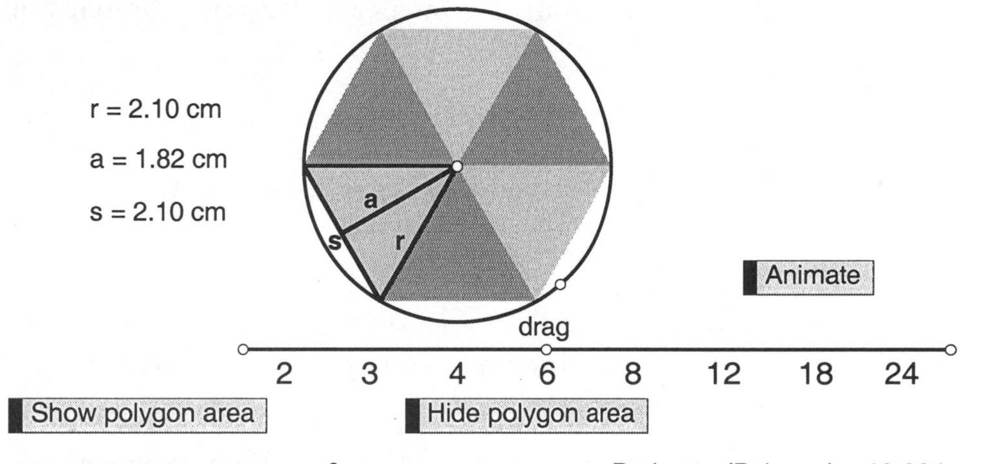

Area(Polygon) = 11.466 cm²
Area(Circle) = 13.864 cm²
Perimeter(Polygon) = 12.604 cm
Circumference(Circle) = 13.20 cm

2. Drag (or animate) point "drag" along its segment. Observe how the polygon and the measurements change.

3. Drag to give the polygon four or more sides.

Q1 Each regular polygon with four or more sides is divided into triangles. Look at the triangle with a thick outline. It has segments labeled *a* for *apothem* and *s* for side. The side is the base of this triangle and the length of the apothem is the height of the triangle. Write a formula for the area of the triangle using *a* and *s*.

Choose **Calculate** from the Measure menu to open the Calculator. Click once on a measurement to enter it into a calculation.

Q2 Use the measurements for *a* and *s* to calculate an expression for the area of the polygon. Press the *Show polygon area* button to confirm that you've made the correct expression. Record your expression below. *Note:* Your calculation will disappear if you change the number of sides of the polygon.

© 2002 Key Curriculum Press

Q3 Change the number of sides of the polygon and calculate a new expression for its area. Check this new expression against the area given in the sketch. Record this expression below.

Q4 If you've successfully calculated expressions for a couple polygons, you should be ready to write a general formula for the area of a regular polygon. Write a formula for area A using a for apothem, s for side length, and n for number of sides.

Q5 Write a formula for the perimeter p of a regular polygon with n sides and with side length s.

Q6 Rewrite your formula in Q4 using p instead of s and n.

4. With the polygon area showing, drag or animate point "drag" some more, focusing on what happens to the polygon as the number of sides increases.

Q7 What happens to the polygon as the number of sides increases?

Q8 What does the apothem approach as the number of sides increases?

Q9 What does the perimeter approach as the number of sides increases?

5. Use the measurements for circumference and for r (radius) to calculate an expression equal to the area of the circle.

Q10 Write a formula for the area of a circle A using C for circumference and r for radius.

Q11 The formula for circumference is $C = 2\pi r$. Substitute $2\pi r$ for C in your formula in Q10 and simplify.

© 2002 Key Curriculum Press

New Area Formulas

Name(s): ______________________

Space scientists have discovered a capsule from an extraterrestrial civilization. Within they found mysterious writings that noted intergalactic linguists translated into the area formulas below.

1. To find the area of a triangle, use $A = mh$, where m is the length of the midsegment of the triangle and h is the height of the triangle.
2. To find the area of a trapezoid, use $A = mh$, where m is the length of the midsegment of the triangle and h is the height of the triangle.
3. To find the area of a rhombus, use $A = rs$, where r and s are the lengths of the diagonals.
4. To find the area of a kite, use $A = rs$, where r and s are the lengths of the diagonals.

Sketch and Investigate

Use Sketchpad to determine if all four formulas always work. Construct polygon interiors and measure the areas. Now measure other quantities (heights, midsegments, and so on) and do calculations to test the formulas. Which work? Which don't? Why? Make sure you manipulate your figures to confirm that the formulas that work always work.

In the space below, write explanations for why the formulas do or don't work. Use algebra and what you know about the standard area formulas for these shapes. Correct any formulas that don't work.

Explore More

1. See if you can come up with other new area formulas for these or other shapes.

This problem is adapted from *Discovering Geometry,* by Michael Serra.
Copyright © 1997 by Michael Serra. Used with permission.

© 2002 Key Curriculum Press

Pick's Theorem

Name(s): ____________________

Pick's theorem is a handy shortcut for finding areas of dot-paper polygons—polygons whose vertices align on a square grid. You will discover Pick's theorem in this activity.

Sketch and Investigate

1. On the Units panel of Preferences, set the Distance Units to **cm**.

In the Graph menu, choose **Show Grid**, then choose **Snap Points**. Select the grid (by clicking on a grid intersection) and choose **Display | Line Width | Dotted**.

2. Show the grid and turn on point snapping.
3. Hide the axes and the two points. Your screen will now look like a piece of dot paper or a geoboard.

Area P_1 = 13.00 cm^2

Polygon p1 has 14 border points and 7 interior points.

Use the **Segment** tool.

4. Construct a many-sided polygon with vertices on grid points.

Select the polygon's vertices in consecutive order; then, in the Construct menu, choose **Polygon Interior**. While the interior is selected, go to the Measure menu and choose **Area**.

5. Construct the polygon's interior.
6. Measure the polygon's area.

Q1 An interior point is any grid point that lies inside the polygon. A border point is any grid point that lies on the border of the polygon. Some border points are vertices of the polygon, but many polygons have border points that are not vertices.

Count the number of border points b and the number of interior points i in your polygon and record these numbers in the chart below. Then calculate $b/2$ and $(b/2) + i$ and complete the first row of the chart.

	b	$\frac{b}{2}$	i	$\frac{b}{2} + i$	Area
Polygon 1					
Polygon 2					
Polygon 3					
Polygon 4					

Q2 Change the shape of your polygon and find the new values for i, b, and the area. Use these values to complete row 2 of the chart.

© 2002 Key Curriculum Press

Q3 Continue changing your polygon and recording new entries in your chart until you see a pattern. The pattern you observe is called Pick's theorem. Write Pick's theorem in the space below.

Explore More

1. It is difficult to explain why Pick's theorem works for every type of polygon. It is not as hard to explain why Pick's theorem works for some triangles, since a triangle is one of the simplest of polygons.

   a. Start a new "dot paper" sketch on your computer screen. Make a small triangle with a base of length 1 unit and a height of 1 unit. Explain why Pick's theorem correctly calculates the area of this simple shape.

   b. Without changing the position of the base or the height of the triangle, drag the top vertex horizontally. Explain why changing the shape of the triangle in this way does not change its area. Also explain why Pick's theorem gives the same result for all these different triangles.

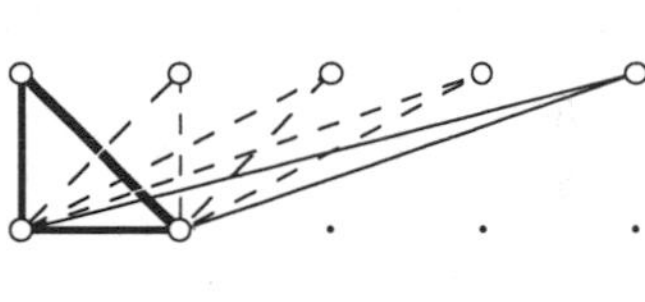

   c. Now follow the procedure from parts a and b, using a triangle with a base of 1 unit and a height of 2 units.

   d. Follow the procedure from parts a and b, using a triangle with a base of 2 units and a height of 2 units.

   e. Continue this procedure for some larger triangles.

2. Explain why Pick's theorem works for any rectangle drawn on dot paper.

© 2002 Key Curriculum Press

Squares and Square Roots

Name(s): ____________________

You can use the Sketchpad grid just like a geoboard or a piece of dot paper. In this activity, you will use squares on a grid to find the square roots of numbers. If you know the area of a square, you can find the square root of its area by measuring one of its sides.

Remember, most square roots are irrational, so many of the values you calculate will be rounded!

Sketch and Investigate

In the Edit menu, choose **Preferences** and go to the Units panel.

1. In Preferences, set the Distance Units to **cm** (centimeters) and the Distance Precision to **thousandths**.

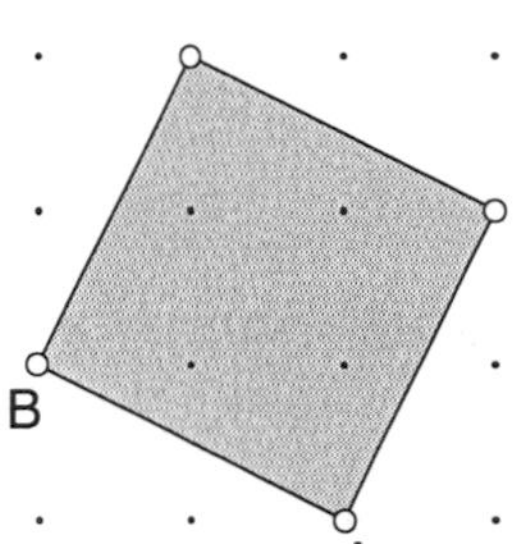

In the Graph menu, choose **Show Grid**, then choose **Snap Points**. Select the grid (by clicking on a grid intersection) and choose **Display | Line Width | Dotted**.

2. Show the grid and turn on point snapping.
3. Hide the axes and the two control points.
4. Use a custom tool to construct a square and its interior by its edge endpoints.

You can use the tool **4/Square (By Edge)** from the sketch **Polygons.gsp**.

5. Measure the area of the square.
6. Measure the length of a side of the square.

Q1 How is a square's side length related to its area?

Select the two measurements. Then, in the Graph menu, choose **Tabulate**.

7. Make a table with these two measurements.
8. Drag a vertex to make the square a different size.

To add an entry, double-click inside the table. If you add an entry that you don't want in your table, choose **Undo** in the Edit menu.

9. Add an entry to your table.
10. Continue adding entries to your square-root table by changing the size of your square.

Q2 Use your table to find the square roots of 12 different numbers less than or equal to 20. Record the numbers and their square roots here.

Square												
Square root												

Q3 Do you think it is possible to find the square root of any whole number using this method? Explain your reasoning.

© 2002 Key Curriculum Press

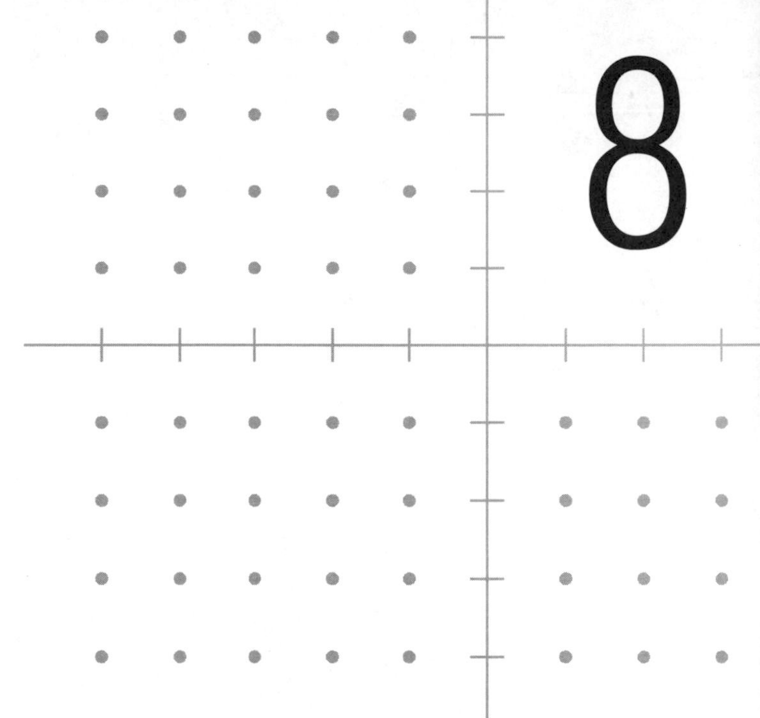

8

The Pythagorean Theorem

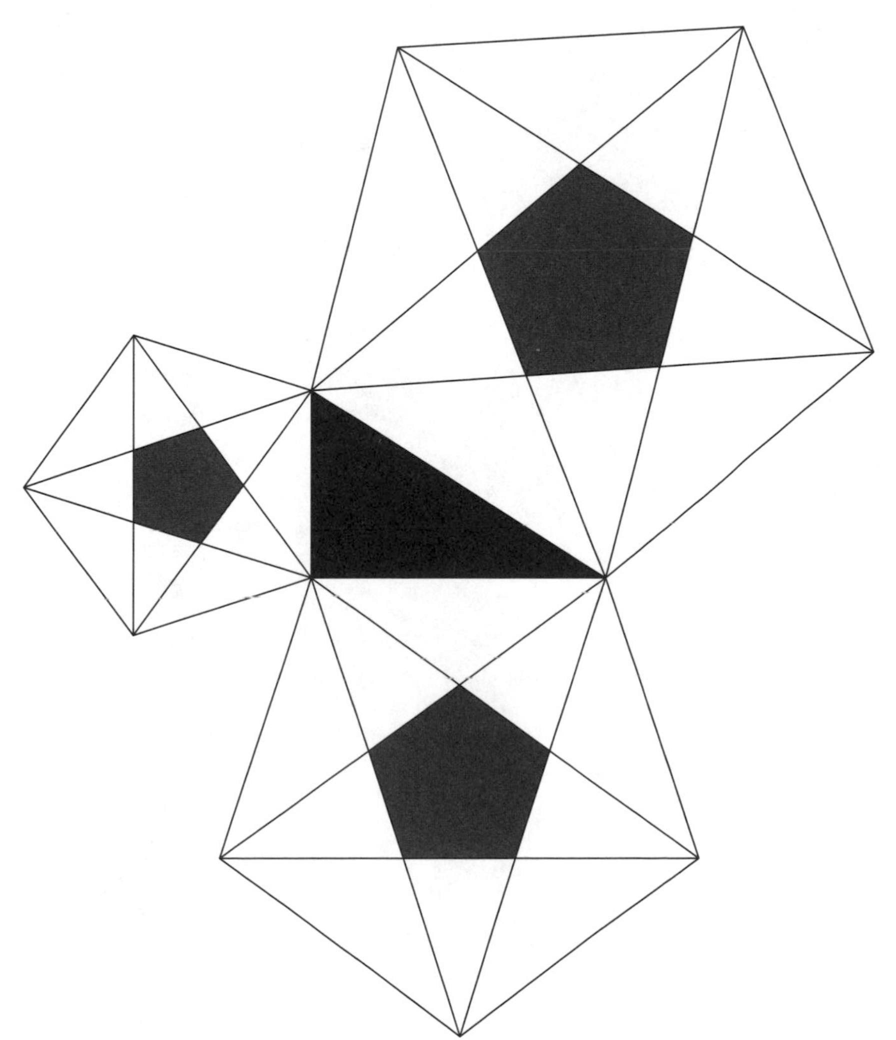

The Pythagorean Theorem

Name(s): ____________________

In this investigation, you'll create a custom tool for constructing a square, then you'll construct squares on the sides of a right triangle. The areas of these squares illustrate perhaps the most famous relationship in mathematics—the Pythagorean theorem.

Sketch and Investigate

1. Construct $\overline{AB}$.

Double-click point *A* to mark it as a center. Select point *B* and $\overline{AB}$; then, in the Transform menu, choose **Rotate**.

2. Mark point *A* as a center and rotate point *B* and $\overline{AB}$ by 90°.
3. Mark point *B*′ as a center and rotate point *A* and $\overline{B'A}$ by 90°.
4. Construct $\overline{A'B}$ to finish the square.

Select the vertices in consecutive order; then, in the Construct menu, choose **Quadrilateral Interior**.

5. Construct the interior.

A B

Step 1

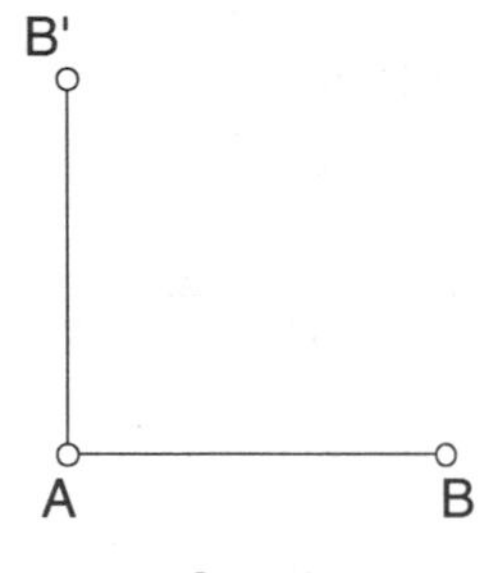

Step 2

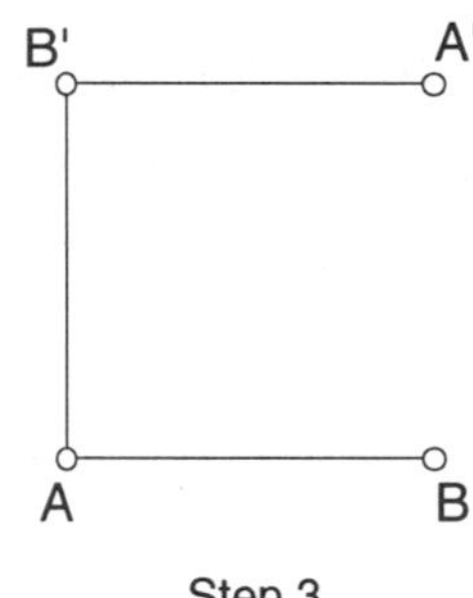

Step 3

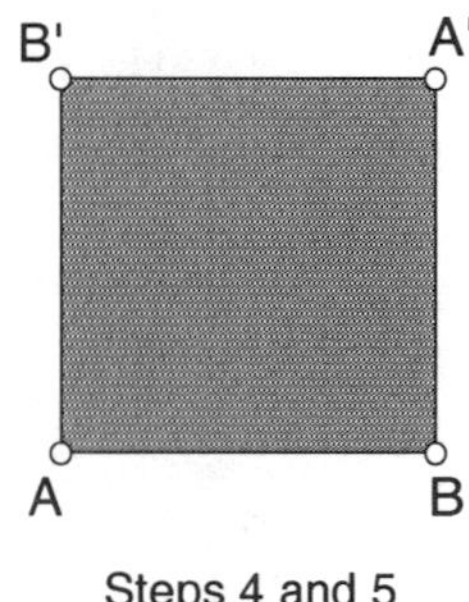

Steps 4 and 5

6. Drag each vertex of the square to make sure it holds together.

Use the **Text** tool and click on each point.

7. Hide the labels.

Select the entire figure; then, in the Custom Tools menu (the bottom tool in the Toolbox), choose **Create New Tool**.

8. Make a custom tool of this construction.

Q1 What properties of a square did you use in this construction?

You might want to save this tool so that you can use it in the future. See the appropriate sections in the help system. (Choose **Toolbox** from the Help menu, then click on the Custom Tools link.)

9. Experiment with using the custom tool to get a feel for the way it works. Note that the direction in which the square is constructed depends on how you use the tool.
10. Open a new sketch.
11. Construct $\overline{AB}$.

Select point *A* and $\overline{AB}$ and, in the Construct menu, choose **Perpendicular Line**.

12. Construct a line through point *A* perpendicular to $\overline{AB}$.
13. Construct $\overline{BC}$, where point *C* is a point on the perpendicular line.

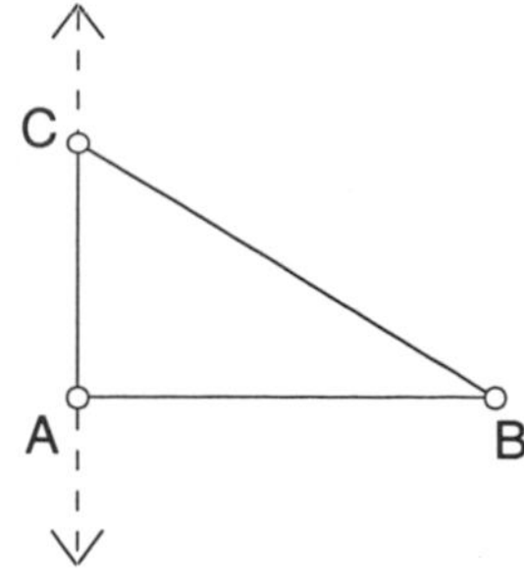

© 2002 Key Curriculum Press

14. Hide the perpendicular line and construct $\overline{AC}$.

15. Drag each vertex to confirm that your triangle stays a right triangle.

Q2 What property of a right triangle did you use in your construction?

To change a label, double-click the label with the finger of the **Text** tool. (The reason for changing these labels is so that your figure will match the way the theorem is usually stated. This may make it easier to remember the theorem.)

16. Change labels so that the right-angle vertex is labeled *C* and the other two vertices are labeled *A* and *B*.

17. Show the labels of the sides. Change them to *a, b,* and *c* so that side *a* is opposite $\angle A$, side *b* is opposite $\angle B$, and side *c* is opposite $\angle C$.

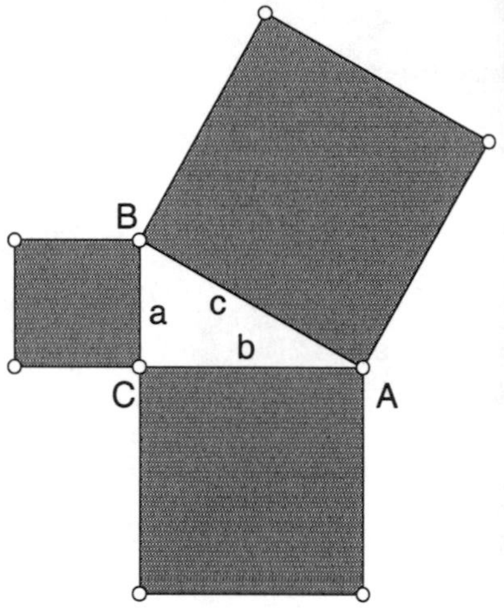

B
a
c
b
C
A

Be sure to attach each square to a pair of the triangle's vertices. If your square goes the wrong way (overlaps the interior of your triangle) or is not attached properly, undo and try attaching the square to the triangle's vertices in the opposite order.

18. Use your square tool to construct squares on the sides of your triangle.

19. Drag the vertices of the triangle to make sure the squares are properly attached.

20. Measure the areas of the three squares.

21. Measure the lengths of sides *a, b,* and *c*.

22. Drag each vertex of the triangle and observe the measures.

Choose **Calculate** from the Measure menu to open the Calculator. Click once on a measurement to enter it into a calculation.

Q3 Describe any relationship you see among the three areas. Use the Calculator to create an expression that confirms your observations.

Q4 Based on your observations about the areas of the squares, write an equation that relates *a, b,* and *c* in any right triangle. (*Hint:* What's the area of the square with side length *a*? What are the areas of the squares with side lengths *b* and *c*? How are these areas related?)

Explore More

1. Do a similar investigation using other figures besides squares. Does your conjecture about the areas still hold?

2. Investigate the converse of the Pythagorean theorem: Construct a nonright triangle and squares on its sides. Measure the areas of the squares and sum two of them. Drag until the sum is equal to the third area. What kind of triangle do you have?

© 2002 Key Curriculum Press

Visual Demonstration of the Pythagorean Theorem

Name(s): ____________________

In this activity, you'll do a visual demonstration of the Pythagorean theorem based on Euclid's proof. By *shearing* the squares on the sides of a right triangle, you'll create congruent shapes without changing the areas of your original squares.

Sketch and Investigate

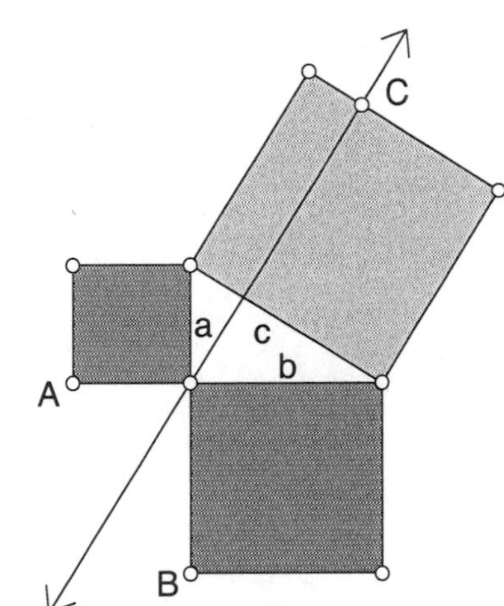

1. Open the sketch **Shear Pythagoras.gsp**. You'll see a right triangle with squares on its sides.

Click on an interior to select it. Then, in the Measure menu, choose **Area**.

2. Measure the areas of the squares.
3. Drag point *A* onto the line that's perpendicular to the hypotenuse. Note that as the square becomes a parallelogram its area doesn't change.
4. Drag point *B* onto the line. It should overlap point *A* so that the two parallelograms form a single irregular shape.

To confirm that this shape is congruent, you can copy and paste it. Drag the pasted copy onto the shape on the legs to see that it fits perfectly.

5. Drag point *C* so that the large square deforms to fill in the triangle. The area of this shape doesn't change either. It should appear congruent to the shape you made with the two smaller parallelograms.

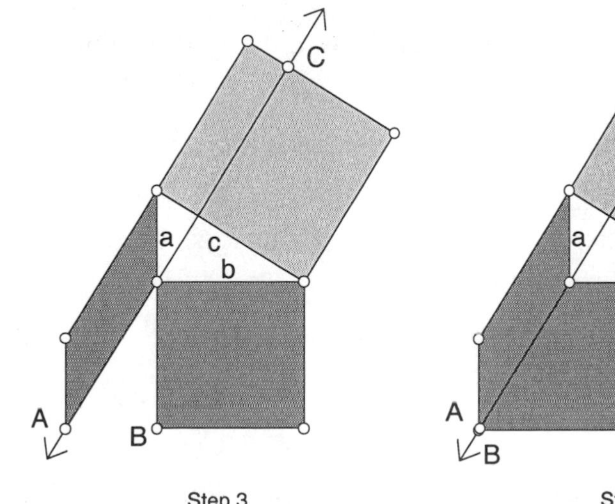

Step 3

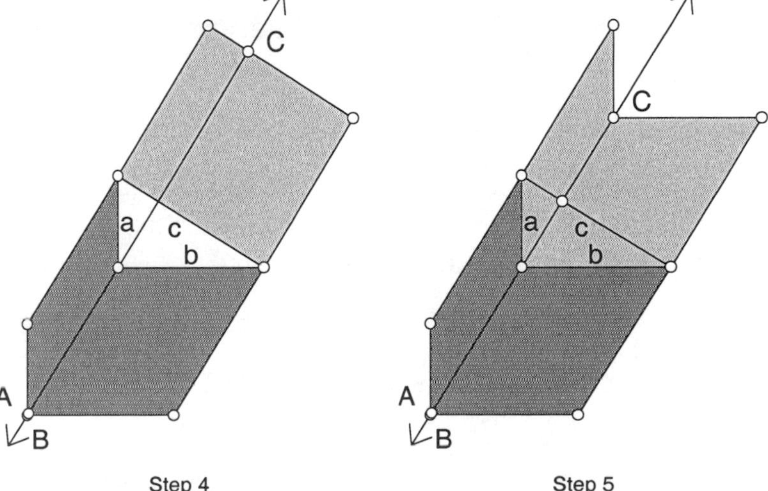

Step 4

Step 5

To confirm that this works for any right triangle, change the shape of the triangle and try the experiment again.

Q1 How do these congruent shapes demonstrate the Pythagorean theorem? (*Hint:* If the shapes are congruent, what do you know about their areas?)

© 2002 Key Curriculum Press

Dissection Demonstration of the Pythagorean Theorem

Name(s): ____________________

Many demonstrations of the Pythagorean theorem involve cutting up the squares on the legs of a right triangle and rearranging them to fit into the square on the hypotenuse. These demonstrations are called *dissections*. Some people might consider a dissection demonstration a proof. Others would require an explanation of why the dissection works.

Sketch and Investigate

1. Construct a right triangle *ABC*. Drag vertices to make sure your triangle is properly constructed.

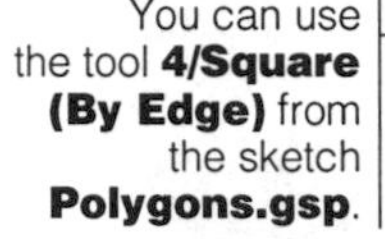

You can use the tool **4/Square (By Edge)** from the sketch **Polygons.gsp**.

2. Use a custom tool to construct squares on the sides. Delete the interiors if necessary.

One way to construct the center is to construct a diagonal and its midpoint. Hide the diagonal.

3. Construct the center of the square on the longer leg.
4. Construct a line through this center, parallel to the hypotenuse.
5. Construct another line through the center, this time perpendicular to the hypotenuse.
6. Construct the four points where these lines intersect the sides of the square. Hide the lines.

Select the vertices of the polygon in consecutive order; then, in the Construct menu, choose **Quadrilateral Interior**.

7. Construct four interiors in this square as shown, using the center as one vertex.
8. Construct the interior of the square on the small leg.

You now have five interiors: four in the large square plus the one small square. Can these five pieces be rearranged to fit in the square on the hypotenuse? Follow steps 9–11 to find out.

9. Select the five interiors. In the Edit menu, choose **Cut**.
10. In the Edit menu, choose **Paste**. The pasted interiors are now free, and you can move them around.

Before you drag, click in a blank area to deselect everything. Then you can drag one piece at a time.

11. Drag each piece into the square on the hypotenuse and arrange them so they fill this square without gaps or overlapping.

Q1 What does this demonstrate about the sides of the right triangle?

© 2002 Key Curriculum Press

Pythagorean Triples

Name(s): ______________________

The Pythagorean theorem states that if a right triangle has side lengths a and b and hypotenuse length c, then $a^2 + b^2 = c^2$. A set of three whole numbers that satisfy the Pythagorean theorem is called a Pythagorean triple. In this activity, you'll find as many right triangles as you can whose side lengths are whole numbers.

Sketch and Investigate

1. Make your sketch window as large as you can.

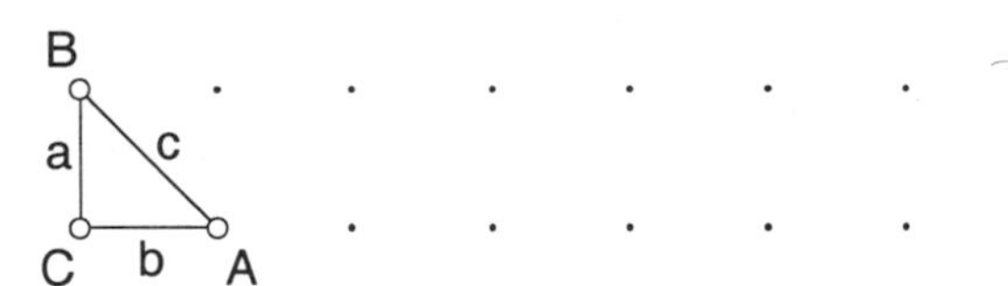

In the Edit menu, choose **Preferences** and go to the Units panel.

2. In Preferences, set the Distance Units to **cm** and the Distance Precision to **hundredths**.

In the Graph menu, choose **Show Grid**, then choose **Snap Points**. Select the grid (by clicking on a grid intersection) and choose **Display | Line Width | Dotted**.

3. Show the grid and turn on point snapping.
4. Hide the axes and the two control points.
5. In the lower left corner of your sketch, draw a right triangle ABC with vertices on the grid.

Using the **Text** tool, click on a segment to show its label. Double-click a label to change it.

6. Show the segment labels and change them to a, b, and c, as shown.
7. Measure the three side lengths.
8. Make the two leg lengths 1 cm each, as shown.

Q1 In this case, you can see that the hypotenuse length is not a whole number. Use the Pythagorean theorem to find the exact hypotenuse length (in radical form) when the side lengths are 1 cm. Show your work.

9. Drag point A one unit to the right.

Q2 When the leg lengths are 1 cm and 2 cm, is the hypotenuse length a whole number?

10. Drag point A one unit to the right again and look to see if the hypotenuse length is a whole number.

© 2002 Key Curriculum Press

You may or may not be able to fill in the whole chart, depending on the thoroughness of your search and the size of your screen. If your screen is very large, you may even need to add rows to the chart.

Q3 Continue a systematic search for Pythagorean triples, dragging point *A* one unit at a time to the right to increase *b* and dragging point *B* one unit up to increase *a*. Any time *c* is a whole number, record the Pythagorean triple in the chart at right.

a	b	c

Refer to your chart and experiment with the sketch to answer the following questions:

Q4 Which sets of triples are side lengths of congruent triangles?

Q5 Which sets of triples are side lengths of similar triangles (triangles with the same shape)?

Q6 Do you think there is a limit to the number of Pythagorean triples possible? Explain.

Q7 In the space below, use the Pythagorean theorem to verify at least three of your sets of triples.

Explore More

1. Euclid's *Elements* demonstrates that Pythagorean triples can be generated by the formulas $m^2 - n^2$, $2mn$, $m^2 + n^2$, where m and n are positive integers and m is greater than n. What triple is generated by $m = 2$ and $n = 1$? Increase m and n and generate some other triples. Can you generate all the triples you recorded in your chart? Can you generate some triples that aren't on your chart? Draw some triangles with these side lengths on the grid to confirm that they're right triangles.

© 2002 Key Curriculum Press

The Isosceles Right Triangle

Name(s): ______________________

In this activity, you'll discover a relationship among the side lengths of an isosceles right triangle. This relationship will give you a shortcut for finding side lengths quickly. You'll start by constructing a square. Dividing this square in half along a diagonal gives you the isosceles right triangle.

Sketch and Investigate

You can use the tool **4/Square (By Edge)** from the sketch **Polygons.gsp**.

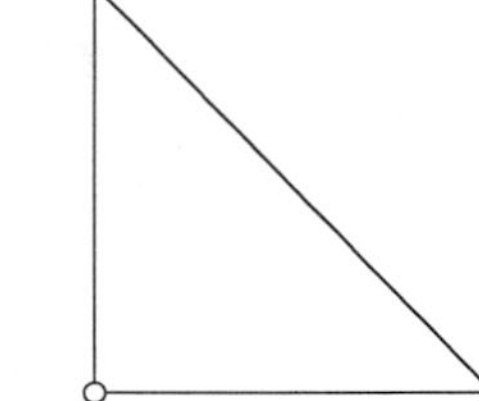

1. Use a custom tool to construct a square *ABCD* by edge endpoints *A* and *B*.
2. Construct diagonal *CA*.

Hide and **Line Width** are in the Display menu.

3. Hide the square's interior, if it has one.
4. Change the line widths of $\overline{CD}$ and $\overline{DA}$ to dashed.

Q1 Explain why ΔABC is an isosceles right triangle.

Q2 Without measuring, state the measures of the acute angles in ΔABC.

5. Measure the three side lengths.

Select the hypotenuse and one of the legs. Then, in the Measure menu, choose **Ratio**.

6. Measure the ratio of the hypotenuse length to one of the leg lengths.
7. Drag point *A* or point *B* and observe this ratio.

Q3 What do you notice about this ratio?

In steps 8 and 9, you'll investigate what this ratio represents geometrically.

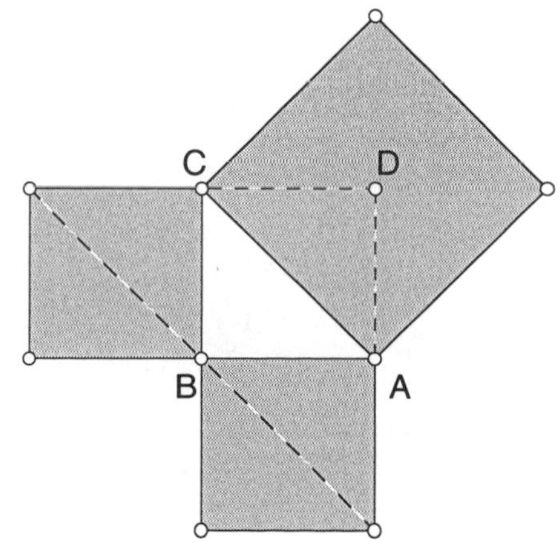

8. Use the square tool to construct squares on the sides of right triangle *ABC*. Drag to make sure the squares are properly attached.
9. Construct one diagonal in each of the smaller squares, as shown at right.

© 2002 Key Curriculum Press

The Isosceles Right Triangle (continued)

Q4 The diagonals you drew in the smaller squares may help you see a relationship between the smaller squares and the square on the hypotenuse. If each of the smaller squares has area x^2, what is the area of the large square? Confirm your conjecture by measuring the areas. Drag the triangle to confirm that this relationship always holds.

Q5 In an isosceles right triangle, if the legs have length x, what is the length of the hypotenuse?

Q6 Use the Pythagorean theorem to confirm your answer to Q5.

Explore More

1. The society of the Pythagoreans discovered that the square root of 2 is *irrational*. Do some research and report on this discovery.

© 2002 Key Curriculum Press

The 30°-60° Right Triangle

Name(s): ______________________

The 30°-60° right triangle—formed by taking half of an equilateral triangle—has special relationships among its side lengths. These relationships make it easy to find all the side lengths if you know just one. In this activity, you'll discover these relationships and why they hold.

Sketch and Investigate

You can use the tool **3/Triangle (By Edge)** from the sketch **Polygons.gsp**. If you need to relabel the triangle, use the **Text** tool. Click once on a point to show its label. Double-click a label to change it.

1. In a new sketch, construct an equilateral triangle *ABC*. Use a custom tool or construct it from scratch. Drag vertices to confirm that the construction is correct.

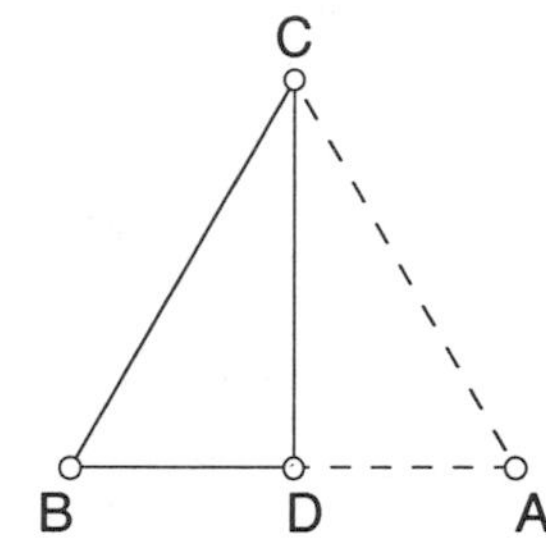

2. Hide the triangle's interior if necessary.
3. Construct the midpoint *D* of $\overline{AB}$.
4. Construct median *CD*.

Select the segments; then, in the Display menu, choose **Line Width | Dashed**.

5. Change the line widths of $\overline{AB}$ and $\overline{AC}$ to dashed.
6. Construct $\overline{BD}$ and make its line width thin.

Q1 Without measuring, state the measure of each angle in ΔCDB. For each angle, explain how you know it has that measure.

Q2 In a 30°-60° right triangle, how does the length of the hypotenuse compare to the length of the short leg? Answer without measuring.

7. Hide point *A*, $\overline{AB}$, and $\overline{AC}$.
8. Use a custom tool to construct squares on the three sides of the triangle as shown at right. Drag to make sure the squares are properly attached.

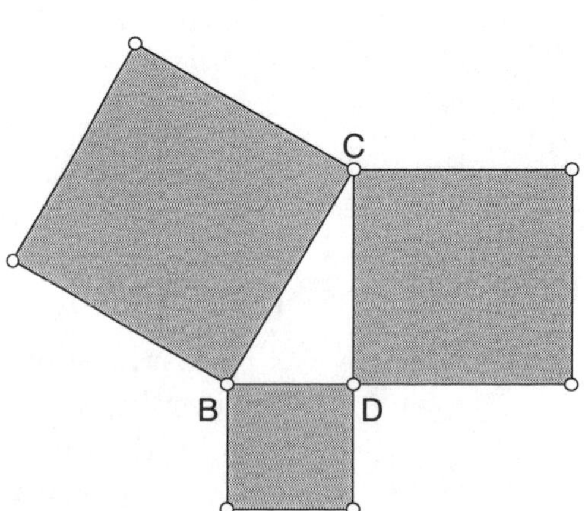

9. Measure the areas of the three squares.

Choose **Calculate** from the Measure menu to open the Calculator. Click once on a measurement to enter it into a calculation.

10. Calculate the ratio of the largest area to the smallest area
11. Drag point *B* and observe this ratio.

© 2002 Key Curriculum Press

Q3 What is this area ratio? Explain why this ratio is what it is. In your explanation, use what you know about the side lengths.

Q4 Now you'll use your answer to Q3 about the square on the hypotenuse and the square on the short leg to help you find the area of the square on the long leg. Answer the following questions:

a. Suppose the smallest square has area x^2. What would be the area of the square on the hypotenuse? ____________

b. Use the Pythagorean theorem to find the area of the square on the long leg. Show your work.

c. State the ratio of the area of the square on the long leg to the area of the square on the short leg. Calculate this ratio in your sketch and drag point *B* to confirm that this ratio applies to all 30°-60° right triangles. ____________

Q5 Suppose the short leg had length x.

a. What would be the length of the hypotenuse? ____________

b. What would be the length of the long leg? ____________

c. What would be the ratio of the length of the long leg to the length of the short leg? (State your answer in radical form.) ____________

Select the hypotenuse and the short leg. Then, in the Measure menu, choose **Ratio**. Measure the other ratio in the same way.

12. To confirm your answers to Q5, measure the ratio of the hypotenuse length to the short leg length. Also measure the ratio of the long leg length to the short leg length. Drag point *B* to confirm that these ratios apply to all 30°-60° right triangles.

Q6 The second ratio you measured in step 12 should be the decimal approximation of the ratio you wrote in Q5c. Write this decimal approximation. ____________

Explore More

1. To test how well you can apply your discoveries, make a Hide/Show action button for each side length measurement. Show one side length and hide the other two. Then calculate the two hidden lengths. Show the hidden lengths to check your calculations. Try this several times, changing the triangle each time and showing different side lengths. Repeat until you think you can calculate the missing side lengths correctly every time.

© 2002 Key Curriculum Press

The Square Root Spiral

Name(s): ____________________

Irrational numbers such as $\sqrt{2}$ and $\sqrt{3}$ correspond to points on a ruler, but you can't find those points precisely by dividing your ruler into fractional parts. However, you can construct square roots with compass and straightedge (or with Sketchpad). In this activity, you'll construct a square root spiral and use it to create a chart of approximate square roots.

Sketch and Investigate

The first part of the spiral is an isosceles right triangle.

Choose **Preferences** from the Edit menu and go to the Units panel.

1. In Preferences, set the Distance Units to **inches** and set Distance Precision to **thousandths**.

With point *A* selected, choose **Translate** in the Transform menu.

2. Construct point *A* and translate it at an angle of 0° by 1 inch to create point *A´*.

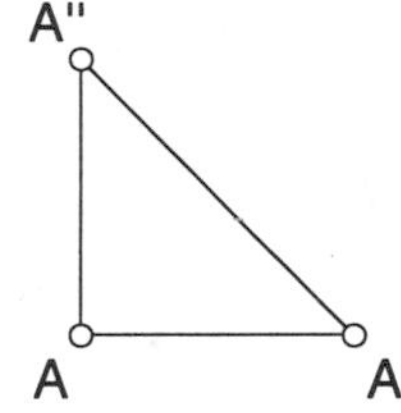

Double-click point *A* to mark it as a center. Select point *A´*; then, in the Transform menu, choose **Rotate**.

3. Mark point *A* as a center and rotate point *A´* by 90°.
4. Connect these points to make isosceles right triangle *AA´A˝*.

Q1 Use the Pythagorean theorem to find the exact value of *A´A˝*. (Use radical form, not a decimal approximation, and show your work.)

In steps 5–9, you'll construct $\sqrt{3}$.

5. Construct a line through point *A´*, perpendicular to $\overline{A'A''}$.
6. Construct circle *A´A*.
7. Construct point *B*, the intersection of the circle with the line, as shown.
8. Hide the circle and line.
9. Construct $\overline{A'B}$ and $\overline{A''B}$.

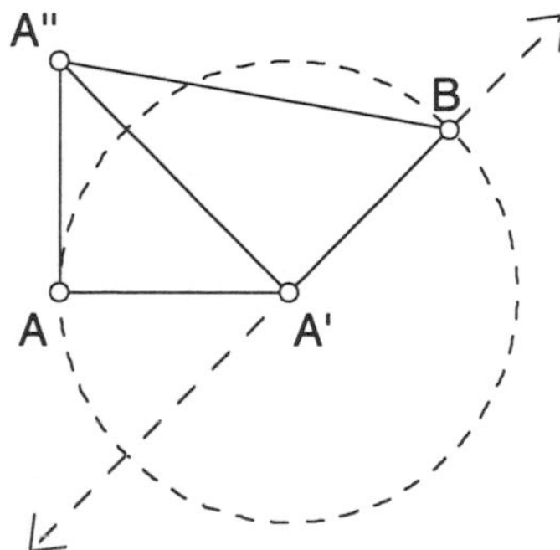

Q2 Explain why *A˝B* is equal to $\sqrt{3}$ inches.

You can continue in this way to construct a spiral that gives you the square roots of as many consecutive positive integers as you like. A custom tool makes the construction process quicker. Follow steps 10–17 to continue your spiral.

© 2002 Key Curriculum Press

10. Construct a line through point B, perpendicular to $\overline{BA''}$.

11. Construct circle BA'.

12. Construct point C, the intersection of the circle with the line, as shown.

13. Hide the circle and line.

14. Construct segments $A''C$ and CB.

Selection order is very important to make the custom tool work.

15. Now create a custom tool. Select, in order, point A', point B, point A'' (these are the tool's *givens*), point C, $\overline{A''C}$, and $\overline{BC}$ (these are the tool's *results*). Choose **Create New Tool** from the Custom Tools menu (the bottom tool in the Toolbox) and name the tool **Next Triangle**.

16. Click on the **Custom** tools icon to select the tool you just created. Click, in order, on point B, point C, and point A'' to create the next right triangle.

17. Use your custom tool to create at least five more right triangles.

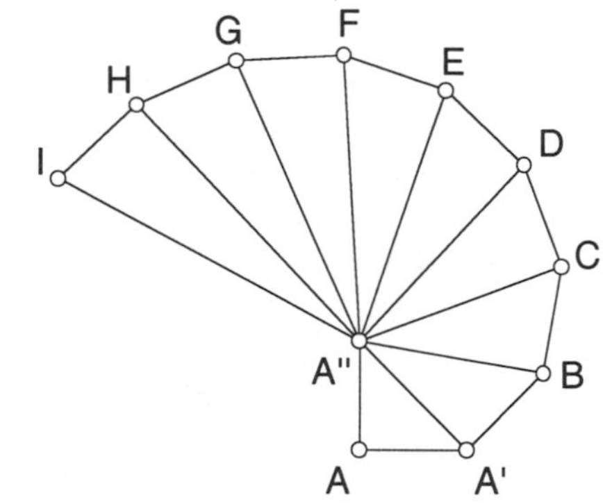

Save this sketch. You can use its custom tool again in Explore More 1, below.

Q3 What are the lengths of all the segments around the outside of the spiral? Write these lengths on the figure at right.

Q4 Using radical form, write the lengths of the spiral arms on the figure above right.

Q5 Measure all the spiral arms, then complete the table below with approximations to the nearest thousandth for square roots of whole numbers from 2 to 10.

$\sqrt{1} = 1$	$\sqrt{2} \approx$	$\sqrt{3} \approx$	$\sqrt{4} =$	$\sqrt{5} \approx$
$\sqrt{6} \approx$	$\sqrt{7} \approx$	$\sqrt{8} \approx$	$\sqrt{9} =$	$\sqrt{10} \approx$

Explore More

1. Draw an arbitrary triangle. Use the **Next Triangle** tool on its three vertices. Now use the tool, in the same order, on the vertices of the newly created triangle. Do this at least eight more times. You should get a spiral (though not a square root spiral) that you can open and close dynamically by dragging the vertices of your original triangle.

© 2002 Key Curriculum Press

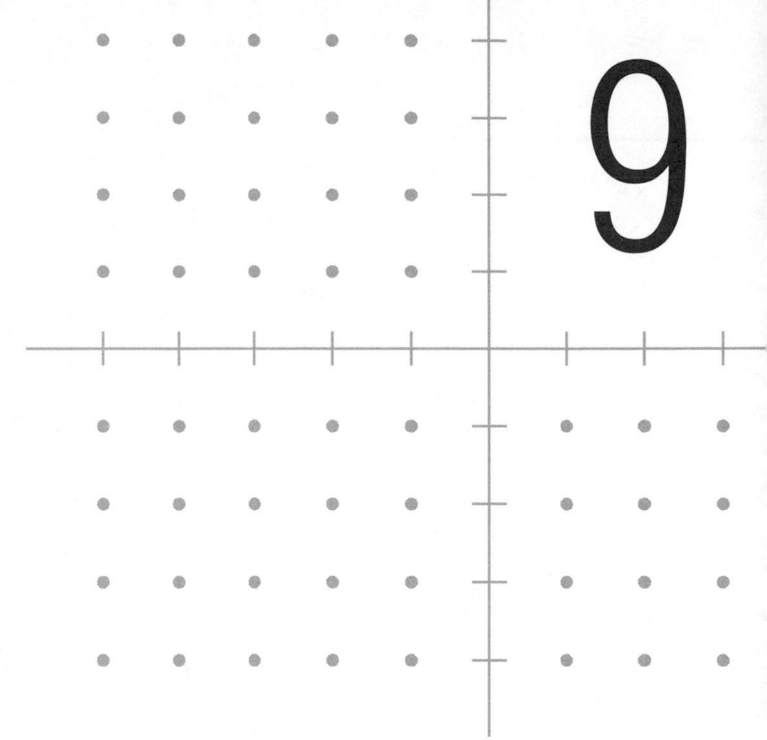

9 Similarity

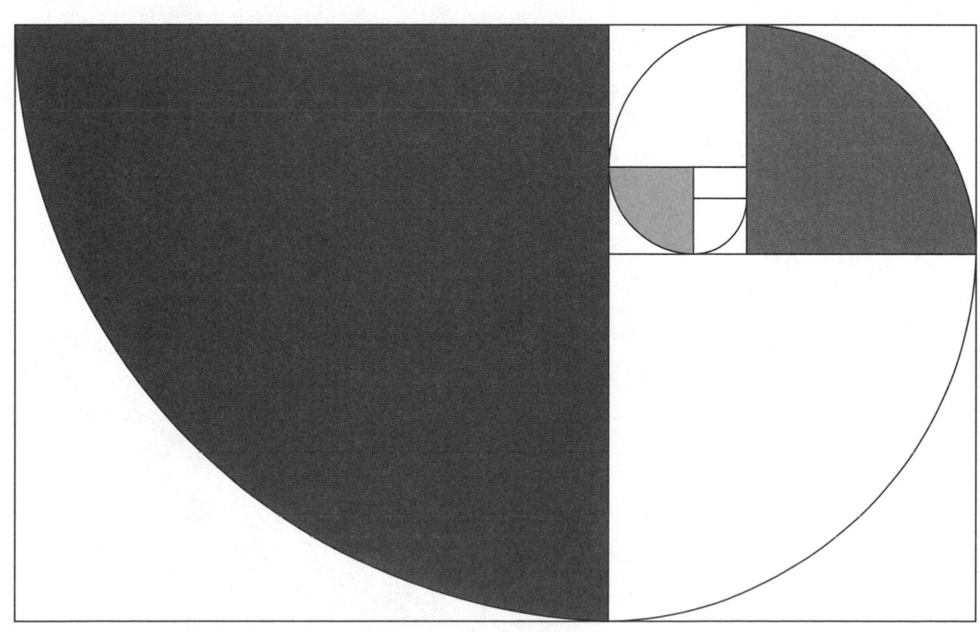

The Golden Rectangle

Name(s): ______________________________

The golden ratio appears often in nature: in the proportions of a nautilus shell, for example, and in some proportions in our bodies and faces. A rectangle whose sides have the golden ratio is called a *golden rectangle.*

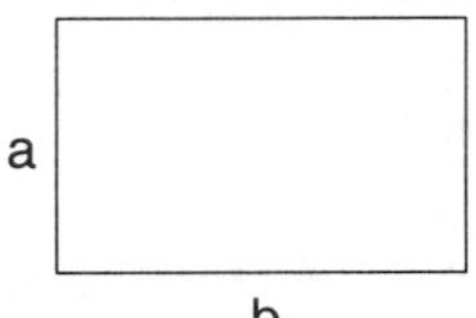

$$\frac{a+b}{b} = \frac{b}{a}$$

In a golden rectangle, the ratio of the sum of the sides to the long side is equal to the ratio of the long side to the short side. Golden rectangles are somehow pleasing to the eye, perhaps because they approximate the shape of our field of vision. For this reason, they're used often in architecture, especially the classical architecture of ancient Greece. In this activity, you'll construct a golden rectangle and find an approximation to the golden ratio. Then you'll see how smaller golden rectangles are found within a golden rectangle. Finally, you'll construct a golden spiral.

Sketch and Investigate

You can use the tool **4/Square (By Edge)** from the sketch **Polygons.gsp**.

1. Use a custom tool to construct a square *ABCD*. Then construct the square's interior.
2. Orient the square so that the control points are on the left side, one above the other (points *A* and *B* in the figure).
3. Construct the midpoint *E* of $\overline{AD}$.
4. Construct circle *EC*.

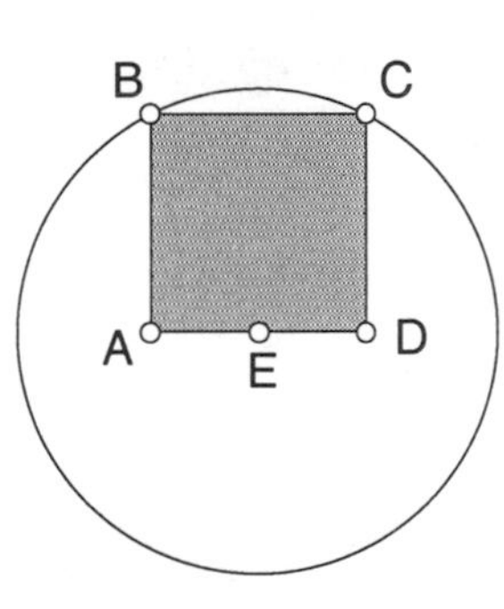

Steps 1–4

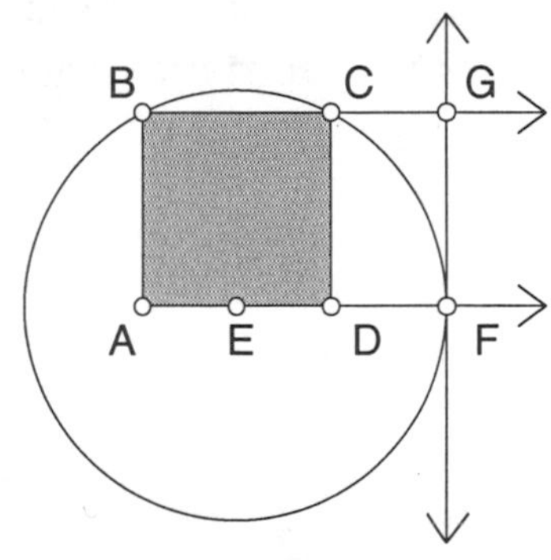

Steps 5–8

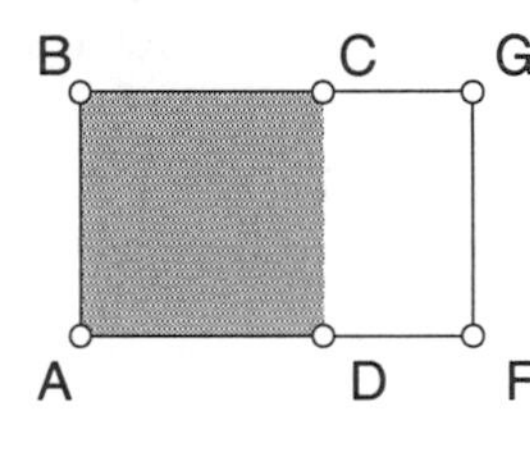

Steps 9–11

Hold down the mouse button on the **Segment** tool to show the Straight Objects palette. Drag right to choose the **Ray** tool.

5. Extend sides *AD* and *BC* with rays, as shown.
6. Construct point *F* where $\overrightarrow{AD}$ intersects the circle.
7. Construct a line perpendicular to $\overrightarrow{AD}$ through point *F*.
8. Construct point *G* where this perpendicular intersects $\overrightarrow{BC}$. Rectangle *AFGB* is a golden rectangle.

Select the objects; then, in the Display menu, choose **Hide Objects**.

9. Hide the lines, the rays, the circle, and point *E*.
10. Hide $\overline{AD}$, $\overline{DC}$, and $\overline{BC}$.

© 2002 Key Curriculum Press

11. Construct $\overline{BG}$, $\overline{GF}$, and $\overline{FA}$.

Select, in order, $\overline{AF}$ and $\overline{AB}$; then, in the Measure menu, choose **Ratio**.

12. Measure AB and AF.
13. Measure the ratio of AF to AB.

Choose **Calculate** from the Measure menu to open the Calculator. Click once on a measurement to enter it into a calculation.

14. Calculate $(AB + AF)/AF$.
15. Drag point A or point B to confirm that your rectangle is always golden.

Q1 The Greek letter phi ($ø$) is often used to represent the golden ratio. Write an approximation for $ø$.

Continue sketching to investigate the rectangle further and to construct a golden spiral.

Select, in order, the circle and points B and D. Then choose **Arc On Circle** from the Construct menu.

Select the entire figure; then choose **Create New Tool** from the Custom Tools menu in the Toolbox (the bottom tool).

If your rectangle goes the wrong way when you use the custom tool, undo and try applying it in the opposite order.

16. Construct circle CB.
17. Construct an arc on the circle from point B to point D, then hide the circle.

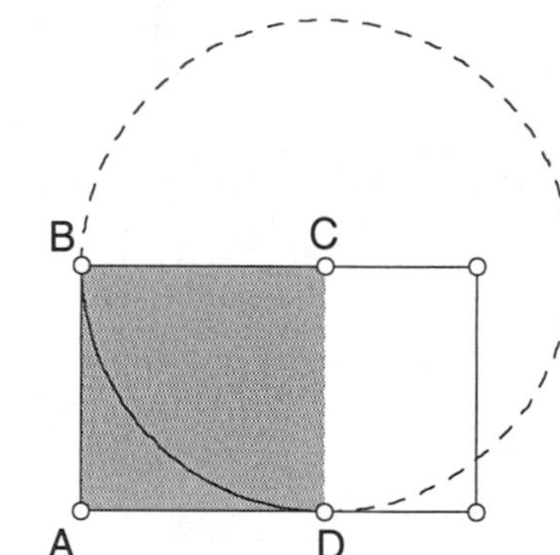

18. Make a custom tool for this construction.
19. Make the rectangle as big as you can, then use the custom tool on points F and D. You should find that the rectangle constructed by your custom tool fits perfectly in the region $DFGC$.

Q2 Make a conjecture about region $DFGC$.

20. Continue using the custom tool within your golden rectangle to create a golden spiral. Hide unnecessary points.

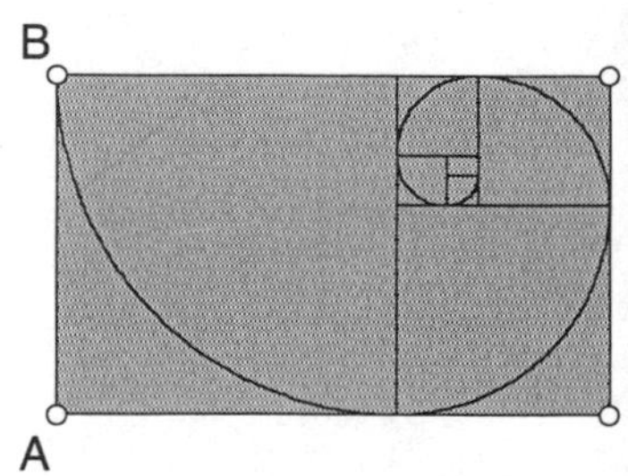

Explore More

1. Let the short side of a golden rectangle have length 1 and the long side have length $ø$. Write a proportion, cross-multiply, and use the quadratic formula to calculate an exact value for $ø$.
2. Calculate $ø^2$ and $1/ø$. How are these numbers related to $ø$? Use algebra to demonstrate why these relationships hold.

© 2002 Key Curriculum Press

Similar Polygons

Name(s): ______________________

Figures are *similar* if they have the same shape. Similar figures don't necessarily have the same size. A *dilation* is a transformation that preserves shape. In this activity, you'll use a dilation to discover principles of similarity. You'll use your discoveries to come up with a definition of similar polygons.

Sketch and Investigate

Double-click the point to mark it as a center.

Select the segments, then, in the Transform menu, choose **Mark Segment Ratio**. The selection order determines the numerator and denominator of the ratio.

Select the polygon; then, in the Transform menu, choose **Dilate**.

1. Construct any polygon.
2. Construct a point outside the polygon and mark it as a center for dilation.
3. Construct two segments of different lengths and mark them as a ratio.
4. Dilate your entire polygon by the marked ratio.

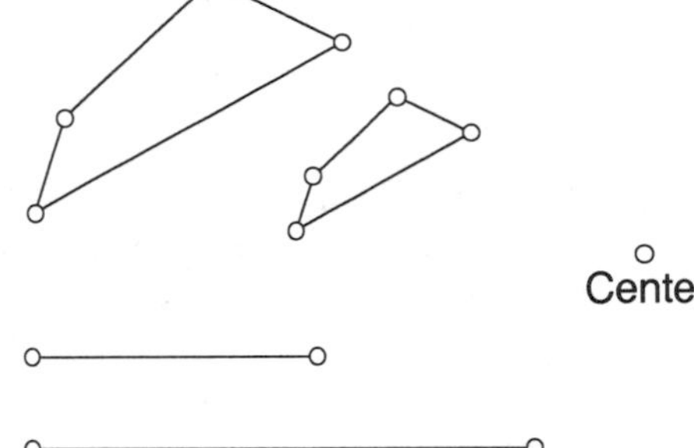

5. Drag the center of dilation. Also change the lengths of your two segments that define the ratio. Observe how these changes affect the similar polygons.

Q1 How can you make the dilated image coincide with the original figure?

6. If necessary, drag the ratio segments so that the polygons don't coincide.

Select the two segments; then, in the Measure menu, choose **Ratio**.

7. Measure the ratio of these segments' lengths.
8. Measure the ratios of some corresponding sides of your polygons.
9. Experiment with dragging different points on the polygon, the ratio segments, and the dilation center. Observe the ratios of corresponding side lengths in the polygon.
10. To compare angles in the two polygons, drag the center of dilation onto each vertex.

Q2 Use your observations to write a definition of similar polygons.

© 2002 Key Curriculum Press

Similar Triangles—AA Similarity

Name(s): ____________

To show that two triangles are similar, you don't need to show that all the corresponding angles are congruent and that all the corresponding sides are proportional. There are several shortcuts. In this activity, you'll construct and investigate triangles with two pairs of congruent corresponding angles.

Sketch and Investigate

1. Construct $\triangle ABC$.
2. Construct $\overleftrightarrow{DE}$ below the triangle.

Double-click point *D* to mark it as a center. Select, in order, points *C*, *B*, and *A*; then, in the Transform menu, choose **Mark Angle**.

3. Mark point *D* as a center of rotation and mark $\angle CBA$ as an angle of rotation.

Select $\overleftrightarrow{DE}$; then, in the Transform menu, choose **Rotate**.

4. Rotate $\overleftrightarrow{DE}$ by the marked angle.

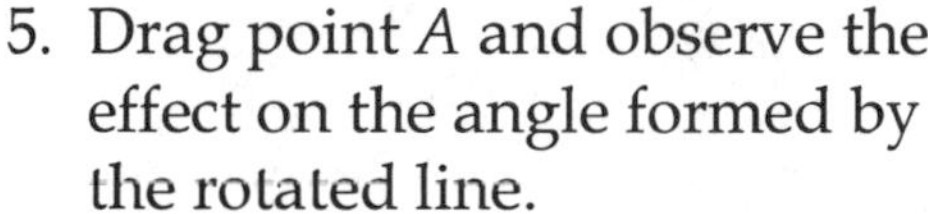

5. Drag point *A* and observe the effect on the angle formed by the rotated line.
6. Mark *E* as a center and mark $\angle BCA$.
7. Rotate $\overleftrightarrow{DE}$ about the new marked center by the new marked angle.
8. Construct point *F*, the point of intersection of these two rotated lines.
9. Hide the lines and replace them with segments.
10. Drag vertices of $\triangle ABC$ and observe the effects on $\triangle FDE$.

Q1 You constructed angles *D* and *E* to be congruent to angles *B* and *C*, respectively. Without measuring, how do you think angles *A* and *F* compare? Explain why they're related in this way.

Select two corresponding segments; then, in the Measure menu, choose **Ratio**. Repeat for the other two pairs of sides.

11. To see if the triangles are similar, measure the ratios of all three pairs of corresponding side lengths. Drag points and observe these ratios.

Q2 Make a conjecture about triangles with two pairs of congruent corresponding angles.

Explore More

1. Investigate AA or AAA similarity for quadrilaterals.

© 2002 Key Curriculum Press

Similar Triangles—SSS, SAS, SSA **Name(s):** ______________

You may have already discovered that if two angles in one triangle are congruent to two angles in another triangle, the triangles are similar. In this activity, you'll experiment with a sketch to discover other shortcuts for determining whether two triangles are similar. These shortcuts involve different combinations of proportional sides and congruent angles.

Sketch and Investigate

1. Open the sketch **Triangle Similarity.gsp**. You'll see a sketch like the one shown below.

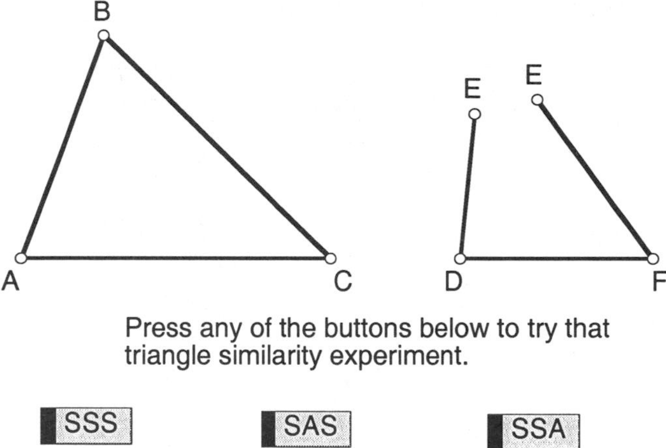

2. Press the SSS action button and follow the instructions on the screen.

Q1 Write your conjecture below.

3. Experiment with the SAS button and the SSA button.

Q2 Of SSS, SAS, and SSA, which combinations of corresponding parts guarantee similarity in a pair of triangles? Which do not?

Explore More

1. Investigate similarity in quadrilaterals. What's the smallest amount of information you need to determine that quadrilaterals are similar?

© 2002 Key Curriculum Press

The Geometric Mean

Name(s): ____________________

What comes next in the number sequence 2, 6, 18, . . .? If you guessed 54, you noticed that each number in the sequence is just the previous term multiplied by 3. Or you may have noticed that there was a constant ratio between successive terms: $54/18 = 18/6 = 6/2 = 3$. A sequence with a constant ratio is called a geometric sequence, and each term is the *geometric mean* or *mean proportional* between the terms on either side of it. For example, 6 is the geometric mean of 2 and 18 because $2/6 = 6/18$. In this activity, you'll discover what a geometric mean is geometrically, and you'll learn how to construct a geometric mean between two lengths.

Sketch and Investigate

1. Construct $\overline{AB}$ and point C on $\overline{AB}$. You will construct the geometric mean of the lengths AC and CB.

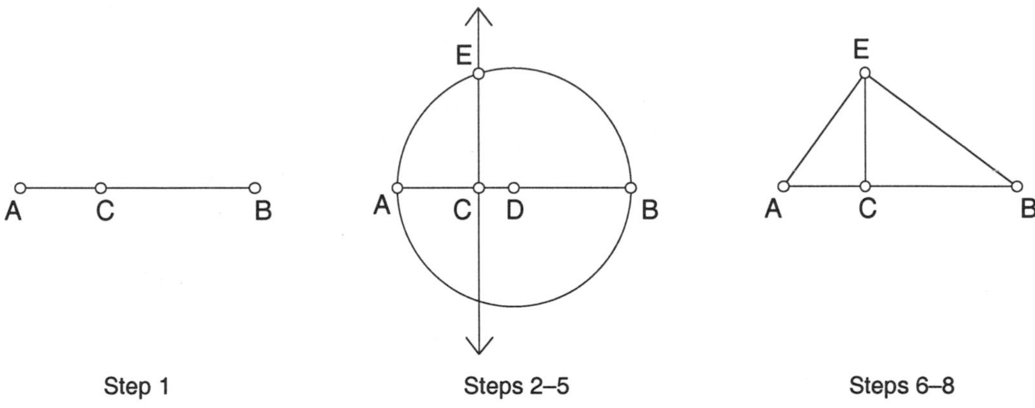

2. Construct the midpoint D of $\overline{AB}$.

Be sure to release the mouse button (or click the second time) with the cursor directly over point *A* so that the circle will be attached at this point.

3. Construct circle DA. Drag point A to make sure the circle is correctly attached.
4. Construct a line through C, perpendicular to $\overline{AB}$.
5. Construct point E where the line and the circle intersect.
6. Construct $\overline{AE}$ and $\overline{EB}$.
7. Hide the circle, the line, point D, and $\overline{AB}$.
8. Construct $\overline{AC}$, $\overline{CE}$, and $\overline{CB}$.

Q1 Drag point C. What kind of triangle is ΔABE? (*Hint:* Recall that it's inscribed in a semicircle.)

© 2002 Key Curriculum Press

Q2 There are three similar triangles in your figure. Write the similarity relationships below and write an explanation of why the triangles are similar.

_________ ~ _________ ~ _________

To measure a ratio, select two segments. Then, in the Measure menu, choose **Ratio**.

Q3 From your similar triangles, figure out which distance is the geometric mean of AC and CB. Measure some ratios to confirm your conjecture. Drag point C to confirm that the distance you found is always the geometric mean. Write a proportion below:

$$\frac{AC}{\quad} = \frac{\quad}{CB}$$

9. Measure CE, AC, and CB.
10. Calculate the product $AC \cdot CB$.

If you don't see the plotted point, drag the point at (1, 0) to scale the axes.

11. Select the measurement CE and the product $AC \cdot CB$. Then, in the Graph menu, choose **Plot As (x, y)**.

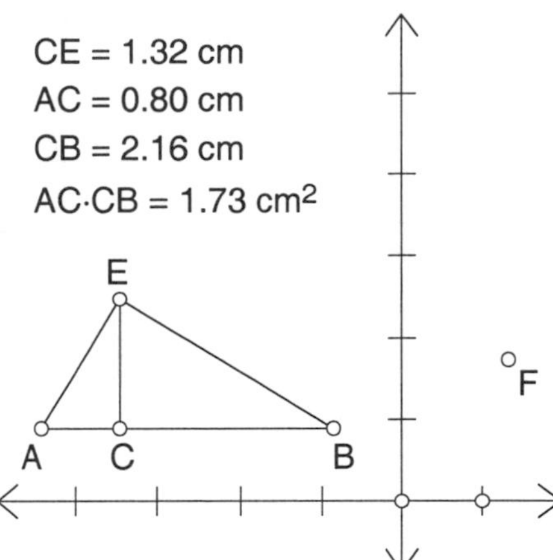

Select the plotted point and point C. Then, in the Construct menu, choose **Locus**.

12. Construct the locus of this plotted point and point C.

Q4 Describe the graph. Explain how it is related to the proportion you wrote in Q3.

Explore More

1. There are two other geometric means in your triangle. Find them and state what they are.
2. Let AE be a, let EB be b, let AC be x, and let CB be $c - x$ (so that AB is c). Use similar triangles to write two proportions. Cross-multiply in each proportion, then add the two resulting equations to combine them into one. Show that $a^2 + b^2 = c^2$ (the Pythagorean theorem).
3. See if you can find a geometric mean in a regular pentagram (five-pointed star).

© 2002 Key Curriculum Press

Finding the Width of a River

Name(s): ____________________

Similar triangles have many problem-solving applications. In this activity, you'll use similar triangles to find a distance that can't be measured directly.

Sketch and Investigate

1. Construct $\overleftrightarrow{AB}$ and a point *C* above $\overleftrightarrow{AB}$.
2. Construct a line parallel to $\overleftrightarrow{AB}$ through point *C*. Imagine that these lines are the banks of a river. You wish to find the distance across the river. (And you can't just measure it—it's a river. So stay away from that Measure menu!)
3. Hide points *A* and *B*.

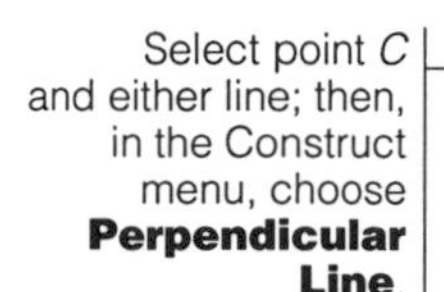

Select point *C* and either line; then, in the Construct menu, choose **Perpendicular Line**.

4. Point *C* represents a tree on the other side of the river from you. To locate yourself directly across the river from point *C*, construct a line through point *C*, perpendicular to the bank of the river.
5. Construct point *D*, where the perpendicular line intersects the other bank. Point *D* is where you start.
6. You walk a few meters and stick a pole into the bank at point *E*. (Construct $\overline{DE}$, where point *E* is on the bank.)

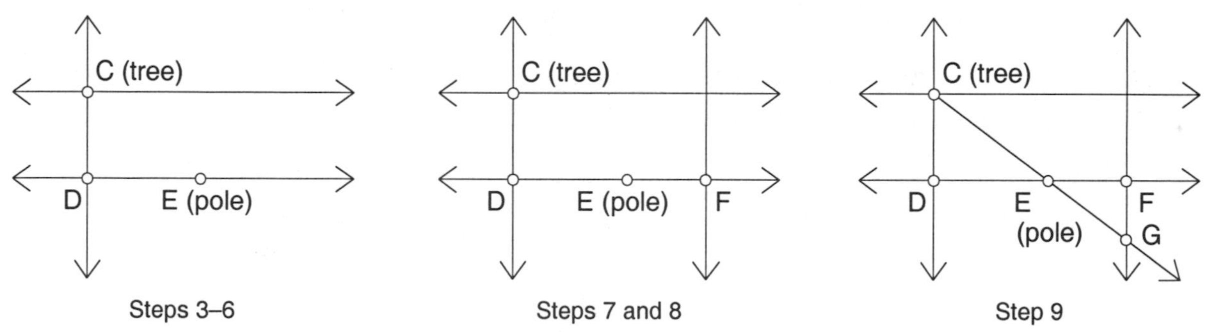

Steps 3–6 | Steps 7 and 8 | Step 9

7. You walk some convenient distance farther. (Construct $\overline{EF}$, where point *F* is on the bank.)
8. Then you make a right turn. (Construct a line through point *F* perpendicular to the bank.)
9. You want to line up the pole you stuck into the ground with the tree on the opposite bank. (Construct $\overrightarrow{CE}$ and point *G* at the intersection of $\overrightarrow{CE}$ and the line through point *F*.)
10. Drag point *C*, *E*, or *F* to see how the model changes. You can also change the width of the river by dragging either line.

© 2002 Key Curriculum Press

Q1 Name two similar triangles in the model and explain how you know they're similar.

Q2 *CD* is the distance you wish to find, and you could measure *DE*, *EF*, and *FG*. But before you measure, write a proportion in terms of these four lengths.

Q3 Solve the proportion above for *CD*.

You can select the segments and measure lengths, or for each distance you can select two points, then, in the Measure menu, choose **Distance**.

11. Now measure *DE*, *EF*, and *FG*.

Choose **Calculate** from the Measure menu to open the Calculator. Click once on a measurement to enter it into a calculation.

12. Calculate an expression that you think will be equal to *CD* using these three measurements.
13. Measure *CD* to confirm your calculation. You can move the banks of the river or the locations of various points to confirm that this method will work under different circumstances.

Q4 What would be the most convenient way to locate points *E* and *F* in order to find *CD* without measuring it directly? Explain.

Explore More

1. Come up with another way to model this problem with Sketchpad using similar triangles.

© 2002 Key Curriculum Press

Finding the Height of a Tree

Name(s): ____________________

You can use similar triangles to calculate the heights of objects you are unable to measure directly. You can find the height of a tall object outdoors by measuring shadows on a sunny day. In Explore More, you will learn a method for finding the height of a tall object that works even when it's cloudy.

Sketch and Investigate

If you hold down the Shift key while you draw, it will be easier to make the line horizontal.

1. Draw a horizontal line. This will represent the ground.
2. Hide the control points of the line.
3. Construct two points on the line. These will represent your feet and the bottom of the tree.

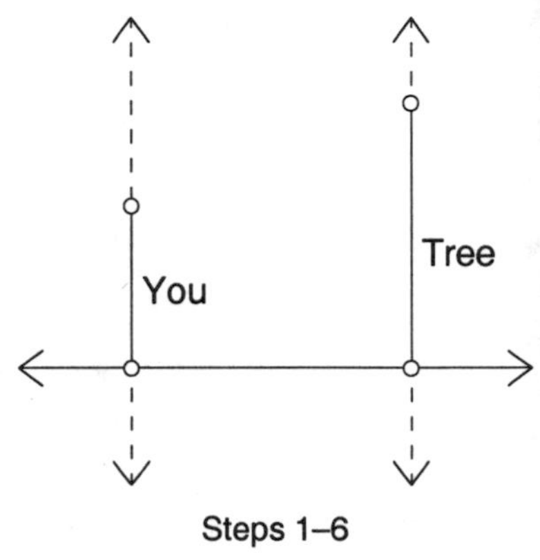

Steps 1–6

To construct the perpendicular lines, first select the points and the ground line.

4. Construct lines through these points perpendicular to the ground.
5. Construct segments on these lines that start at the ground and go up. Hide the lines. (The lines to hide are shown as dashed in the figure above.)

Using the **Text** tool, click once on a segment to show its label. Double-click the label to change it.

6. Label the two perpendicular segments. Change the labels so that one segment is named after you and the other is called *Tree*. Adjust the heights so that the tree is much taller than you.

You shouldn't think of this line's control point as representing the sun. (The sun is much too big and much too far away to fit into your sketch!) You can, however, control the direction from which the sun shines with this point.

7. Draw a line from the sky above and to the right of the tree, down to the ground. This line represents a ray of sunlight.

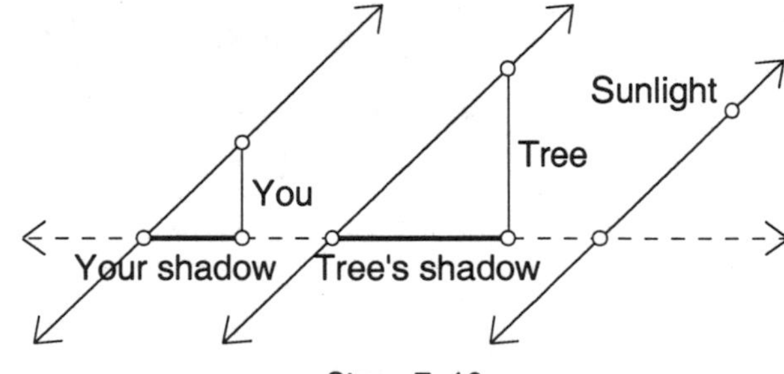

Steps 7–10

8. Since the sun is so far away and so large, when its rays reach the earth, they are essentially parallel. Construct lines parallel to the line of sunlight through the point at the top of *You* and through the point at the top of *Tree*.
9. Construct the points where the parallel lines intersect the ground, then hide the ground line.

The **Line Width** submenu is in the Display menu.

10. Construct segments to represent your shadow and the tree's shadow. Change the line width of these shadows to thick and label them to represent their objects.

© 2002 Key Curriculum Press

Finding the Height of a Tree (continued)

11. Measure the three things that you would actually be able to measure directly in the real situation: your height, the length of your shadow, and the length of the tree's shadow.

12. Drag different points in your model to see what they do. Think about what these movements represent in the physical situation (for example, the sun going up or down, shadows getting longer, you getting taller, and so on). Be careful—it's possible to represent situations with your model that are physically impossible!

You might want to animate a sunset and sunrise. →

Q1 What happens to shadows as the sun gets lower in the sky?

Q2 What happens to the length of your shadow if you make yourself shorter in your model?

Q3 Drag your "feet" along the ground to simulate walking. Does walking the short distances represented in this model do anything to the length of your shadow? Explain.

13. Your model is a scale drawing you can use to solve problems. Drag the top point of the segment that represents you until its length corresponds conveniently with your height (for example, if you're 60 inches tall, you could make the segment .60 cm or inches long.) Drag your tree to a good height (taller than you!) and adjust the sun's rays to a reasonable angle.

Q4 Explain why the triangles formed by you and your shadow and by the tree and its shadow are similar.

Q5 Using *only the three measurements you have already made,* figure out the height of the tree. Show and explain all your work.

© 2002 Key Curriculum Press

14. You can check your reasoning in Q5 by measuring the height of the tree in your model. Find this length.

Q6 How well do your calculations match the measurement for the tree's height in your sketch? If your calculations don't match the measurement, explain what went wrong and try the calculations again.

Explore More

1. Drag parts of your model until it represents a situation that is physically impossible. Describe the situation.
2. Suppose you measured the shadows of two objects, each at a different time of day. Is it possible for the objects and their shadows to create similar triangles?
3. It's possible to make indirect measurements using similar triangles even on a cloudy day, when no shadows are cast. The method pictured at right uses mirrors. Use Sketchpad to model this method. (*Hint:* Since the method involves reflection in a mirror, your sketch will require a reflection, too.) Explain your method and why it works.

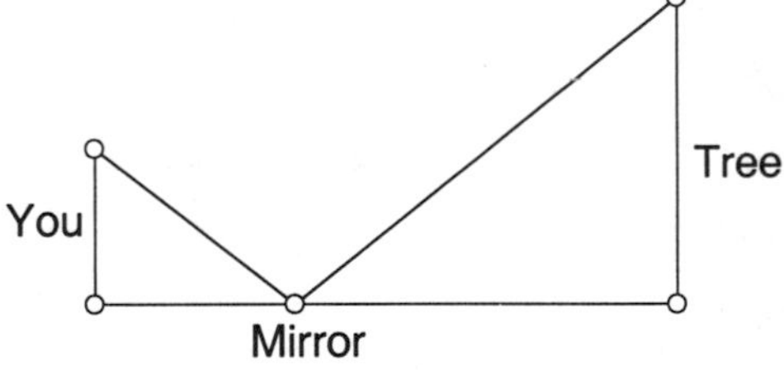

© 2002 Key Curriculum Press

Measuring Height with a Mirror

Name(s): ____________________

You can measure the height of a tall object such as a flagpole by putting a mirror on flat ground then locating yourself so that you can see the top of the flagpole in the mirror. Measure the height to your eye, the distance from your feet to the mirror, and the distance from the mirror to the base of the flagpole. Use these measurements and similar triangles to calculate the height of the flagpole. You might go outside and try it first. Then you can model the situation using Sketchpad.

Sketch and Investigate

If you hold down the Shift key while you draw, it will be easier to make the line horizontal.

1. Draw a horizontal line *AB*. This will represent the ground.
2. Hide points *A* and *B*.
3. Construct points *C* and *D* on the line. These will represent your feet and the bottom of the flagpole.

To construct the perpendicular lines, first select the points and the ground line.

4. Construct lines through these points perpendicular to the ground.

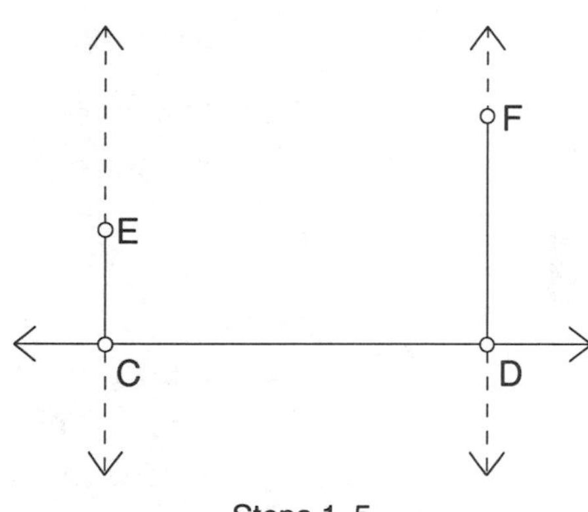

Steps 1–5

5. Construct segments *CE* and *DF* on these lines, starting from the ground and going up. Hide the lines. (The lines to hide are shown as dashed in the figure above.)
6. Construct point *G* on the horizontal line between you and the flagpole. This point represents the place where you locate a mirror.
7. Construct $\overrightarrow{FG}$. This represents the path of a ray of light from the top of the flagpole to the mirror.

Double-click the line to mark it as a mirror. Select point *F*, the flagpole segment, and the ray; then, in the Transform menu, choose **Reflect**.

8. Mark the horizontal line as a mirror and reflect point *F*, the flagpole, and the ray over it.

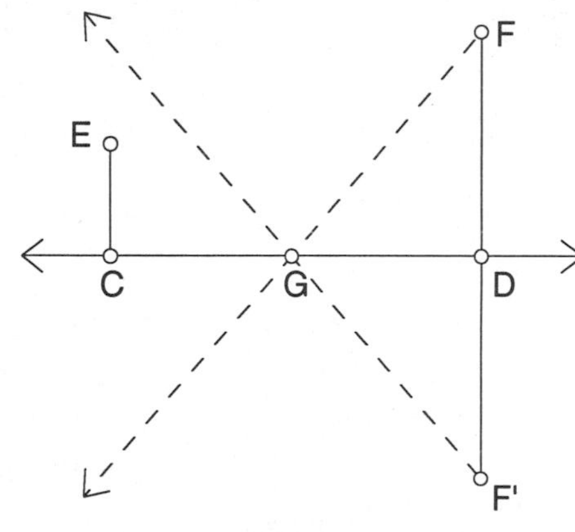

Steps 6–8

The reflected ray *F′G* represents the apparent path of a ray of light from the flagpole's mirror image through the mirror. From point *G* on, the ray represents the path of a ray of light from point *F* as it is reflected off the mirror.

9. You want to position yourself so that you can see the top of the flagpole in the mirror. Drag point *C* (your feet) until $\overrightarrow{F'G}$ passes through point *E* (your eye).

© 2002 Key Curriculum Press

Q1 Explain why $\angle FGD \cong \angle EGC$.

Q2 Name the two similar triangles and explain why they're similar.

10. Experiment by moving the mirror, then finding out where to locate yourself to see the top of the flagpole given the new mirror location.

Q3 If you move the mirror closer to the flagpole, do you have to move closer to or farther from the mirror?

Q4 Remember, in the actual experiment you can't measure *FE* because the flagpole is too tall. What three distances could you measure easily (with the help of a partner)?

Q5 Before you measure, set up a proportion to find the height of the flagpole, *DF,* in terms of three other distances.

$$\frac{DF}{\quad} = \frac{\quad}{\quad}$$

Select points *E* and *C*; then, in the Measure menu, choose **Distance**. Repeat for *CG* and *GE*. Choose **Calculate** from the Measure menu to open the Calculator. Click once on a measurement to enter it into a calculation.

11. Now measure *EC, CG,* and *GD*. Calculate an expression that you think will be equal to *DF*. Measure *DF* to confirm your calculation. If you're off just a bit, it's probably because *E* can't be located exactly on $\overrightarrow{F'G}$. You can relocate the mirror and try again from different positions. You can even change your height or the flagpole's height to change the problem.

Q6 Would you get a different height for the flagpole if you located the mirror in a different place? Explain why or why not.

Explore More

1. See if you can come up with other ways to model this problem with Sketchpad using similar triangles. (*Hint:* If you use shadows, you can solve the problem without any mirrors.)

© 2002 Key Curriculum Press

Parallel Lines in a Triangle

Name(s): ______________________

When you cut through a triangle with a line parallel to a side, you create similar triangles. In this activity, you'll investigate proportions that result from these similar triangles.

Sketch and Investigate

1. Construct $\triangle ABC$.
2. Construct point D on $\overline{AB}$.

Select point D and $\overline{AC}$; then, in the Construct menu, choose **Parallel Line**.

3. Construct a line through point D, parallel to $\overline{AC}$.
4. Construct point E where the line intersects $\overline{BC}$.

5. Hide the line and construct $\overline{DE}$.
6. Drag point D and observe the segment inside the triangle.

Q1 Name a pair of similar triangles and explain why they're similar.

Q2 Write three equal ratios involving the sides of the triangles.

______ = ______ = ______

Select a segment to measure a length. Or select two points and measure the distance between them.

7. Measure BD, DA, BE, and EC.
8. Drag point D again and observe these measurements.

Choose **Calculate** from the Measure menu to open the Calculator. Click once on a measurement to enter it into a calculation.

Q3 There's another proportion involving the segments into which the parallel line divides the sides of the triangle. Calculate ratios to discover a proportion involving BD, DA, BE, and EC. Write this proportion below.

______ = ______

Explore More

1. Show how the proportions involving BD, DA, BE, and EC can be derived using algebra and the similar triangles' proportions.
2. Show that the converse of your conjecture is true. That is, show that if a line divides the sides of a triangle proportionally, it's parallel to the third side.

© 2002 Key Curriculum Press

Dividing a Segment into Equal Parts

Name(s): ______________

You may already know how to construct a midpoint using a compass and straightedge. In this activity, you'll learn a method for dividing a segment into three or more equal parts using Sketchpad's tools and the Construct menu. This method is equivalent to the compass-and-straightedge method that Euclid describes in the *Elements*.

Sketch and Investigate

1. Construct $\overline{AB}$. This is the segment that you'll divide into three parts.

Hold the mouse button down on the **Segment** tool and drag right to switch to the **Ray** tool. →

2. Construct $\overrightarrow{AC}$ at an angle from $\overline{AB}$. Locate point C no more than an inch from point A.

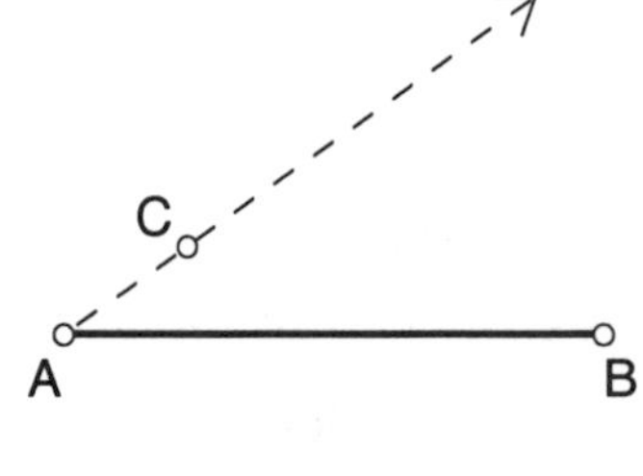

Steps 1 and 2

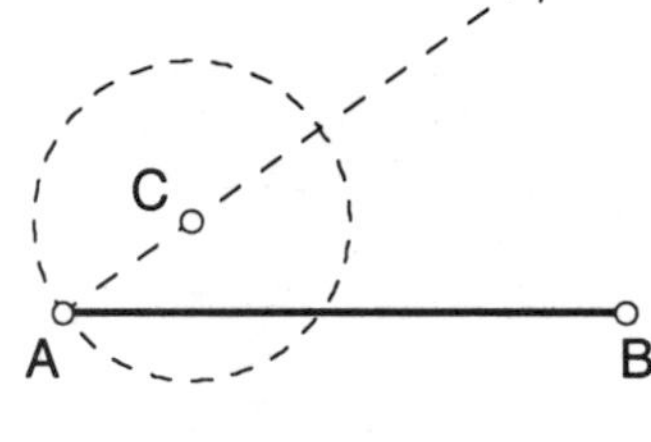

Step 3

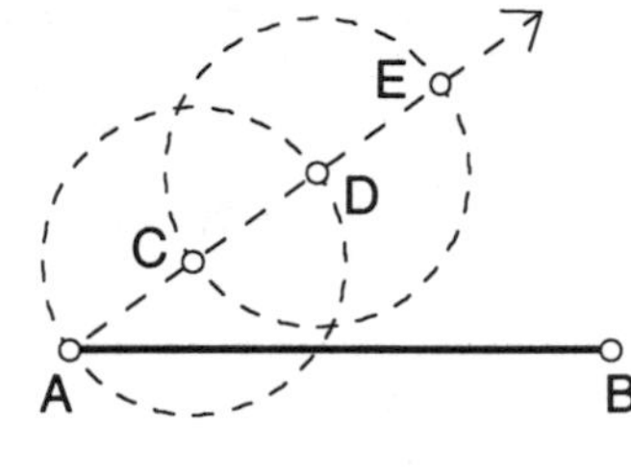

Steps 4 and 5

Be sure to release the mouse button (or click the second time) with the cursor directly over point *A* so that the circle will be properly attached. →

3. Construct circle CA.
4. Construct circle DC, where point D is the intersection of the first circle with the ray.
5. Construct point E at the intersection of circle DC and the ray.

Q1 You've now marked off three equal distances on $\overrightarrow{AC}$. Name the equal distances and explain why they are equal.

Next, you'll use the three equal distances on $\overrightarrow{AC}$ to construct equal distances on $\overline{AB}$.

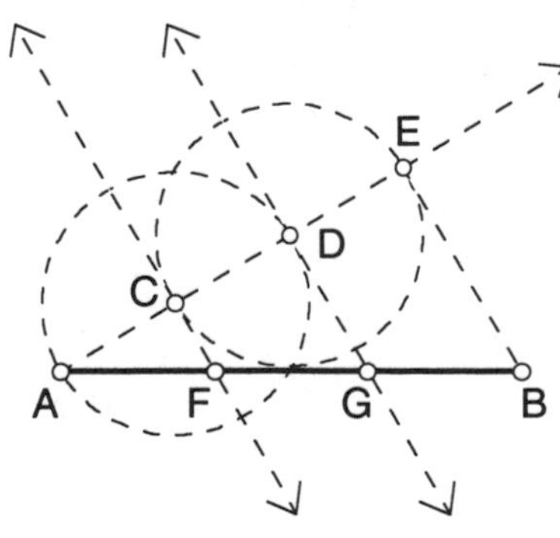

6. Construct $\overline{EB}$.

Select point *D*, point *C*, and $\overline{EB}$; then, in the Construct menu, choose **Parallel Lines**. →

7. Construct lines through points D and C, parallel to $\overline{EB}$.
8. Construct points F and G where these lines intersect $\overline{AB}$.
9. Drag point A or point B to observe that points F and G always divide $\overline{AB}$ into equal thirds. (Measure if you wish to confirm your observation.)

© 2002 Key Curriculum Press

Q2 Using similar triangles, explain why $AF = FG = GB$.

10. Hide everything but $\overline{AB}$ and points *A*, *F*, *G*, and *B*. Drag point *A* or point *B* to enjoy your trisection without having the rest of the construction block your view.

Explore More

1. Use this procedure to divide a segment into five equal parts.
2. Tenth-grade students Dan Litchfield and Dave Goldenheim used Sketchpad to discover a different method for dividing a segment. With the help of their teacher, Charles Dietrich, they published their findings in *The Mathematics Teacher* (vol. 90, no. 1, January 1997, pp. 8–12) in an article titled "Euclid, Fibonacci, GLaD." (They called their construction the GLaD construction, for Goldenheim, Litchfield, and Dietrich.) Part of their construction is shown below. *ABCD* is a rectangle. Point *M* is a midpoint. Points P_3, P_5, and P_7 divide $\overline{AB}$ at 1/3, 1/5, and 1/7 of its length. Try the GLaD construction and confirm that it works. Add to it to show fractions with even denominators, such as 1/2, 1/4, and so on.

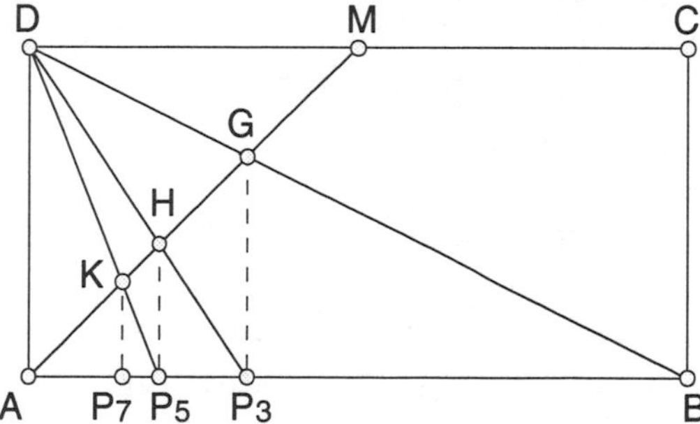

3. See if you can discover other methods for dividing a segment into equal parts.

© 2002 Key Curriculum Press

Spacing Poles in Perspective

Name(s): ________________

When you look at a long line of telephone poles or fence posts disappearing into the distance, the farther away the poles are, the shorter they appear to be. Distant poles also appear to be closer together. In this activity, you'll learn to draw fence posts in perspective so that their spacing appears realistic.

Sketch and Investigate

Hold down the mouse button on the current **Straightedge** tool and drag right to switch between the **Segment** and **Line** tools. Holding down the Shift key while you draw makes it easier to create horizontal and vertical lines.

1. Construct a horizontal line $\overleftrightarrow{AB}$. This is your horizon line. Point *B* will be your vanishing point.
2. Construct vertical segment $\overline{CD}$. This is your first fence post (or telephone pole).
3. Construct $\overline{CB}$ and $\overline{DB}$.
4. Construct point *E* on $\overline{DB}$. This is the foot of your second fence post.

Select point *E* and $\overline{CD}$; then, in the Construct menu, choose **Parallel Line**.

5. Construct a line through point *E* parallel to $\overline{CD}$.
6. Construct point *F* where this line intersects $\overline{CB}$.
7. Hide line *EF*.
8. Construct $\overline{EF}$.
9. Construct point *G*, the midpoint of $\overline{EF}$.
10. Construct $\overrightarrow{CG}$.
11. Construct point *H* where $\overrightarrow{CG}$ intersects $\overline{DB}$. Point *H* is the foot of your third fence post.
12. Hide $\overrightarrow{CG}$ and point *G*.
13. Construct the third fence post just as you constructed the second in steps 5–8.

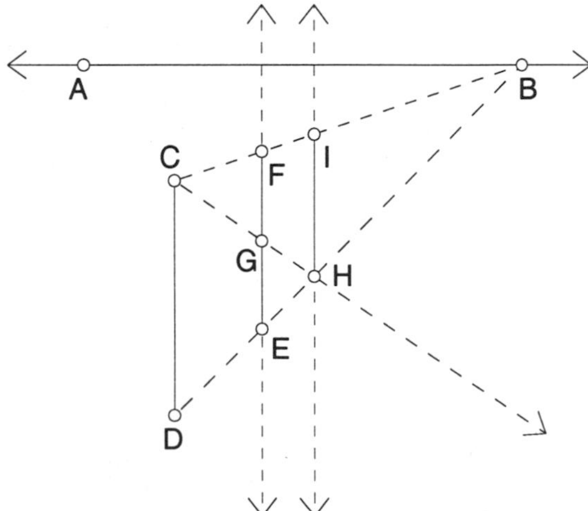

You can create a custom tool to construct all the rest of your fence posts.

Select point *E*; then, in the Edit menu, choose **Split Point From Segment**.

14. Split point *E* from $\overline{DB}$.
15. Select, in order, points *B*, *D*, *C*, *E*, *H*, and *I* and segment *HI*. (The first four selections will be the *givens* of the new tool; the last three will be the *results*.)

© 2002 Key Curriculum Press

16. In the Custom Tools menu, choose **Create New Tool**. (The Custom Tools menu is the bottom tool in the Toolbox.) Name the tool **Next Pole**.

Select point *E* and $\overline{DB}$; then, in the Edit menu, choose **Merge Point To Segment**.

17. Merge point *E* back onto $\overline{DB}$.

18. Click on the **Custom** tools icon to choose your new tool. Now click, in order, on points *B, E, F,* and *H*. The next fence post should be constructed.

19. Construct at least five more fence posts in the same way. In each case, click on point *B* first, then on the lower endpoint of the second-to-last fence post, then on the upper endpoint of the second-to-last fence post, then on the lower endpoint of the last fence post.

20. Hide $\overline{CB}$ and $\overline{DB}$.

Click in a blank area to make sure nothing is selected, then choose the **Point** tool. In the Edit menu, choose **Select All Points**. Then choose **Edit | Action Button | Hide/Show**.

Show Points

21. Select all the points, then make a Hide/Show action button. Press the button to hide the points.

22. Your static sketch may not look like much, but drag the first post to see the effect on your sketch. Can you imagine you're a bird swooping down on some abandoned telephone poles in the desert? Try lifting the poles so that their bases are above the horizon line.

23. Press the Hide/Show button to show the points again.

24. Experiment with dragging points to change your sketch. For example, drag point *E* to change the spacing between posts. Drag point *C* or point *D* to change the heights of the posts.

25. To see why this method gives the correct spacing, construct a segment from the top of the first post to the bottom of the third post. Construct another segment from the bottom of the first post to the top of the third post.

Q1 What do you notice about the place where the second post is located? Explain why this spacing appears realistic.

© 2002 Key Curriculum Press

Proportions with an Angle Bisector in a Triangle

Name(s): ____________________

Quick! Where does an angle bisector intersect the opposite side in a triangle? Did you guess the midpoint? A quick check will show that this works only in special cases. In this activity, you'll discover a proportion relationship of angle bisectors in triangles.

Sketch and Investigate

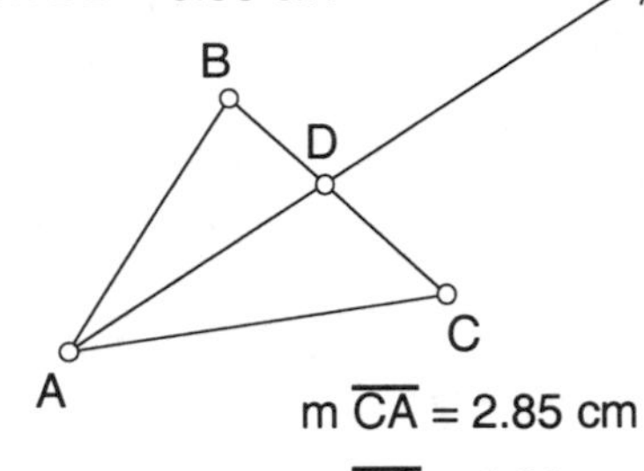

1. Construct ΔABC.

Select, in order, points *B*, *A*, and *C*. Then, in the Construct menu, choose **Angle Bisector**.

2. Construct the bisector of $\angle BAC$.
3. Construct point *D* where the bisector intersects $\overline{BC}$.
4. Drag vertices of the triangle and observe point *D*.

Q1 Is point *D* the midpoint of $\overline{BC}$? __________

5. Hide $\overline{BC}$ and construct $\overline{BD}$ and $\overline{DC}$.
6. Measure *AB*, *BD*, *DC*, and *AC*.

Q2 Drag some more. Under what conditions will point *D* be the midpoint of $\overline{BC}$?

Q3 How do *BD* and *CD* compare when *AB* is greater than *AC*?

To measure a ratio, select two segments. Then, in the Measure menu, choose **Ratio**.

Q4 Your answer to Q3 may give you an idea for a proportion. Measure ratios involving *AB*, *AC*, *BD*, and *CD* to see if you can create equal ratios (a proportion). Write the proportion below.

7. Manipulate your triangle to make sure your proportion holds for any triangle.

Q5 Write your findings as a conjecture.

Explore More

1. Construct a segment. Use your conjecture to figure out a construction that divides the segment into a given ratio, say 2:3.

© 2002 Key Curriculum Press

Modeling a Pantograph

Name(s): ______________________

A pantograph is a simple mechanical device that uses two pens to copy and enlarge or reduce drawings and maps. Thomas Jefferson made one, hoping he could use it to write more than one letter at a time. In this activity, you'll do a very simple construction that does what a pantograph does. Then, if you're brave and if you have enough time, you'll construct a model that more closely resembles a physical pantograph.

Sketch and Investigate

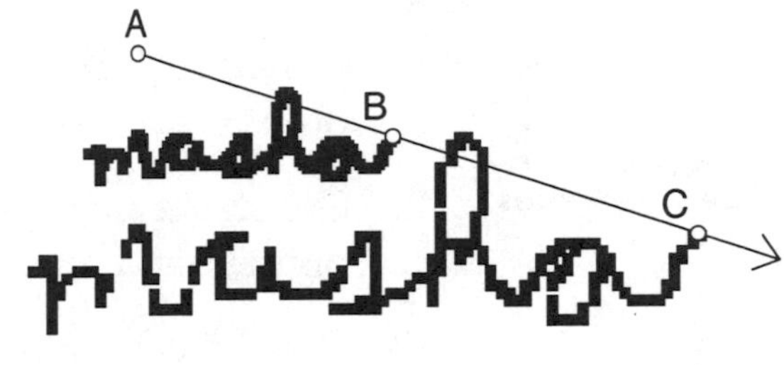

1. Construct $\overrightarrow{AB}$.
2. Construct point *C* on $\overrightarrow{AB}$, beyond point *B*.
3. Select points *B* and *C*; then, in the Display menu, turn on **Trace Point**.
4. Drag point *B* to write your name. Choose **Erase Traces** from the Display menu when you wish to erase all traces from the screen.
5. Measure *AB* and *AC*.

   (Select points *A* and *B*; then, in the Measure menu, choose **Distance**. Repeat for *AC*.)
6. Calculate *AB*/*AC*.

   (Choose **Calculate** from the Measure menu to open the Calculator. Click once on a measurement to enter it into a calculation.)
7. Draw something with point *B*. Notice that point *C* moves on the ray so that the ratio *AB*/*AC* stays constant.
8. Move point *C* to make a different ratio. Experiment with drawing things with point *B* using different ratios.

Q1 What does the ratio have to do with the traces of points *B* and *C*?

An actual, physical pantograph is constructed of rigid material, such as strips of wood. These pieces don't stretch the way a dynamic Sketchpad ray does. So an actual pantograph depends on linkages that make it flexible.

The following pages describe a construction that models a physical pantograph.

© 2002 Key Curriculum Press

Modeling an Actual Pantograph

9. In a new sketch, construct $\overline{AB}$. (This is not part of the pantograph, but it's a control segment that will make parts of your pantograph both rigid and adjustable.)

A B C D E

Steps 9–15

Hold down the mouse button on the **Segment** tool to show the **Straightedge** palette. Drag right to choose the **Ray** tool.

10. Construct $\overrightarrow{CD}$.

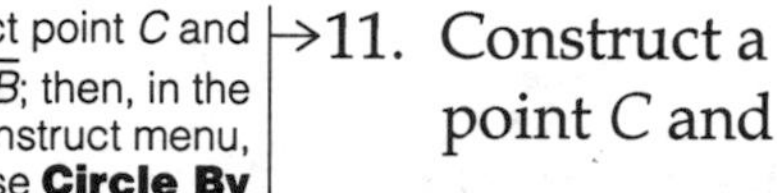

Select point *C* and $\overline{AB}$; then, in the Construct menu, choose **Circle By Center+Radius**.

11. Construct a circle with center point *C* and radius *AB*.

12. Construct a circle with center point *D* and radius *AB*.

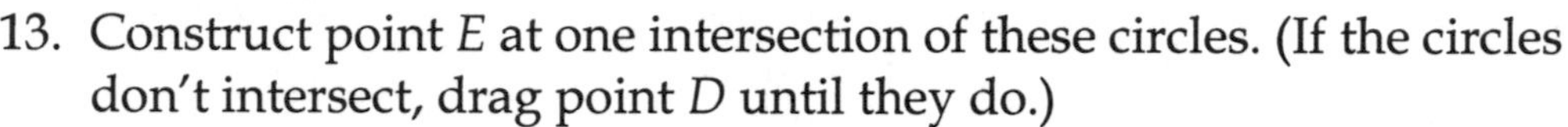

13. Construct point *E* at one intersection of these circles. (If the circles don't intersect, drag point *D* until they do.)

14. Construct $\overrightarrow{CE}$.

15. Construct $\overline{DE}$.

16. Hide the circles.

17. Construct $\overline{EF}$ on $\overrightarrow{CE}$.

Select point *F* and $\overline{DE}$; then, in the Construct menu, choose **Parallel Line**.

18. Construct a line through point *F* parallel to $\overline{DE}$.

19. Construct a line through point *D* parallel to $\overrightarrow{CE}$.

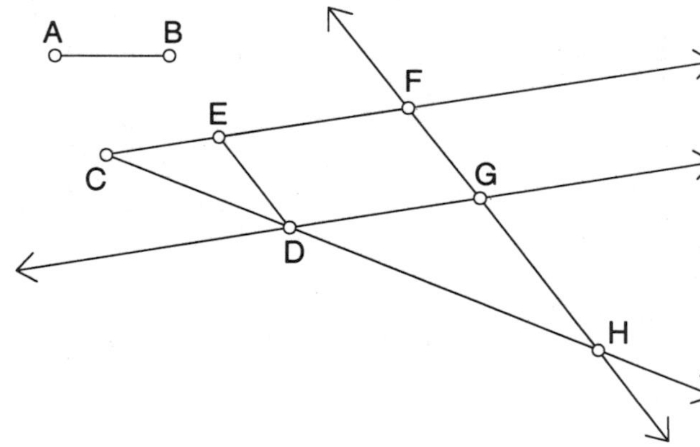

Steps 16–21

20. Construct point *G* where these lines intersect.

21. Construct point *H* at the intersection of $\overleftrightarrow{FG}$ and $\overrightarrow{CD}$.

22. Hide $\overrightarrow{CE}$, $\overrightarrow{CD}$, $\overleftrightarrow{FG}$, and $\overleftrightarrow{DG}$.

23. Construct $\overline{CE}$, $\overline{FG}$, $\overline{DG}$, and $\overline{GH}$. This is something like what a real pantograph looks like.

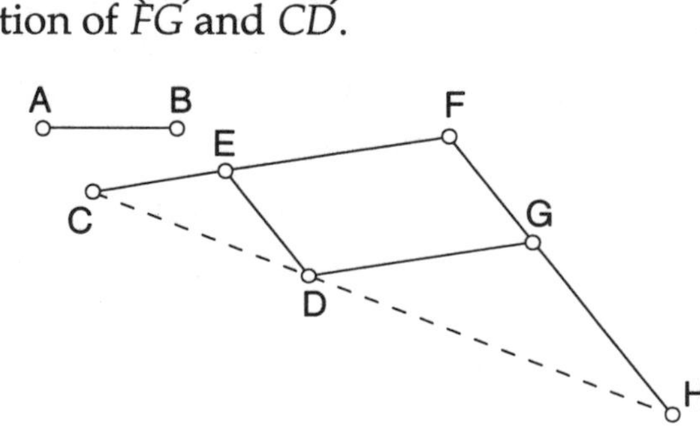

© 2002 Key Curriculum Press

After you draw $\overline{CD}$, choose **Display | Line Width | Dashed**.

24. Construct $\overline{CD}$ and $\overline{DH}$ and make these segments dashed. These segments wouldn't appear on a real pantograph, but they can help you see how a pantograph works.

25. Drag point *D* to observe how the pantograph behaves. Note that it falls apart if you drag point *D* too far from point *C*. You can extend its range by lengthening $\overline{AB}$.

26. Turn on **Trace Points** for points *D* and *H*.

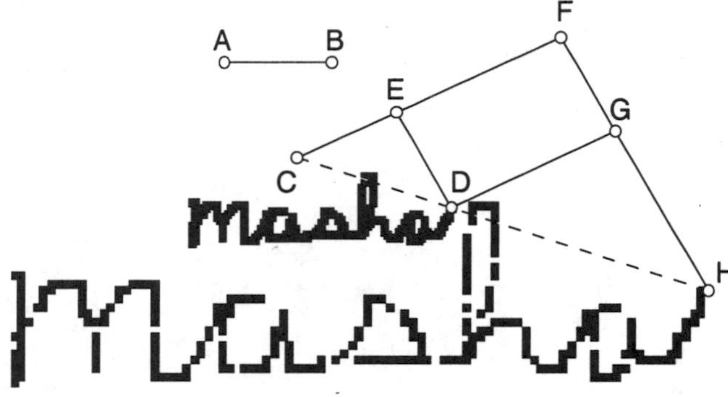

This may take several tries. Experiment with different starting places for point *D*. If necessary, make $\overline{AB}$ longer and move point *F* farther from point *E*.

27. Drag point *D* to trace out your name.

28. Move point *F*, then drag point *D* to see how the location of point *F* affects the trace of point *H*.

Q2 How would you locate point *F* so that the trace of point *H* was twice as large as the trace of point *D*? Use similar triangles to explain why.

Explore More

1. Build an actual pantograph out of old rulers, small bolts, and wing nuts.

© 2002 Key Curriculum Press

Proportions with Area

Name(s): ______________________

In this exploration, you'll discover a relationship between the areas of similar figures.

Sketch and Investigate

To construct the interior, select the vertices. Then, in the Construct menu, choose **Polygon Interior**.

Double-click the center point to mark it as a center.

1. Construct segments $\overline{AB}$ and $\overline{CD}$, where $\overline{AB}$ is longer than $\overline{CD}$.
2. Construct any polygon and its interior.
3. Construct a point outside the polygon and mark it as a center.

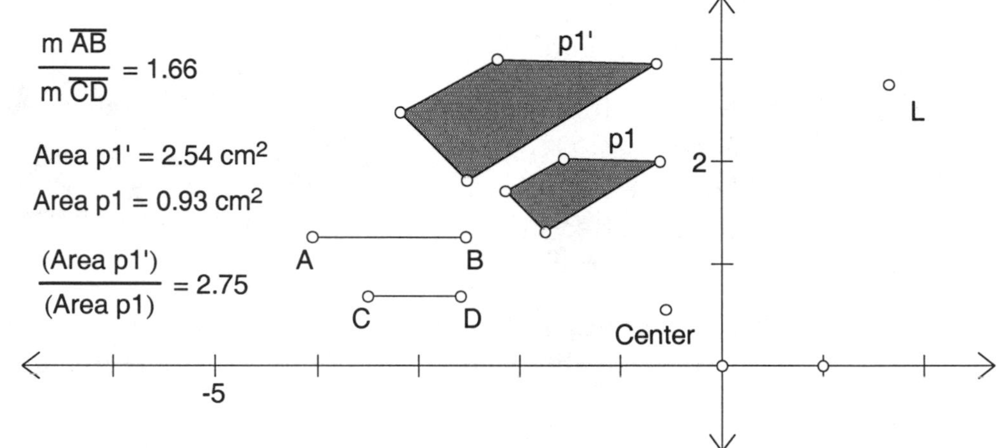

Select $\overline{AB}$ and $\overline{CD}$; then, in the Transform menu, choose **Mark Segment Ratio**.

Select $\overline{AB}$ and $\overline{CD}$ again, then go to the Measure menu and choose **Ratio**.

Select the polygon; then, in the Transform menu, choose **Dilate**.

4. Mark the ratio of *AB* to *CD*.
5. Measure the ratio of *AB* to *CD*.
6. Dilate the vertices, sides, and interior of the polygon by the marked ratio. (If $\overline{AB}$ is longer than $\overline{CD}$, the image should be bigger than the original.)
7. Measure the ratio of a side on the dilated polygon to the corresponding side on the original polygon.
8. Measure the ratio of a different pair of corresponding sides.
9. Drag points and observe the ratios you have measured.

Q1 How is the ratio of a pair of corresponding side lengths related to the dilation ratio?

Choose **Calculate** from the Measure menu to open the Calculator. Click once on a measurement to enter it into a calculation.

10. Measure the areas of the polygons.
11. Calculate the ratio of the area of the dilated polygon to the area of the original.

© 2002 Key Curriculum Press

12. Select, in order, the measure of the ratio of the side lengths and the calculation of the ratio of the areas. In the Graph menu, choose **Plot As (x, y)**. You'll get a pair of axes and a point whose coordinates are the two numbers you selected. If you can't see the plotted point, drag the point at (1, 0) closer to the origin to scale the axes.
13. While this point is selected (point *L* in the diagram on the previous page), choose **Trace Plotted Point** in the Display menu.
14. Drag point *B* to experiment with different scale factors. The point you plotted will trace out a graph of the side-length ratio versus the ratio of the areas for different similar figures.

Q2 To help you see the relationship between side lengths and areas, complete the table below for some specific side-length ratios, then generalize for any scale factor a/b.

Side-length ratios	2	3	1	1/2	1/10	a/b
Area ratios						

Q3 State your findings as a conjecture.

Q4 Explain how the shape of the graph in your sketch supports your conjecture.

Explore More

1. Move point *A* close to point *C*. Merge point *B* to $\overline{CD}$, then make an action button to animate the point along the segment. Describe what the button does.
2. Drag the center of dilation. Explain why point *L* (the plotted point) doesn't move.
3. How does the ratio of the volumes of similar solids compare to the ratio of their surface areas and the ratio of their corresponding lengths? Investigate by calculating the volumes and surface areas of two boxes, one twice as long, wide, and tall as the other.

© 2002 Key Curriculum Press

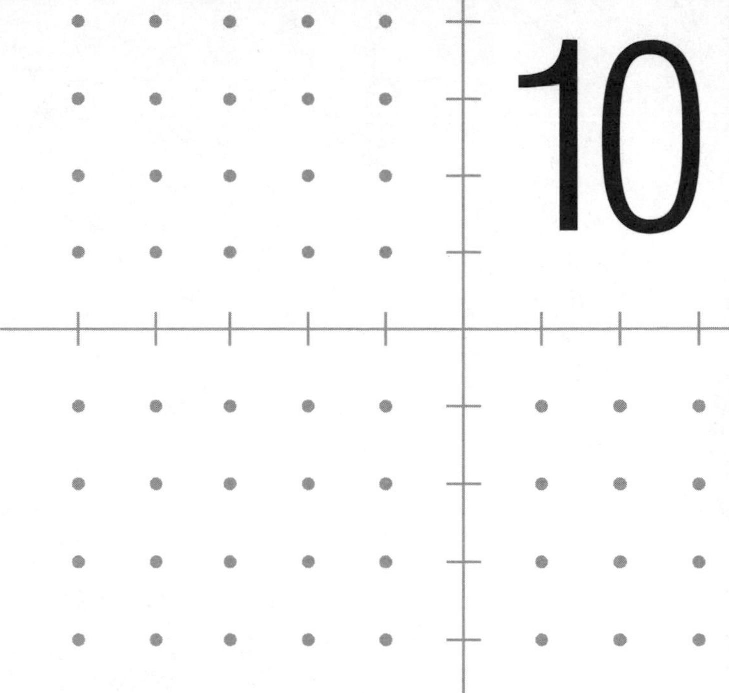

10

Trigonometry and Fractals

Trigonometric Ratios

Name(s): ______________________

Right-triangle trigonometry builds on similar-triangle concepts to give you more ways to find unknown measures in triangles. In this activity, you'll learn about trigonometric ratios and how you can use them.

Sketch and Investigate

In steps 1–5, you'll construct a right triangle.

m∠CAB = 31°

$\frac{\text{m opposite}}{\text{m hypotenuse}} = 0.51$

$\frac{\text{m adjacent}}{\text{m hypotenuse}} = 0.86$

$\frac{\text{m opposite}}{\text{m adjacent}} = 0.60$

hypotenuse

C

opposite

A

adjacent

B

1. Construct $\overline{AB}$.

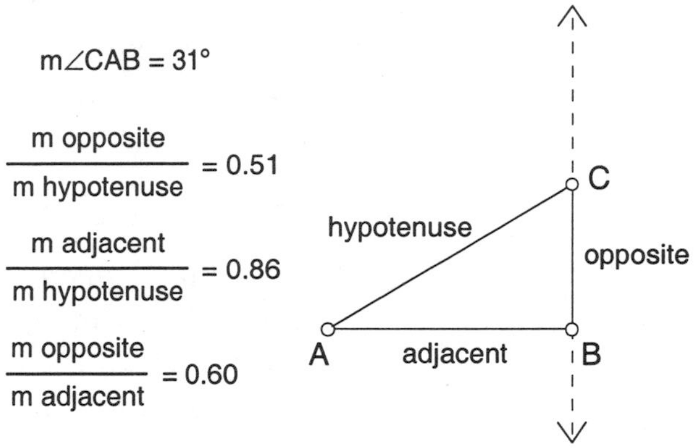

Select point *B* and $\overline{AB}$; then, in the Construct menu, choose **Perpendicular Line**.

2. Construct a line through point *B* perpendicular to $\overline{AB}$.
3. Construct $\overline{AC}$, where point *C* is a point on the perpendicular line.
4. Hide the line.
5. Construct $\overline{BC}$ to finish the right triangle.

Using the **Text** tool, click once on a segment to show its label. Double-click the label to change it.

6. Show the three segments' labels and change the labels to match the figure above right.

Select, in order, points *C*, *A*, and *B*. Then, in the Measure menu, choose **Angle**.

7. Measure angle *CAB*.

For each ratio, select the two segments in order. Then, in the Measure menu, choose **Ratio**.

8. Measure the ratios *opposite/hypotenuse, adjacent/hypotenuse,* and *opposite/adjacent*.

Q1 Drag point *C* to change the angles. When the angles change, do the ratios also change?

Q2 Drag point *A* or point *B* to scale the triangle. What do you notice about the ratios when the angles don't change? Explain why you think this happens.

Your observations in Q2 give you a useful fact about right triangles. For any right triangle with a given acute angle, each ratio of side lengths has a given value, regardless of the size of the triangle. The three ratios you measured are called *sine, cosine,* and *tangent.*

Choose **Calculate** from the Measure menu to open the Calculator. In the Functions pop-up menu, choose **sin**. Click in the sketch on the measure of ∠*CAB*, then click OK. Use the same process to calculate cosine and tangent.

9. The sine, cosine, and tangent functions can be found on all scientific calculators, commonly abbreviated as sin, cos, and tan. Use Sketchpad's Calculator to calculate the sine, cosine, and tangent of ∠*CAB*. Match these calculations with the ratios they are equal to.

© 2002 Key Curriculum Press

Q3 Complete the ratios for cosine and tangent below.

$$\text{sine } \angle A = \frac{\text{length of leg opposite } \angle A}{\text{length of hypotenuse}}$$

cosine $\angle A$ = ____________________

tangent $\angle A$ = ____________________

Q4 Drag point C so that $\angle A$ measures as close to 30° as you can get it. Write approximate values for the sine, cosine, and tangent of 30° below. Use the definitions in Q3 and refer to the calculations in your sketch to find these values.

sin 30° = ________ cos 30° = ________ tan 30° = ________

Q5 Without measuring, figure out the measure of $\angle C$ and write down that number. Calculate the sine of that angle measure. The sine of $\angle C$ should be close to one of the trigonometric ratios for $\angle A$. Which one? Explain why this is so.

Q6 Drag point C and answer the following questions.

a. What's the smallest possible value for the sine of an angle in a right triangle? What angle has this value? ____________

Hint: Make $\overline{AB}$ short so that you can drag point C up farther.

b. What's the greatest possible value for the sine of an angle in a right triangle? What angle has this value? ____________

c. Why can't you make m$\angle CAB$ exactly equal to 90°?

d. Even though you can't make m$\angle CAB$ exactly equal to 90°, what do you think is the value of tan 90°? Explain.

e. For what angle is the tangent equal to 1? Why?

f. For what angle are the sine and cosine equal? Why?

g. Suppose an angle has measure x. Complete this equation:

sin x = cos ____________.

© 2002 Key Curriculum Press

Modeling a Ladder Problem

Name(s): ______________________

Drawing diagrams is a useful method to help solve many types of realistic problems. Dynamic diagrams can be even more useful. Here's a problem that can be solved with a Sketchpad sketch.

The Occupational Safety and Health Administration (OSHA) recommends that when you use a ladder, you should lean it against a wall so that the height at which it touches the wall is four times the distance from the wall to the foot of the ladder. Any more and you risk tipping the ladder backward. Any less and you risk having the bottom slide out from under the ladder. What's the height from the floor that you can reach with a 20-foot ladder? What angle will the ladder make with the floor?

Sketch and Investigate

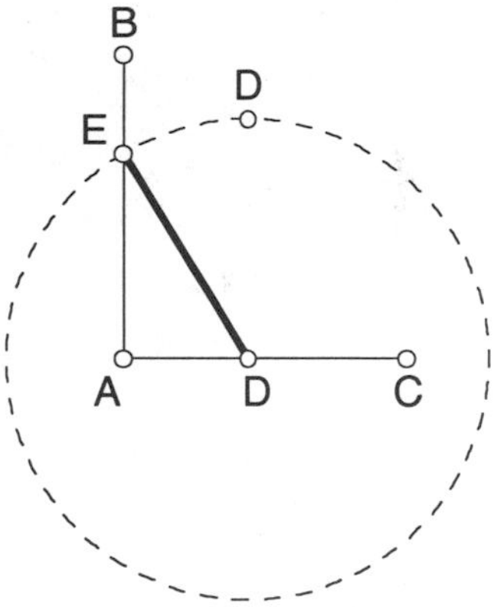

Choose **Preferences** from the Edit menu and go to the Units panel.

1. Set Preferences to display the Distance Units in **inches**.

Holding down the Shift key while you draw makes it easier to draw vertical and horizontal segments.

2. Construct vertical segment *AB* and horizontal segment *AC*. These segments represent the wall and the floor.

3. Construct point *D* on the floor. This point will be the foot of your ladder.

Select point *D*; then, in the Transform menu, choose **Translate**.

4. Translate point *D* vertically by 2 inches. The 2 inches will represent the length of your ladder, so the scale of your drawing will be 1 in. = 10 ft.
5. Construct circle *DD′*.
6. Construct point *E* where the circle intersects the wall. You may have to move point *D* first so that the circle and the wall intersect.
7. Construct $\overline{DE}$. This segment represents your ladder. Its length can't change because the radius of the circle is fixed at 2 inches.
8. Hide the circle and point *D′*.
9. Drag point *D* back and forth. You should see the top of the ladder move up and down the wall.

Select, in order, points *E*, *D*, and *B*. Then, in the Measure menu, choose **Angle**. Select points *E* and *A*; then, in the Measure menu, choose **Distance**. Repeat for *AD*.

10. Measure $\angle EDA$, *EA*, and *AD*. (*EA* represents the height on the wall that your ladder is reaching.) Calculate *EA*/*AD*.

Q1 Drag point *D*. Given the constraints in the problem, how high can the ladder reach? What angle does it make with the floor?

© 2002 Key Curriculum Press

Q2 Confirm your answers using trigonometry. Show your work.

Explore More

1. Suppose a ladder is propped against one wall in the corner of a room. To one side of the ladder is another wall. A wet paintbrush rests on the center rung of the ladder, just touching the side wall. Suddenly, the foot of the ladder slips and the paintbrush falls with it, painting a streak on the side wall as it falls! What does the streak look like? To model this in your sketch, construct the midpoint of your ladder. While it's selected, choose **Trace Point** in the Display menu. Animate point D along $\overline{BC}$.

2. Select the measurements for EA and AD and choose **Plot As (x, y)** in the Graph menu. Drag the foot of the ladder. What kind of graph do you get? If you were to drag the foot of a ladder away from a wall at a constant rate, would the top of the ladder fall at a constant rate? Why or why not?

3. Write one or more other problems that could be modeled with this sketch.

© 2002 Key Curriculum Press

A Sine Wave Tracer

Name(s): ______________________________

In this exploration, you'll construct an animation "engine" that traces out a special curve called a *sine wave*. Variations of sine curves are the graphs of functions called *periodic functions,* functions that repeat themselves. The motion of a pendulum and ocean tides are examples of periodic functions.

Sketch and Investigate

1. Construct a horizontal segment *AB*.

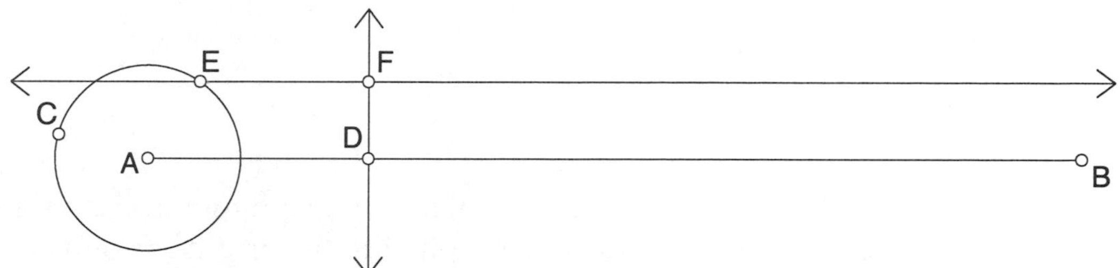

2. Construct a circle with center *A* and radius endpoint *C*.
3. Construct point *D* on $\overline{AB}$.
4. Construct a line perpendicular to $\overline{AB}$ through point *D*.
5. Construct point *E* on the circle.
6. Construct a line parallel to $\overline{AB}$ through point *E*.
7. Construct point *F*, the point of intersection of the vertical line through point *D* and the horizontal line through point *E*.

Select point *D* and $\overline{AB}$; then, in the Construct menu, choose **Perpendicular Line**.

Q1 Drag point *D* and describe what happens to point *F*.

Don't worry, this isn't a trick question!

Q2 Drag point *E* around the circle and describe what point *F* does.

Q3 In a minute, you'll create an animation in your sketch that combines these two motions. But first try to guess what the path of point *F* will be when point *D* moves to the right along the segment at the same time that point *E* is moving around the circle. Sketch the path you imagine below.

© 2002 Key Curriculum Press

Select points D and E and choose **Edit | Action Buttons | Animation**. Choose **forward** in the Direction pop-up menu for point D.

8. Make an action button that animates point D forward along $\overline{AB}$ and point E forward around the circle.

9. Move point D so that it's just to the right of the circle.

10. Select point F; then, in the Display menu, choose **Trace Point**.

11. Press the Animation button.

Q4 In the space below, sketch the path traced by point F. Does the actual path resemble your guess in Q3? How is it different?

12. Select the circle; then, in the Graph menu, choose **Define Unit Circle**. You should get a graph with the origin at point A. Point B should lie on the x-axis. The y-coordinate of point F above $\overline{AB}$ is the value of the sine of $\angle EAD$.

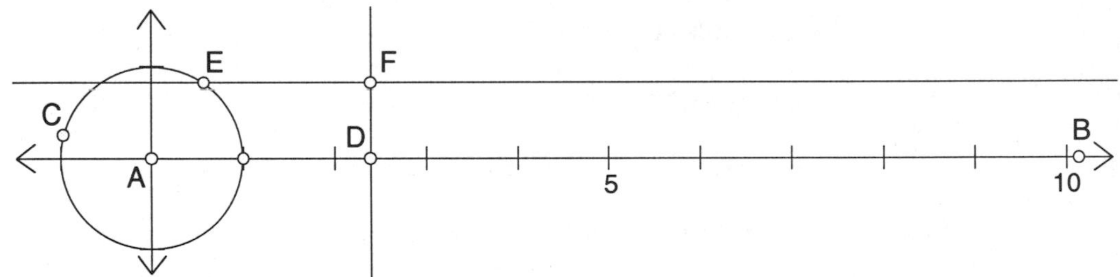

Q5 If the circle has a radius of 1 grid unit, what is its circumference in grid units? (Calculate this yourself; don't use Sketchpad to measure it because Sketchpad will measure in inches or centimeters, not grid units.)

13. Measure the coordinates of point B.

14. Adjust the segment and the circle until you can make the curve trace back on itself instead of drawing a new curve every time. (Keep point B on the x-axis.)

Q6 What's the relationship between the x-coordinate of point B and the circumference of the circle (in grid units)? Explain why you think this is so.

© 2002 Key Curriculum Press

Modeling Pendulum Motion

Name(s): ______________________

A pendulum swings back and forth, slowing down to a momentary stop at each end of its swing and reaching its greatest speed at the bottom of its swing. This motion is periodic, and as long as the pendulum doesn't swing too far, the motion can be described with a sine function. If you did the activity A Sine Wave Tracer, the method for constructing a pendulum model will seem familiar to you.

Sketch and Investigate

1. Construct a circle *AB* near the bottom of your sketch.
2. Construct point *C* on the circle.
3. Construct a horizontal segment *DE* above the circle.
4. Construct a line through point *C* perpendicular to $\overline{DE}$.

   Select point *C* and $\overline{DE}$; then, in the Construct menu, choose **Perpendicular Line**.

5. Construct point *F* where this line intersects $\overline{DE}$.
6. Drag point *C* and observe the motion of point *F*. You'll use this back-and-forth motion to drive a pendulum.
7. Construct a large circle *GH* above $\overline{DE}$.
8. Construct $\overline{GF}$.
9. Construct point *I* where $\overline{GF}$ intersects the circle.
10. Drag point *C* and observe the motion of point *I*. Point *I* will be the bottom point of your pendulum.
11. Make an action button to animate point *C* around the circle.

    Select point *C*; then choose **Edit | Action Buttons | Animation**.

12. Hide everything but the Animation button, point *G*, and point *I*.

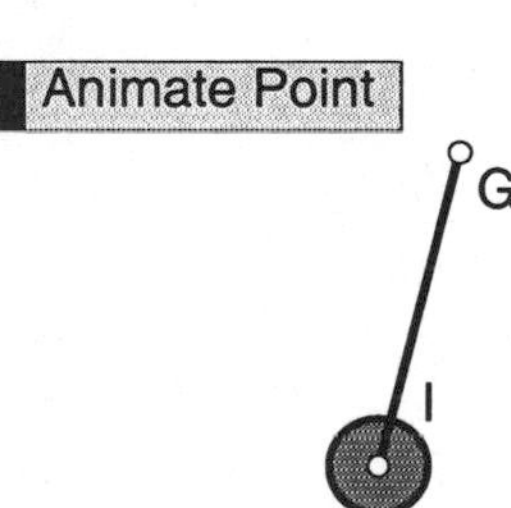

13. Construct $\overline{GI}$. This is your pendulum string.
14. To make a nice pendulum bob, translate point *I* by 0.5 cm or 0.2 inches. Construct circle *II′* and its interior. Hide point *I′*.
15. Press the Animation button to set your pendulum in motion. Press it again to stop the motion.

    If you wish to adjust the pendulum's speed, select the action button; then, in the Edit menu, choose **Properties**. Go to the Animate panel and use the Speed pop-up menu.

© 2002 Key Curriculum Press

Creating a Hat Curve Fractal

Name(s): ____________________

By using the **Iterate** command, you can repeat an action again and again on the same figure. Repeatedly taking the result of an action and applying the action to that result again is called *iteration* in mathematics and is central to the creation of fractals. In this activity, you'll create the first few stages of a fractal called the *hat curve.* A true hat curve, created in infinitely many stages, has dimension between 1 and 2.

Sketch and Investigate

1. In a new sketch, construct a long horizontal segment $\overline{AB}$ near the bottom of the sketch window.

Double-click point *A* to mark it as a center. Select point *B*; then, in the Transform menu, choose **Dilate**.

2. Mark point *A* as a center and dilate point *B* by a scale factor of 1/3.

A B' B

Steps 1 and 2

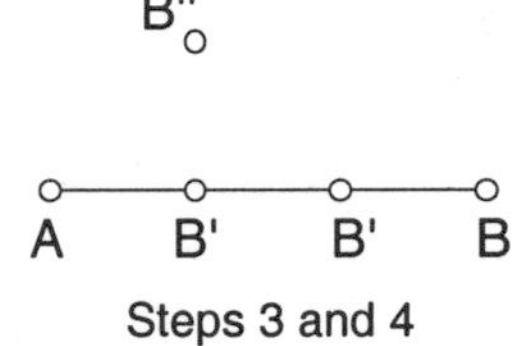

Steps 3 and 4

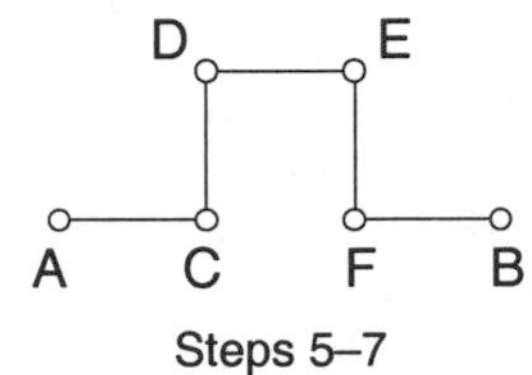

Steps 5–7

3. Also dilate point *B* by a scale factor of 2/3.
4. Mark the first (left) point *B´* as a center and rotate the other (right) point *B´* by 90°.
5. Mark point *B´´* as a center and rotate the first (left) point *B´* by 90°.
6. Hide $\overline{AB}$.

Using the **Text** tool, click once on a point to show its label. Double-click the label to change it.

7. Connect the six points with segments to form a hat, as shown above right. Relabel the points to match the figure.

Take a moment to think about what you've "done" to segment *AB:* you've transformed it from a simple segment to a hat shape made up of five smaller segments. Now imagine doing the same thing (*iterating* the construction) to segment *AC,* and then to the other four smaller segments. Make a drawing in the margin of what the resulting figure (the *first iteration*) would look like.

Can you imagine what the second iteration would look like (in other words, if you now applied the iteration rule to each of the very small segments in your drawing above)? You'll now use Sketchpad's **Iterate** command to construct an iterated image that can show several different stages of the iteration.

8. Select, in order, point *A* and point *B*. Choose **Iterate** from the Transform menu. The Iterate dialog box appears.
9. Choose **Final Iteration Only** from the Display pop-up menu. This tells Sketchpad to hide segments once they get iterated on.

© 2002 Key Curriculum Press

Drag the dialog box by its title bar if you can't see a point in the sketch below.

10. Click first on point *A* in the sketch, then on point *C*. This tells Sketchpad to "do to segment *AC* what was done to segment *AB*."

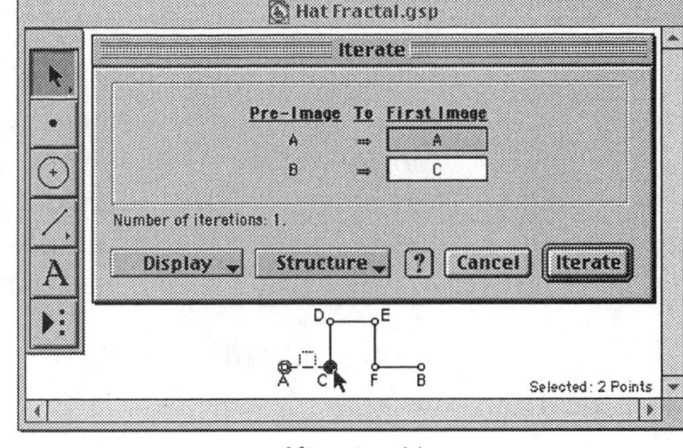

After step 11

11. Press the – key twice so that you see just one iteration.

12. Choose **Add New Map** from the Structure menu so that you can iterate on a new segment.

13. Click on point *C* first, then on point *D*.

If one of the cells in your dialog box has the wrong letter, highlight it and click on the proper point in the sketch.

14. Repeat steps 12 and 13 three more times, once for each remaining segment. When you're done, the Iterate dialog box should look like the one at right. Click Iterate.

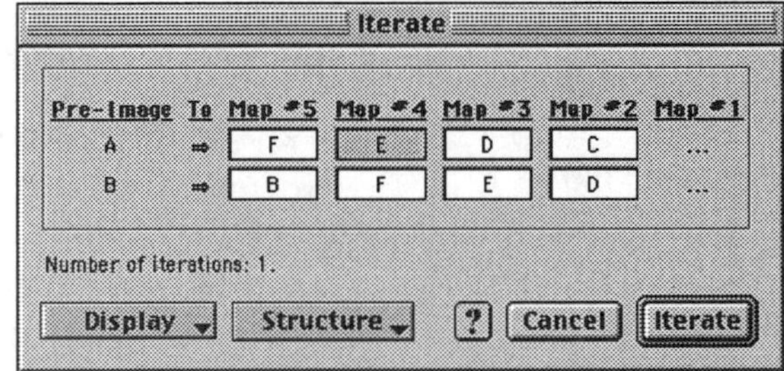

15. Hide segments *AC, CD, DE, EF,* and *FB*. You now should see a stage 1 hat curve. How does it compare to your drawing on the previous page?

16. Explore other stages of the hat curve by selecting part of the iterated image and pressing the + and – keys.

Q1 Sketch a stage 2 hat curve on a blank piece of paper.

Q2 What stage hat curve is shown at right?

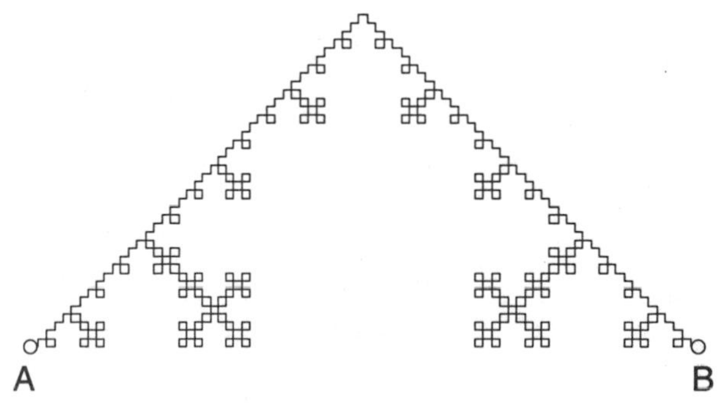

Q3 Suppose the original segment *AB* had length 1 unit. A stage 0 hat curve is five segments, each 1/3 the length of the original, so its length is 5/3. Complete the chart below. What would be the length of a stage infinity hat curve?

Stage	0	1	2	3	*n*
Length	5/3				

© 2002 Key Curriculum Press

Creating a Sierpiński Gasket Fractal **Name(s):** ______________

By using the **Iterate** command, you can repeat an action again and again on the same figure. Repeatedly taking the result of an action and applying the action to that result again is called *iteration* in mathematics and is central to the creation of fractals. In this activity, you'll create the first few stages of a fractal called the *Sierpiński gasket*. A true Sierpiński gasket, created in infinitely many stages, has dimension between 1 and 2 and its perimeter and area have strange properties.

Sketch and Investigate

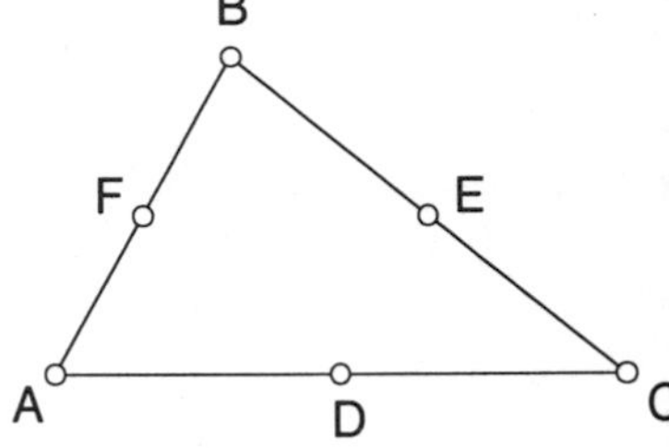

1. In a new sketch, construct a triangle *ABC*, with point *A* at the bottom left corner.
2. Construct the midpoints of the three sides.
3. If necessary, change labels to match the diagram.

Using the **Text** tool, click once on a point to show its label. Double-click the label to change it.

4. Construct the interior of the triangle.

Select the vertices; then, in the Construct menu, choose **Triangle Interior**.

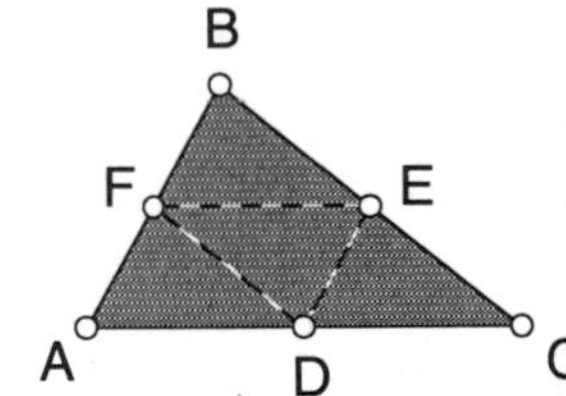

As shown at right, the three midpoints help define four "subtriangles" of ΔABC, namely ΔAFD, ΔFBE, ΔDEC, and ΔEDF. (The dotted lines are shown for illustration only—they shouldn't be in your sketch.)

Take a moment to think about what you've "done" to triangle *ABC:* You've constructed its midpoints and its interior. Now imagine doing the same thing (*iterating* the construction) to ΔAFD, then to ΔFBE and ΔDEC (but *not* to ΔEDF), and then hiding the original interior. Make a drawing below of what the resulting figure (the *first iteration*) would look like.

Can you imagine what the second iteration would look like (in other words, if you now applied the iteration rule to the three outer subtriangles in your drawing above)? You'll now use Sketchpad's **Iterate** command to construct an iterated image that can show several stages of the iteration.

5. Select, in order, points *A*, *B*, and *C*. Choose **Iterate** from the Transform menu. The Iterate dialog box appears.
6. Choose **Final Iteration Only** from the Display pop-up menu. This tells Sketchpad to hide triangle interiors once they get iterated on.

© 2002 Key Curriculum Press

Creating a Sierpiński Gasket Fractal (continued)

Drag the dialog box by its title bar if you can't see a point in the sketch.

7. Click on point A first, then on point F, and then on point D. This tells Sketchpad to "do to triangle AFD what was done to triangle ABC."

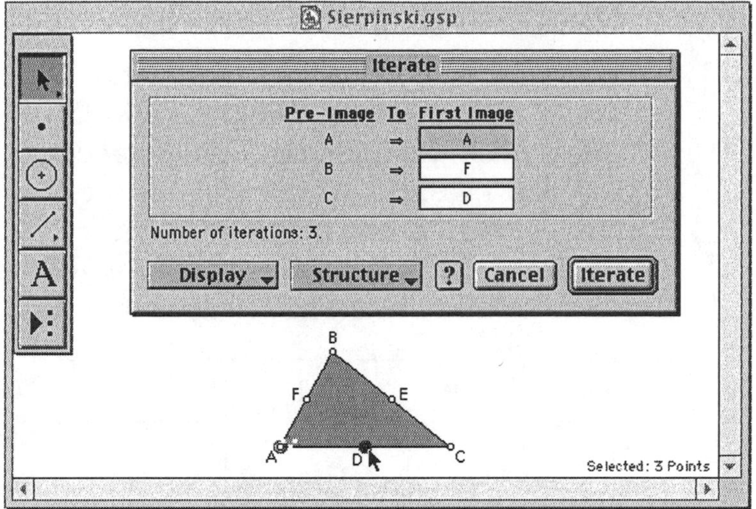

After step 7

8. Choose **Add New Map** from the Structure menu.
9. Repeat step 7 for points F, B, and E, choose **Add New Map**, then repeat step 7 for points D, E, and C. When you're done, the Iterate dialog box should look like the one at right. Click Iterate.

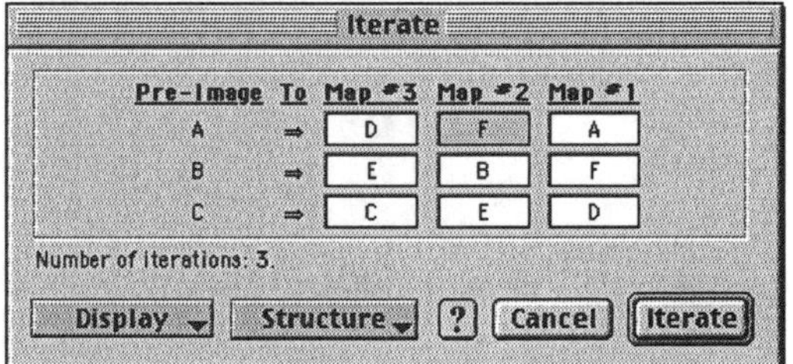

10. Deselect all objects. Now click in the center of ΔABC to select its interior, then hide it.
11. Hide the midpoints.
12. Select the iterated image and press the – key until nothing changes. This is the stage 1 iteration. How does it compare with your drawing on the previous page?

Q1 With the iterated image still selected, press the + key once to show the stage 2 iteration. Sketch the resulting figure below.

© 2002 Key Curriculum Press

13. Use the + and – keys to explore other stages of the Sierpiński iteration.

Q2 What stage gasket is shown in the figure at right? ___________

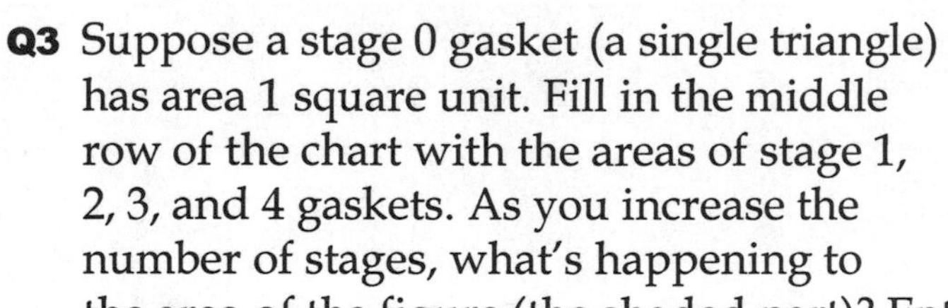

Q3 Suppose a stage 0 gasket (a single triangle) has area 1 square unit. Fill in the middle row of the chart with the areas of stage 1, 2, 3, and 4 gaskets. As you increase the number of stages, what's happening to the area of the figure (the shaded part)? Enter an expression in the chart for the area of a stage n gasket.

Stage	0	1	2	3	4	n
Area	1					
Perimeter	3					

Q4 Suppose the stage 0 gasket started with perimeter 3 units. What happens to the perimeter, including the perimeters around all the little shaded triangles inside, as the stages increase? Complete the bottom row of the chart for perimeter.

Q5 What would the area of a Sierpiński gasket be at stage infinity? ___________

Q6 What would the perimeter of a Sierpiński gasket be at stage infinity? ___________

© 2002 Key Curriculum Press

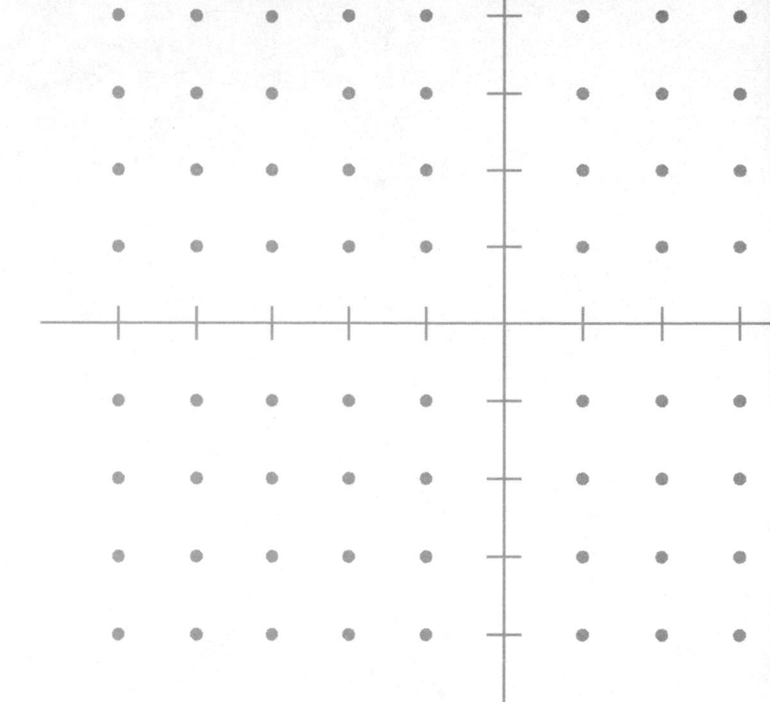

Activity Notes

Introducing Points, Segments, Rays, and Lines (page 3)

Prerequisites: None. The lesson introduces points, segments, and rays, as well as notation used to represent these objects.

Sketchpad Proficiency: Absolute beginner. This lesson is designed as a possible first experience with Sketchpad. Students use the basic tools and create a simple animation.

Activity Time: 25–40 minutes

Example Sketch: Segs Rays Lines.gsp

Sketch and Investigate

Q1 You can make the distance between two points zero by dragging one point onto the other.

Q2 The length of a segment is equal to the distance between the segment's endpoints.

Q3 The midpoint traces a straight path. This path is parallel to segment *AB* and half as long.

Q4 Ray *AB* could not be called ray *BA*. Ray *BA* has endpoint *B* and passes through point *A*.

Q5 You can't measure the length of a ray because it is infinitely long.

Q6 You can't find the midpoint of a ray because a ray only has one endpoint and is infinitely long.

Q7 $\overrightarrow{AB}$ and $\overrightarrow{AC}$

Q8 Lines and rays are infinitely long; segments are finite.

A line has no endpoints, a ray has one endpoint, and a segment has two endpoints.

Lines, rays, and segments are all straight.

The notation for a line, ray, or segment uses two letters. Each letter represents a point on that object. In the notation for a ray, one of the points must be an endpoint. In the case of a segment, both of the points must be endpoints. In the case of a line, both points are any (distinct) points on the line.

Q9 $\overrightarrow{AB}$ and $\overrightarrow{BA}$ are rays. $\overline{AB}$ is a segment.

Q10 Students are most likely to use the **Ray** tool to construct $\overrightarrow{AB}$ and $\overrightarrow{AC}$, then adjust point *A* so that it's between points *B* and *C*. This is fine, but it won't remain a line when dragged. If you construct $\overrightarrow{AB}$ and use the same two control points to construct $\overrightarrow{BA}$, the rays will remain a line when dragged.

Introducing Angles (page 7)

Prerequisites: None. This activity provides an introduction to angle notation, but could also serve as a review of angle notation.

Sketchpad Proficiency: Absolute beginner. This lesson is designed as a possible first experience with Sketchpad. Students use the basic tools and create a simple animation.

Activity Time: 25–40 minutes

Example Sketches: **Angle Measure.gsp** and **Clock.gsp**

Sketch and Investigate

Q1 The vertex of the angle is point *A*.

Q2 $\angle BAC$, $\angle CAB$

Q3 The least angle measure is 0°. The greatest is 180°. (Sketchpad, like most protractors, does not measure reflex angles. See Q9 below.)

Q4 An angle with measure 0° is a single ray.

Q5 An angle with measure 90° has perpendicular sides.

Q6 An angle with measure 180° is a straight line.

Q7 See student work.

Q8 See student work.

Q9 The largest angle would measure 360°.

Q10 If an angle has segments for sides, it's possible to lengthen the sides while actually decreasing the angle measure. This should help students overcome the common misconception that an angle's measure is related to the lengths of its sides. See the sketch **Angle Measure.gsp**.

Explore More

1. This is a fairly involved assignment, so you may wish to assign it as a long-term challenge or project. Construct a circle. Construct both the hour and minute hands as radii of this circle. (Later, you'll construct a shorter segment along the current hour-hand radius.) Make an Animation action button, setting the speed of the minute hand to be 12 times that of the hour hand. (Try a speed of 1/12 for the hour hand and 1 for the minute hand, for example.) Choose **clockwise** for the Direction of each animation. Improve the looks of your clock by hiding objects and adding numbers and color. See the example sketch **Clock.gsp**.

© 2002 Key Curriculum Press

Euclid's Proposition 1—An Equilateral Triangle (page 10)

Prerequisites: Students need to understand the term *equilateral.* A discussion of Euclid's tools and how they differ from the modern compass and straightedge should interest students.

Sketchpad Proficiency: Beginner

Activity Time: 15–30 minutes

Example Sketch: **Equilateral Triangle.gsp.** This sketch contains the custom tool **Equilateral Triangle**.

Sketch and Investigate

Q1 The triangle will stay equilateral no matter which vertex you drag. (Dragging *A* or *B* will scale the triangle. Dragging *C* will translate it.) If the triangle does not stay equilateral, it was not constructed correctly.

Q2 $\overline{AB}$ is a radius of both circles, so the circles are congruent. Each of the three sides is a radius of one circle or the other, so all three sides are congruent. Therefore the triangle is equilateral.

Q3 The angles in an equilateral triangle are all congruent. Each angle measures 60°.

Explore More

1. Equilateral triangles can tile the plane, meaning they can fill the plane without gaps or overlap. Because every angle in an equilateral triangle is 60°, six triangles fit around a vertex to complete a 360° revolution without gaps or overlap. Also, because the sides of an equilateral triangle are all congruent, the triangles fit together side-to-side.

   For tips on making and using custom tools, see the appropriate sections in the help system. (Choose **Toolbox** from the Help menu, then click on the Custom Tools link.)

2. There are several translations from the ancient Greek of Euclid's *Elements*, and they may be difficult for students to follow. Nevertheless, students will notice that the construction and explanation in this activity match Euclid's construction and proof almost exactly. In this activity, students perform essentially the same mathematics as Euclid—2000 years later, on a computer.

Daisy Designs (page 11)

Prerequisites: None

Sketchpad Proficiency: Beginner

Activity Time: 15–20 minutes

Example Sketch: **Hex Designs.gsp**. This sketch contains the custom tool **Daisy**.

Presenting the Sketch

Since this activity does not ask for a written response, you might want students to print out their daisy designs or save them electronically. If they print the designs, remind them that color will not print (unless you have a color printer). You might have them print the outlines of the designs and take them home to color them in. If they save the sketches electronically, remind them to use the **Text** tool to put their names on the sketches and possibly to describe their constructions and designs.

Explore More

In the initial construction, the points along the circle mark the vertices of a regular hexagon. Connect these points using the **Segment** tool and hide all the circles. For tips on making and using custom tools, see the appropriate sections in the help system. (Choose **Toolbox** from the Help menu, then click on the Custom Tools link.)

© 2002 Key Curriculum Press

Duplicating a Line Segment (page 13)

Prerequisites: Students should know how to duplicate a segment using a compass and straightedge.

Sketchpad Proficiency: Beginner

Activity Time: 15–25 minutes

Example Sketch: **Duplicate Segment.gsp**. This sketch contains the custom tool **Duplicate Segment**.

Sketch and Investigate

Q1 Dragging either point *C* or point *D* does not change the length of $\overline{CD}$, because its length is determined by $\overline{AB}$. Point *D* swings in the arc of the hidden circle without moving point *C*. Dragging point *C* moves the entire segment.

Q2 As you drag point *A* or point *B*, $\overline{CD}$ adjusts its length to match that of $\overline{AB}$.

Q3 The Sketchpad command **Circle By Center+Radius** uses the radius of the first circle to define the radius of a second circle. The two segments are congruent because they're radii of congruent circles. When you duplicate a segment with a compass, you open the compass radius to the length of the first segment, then move the compass to another point and swing an arc with this radius to define the length of the second segment. Keeping the same compass setting is like using **Circle By Center+Radius** in Sketchpad. Sketchpad's **Compass** tool does not allow you to keep the same compass setting after you've drawn a circle.

Explore More

1. Use **Circle By Center+Radius** to duplicate the first segment. Then use **Circle By Center+Radius** two more times to duplicate the other two segments, using the endpoints of the first segment as centers. The construction will look something like this:

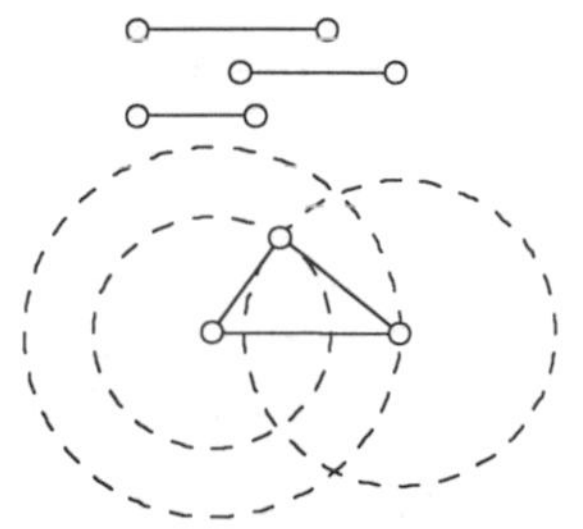

   a. The segments can make a triangle only if the sum of any two lengths is longer than the third. (See Triangle Inequalities in Chapter 3 for an activity devoted to this concept.)

   b. Follow the same procedure used in the first construction to construct the second triangle. The two triangles will be congruent. (See Triangle Congruence in Chapter 3 for an activity devoted to this idea.)

2. Euclid's construction is very complicated because Euclid had a collapsible compass. (He obviously couldn't use **Circle By Center+Radius**, either.) Euclid uses Proposition 1, in which he constructs an equilateral triangle, in his construction for Proposition 2. (See the activity Euclid's Proposition 1—Constructing an Equilateral Triangle, earlier in this chapter.) If nothing else, students can observe how much simpler the construction is both on Sketchpad and with a modern compass. If they are persistent and have a good translation of the *Elements*, they can try to follow Proposition 2 on the computer, step by step.

© 2002 Key Curriculum Press

Duplicating an Angle (page 14)

Prerequisites: It will help if students can duplicate an angle using traditional compass and straightedge tools. It will also help if students have done the previous activity, Duplicating a Line Segment.

Sketchpad Proficiency: Beginner/Intermediate

Activity Time: 15–30 minutes

Example Sketch: **Duplicate Angle.gsp**. This sketch contains the custom tool **Duplicate Angle**.

Sketch and Investigate

Q1 The angles have the same measure because triangles *AFG* and *DHI* are congruent. The triangles are congruent because the sides of triangle *DHI* are constructed by duplicating the sides of triangle *AFG*. Circle *DH* was constructed using length *AF*, so *DH* = *AF* and *DI* = *AG*. Circle *HI* was constructed using length *FG*, so *HI* = *FG*. This is a use of the SSS congruence postulate. (Students may not be familiar with it yet.)

Explore More

1. This construction will probably seem simpler to students because it requires fewer steps. Constructions using the Transform menu are often more straightforward than the strictly Euclidean constructions using only the tools and the Construct menu. In the future, students might prefer this construction method when they need to duplicate an angle in a construction.
2. Duplicate the segments on the sides of the angle using **Circle By Center+Radius** in the Construct menu. All triangles constructed from these parts will be congruent. This demonstrates the SAS congruence postulate. See the activity Triangle Congruence in Chapter 3.

Angles Formed by Intersecting Lines (page 15)

Prerequisites: Students should be familiar with angle notation and the measurement of angles.

Sketchpad Proficiency: Beginner

Activity Time: 15–30 minutes

Example Sketch: **Intersecting Lines.gsp**

Sketch and Investigate

Q1 a. $\angle BEC$ and $\angle AED$ are another pair of vertical angles.

b. Vertical angles are always congruent.

Q2 a. Besides $\angle CEB$ and $\angle DEB$, the following pairs of angles are also linear pairs:
$\angle CEB$ and $\angle CEA$
$\angle CEA$ and $\angle AED$
$\angle AED$ and $\angle DEB$

b. Angles in a linear pair are always supplementary. If students use Sketchpad's Calculator to add two angle measures in a linear pair, they will observe that the angle measures always sum to 180°.

Q3 All four angles are right angles.

Q4 The other angles will measure 117°, 63°, and 117°. If students have the precision set to be very precise, they may find it hard to drag until a measurement is exactly 63°. In this case, they can change their precision settings in **Preferences** in the Edit menu.

Explore More

1. a. If you know two different angle measures, you can find the other four (provided that the two you know aren't a pair of vertical angles).

   b. If any two angles that are not a pair of vertical angles measure 60°, all six angles will measure 60°.
2. If you know three angle measures, no two of which are a pair of vertical angles, you can find the other five. If the angles are congruent, they all measure 45°.
3. If *n* lines intersect to form 2*n* angles, you need to know the measures of *n* – 1 angles (no two of which are a pair of linear angles) to find the remaining angle measures.

© 2002 Key Curriculum Press

Properties of Parallel Lines (page 17)

Prerequisites: Students should be familiar with angle notation and angle measurement. This activity introduces the terms *transversal, corresponding* angles, *alternate interior* angles, *alternate exterior* angles, *same-side interior* angles, and *same-side exterior* angles.

Sketchpad Proficiency: Beginner

Activity Time: 25–35 minutes

Example Sketch: **Parallel Lines.gsp**

Sketch and Investigate

Q1 Students should complete the chart as shown below.

Angle Type	Pair 1	Pair 2	Rel'ship
Corresponding	$\angle FCE$, $\angle CAB$	See Q2 below.	Equal measure (or congruent)
Alternate interior	$\angle ECA$, $\angle CAG$	$\angle DCA$, $\angle CAB$	Equal measure
Alternate exterior	$\angle FCE$, $\angle HAG$	$\angle HAB$, $\angle DCF$	Equal measure
Same-side interior	$\angle ECA$, $\angle BAC$	$\angle DCA$, $\angle GAC$	Supple-mentary
Same-side exterior	$\angle FCD$, $\angle HAG$	$\angle FCE$, $\angle HAB$	Supple-mentary

Q2 There are more than two pairs of corresponding angles. The three more pairs of corresponding angles not listed in the second row above are $\angle ECA$ and $\angle BAH$, $\angle HAG$ and $\angle ACD$, and $\angle GAC$ and $\angle DCF$. Students should have recorded one of these pairs in the chart above. The relationship between angles in each pair is that they have equal measure.

Q3 The lines must be parallel.

Explore More

1. The last step is to rotate $\overleftrightarrow{AC}$ by the marked angle. Because the alternate interior angles were constructed to be congruent, the new line will be parallel to $\overleftrightarrow{AB}$.

Constructing a Perpendicular Bisector (page 19)

Prerequisites: Students should know or be introduced to the terms *perpendicular* and *bisector*.

Sketchpad Proficiency: Beginner

Activity Time: 15–30 minutes

Example Sketch: **Perpendicular Bisector.gsp.** This sketch contains the custom tool **Perpendicular Bisector.**

Sketch and Investigate

Q1 $AC = BC$ and $AD = BD$

Q2 Point E is the midpoint of $\overline{AB}$. It is also the midpoint of $\overline{CD}$.

Q3 Any point on a perpendicular bisector is equidistant from the endpoints of the bisected segment.

Explore More

1. Select the segment, then choose **Midpoint** in the Construct menu. Then select the segment and the midpoint and choose **Perpendicular Line** in the Construct menu.
2. The converse of Q3 is "Any point equidistant from the endpoints of a segment is on the perpendicular bisector." Students should discover that when $GA = GB$, point G lies on the perpendicular bisector. (To enhance this demonstration, select point G and choose **Trace Point** in the Display menu. Then drag point G, keeping GA and GB as close to equal as possible. The point should trace the perpendicular bisector.)
3. Use the Transform menu to mark the mirror and also to reflect the point. The mirror line is the perpendicular bisector of the segment.
4. This concept is explored in depth in the activity Perpendicular Bisectors in a Triangle, in Chapter 3.

© 2002 Key Curriculum Press

The Slope of a Line (page 20)

Prerequisites: Students should be familiar with the coordinate plane. Students do not need any prior knowledge about slope, although this activity could be a good review.

Sketchpad Proficiency: Beginner

Activity Time: 30 minutes without the Explore More section. Also, you may want to allow more time for a few more rounds of the Slope Game.

Example Sketch: **Slope of a Line.gsp**

Sketch and Investigate

Q1 a. Lines with positive slope rise from left to right. Lines with negative slope fall from left to right.

b. Zero

c. Steeper lines have slopes with greater absolute value.

d. Undefined

Q2 Check students' work.

Explore More

1. Students' drawings should resemble the figure below. They should calculate slopes of 2/3 and –2/3.

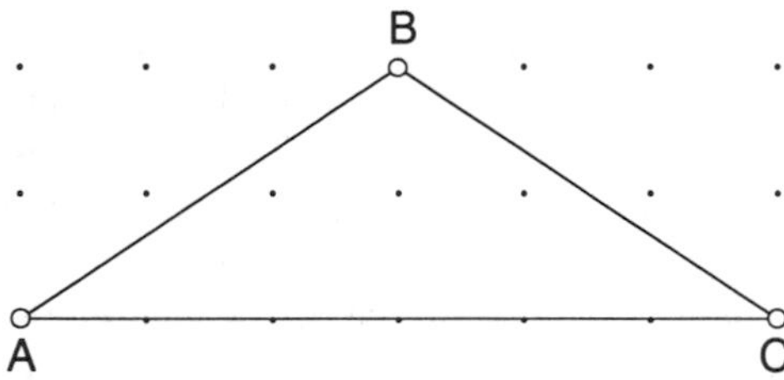

2. Students should informally explain that slope is calculated by dividing the difference in y-coordinates by the difference in corresponding x-coordinates. Formally stated, if two points have coordinates (x_1, y_1) and (x_2, y_2), the slope of the line through them is $(y_2 - y_1)/(x_2 - x_1)$.

Equations of Lines (page 22)

Prerequisites: Students should understand *slope*. They'll be introduced to *y-intercept*.

Sketchpad Proficiency: Beginner

Activity Time: 15–30 minutes

Example Sketch: **Line Equation.gsp**

Demonstration Sketch: **Slope-Intercept Form.gsp**

Sketch and Investigate

Q1 m represents the slope of the line and b represents the y-coordinate of the y-intercept.

Q2 See student work.

Q3 Answers will vary. Assuming you know the scale of the axes, you can estimate the slope, m, and the y-intercept, b. Then you can write an equation in the form $y = mx + b$.

Explore More

1. If two parallel lines have y-intercepts that are 2 units apart, the lines themselves are 2 units apart only if they are horizontal. If the distance between their y-intercepts is kept constant as the absolute value of their slope increases, the distance between the lines decreases.

© 2002 Key Curriculum Press

Slopes of Parallel and Perpendicular Lines (page 24)

Prerequisites: Students should understand the terms *parallel* and *perpendicular*. Students do not need to be familiar with slope.

Sketchpad Proficiency: Beginner/Intermediate

Activity Time: 25–40 minutes

Example Sketch: Slopes.gsp

Sketch and Investigate

Q1 The angle measurement approaches 0° and should eventually disappear when the slopes are equal.

Q2 The vertex E of $\angle AEC$ is the point of intersection of the lines. Lines with equal slope do not intersect, so the intersection point disappears when the slopes are the same; therefore, the angle also disappears.

Q3 If two lines have equal slopes, then the lines are parallel.

Q4 The product of the slopes of perpendicular lines is always –1 (as long as one of the lines is not horizontal).

Q5 If two lines are perpendicular, one of the slopes must be positive and the other negative. The product of a positive number and a negative number is always a negative number.

Q6 The slope of a vertical line is undefined, so the product of an undefined quantity with any other number is also undefined.

Explore More

1. Select the line and choose **Equation** in the Measure menu. The coefficient of the x term in the equation equals the slope of the line (unless the line is vertical and has an undefined slope). For further development of this topic see the activity The Slope of a Line, earlier in this chapter.
2. Students should locate the second point by using the same rise and run as the two points on the first line.
3. If students construct parallel lines, the slopes will always be exactly equal. The product of the slopes of constructed perpendicular lines will always be exactly –1.

Distance from a Point to a Line (page 25)

Prerequisites: Students should know, or be introduced to, the term *perpendicular*.

Sketchpad Proficiency: Beginner

Activity Time: 10–20 minutes

Example Sketches: Pt Line Distance.gsp and Sewer River.gsp

Sketch and Investigate

Q1 When CD is minimized, it equals the distance from C to $\overleftrightarrow{AB}$. (You might want to change the Distance Precision in Preferences to make these measurements match up more precisely.)

Q2 $\overline{CD}$ is perpendicular to $\overleftrightarrow{AB}$.

Q3 The distance from a point to a line is measured along a perpendicular to the line through the given point. (This is the shortest distance.)

Explore More

1. The figure below shows the sewage plant where the two rivers meet. The circle represents the 5-mile radius and the home is located on the circle. Perpendicular segments represent the shortest paths to the two rivers. Surprisingly, the optimal location for the house is on one of the riverbanks (assuming you don't mind walking to the other river through the sewage zone). This becomes clear when you drag point Home toward a river. One of the two lengths becomes zero, leaving a single, straight path to the other river. Because the shortest paths from the home to each river lead into the sewage zone, some students may model the problem differently, arguing that they don't want to fish in a sewage zone any more than they want to live in one.

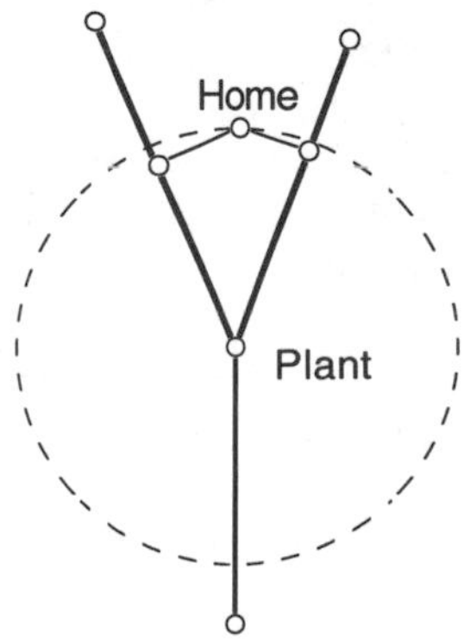

© 2002 Key Curriculum Press

Angle Bisectors (page 26)

Prerequisites: Students should know, or be introduced to, the term *angle bisector.*

Sketchpad Proficiency: Beginner

Activity Time: 15–30 minutes

Example Sketch: **Angle Bisector.gsp**. This sketch contains the custom tool **Angle Bisector**.

Sketch and Investigate

Q1 Students should guess that D is the same distance to both sides of the angle.

Q2 $\angle BAD$ and $\angle DAC$ have the same measure.

Q3 Any point on the angle bisector of an angle is equidistant from both sides of the angle.

Explore More

1. $\overrightarrow{AC}$ is the angle bisector of the angle formed by $\overrightarrow{AB}$ and its reflected image.
2. The figure below shows the construction. Start with rays AB and AC. Construct circle AB. Construct circle BD, where point D is the point of intersection of circle AB and $\overrightarrow{AC}$. Construct circle DB. Point E, where the congruent circles intersect, is on the angle bisector.

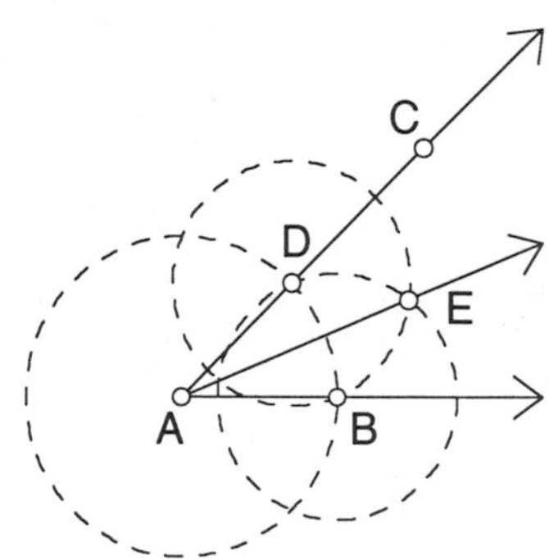

3. The converse of Q3 is "Any point equidistant from both sides of an angle is on the angle bisector." This converse is true. To demonstrate this with Sketchpad, construct an angle and a point in its interior and measure the distances from the point to each side. (Select the point and a side and choose **Distance** from the Measure menu.) Drag the point until the distances are equal. Choose **Trace Point** in the Display menu and continue to drag the point, keeping the distances as close to equal as possible. The point will trace the angle bisector.
4. This is the subject of an activity in Chapter 3: Angle Bisectors in a Triangle.

Trisecting an Angle (page 27)

Prerequisites: Students should know what an *angle bisector* is.

Sketchpad Proficiency: Beginner

Activity Time: 20–30 minutes

Example Sketch: **Angle Trisector.gsp**. This sketch contains the custom tool **Angle Trisector**.

Sketch and Investigate

Q1 The angles are trisectors because the two interior rays were constructed by rotating a side of the original angle by 1/3 of the original angle's measurement.

Explore More

1. See the activity Morley's Theorem in Chapter 3. An equilateral triangle can be found among the intersections of the angle trisectors.
2. This construction does not correctly trisect the angle. Students can measure all three angles to check this. (They might want to return the angle measure to degrees instead of directed degrees in the Preferences dialog box.) The inequality among the angles is most evident when $\overline{BC}$ is long and $\angle BAC$ is large.

© 2002 Key Curriculum Press

Drawing a Box with Two-Point Perspective (page 28)

Prerequisites: You may want to introduce the terms *horizon line* and *vanishing points,* or let students do the construction to discover what these terms mean by observing their own sketches.

Sketchpad Proficiency: Beginner

Activity Time: 20–30 minutes

Example Sketches: **2 Point Perspective Box.gsp** and **Cabin.gsp**

Presenting the Sketch

Since this activity does not ask for a written response, you might want students to print their sketches or save them electronically. If they print the design, you might have them take it home to color it in. If they save the sketch electronically, remind them to use the **Text** tool to put their name on the sketch and possibly describe their construction.

As a nice extension, students can add to their box to create a building or even an entire city block viewed in perspective. See the example sketch **Cabin.gsp**. Also, they could create a box with one-point perspective like the one below.

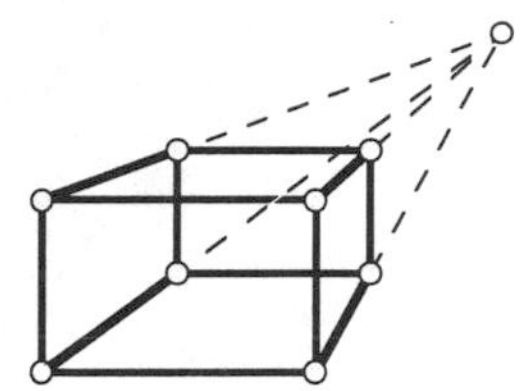

Introducing Transformations (page 33)

Prerequisites: None. This activity provides an introduction to the basic transformations: translations, rotations, and reflections.

Sketchpad Proficiency: Beginner

Activity Time: 25–40 minutes

Demonstration Sketches: **Translate.gsp**, **Rotate.gsp**, and **Reflect.gsp**

Sketch and Investigate

Q1 The original image and the translated image have the same shape, size, and orientation. They both face the same way. The only difference between them is that they are in different locations. The translated image is a copy of the original after a slide.

Q2 The original image and the rotated image have the same shape, size, and orientation. The only difference between them is that the rotated image is turned.

Q3 The original image and the reflected image have the same shape and size, but different orientations. The reflected image is flipped to face in the opposite direction. It is the mirror image of the original.

Q4 The translated image lies directly on top of the original when the translation vector has length zero. The rotated image lies directly on top of the original when the angle of rotation is zero. The reflected image cannot lie directly on top of the original unless the original shape has reflection symmetry and the mirror line is a line of symmetry.

Explore More

1. Answers will vary. Ask students to describe the different transformations in their designs. (Perhaps you might require that each design contain at least one example of each of the three basic isometries.)
2. Two reflections in succession over intersecting lines are equivalent to a single rotation. See the activity Reflections over Two Intersecting Lines in Chapter 2.
3. Two reflections in succession over parallel lines are equivalent to a single translation. See the activity Reflections over Two Parallel Lines in Chapter 2.

© 2002 Key Curriculum Press

Properties of Reflection (page 36)

Prerequisites: None

Sketchpad Proficiency: Beginner

Activity Time: 30–45 minutes (The first part, Mirror Writing, takes about 5 minutes and can be done independently of the rest of the activity.)

Example Sketch: Reflection.gsp

Demonstration Sketch: Reflect.gsp

Sketch and Investigate

Q1 Point C' traces the mirror image of the student's name.

Q2 Reflection preserves lengths and angle measures.

Q3 A figure and its reflected image are always congruent.

Q4 The vertices of the triangle *CDE* go from *C* to *D* to *E* in a counter-clockwise direction. The vertices of the reflected triangle $C'D'E'$ go from C' to D' to E' in a clockwise direction.

Q5 The mirror line is the perpendicular bisector of any segment connecting a point and its reflected image.

Explore More

1. Here is one way to perform this construction: Construct a line through the given point, perpendicular to the given mirror line. Then construct a circle from the intersection of the line and the perpendicular to the original point. The other intersection of the circle and the perpendicular is the reflected image of the original point. For an extra challenge, try doing this construction using only the Euclidean tools, that is, not using the menu at all.
2. Reflect a point across a line. Connect the point with its image point. Also connect each of these points with a third point on the line.
3. Students will notice that they have to flip one of the triangles in order to match the other exactly. Only one triangle will have the shaded side facing up. This is another demonstration that the triangles have opposite orientations.
4. This construction creates an isosceles trapezoid. If the segment connecting two points on one side of the mirror is parallel to the mirror, the points and their images form a rectangle. If the distance from each point to the mirror line is half the distance between the points, the points and their images form a square.
5. Note that this construction creates an angle that is defined by its bisector. It doesn't so much involve bisecting an angle as it does doubling one.
6. The ruler and its image should form a straight line. The apparent distance from your nose to your nose's mirror image is twice the length of the ruler.

© 2002 Key Curriculum Press

Reflections in the Coordinate Plane (page 38)

Prerequisites: Students should understand the (x, y) notation of a point in the coordinate plane. Some previous familiarity with reflections is also helpful.

Sketchpad Proficiency: Beginner/Intermediate

Activity Time: 30–40 minutes

Example Sketch: Coordinate Reflect.gsp

Sketch and Investigate

Q1 The y-coordinates of the point and its image are the same. The x-coordinates are opposites. A point with coordinates (a, b) has image coordinates $(-a, b)$. (Make sure students drag an original vertex into different quadrants so they can see these coordinates take on negative values.)

Q2 This time, the x-coordinates of the point and its image are the same and the y-coordinates are opposites. A point with coordinates (a, b) has image coordinates $(a, -b)$.

Explore More

1. The coordinates of the image of a point after a reflection across the line $y = x$ are reversed. So a point with coordinates (a, b) has image coordinates (b, a).
2. Both coordinates change sign. A point with coordinates (a, b) has second-image coordinates $(-a, -b)$. The second image is a rotation of 180° about the origin.

Translations in the Coordinate Plane (page 39)

Prerequisites: Students should understand the (x, y) notation of a point in the coordinate plane. Some previous familiarity with translations is also helpful.

Sketchpad Proficiency: Beginner/Intermediate

Activity Time: 35–45 minutes

Example Sketch: Coordinate Translate.gsp

Sketch and Investigate

Q1 If you drag point B along the x-axis, the y-coordinates of a vertex and its image point will be equal, but the x-coordinates will differ.

Q2 If you drag point B along the y-axis, the x-coordinates of a vertex and its image point will be equal, but the y-coordinates will differ.

Q3 If the vector translates the triangle up and to the left, point B is in the second quadrant. Its x-coordinate is negative (causing the movement to the left) and its y-coordinate is positive (causing the movement up).

Q4 The image of (x, y) under a translation by (a, b) is the point $(x + a, y + b)$.

Explore More

1. These two translations combined are equivalent to a single translation by a vector from the origin to the second vector tip.

© 2002 Key Curriculum Press

The Burning Tent Problem (page 40)

Prerequisites: None. You might need to explain the terms *incoming angle* and *outgoing angle* if students are not already familiar with them.

Sketchpad Proficiency: Intermediate

Activity Time: 30–40 minutes

Example Sketch: Burning Tent.gsp

Sketch and Investigate

Q1 The incoming angle is equal to the outgoing angle.

Q2 The shortest distance between any pair of points lies along a straight line, so $\overline{CD'}$ is the shortest path from point C to point D'.

Q3 Point E should be located at the intersection of $\overline{CD'}$ and $\overline{AB}$ for $CE + ED$ to be minimized.

Explore More

1. Construct the segment representing the river and the points for the camper and her tent. Then reflect the tent point across the river. Connect this image point with the camper point to locate the point on the river where the camper should fill her bucket. Then construct two segments of the camper's path using this intersection point.
2. The mirror needs to be only half as long as your height for you to see your full reflection. This is true no matter how tall you are or how far away you stand from the mirror. This problem makes a nice project. Students can try it out with a real mirror and report their results. They can also use their sketch to help them prove their results.

The Feed and Water Problem (page 42)

Prerequisites: It will be helpful if students have solved a problem similar to the Burning Tent Problem in the preceding activity.

Sketchpad Proficiency: Intermediate

Activity Time: 25–35 minutes

Example Sketch: Feed and Water.gsp

Sketch and Investigate

Q1 In each case, the incoming angle should be equal to the outgoing angle. It takes several iterations to make the angles match at both the pasture and the river. After one set is adjusted to match, the others will no longer match. As students keep adjusting each pair of angles, the total distance traveled by the rider and his horse should decrease.

Explore More

1. The figure below shows the construction. The segment $E'D'$ is the shortest path between these two points because it is straight. Because reflection preserves congruence, the path of the rider shown here is the same length as $E'D'$ and is a minimal path.

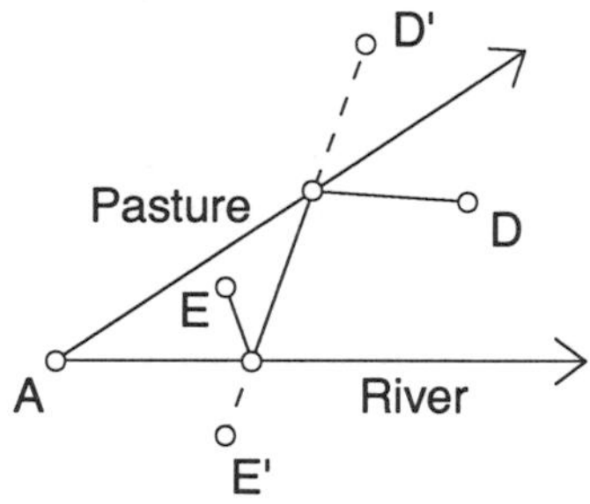

2. It does matter whether the rider visits the river first or the pasture first. One path will usually be shorter than the other. To determine which to visit first, construct ray DE. If this ray intersects the river, the rider should visit the pasture first. If the ray intersects the pasture, the rider should visit the river first. These Explore More problems are fairly sophisticated, and therefore work well together as a long-term assignment or project. Ask students to explain the different minimal paths and how they found them.

© 2002 Key Curriculum Press

Planning a Path for a Laser (page 43)

Prerequisites: Students should have previous experience constructing a path involving a single reflection. Experience constructing a path involving more than one reflection is helpful. The previous activities, The Burning Tent Problem and The Feed and Water Problem, are good prerequisites.

Sketchpad Proficiency: Intermediate

Activity Time: 40 minutes for measuring the room and building the Sketchpad model. If you plan to test your models, the time allowance depends on the number of groups you will have setting up and testing. For eight or nine groups, plan another 100 minutes for testing all the models. (See more suggestions below in Explore More.)

Example Sketch: Laser Path.gsp

Sketch and Investigate

Q1 Look at the picture below and imagine you are standing at the laser position.

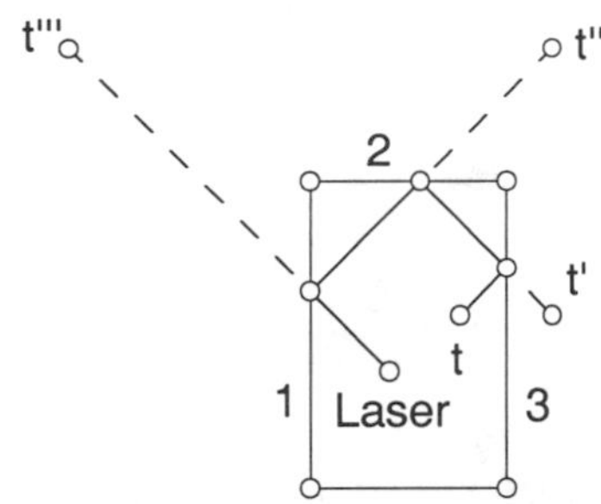

If you look into the mirror on wall 1, you can see the target point *t*. You are really seeing the image of the target after three reflections. That's why your line of sight connects to the point *t‴*. The triple prime indicates that the original target has undergone three reflections. If you stand at the mirror on wall 1 and look toward the mirror on wall 2, you see the target after two reflections, which is why your line of sight connects to the point *t″*. If you stand at the mirror on wall 2 and look toward the mirror on wall 3, you are looking at the target after only one reflection, so your line of sight connects to the point *t′*. It is possible to build this sketch correctly using other reflections. For example, you can use the same reasoning to reflect the laser point off the three walls. Also, you can construct a correct sketch using combinations of reflections of the target point and reflections of the laser. As long as the angle of approach equals the angle of departure for each reflection, the sketch is correct.

Explore More

1. The actual testing is very rewarding for students. It does require class time and equipment. Make sure you can get your room dark, and toss some flour (if you have some) in the air to see the path of the laser. A flashlight beam will diffuse too much in a classroom, so you really need a laser. Make sure you have something for students to work on while each group is setting up, since measuring and marking the right spots in the room can take some time. If you want to make it easier, use larger mirrors. Try to have each group of students follow the written directions of another group without talking to them. *Make sure that students are not at eye level with the laser.* One problem is that it's hard for the person with the laser to hold it still. To avoid this problem, you might have students set the laser on a pile of books or boxes. It's also important that the mirrors be positioned perfectly flat against the walls.

   If you do not have a laser in your school, try one of these alternatives:

- Find or purchase a laser presentation pointer. These are fairly inexpensive and work quite well.
- Don't use a laser at all, but check your models by testing the line of sight. Have a student stand at the position for the laser and look into the third mirror to find out if he or she can see the target.
- Have students use a very small room and a very strong flashlight. You might have them use a bathroom or a closet at home. (A flashlight will diffuse too much in a classroom.)

2. This is very challenging, but is still within the range of high school students. They will need to make two scale drawings. One shows the plan from above; the other, the plan from the side. In both plans, the angle of approach will equal the angle of departure, even though you are viewing the paths at an angle.

© 2002 Key Curriculum Press

Reflections over Two Parallel Lines (page 44)

Prerequisites: Students should be familiar with a reflection over one line before they work with reflections over two lines.

Sketchpad Proficiency: Intermediate

Activity Time: 30–45 minutes

Example Sketch: Reflection-Parallel.gsp

Demonstration Sketch: Reflect-Parallel.gsp

Sketch and Investigate

Q1 Two reflections over a pair of parallel lines are equivalent to a translation.

Q2 $AA'' = 2EF$

Q3 $\overline{EF}$ is perpendicular to both lines. Because parallel lines are everywhere equidistant, EF represents the distance between them.

Q4 The translation along the vector AA' moves the original figure onto the second reflected image. This demonstrates that reflecting a figure over two parallel lines is equivalent to a single translation. The translation vector is perpendicular to the lines and is twice the distance between the lines.

Q5 a. $AE = EA'$

b. $A'F = FA''$

c. $AA' + A'A'' = AA''$

d. Because $AE = EA'$, $(1/2)A'A = EA'$. Because $A'F = FA''$, $(1/2)A'A'' = A'F$. Also, the distance between the parallel lines, $EF = EA' + A'F$. Substituting from above gives: $EF = (1/2)A'A + (1/2)A'A'' = (1/2)AA''$.

Explore More

1. If you reverse the order of the lines in the two reflections, the translation goes in the opposite direction.
2. Construct a segment connecting a point with its translated image. Construct the perpendicular bisector of this segment and a line parallel to the perpendicular bisector through one of the segment's endpoints. Reflections over these two parallel lines will be equivalent to the translation.

Reflections over Two Intersecting Lines (page 46)

Prerequisites: Students should be familiar with a reflection over one line before they work with reflections over two lines.

Sketchpad Proficiency: Intermediate

Activity Time: 25–40 minutes

Example Sketch: Reflection Intersecting.gsp

Demonstration Sketch: Reflect Intersecting.gsp

Sketch and Investigate

Q1 The combination of two reflections over intersecting lines is equivalent to a single rotation.

Q2 $m\angle ABA'' = 2 \cdot m\angle CBD$.

Q3 A rotation about the point of intersection of two lines is equivalent to a combination of two reflections over the lines. The angle of rotation is twice one of the angles formed by the intersecting lines.

Q4 a. $m\angle ABC = (1/2)\ m\angle ABA'$

b. $m\angle A'BD = (1/2)\ m\angle A'BA''$

c. $m\angle ABA' + m\angle A'BA'' = m\angle ABA''$

d. Since $m\angle ABC = m\angle CBA'$,
and $m\angle CBA' + m\angle A'BD = m\angle CBD$,
then, by substitution,
$m\angle ABC + m\angle A'BD = m\angle CBD$.
$(1/2)\ m\angle ABA' + (1/2)\ m\angle A'BA'' = m\angle CBD$,
therefore, $(1/2)\ m\angle ABA'' = m\angle CBD$.

Explore More

1. Changing the order of the two reflections reverses the direction of the rotation (from clockwise to counter-clockwise or vice versa).
2. The image after being reflected over a pair of parallel lines is a translation.
3. Construct a segment connecting a point and its rotated image. Construct the perpendicular bisector. Repeat for another pair of points. The center of rotation is located where the two perpendicular bisectors intersect.

© 2002 Key Curriculum Press

Glide Reflections (page 48)

Prerequisites: Students should be familiar with translations and reflections. Students need to know that a translation is equivalent to a combination of reflections over two parallel lines.

Sketchpad Proficiency: Intermediate

Activity Time: 30–40 minutes

Example Sketch: **Glide Reflect.gsp**

Demonstration Sketch: **Threeflect.gsp**

Sketch and Investigate

Q1 A glide reflection is the product of a reflection and a translation.

Q2 A translation is the product of two reflections over parallel lines.

Q3 A glide reflection is the product of three reflections. Two of the reflection lines can be parallel, although they do not have to be (see Explore More 3, below).

Explore More

1. First, split point *G* from line *EF*. (Select point *G* and choose **Split Point From Line** from the Edit menu.) Then select, in order, the original polygon, point *E*, point *F*, point *G*, and the first glide-reflected image. Choose **Create New Tool** from the Custom Tools menu (the bottom icon in the Toolbox). Name the tool "Glide Reflection." Now merge point *G* back to line *EF*. To use the new tool, click on the **Custom** tools icon in the Toolbox, then click on objects in the sketch as instructed in the Status Line. To make the tool easier and quicker to use, choose **Show Script View** from the Custom Tools menu, double-click point *E* in the Given list, and check Automatically Match Sketch Object in the dialog box that appears. Do the same for points *F* and G. From now on, students will only have to click on the pre-image to use the tool (as long as the mirror line is defined by points labeled *E* and *F* and there's a point on the line labeled *G*).
2. This takes some time, but has fun results and is a good introduction to action buttons. Students can complete it as a long-term assignment or project. The Presentation can be refined by choosing the individual Hide/Show buttons, choosing **Properties** from the Edit menu, and changing settings on the Hide/Show panel.
3. If students try reflecting over three random lines, they will discover that this is a glide reflection as well (though it may not be obvious). They can confirm this by selecting the image, the original, and the three lines and defining the three reflections as a custom tool. When they apply this repeatedly, they'll see the glide reflection pattern.
4. A rotation followed by a reflection is a glide reflection (or, in the special case where the center of rotation is a point on the reflection line, a simple reflection). A rotation followed by a translation is a rotation by a different angle with a different center.

© 2002 Key Curriculum Press

Symmetry in Regular Polygons (page 50)

Prerequisites: Students should know the terms *regular polygon, perpendicular bisector, reflection, rotation, symmetry,* and *axis of symmetry* or *axis of reflection*. You might want to introduce reflection and rotation symmetry with examples in nature: butterflies, flowers, starfish, snowflakes, and so on.

Sketchpad Proficiency: Intermediate/Advanced

Activity Time: 40–50 minutes. If you have less time, it's also possible to investigate only reflection symmetry (and not rotational symmetry) and stop at the bottom of the first page. This would take about 30 minutes.

Example Sketch: Polygon Symmetry.gsp

Demonstration Sketches: Reflection Symmetry.gsp and Rotation Symmetry.gsp

Sketch and Investigate

Q1 Every line of symmetry passes through the center of the polygon. If the regular polygon has an odd number of sides, each line of symmetry is a perpendicular bisector of one side and passes through an opposite vertex. If the regular polygon has an even number of sides, each line of symmetry either is a perpendicular bisector of a pair of opposite sides or passes through a pair of opposite vertices.

Q2 Students will fill in one entry in row 2 below, depending on which polygon they were working with.

# of sides of regular polygon	3	4	5	6
# of reflection symmetries	3	4	5	6
# of rotation symmetries	3	4	5	6

Q3 Answers will vary depending on the student's polygon. Also, for any given regular polygon, there are many correct answers. To check a student's answer, calculate $360°/n$, where n is the number of sides in the polygon, and make sure their rotation angle is some integer multiple of this quotient.

Q4 Students will fill in one entry in row 3 in the chart shown above, depending on which polygon they were working with.

Q5 Students complete the chart shown above.

Q6 A regular n-gon has n axes of reflection symmetry and n rotation symmetries. The smallest angle of rotation symmetry larger than 0° is $360°/n$.

Explore More

1. Answers will vary. A quick way to construct a regular polygon is to rotate by a central angle. For example, to construct a pentagon, construct two points and rotate one point around the other five times, by 72° each time.
2. Have students pick a shape, define the shape, and report on its symmetry. Make sure they address special cases, such as rectangles that are also squares, because these cases can have more symmetry. This Explore More can make a nice long-term assignment or project. Students might describe their results as a poster, or create a sketch with color, text, a Show/Hide button, and animation.

© 2002 Key Curriculum Press

Tessellating with Regular Polygons (page 52)

Prerequisites: Students should be familiar with *regular polygons* and their properties. Previous experience with tessellations is also helpful.

Sketchpad Proficiency: Intermediate/Advanced

Activity Time: 30–45 minutes

Example Sketch: **Polygons.gsp**. This sketch contains custom tools for all of the regular polygons required in the activity. Make sure students use tools that say "By Edge."

Sketch and Investigate

Q1 Equilateral triangles tessellate because their angles are each 60° and their sides are equal. Because 60° divides evenly into 360°, the angles of the triangles collect around a single point without gaps or overlaps. Because the sides are equal, they can match up.

Q2 The only regular polygons that tessellate are those whose angles divide evenly into 360°: equilateral triangles, squares, and regular hexagons.

Q3 A regular heptagon has angles of $128\ {}^4/_7°$. This means two heptagons could meet to make an angle of $257\ {}^1/_7°$, which is less than 360° and would leave a gap. Three would meet to make an angle of $385\ {}^5/_7°$, which is more than 360° and would make an overlap. So regular heptagons cannot tessellate.

Explore More

1. Starting with a single polygon, students can tessellate by reflecting polygons over sides, by translating, by rotating 180° about midpoints of sides, or by rotating by the appropriate angles around the polygon's vertices.
2. These tessellations can use polygons with more than six sides. There are only eight *semiregular* tilings: tessellations in which two or more types of regular polygons are used and the polygons are arranged at every vertex in the same way. More tessellations are possible with polygons arranged differently at different vertices.
3. Any rhombus will tessellate.
4. Answers will vary.

A Tumbling-Block Design (page 53)

Prerequisites: Students should know what a *regular hexagon* is and know or be introduced to the term *translation*.

Sketchpad Proficiency: Intermediate/Advanced

Activity Time: 25–35 minutes

Example Sketches: **Tumbling Blocks.gsp** and **Polygons.gsp**. The latter sketch contains the custom tool **6/Hexagon (Inscribed)**, which students can use to construct the first hexagon.

Sketch and Investigate

Q1 Each hexagon is composed of three rhombuses.

Q2 The shading on the hexagons makes them appear three-dimensional so that they look like cubes. The cubes sometimes appear to pop in and out of the page as the eye moves over the design.

Q3 Answers will vary.

Presenting the Sketch

You might want students to print their tumbling-block designs or save them electronically. If they print the designs, remind them that color will not print (unless you have a color printer). You might have them print the outline of the design and take it home to color it in. If they save the sketch electronically, remind them to use the **Text** tool to put their names on the sketches and possibly to describe their constructions and designs.

© 2002 Key Curriculum Press

Tessellating with Triangles (page 55)

Prerequisites: Students should understand what a *tessellation* is. Experience with rotations and translations is also helpful.

Sketchpad Proficiency: Intermediate/Advanced

Activity Time: 20–30 minutes

Example Sketch: Triangle Tiles.gsp

Sketch and Investigate

Q1 The two triangles form a parallelogram.

Q2 The fact that the top and bottom edges are straight demonstrates that the angles of a triangle sum to 180°. The sketch below demonstrates how the angles around point *C* that form a straight line are each congruent to an angle of the original triangle on the left.

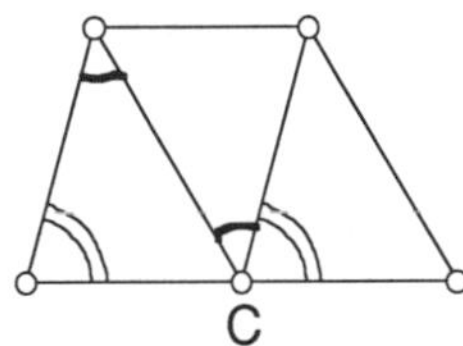

Q3 The sum of the angles surrounding a point is 360°. Among the angles around any point in this tessellation, there are two copies of each angle from the original triangle. Since one set of these angles sums to 180°, two sets sum to 360°.

Explore More

1. Any quadrilateral will tessellate. Rotate the quadrilateral by 180° about the midpoint of each side. Do the same with the rotated images. Continue in this way to tile the plane. The four angles of the quadrilateral will meet at each vertex without gaps or overlap, because the sum of the angles in any quadrilateral is 360°.

Tessellations Using Only Translations (page 56)

Prerequisites: Students should understand the terms *parallelogram, tessellation,* and *translation.*

Sketchpad Proficiency: Intermediate

Activity Time: 25–35 minutes

Example Sketch: Translation Tessellation.gsp

Presenting the Sketch

Since this activity does not ask for a written response, you might want students to print their tessellations or save them electronically. If they print the design, remind them that color will not print (unless you have a color printer). You might have them print the outline of the tessellation and take it home to color it in and decorate it with details. If they save the sketch electronically, remind them to use the **Text** tool to put their names on the sketch and possibly describe their constructions and tile patterns.

Explore More

1. This is a quick way to introduce the animation button, with potentially exciting results. Have students try it even if you have only an extra minute or two.
2. The process is the same for a regular hexagon, except that there are three pairs of parallel sides instead of two. So students can make three different irregular edges on adjacent sides, which they then translate across the hexagon to the opposite sides. This tiling is more interesting, but also more complex.

© 2002 Key Curriculum Press

Tessellations That Use Rotations (page 58)

Prerequisites: Students should understand the terms *equilateral triangle, tessellation,* and *rotation.*

Sketchpad Proficiency: Intermediate/Advanced

Activity Time: 35–45 minutes

Example Sketch: Twisted Triangles.gsp

Sketch and Investigate

Q1 The tessellation would have 60° rotation symmetry around point *A*. Notice that claiming the tessellation has 60° rotation symmetry disregards the different shading of the tiles and takes only their outlines into account. Students might point out, correctly, that the tessellation has 120° rotational symmetry if you take into account the alternate-shading pattern.

Q2 The tessellation would have 180° rotation symmetry about point *F*. (Again, this symmetry is only for the outline of the tiles and disregards the shading pattern.)

Q3 The tessellation will have 120° rotation symmetry about points *B* and *C*. Students should notice that every other tile matches around each of these points. Students should rotate appropriate tiles by 120° around points *B* and *C* to fill in more of the tessellation.

Defining Triangles (page 63)

Prerequisites: Students should be familiar with the notation for describing a triangle using three vertices.

Sketchpad Proficiency: Absolute beginner. This activity is designed as a possible first experience with Sketchpad.

Activity Time: 30–45 minutes

Required Sketch: Classify Triangles.gsp

Q1 Answers will vary. One possible answer is that triangle *ABC* is the most flexible because it has no constraints. However, students may have different views of what *flexible* means. (For example, students have argued that triangle *ABC* is the least flexible because it is "stuck in the corner.") Have the class discuss what it means for a shape to be flexible as opposed to constrained, since this is an important concept in working with Sketchpad.

Q2 Answers will vary. One possible answer is that triangle *HIG* is the least flexible. All you can do is scale it; you can't change its shape.

Q3 A triangle can have either two or three acute angles.

Q4 A triangle can have either zero or one obtuse angle.

Q5 Triangle *DEF* can be either acute or obtuse.

Q6 Triangle *LMN* is always a right triangle.

Q7 Triangle *IGH* is always an equiangular triangle.

Q8 Triangle *ABC* is scalene most of the time. (However, it is possible to drag it and make one or more of its sides equal, in which case it is no longer scalene.)

Q9 Triangle *LMN* is scalene most of the time.

Q10 Triangles *EFD* and *IGH* are always isosceles.

Q11 Triangle *IGH* is always equilateral.

Q12 a. An obtuse isosceles triangle is a possible shape. Students can use triangle *EDF* to demonstrate this. Check students' work for appropriate sketches.

b. An acute right triangle is impossible because one angle will always be 90°.

c. An obtuse equiangular triangle is impossible because each angle must be 60°.

Continued on next page.

© 2002 Key Curriculum Press

Defining Triangles

Continued from previous page.

d. An isosceles right triangle is a possible shape. Triangle *LMN* and triangle *EDF* can both demonstrate this. Check students' work for an appropriate sketch.

e. An acute scalene triangle is a possible shape. Triangle *ABC* can demonstrate this. Check students' work for an appropriate sketch.

Q13 An *acute triangle* is a triangle with three acute angles.

An *obtuse triangle* is a triangle with one obtuse angle.

A *right triangle* is a triangle with a 90° angle.

A *scalene triangle* is a triangle with all three sides of unequal length.

An *isosceles triangle* is a triangle with at least two sides of equal length.

An *equilateral triangle* is a triangle with all three sides of equal length.

Explore More

1. There are several ways to construct each of these triangles. For a method of constructing an equilateral triangle, see the activity Euclid's Proposition 1—An Equilateral Triangle, in Chapter 1. For methods of constructing an isosceles triangle, see the Activity Notes for the activity Constructing Isosceles Triangles in Chapter 3. For a method of constructing a right triangle, see the activity The Pythagorean Theorem in Chapter 8.

Triangle Sum (page 65)

Prerequisites: None

Sketchpad Proficiency: Beginner/Intermediate

Activity Time: 30–45 minutes (The first part takes only 5–10 minutes and is suitable for a beginning user. The second part takes more time and more skill.)

Example Sketch: **Triangle Sum.gsp**

Demonstration Sketch: **Triangle Sum 2.gsp**

Sketch and Investigate

Q1 The sum of the angles in any triangle is 180°.

Q2 We need to show that the three angles that form a straight angle at point *B* are congruent to the three angles of the original triangle. Because the horizontal line was constructed parallel to the opposite side of the triangle, the angles marked below with a single arc are congruent because they are alternate interior angles. The same argument holds for the angles marked with two arcs. The third unmarked angle at point *B* is the remaining angle of the original triangle. So the three angles, which form a straight angle at point *B* (and whose measures thus add up to 180°), are each congruent to the three angles of the original triangle. Therefore, the three angle measures of the triangle must also add up to 180°.

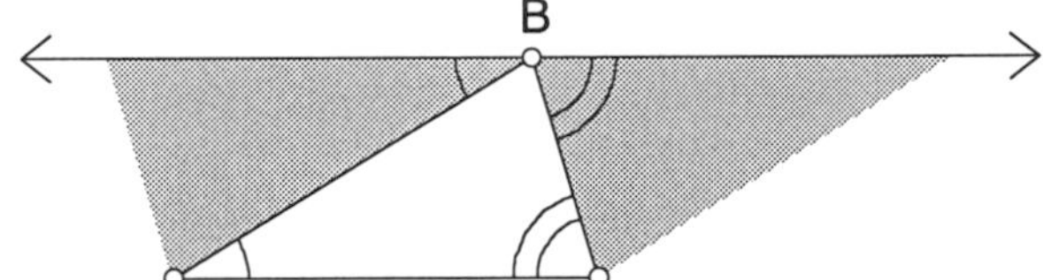

Explore More

1. Students should discover that the angle sum for any n-gon is $180°(n - 2)$.

© 2002 Key Curriculum Press

Exterior Angles in a Triangle (page 66)

Prerequisites: In this activity, students are introduced to the terms *exterior angle* and *remote interior angle*. While *remote interior* is not defined, it should be clear from the context.

Sketchpad Proficiency: Beginner/Intermediate

Activity Time: 25–45 minutes (The first part takes only 10–15 minutes and is suitable for a beginning user. The second part takes more time and more skill.)

Example Sketch: Ext Angles in Triangle.gsp

Sketch and Investigate

Q1 The sum of the measures of the two remote interior angles equals the measure of the exterior angle.

Q2 The triangles created by rotation and translation are congruent to the original triangle, so their corresponding angles are also congruent. The two angles that fill the exterior angle correspond to the two remote interior angles of the original triangle, as marked below, so this shows that the measures of the remote interior angles sum to the measure of the exterior angle.

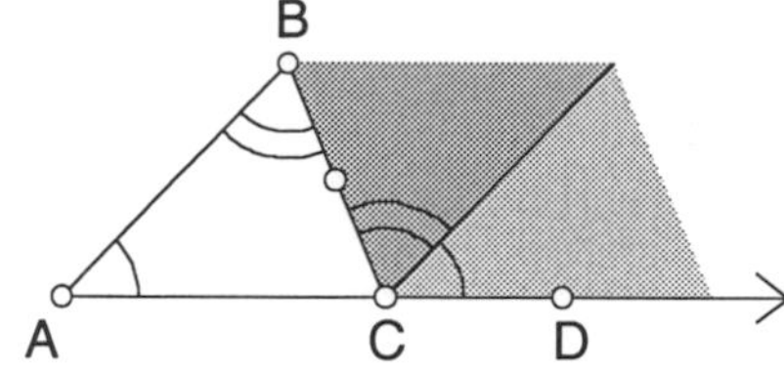

Triangle Inequalities (page 67)

Prerequisites: None

Sketchpad Proficiency: Beginner

Activity Time: 25–40 minutes

Example Sketch: Triangle Inequality.gsp

Sketch and Investigate

Q1 If the sum of two side lengths equals the third side length, two sides of the triangle collapse onto the third side, forming a segment instead of a triangle.

Q2 It's impossible for the sum of the lengths of any two sides of a triangle to be less than the length of the third side. If the sum of the lengths of the two segments (sides) is less than the length of the third side, the two short segments together are not long enough to meet and create a closed shape.

Q3 The length of any one side of a triangle must be less than the sum of the lengths of the other two sides.

Q4 Students should fill in the chart with the following angles. First row: $\angle C$, $\angle B$, $\angle A$
Second row (the same): $\angle C$, $\angle B$, $\angle A$

Q5 The largest angle in a triangle is always opposite the longest side and the smallest angle is always opposite the shortest side.

Explore More

1. The longest median and the longest altitude are to the shortest side. The shortest median and the shortest altitude are to the longest side.

© 2002 Key Curriculum Press

Triangle Congruence (page 68)

Prerequisites: Students should know the term *congruent*. This could be the students' introduction to the different possible triangle congruence properties, or it could serve as a review.

Sketchpad Proficiency: Beginner

Activity Time: 30–40 minutes

Required Sketch: Triangle Congruence.gsp

Sketch and Investigate

Q1 No. Three sides determine a unique triangle.

Q2 If two triangles have three pairs of congruent sides, then the triangles are congruent (SSS).

Q3 These combinations of parts guarantee congruence: SSS, SAS, ASA, AAS. For AAS, it's important to state that the sides must correspond. (The correspondence is forced by the order in the cases: It's impossible for the parts not to correspond.)

SSA and AAA do not guarantee congruence.

Explore More

1. Counterexample for SSA:

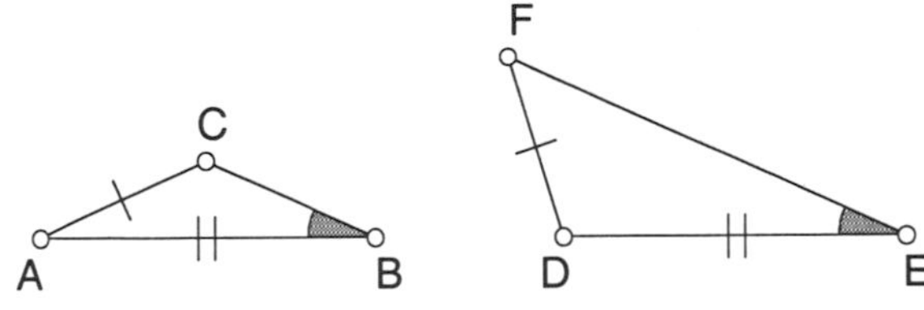

Counterexample for AAA:

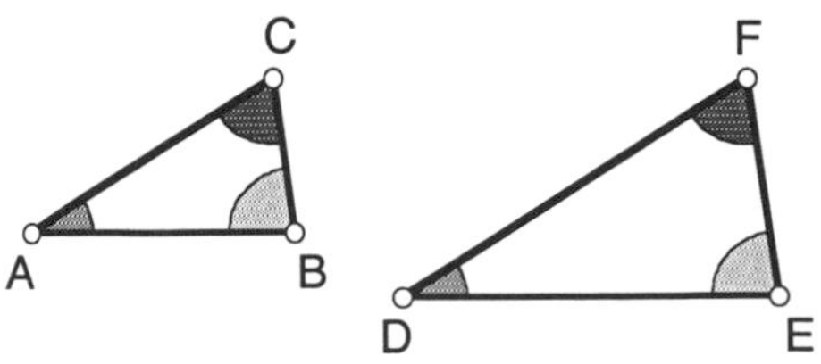

Properties of Isosceles Triangles (page 69)

Prerequisites: This activity introduces the terms *isosceles* and *base angles*.

Sketchpad Proficiency: Beginner

Activity Time: 15–30 minutes

Example Sketch: Isosceles.gsp

Sketch and Investigate

Q1 Two sides of the triangle are radii of the same circle. This guarantees that two sides of the triangle are always congruent. Therefore, the triangle is always isosceles.

Q2 The base angles of an isosceles triangle have equal measure. The vertex angle usually has a different measure.

Explore More

1. Students should find that a triangle with congruent base angles is isosceles, although the measures may be slightly off depending on the precision. (Students can change Angle Precision on the Units panel of **Preferences**, in the Edit menu.)
2. Students should find that a triangle is equilateral if and only if the triangle is equiangular. For directions on constructing an equilateral triangle, see the activity Euclid's Proposition 1—An Equilateral Triangle, in Chapter 1. To construct an equiangular triangle, students can rotate a segment around one of its endpoints by 60° using the Transform menu.

© 2002 Key Curriculum Press

Constructing Isosceles Triangles (page 70)

Prerequisites: Students need to know what an *isosceles triangle* is and should know some of its properties. In the preceding activity, Properties of Isosceles Triangles, students learn one of the methods described below.

Sketchpad Proficiency: Beginner/Intermediate/Advanced, depending on how many different construction methods you expect from students and how many hints you are willing to give them.

Activity Time: 15–50 minutes

Example Sketch: **Isosceles Tools.gsp**. This sketch contains the custom tools **Isosceles 1–4**, which perform the four constructions listed below.

The more time you give students, the more methods they will come up with. Have students drag vertices of their figures to make sure their constructions are correct. Isosceles triangles that fall apart and can turn into other shapes are underconstrained. A construction that stays an isosceles triangle but that can't take on all possible shapes of an isosceles triangle is overconstrained. Here are various methods for constructing an isosceles triangle that is neither overconstrained nor underconstrained.

Method: Construct a circle *AB* and radii *AB* and *AC*. Construct $\overline{BC}$.
Property: An isosceles triangle has two equal sides.

Method: Construct a line *AB* and a point *C* not on the line. Reflect point *C* across the line. Triangle *ACC'* is isosceles.
Property: An isosceles triangle has reflection symmetry.

Method: Construct $\overline{AB}$ and its midpoint *C*. Construct a perpendicular through point *C*. Construct point *D* on the perpendicular. Triangle *ABD* is isosceles.
Property: The perpendicular bisector of the base of an isosceles triangle passes through the vertex of the vertex angle.

Method: Construct $\overrightarrow{AB}$ and $\overrightarrow{AC}$. Construct the angle bisector of $\angle BAC$. Construct point *D* on the angle bisector and a line through point *D* perpendicular to the angle bisector. Construct the points of intersection *E* and *F* of this line with $\overrightarrow{AB}$ and $\overrightarrow{AC}$. Triangle *AEF* is isosceles.
Property: The angle bisector of the vertex angle of an isosceles triangle is perpendicular to the base.

Method: Construct $\overline{AB}$, $\overrightarrow{BA}$, and $\overrightarrow{AC}$. Select points *C*, *A*, and *B* and, in the Transform menu, choose **Mark Angle**. Mark point *B* as a center. Rotate $\overrightarrow{BA}$ by the marked angle. Construct the point of intersection, *D*, of this ray and $\overrightarrow{AC}$. Triangle *ABD* is isosceles.
Property: The base angles of an isosceles triangle are equal in measure.

© 2002 Key Curriculum Press

Medians in a Triangle (page 71)

Prerequisites: Students should know, or be introduced to, the terms *midpoint* and *median*. It would be helpful for students to know how to classify triangles.

Sketchpad Proficiency: Beginner/Intermediate

Activity Time: 30–40 minutes

Example Sketch: **Medians.gsp.** This sketch contains the custom tool **Centroid**, which constructs the centroid of a triangle given three points (the vertices).

Demonstration Sketch: Triangle Points.gsp

Sketch and Investigate

Q1 The third median intersects the other two at their point of intersection. The three medians are concurrent.

Q2 Students could record either one of the calculations below.

$$\frac{BCe}{CeF} = 2.000 \qquad \frac{CeF}{BCe} = 0.500$$

Q3 The centroid divides each median into two parts. One part is twice the length of the other.

Q4 The slope of the line is 1/2 (or 2, depending on which way students build their tables). This represents the ratio between the lengths of the segments the centroid creates on a median.

Explore More

1. For tips on making and using custom tools, see the appropriate sections in the help system. (Choose **Toolbox** from the Help menu, then click on the Custom Tools link.) This custom tool will be especially useful in the activity The Euler Segment, later in this chapter. A sample centroid tool is included in the sketch **Triangle Centers.gsp**.

Perpendicular Bisectors in a Triangle (page 73)

Prerequisites: Students should know the term *perpendicular bisector*. It would be helpful for students to know how to classify triangles.

Sketchpad Proficiency: Beginner

Activity Time: 20–30 minutes

Example Sketch: **Perp Bisectors.gsp.** This sketch contains the custom tool **Circumcenter**, which constructs the circumcenter and circumcircle of a triangle given three points (the vertices).

Demonstration Sketch: Triangle Points.gsp

Sketch and Investigate

Q1 The third perpendicular bisector intersects the other two at their point of intersection. The three perpendicular bisectors are concurrent.

Q2 Point G is outside the triangle when the triangle is obtuse. Point G is inside the triangle when the triangle is acute.

Q3 When point G is on the triangle, the triangle is right. Point G lies on the midpoint of the hypotenuse.

Q4 The distances are the same from the circumcenter to each vertex.

Explore More

1. For tips on making and using custom tools, see the appropriate sections in the help system. (Choose **Toolbox** from the Help menu, then click on the Custom Tools link.) This custom tool will be especially useful in the activity The Euler Segment, later in this chapter. A sample circumcenter tool is included in the sketch **Triangle Centers.gsp**.
2. The circumcenter is equidistant from vertices A and B because it lies on the perpendicular bisector of $\overline{AB}$. It is equidistant from vertices B and C because it lies on the perpendicular bisector of $\overline{BC}$. Therefore (using the transitive property), it is equidistant from A and B and C.
3. If students try to circumscribe quadrilaterals, they will discover that, unlike triangles, not all quadrilaterals can be circumscribed. Those that can be circumscribed are called *cyclic quadrilaterals*. Students can inscribe a quadrilateral in a circle and look for properties of cyclic quadrilaterals. One property is that opposite angles are supplementary. Other polygons are cyclic when their perpendicular bisectors are concurrent.

© 2002 Key Curriculum Press

Altitudes in a Triangle (page 75)

Prerequisites: Students should know the terms *perpendicular, acute,* and *obtuse*. The activity introduces the term *altitude*.

Sketchpad Proficiency: Intermediate

Activity Time: 30–50 minutes for the entire activity. If you have less time, you can provide a basic introduction to altitude by stopping after Q2 (about 15 minutes); or stop after Q3 (25–30 minutes), where students get a sense of the concurrency of altitudes.

Example Sketch: Altitudes.gsp. This sketch contains the custom tools **Altitude** and **Orthocenter**, which construct the altitudes and orthocenter of a triangle given three points (the vertices).

Demonstration Sketch: Triangle Points.gsp

Sketch and Investigate

Q1 If an altitude falls outside the triangle, the triangle is obtuse.

Q2 When $\angle A$ is right, altitude BD lies on side BA.

Note: An altitude tool is provided on the accompanying disk. For tips on making and using custom tools, see the appropriate sections in the help system. (Choose **Toolbox** from the Help menu, then click on the Custom Tools link.)

Q3 When the triangle is acute, the three altitudes intersect at the same point inside the triangle.

Q4 When the triangle is obtuse, two altitudes fall outside the triangle and the third falls inside.

Q5 All three lines containing the altitudes always intersect at the orthocenter of the triangle. The orthocenter lies inside an acute triangle and outside an obtuse triangle.

Explore More

1. For tips on making and using custom tools, see the appropriate sections in the help system. (Choose **Toolbox** from the Help menu, then click on the Custom Tools link.) This custom tool will be especially useful in the activity The Euler Segment, later in this chapter. A sample orthocenter tool is included in the sketch **Triangle Centers.gsp**.
2. Each point is the orthocenter of the other three. In other words, if point D is the orthocenter of $\triangle ABC$, then point C is the orthocenter of $\triangle ABD$, point B is the orthocenter of $\triangle ACD$, and point A is the orthocenter of $\triangle BCD$.
3. Students should calculate $(1/2)bh$ for each of the three bases and corresponding altitudes.

Angle Bisectors in a Triangle (page 77)

Prerequisites: Students should know, or be introduced to, the term *angle bisector*.

Sketchpad Proficiency: Beginner

Activity Time: 20–30 minutes

Example Sketch: Angle Bisectors.gsp. This sketch contains the custom tool **Incenter**, which constructs the incenter and incircle of a triangle given three points (the vertices).

Demonstration Sketch: Triangle Points.gsp

Sketch and Investigate

Q1 The third angle bisector intersects the other angle bisectors at their point of intersection.

Q2 The distance from the incenter to each of the three sides of a triangle is the same.

Explore More

1. In the figure below, point D is the incenter. Line DE is perpendicular to $\overline{AC}$. Point E is the radius point of the circle. If students don't construct a point such as point E to anchor the circle, their sketches will fall apart when dragged.

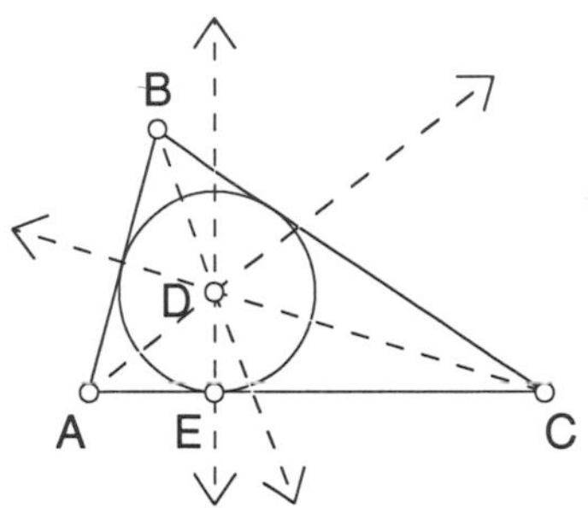

2. For tips on making and using custom tools, see the appropriate sections in the help system. (Choose **Toolbox** from the Help menu, then click on the Custom Tools link.) This custom tool will be especially useful in the activity The Euler Segment, later in this chapter.
3. Any point on an angle bisector is equidistant from two sides of the angle being bisected. The incenter is on all three angle bisectors, so it is equidistant from all three sides of the triangle. Thus, a circle whose radius is this distance will just touch the three sides.
4. You can inscribe a circle in any quadrilateral with concurrent angle bisectors. This type of quadrilateral includes rhombuses and kites, but not most rectangles or parallelograms.

   In general, a polygon must have concurrent angle bisectors in order to have an inscribed circle.

© 2002 Key Curriculum Press

The Euler Segment (page 78)

Prerequisites: Students should know the names of the different triangle centers: *incenter, circumcenter, orthocenter,* and *centroid.* This activity introduces them to the *Euler segment.*

Sketchpad Proficiency: Intermediate/Advanced. Students will be using custom tools.

Activity Time: 30–45 minutes

Required Sketch: Triangle Centers.gsp

Sketch and Investigate

Q1 The orthocenter, the centroid, and the circumcenter are always collinear.

Q2 Here are some of the observations students could make: In an equilateral triangle, all four points are coincident. In an isosceles triangle, all four points are collinear and lie along the median to the vertex angle. In an acute triangle, all four points lie inside the triangle. In an obtuse triangle, the circumcenter and orthocenter lie outside the triangle. In a right triangle, the orthocenter lies on the vertex of the right angle, and the circumcenter lies on the midpoint of the hypotenuse.

Q3 The circumcenter and the orthocenter are the endpoints of the Euler segment. The centroid lies between them.

Q4 The distance from the orthocenter to the centroid is twice the distance from the centroid to the circumcenter.

Explore More

1. Three of the points are the midpoints of the sides of the original triangle. Three other points are the points where the altitudes intersect the opposite sides of the triangle (the *feet* of the altitudes). The last three points are the midpoints of the segments connecting the orthocenter with each vertex.
2. In an equilateral triangle, three pairs of points coincide, reducing the nine points to six. In a right triangle, three points coincide at the right angle vertex, and a pair of points coincide at each of two side midpoints, so the nine points are reduced to five. In an isosceles right triangle, the foot of the third altitude coincides with the midpoint of a side, so the five points in a right triangle are reduced to four.

Excircles of a Triangle (page 80)

Prerequisites: Students should understand the terms *inscribed circle, angle bisector, incenter, tangent, interior angle,* and *exterior angle* of a triangle.

Sketchpad Proficiency: Beginner

Activity Time: 15–30 minutes

Required Sketch: Excircles.gsp

Sketch and Investigate

Q1 The incircle is inscribed in the triangle. This means it is always tangent to all three sides.

Q2 Each excircle is always tangent to one side and also tangent to lines that extend the other two sides.

Q3 The center of the circle inscribed in an angle must lie on the angle bisector. The complete construction is shown below. $\overline{BF}$ is constructed to be perpendicular to the side of the circle, and point F is on the angle bisector.

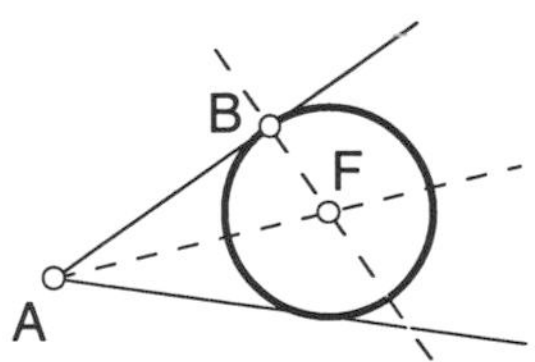

Q4 The ray is an angle bisector. In Q3, students discovered that the center of the circle inscribed in an angle must lie on the angle bisector.

Q5 Students should have constructed nine rays. Each ray has its first control point at a triangle vertex and its second control point at the center of an excircle. Below are some conjectures they might make about the sketch:

The angle bisectors of the interior angles in a triangle intersect at the center of the inscribed circle (also called the incenter).

Each angle bisector of an interior angle of a triangle intersects the center of an excircle.

Each angle bisector of an exterior angle of a triangle intersects the center of an excircle.

Just as the center of the incircle is the intersection of three angle bisectors, so is the center of each excircle. In the case of an excircle, two of the angle bisectors bisect exterior angles.

The centers of any two excircles are collinear with a vertex of the triangle.

© 2002 Key Curriculum Press

The four circles have a lot in common: The three excircles are inscribed in three-sided regions that have infinite area (open regions) and the incircle is inscribed in a three-sided region that is closed and has finite area. (*Note:* If the same construction were made on a sphere, all four regions would be closed and finite.)

The Surfer and the Spotter (page 82)

Prerequisites: Students should know the term *equilateral triangle* and know how to construct one with Sketchpad (or at least know how to use a custom tool to construct one).

Sketchpad Proficiency: Intermediate/Advanced

Activity Time: 25–45 minutes

Example Sketch: **Surfer_Spotter.gsp**

Sketch and Investigate

Q1 Spencer's hut (point *D*) is best located in the center of the island (this center point is at once the incenter, the circumcenter, the orthocenter, and the centroid of the equilateral triangle). The center point minimizes the sum of the distances to the three vertices.

Sarah's hut (point *E*) can be located anywhere on the island, because every location has the same sum of distances to all three beaches. This may seem surprising, but it can be confirmed by dragging. As point *E* approaches any vertex, the three paths converge into a single path that is an altitude in the triangle. The sum of the lengths of the three paths is equal to the length of an altitude, regardless of where point *E* is located.

© 2002 Key Curriculum Press

Morley's Theorem (page 83)

Prerequisites: Students should understand the idea of *trisecting an angle*. They also need to be able to identify an *equilateral triangle*.

Sketchpad Proficiency: Advanced

Activity Time: 25–40 minutes

Example Sketch: **Morley's Theorem.gsp**

Sketch and Investigate

Q1 The intersections of the adjacent angle trisectors in any triangle are the vertices of an equilateral triangle. (This conjecture is difficult to word. Students might find it easier to explain the conjecture with the help of a diagram.)

Explore More

1. The three triangles surrounding the equilateral triangle are all isosceles. There are numerous angle relationships that students may discover. These undoubtedly play a role in the proof. You might ask students to try to prove the theorem, but the proof is beyond the scope of this book (that is, at the moment it's beyond the author, who's working under a deadline!).
2. Rays from the original triangle's vertices through the opposite vertices of the equilateral triangle are concurrent. Students may expect them to be angle bisectors, but they're not.
3. Trisectors of one set of exterior angles intersect to form a hexagon. One set of alternating vertices of this hexagon includes the vertices of the original triangle. The other set forms an equilateral triangle.

See Coxeter and Greitzer, *Geometry Revisited*, for more on Morley's theorem.

Napoleon's Theorem (page 85)

Prerequisites: Students should know the terms *equilateral triangle*, *midpoint*, *median*, and *centroid*.

Sketchpad Proficiency: Advanced. This is not a very difficult construction, but is rated for the advanced user because it suggests using a custom tool. This investigation is a good way to introduce using custom tools to speed up a construction.

Activity Time: 30–45 minutes

Example Sketch: **Napoleon's Theorem.gsp**

Sketch and Investigate

One method of constructing an equilateral triangle is described in the activity Euclid's Proposition—An Equilateral Triangle, in Chapter 1. A sample equilateral triangle custom tool is included in the sketch **Polygons.gsp**. For tips on making and using custom tools, see the appropriate sections in the help system. (Choose **Toolbox** from the Help menu, then click on the Custom Tools link.)

Q1 Segments joining the centroids of equilateral triangles constructed on the sides of any triangle form another equilateral triangle.

Explore More

1. The segments that each connect a vertex of the original triangle with the most remote vertex of the equilateral triangle on the opposite side are all congruent.
2. The difference between the areas of the inner and outer Napoleon triangles equals the area of the original triangle.
3. *An Introduction to the History of Mathematics*, by Howard Eves, makes some interesting references to Napoleon and his interest in math and mathematicians. H. S. M. Coxeter, in *Geometry Revisited*, recounts that Laplace once told Napoleon, "General, the last thing we need from you is a geometry lesson."

© 2002 Key Curriculum Press

Defining Special Quadrilaterals (page 89)

Prerequisites: None. You could use this activity as a review of the terms *kite, trapezoid, parallelogram, square, rhombus,* and *rectangle*. But this could also serve as an introduction to these terms.

Sketchpad Proficiency: Absolute beginner

Activity Time: 25–45 minutes

Required Sketches: Special Quads.gsp

Sketch and Investigate

Q1 A trapezoid is a quadrilateral with (at least/exactly) one pair of parallel sides. *Note:* Some geometry texts say *at least* and some say *exactly*. Since you can drag the trapezoid in the sketch to form a parallelogram, the "at least" definition might be appropriate here. Discuss the differences between these definitions.

Q2 A kite is a quadrilateral with (at least/exactly) two pairs of congruent, adjacent sides. *Note:* Some geometry texts say *at least* and some say *exactly*. Since you can drag the kite in the sketch to form a rhombus, the "at least" definition might be more appropriate here. Discuss the differences between these definitions.

Q3 A parallelogram is a quadrilateral with two pairs of opposite sides parallel.

Q4 A rectangle is a quadrilateral with four right angles.

Q5 A rhombus is a quadrilateral with four equal sides.

Q6 A square is a quadrilateral with equal sides and equal angles.

Q7 A square

Q8 A square

Q9 A square is a quadrilateral that is both a rhombus and a rectangle.

Q10 a. sometimes; b. sometimes; c. always; d. always; e. never

Explore More

1. The Activity Notes of the following activities in Chapter 4 describe ways of constructing these different parallelograms: Constructing Parallelograms, Constructing Rectangles, Constructing Rhombuses, and Constructing Isosceles Trapezoids.

Properties of Parallelograms (page 91)

Prerequisites: Students should know the definition of a *parallelogram*.

Sketchpad Proficiency: Beginner

Activity Time: 25–40 minutes

Example Sketch: Parallelogram.gsp

Sketch and Investigate

Q1 Opposite sides in a parallelogram are equal in length.
Opposite angles in a parallelogram are equal in measure.
Consecutive angles in a parallelogram are supplementary.

Q2 Diagonals in a parallelogram bisect each other. Students might also notice that the diagonals in a parallelogram divide the parallelogram into four pairs of congruent triangles.

Explore More

1. A parallelogram does not have reflection symmetry unless it is also a rhombus or a rectangle. A parallelogram does always have 180° rotation symmetry around the intersection of its diagonals.
2. See the Activity Notes for the next activity, Constructing Parallelograms, for descriptions of some construction methods.

© 2002 Key Curriculum Press

Constructing Parallelograms (page 92)

Prerequisites: Students should be familiar with the definition of a parallelogram and also with various properties of a parallelogram.

Sketchpad Proficiency: Beginner/Intermediate/Advanced. The more advanced the user, the more construction methods that user will discover.

Activity Time: 20–45 minutes (depends entirely on how long you choose to set students loose)

Example Sketch: **Parallelogram Tools.gsp**. This sketch contains the custom tools **Parallelogram 1–6**, which perform the six constructions listed below.

The more time you give students, the more methods they'll come up with. Have students drag vertices of their figures to make sure their constructions are correct. Parallelograms that fall apart and can turn into other shapes are underconstrained. Constructions that remain parallelograms but that can't take on all the shapes of a parallelogram are overconstrained. Here are various methods for constructing a parallelogram that is neither overconstrained nor underconstrained.

Method: Construct segments *AB* and *AC*. Construct a line through point *B* parallel to $\overline{AC}$ and a line through point *C* parallel to $\overline{AB}$. Construct the intersection of these lines, then hide the lines. Construct the missing segments. (This method is described in more detail in the student pages of the previous activity, Properties of a Parallelogram.)
Properties: This uses the definition of a parallelogram, which states that opposite sides are parallel.

Method: Construct a triangle. Construct the midpoint of one of its sides. Mark the midpoint as a center of rotation and rotate the triangle about this point by 180°.
Properties: A parallelogram has rotational symmetry about the midpoints of its diagonals. Also, this uses the property that a parallelogram consists of two congruent triangles, separated by a diagonal.

Method: Construct a segment and a point not on the segment. Mark the endpoints of the segment as a vector. Translate the point not on the segment by the marked vector. Construct the missing sides.
Properties: A parallelogram has one pair of opposite sides that are both parallel and congruent.

Method: Construct a segment and a point not on the segment. Select the segment and the point and, in the Construct menu, choose **Circle By Center+Radius**. Construct a line through the point, parallel to the segment. Find the point where the circle and the line intersect. This is the fourth vertex of the parallelogram.
Properties: A parallelogram has one pair of opposite sides that are both parallel and congruent.

Method: Construct a segment and its midpoint. Construct a line through the segment attached at the midpoint. Construct a circle centered at the midpoint. Find the two points where the circle intersects the line. These two points and the original endpoints of the segment are the vertices of the parallelogram.
Properties: The diagonals of a parallelogram bisect each other.

Method: Construct a pair of concentric circles. Construct two lines that both contain the center point. Find the two points of intersection of one of the lines with one of the circles, and of the other line with the other circle. These four points are the points of intersection of the parallelogram.
Properties: The diagonals of a parallelogram bisect each other.

© 2002 Key Curriculum Press

Properties of Rectangles (page 93)

Prerequisites: Students should know the definition of *rectangle.*

Sketchpad Proficiency: Beginner

Activity Time: 25–40 minutes

Example Sketch: Rectangle.gsp

Sketch and Investigate

Q1 Opposite sides of a rectangle are congruent.

Q2 Diagonals in a rectangle are congruent and bisect each other.
The diagonals in a rectangle divide the rectangle into two pairs of congruent isosceles triangles.

Explore More

1. Rectangles have all the properties of parallelograms; they also have congruent diagonals.
2. A rectangle has 180° rotation symmetry about the intersection of its diagonals and two lines of reflection symmetry through midpoints of opposite sides. A rectangle that is also a square has additional symmetries.
3. See the Activity Notes for the next activity, Constructing Rectangles, for various construction methods that use different properties.

Constructing Rectangles (page 94)

Prerequisites: Students should be familiar with the definition of *rectangle* and also with various properties of a rectangle.

Sketchpad Proficiency: Beginner/Intermediate/Advanced. The more advanced the user, the more construction methods that user will discover.

Activity Time: 20–45 minutes (depends entirely on how long you choose to set students loose)

Example Sketch: Rectangle.gsp. This sketch contains the custom tools **Rectangle 1–6**, which perform the six constructions listed below.

The more time you give students, the more methods they'll come up with. Have students drag vertices of their figures to make sure their constructions are correct. Rectangles that fall apart and can turn into other shapes are underconstrained. Constructions that remain rectangles but that can't take on all the shapes of a rectangle are overconstrained. Here are various methods for constructing a rectangle that is neither overconstrained nor underconstrained.

Method: Construct a segment. Construct perpendicular lines through the endpoints. From a point on one of the perpendiculars, construct a perpendicular line (or a line parallel to the original segment).
Properties: A rectangle is a quadrilateral with four right angles.

Method: Construct a segment AB. Construct a line through point A, perpendicular to $\overline{AB}$. Construct $\overline{AC}$ on this line. Construct a circle with center C and radius AB. Construct a circle with center B and radius AC. Construct $\overline{BD}$ and $\overline{CD}$, where D is the intersection of the circles.
Properties: A rectangle has at least one right angle and the opposite sides are congruent.

Method: Construct a segment AB and its midpoint, C. Construct circle CA. Construct ray $\overrightarrow{DC}$, where point D is on the circle. Construct point E, the intersection of the ray and the circle. Construct $\overline{AD}$, $\overline{DB}$, $\overline{DE}$, and $\overline{EA}$.
Properties: The diagonals of a rectangle are equal and bisect each other.

Continued on next page.

© 2002 Key Curriculum Press

Constructing Rectangles

Continued from previous page.

Method: Construct a segment AB and its midpoint C. Construct a line through point C, perpendicular to $\overline{AB}$. Construct circle CD, where point D is on the perpendicular line. Construct point E, the other intersection of the circle with the line. Construct lines through points D and E, perpendicular to $\overline{DE}$ (or parallel to $\overline{AB}$). Construct lines through points A and B, perpendicular to $\overline{AB}$ (or parallel to $\overline{DE}$).
Properties: The segments connecting midpoints of opposite sides of a rectangle bisect each other and are perpendicular to the sides of the rectangle. A rectangle has two perpendicular lines of symmetry.

Method: Construct a segment AB. Construct a line perpendicular to $\overline{AB}$, through point A. Construct $\overline{AC}$ on this line. Construct $\overline{CB}$ and point D, the midpoint of $\overline{CB}$. Rotate A, $\overline{AB}$, and $\overline{AC}$ 180° about point D.
Properties: A rectangle has at least one right angle and has 180° rotation symmetry.

Method: Construct two perpendicular lines. Construct a point not on either line. Reflect it across one of the lines. Now reflect the two points across the other line.
Properties: A rectangle has two perpendicular lines of symmetry.

Different methods are interesting because they yield different control points for manipulating the rectangle. The most efficient custom tool can be made for the last method, although that tool has three givens. Each of these methods has a corresponding example custom tool.

Properties of Rhombuses (page 95)

Prerequisites: Students should know the definition of a *rhombus*.

Sketchpad Proficiency: Beginner

Activity Time: 25–40 minutes

Example Sketch: **Rhombus.gsp**

Sketch and Investigate

Q1 Opposite sides of a rhombus are parallel. (A rhombus is a parallelogram.)
Opposite angles of a rhombus are equal and consecutive angles are supplementary.

Q2 The diagonals of a rhombus are perpendicular bisectors of each other.
The diagonals of a rhombus bisect the angles.
The diagonals of a rhombus are lines of reflection symmetry.

Explore More

1. Answers will vary. Students should point out that rhombuses have all the properties of an ordinary parallelogram in addition to their own special properties, listed in Q1 and Q2 above.
2. A rhombus has 180° rotation symmetry. It has two axes of reflection symmetry, one along each diagonal.
3. For methods of constructing rhombuses, see the Activity Notes that follow for the activity Constructing Rhombuses.

© 2002 Key Curriculum Press

Constructing Rhombuses (page 96)

Prerequisites: Students should be familiar with the definition of a rhombus and also familiar with various properties of a rhombus.

Sketchpad Proficiency: Beginner/Intermediate/Advanced. The more advanced the user, the more construction methods that user will discover.

Activity Time: 20–45 minutes (depends entirely on how long you choose to set students loose)

Example Sketch: **Rhombus.gsp**. This sketch contains the custom tools **Rhombus 1–8**, which perform the eight constructions listed below.

The more time you give students, the more methods they'll come up with. Have students drag vertices of their figures to make sure their constructions are correct. Rhombuses that fall apart and can turn into other shapes are underconstrained. Constructions that remain rhombuses but that can't take on all the shapes of a rhombus are overconstrained. Here are various methods for constructing a rhombus. The first is a popular one that is overconstrained. The rest are neither overconstrained nor underconstrained.

Method: Construct circles *AB* and *BA*. Construct a rhombus connecting the centers and the two points of intersection of the circles. (This is a special rhombus, composed of two equilateral triangles.)
Properties: A rhombus has four equal sides.

Method: Construct circles *AB* and *BA*. Construct circle *CA*, where point *C* is a point on circle *AB*. Construct point *D* at the point of intersection of circles *BA* and *CA*. *ABDC* is a rhombus.
Properties: A rhombus has four equal sides.

Method: Construct a circle *AB* and two radii. Construct a parallel to each radius through the endpoint of the other.
Properties: A rhombus has equal consecutive sides and parallel opposite sides.

Method: Construct a segment *AB* and its midpoint *C*. Construct a line through point *C*, perpendicular to $\overline{AB}$. Construct circle *CD*, where point *D* is on the perpendicular line. Construct point *E*, the other intersection of the circle with the line. *ADBE* is a rhombus.
Properties: The diagonals of a rhombus bisect each other.

Method: Construct a circle *AB* and then $\overline{BC}$, where point *C* is on the circle. Reflect point *A* across $\overline{BC}$. *ABA′C* is a rhombus.
Properties: A rhombus has a pair of equal consecutive sides and a line of symmetry through their unshared endpoints.

Method: Construct a segment *AB* (to be a diagonal) and its midpoint, *C*. Construct a perpendicular through point *C*. Construct point *D* on the perpendicular. Reflect point *D* across $\overline{AB}$. *ADBD′* is a rhombus.
Properties: The diagonals of a rhombus are perpendicular and are axes of reflection symmetry.

Method: Construct a segment *AB* to serve as half a diagonal. Construct a perpendicular through point *B*. Construct point *C* on the perpendicular. Rotate points *A* and *C* 180° about point *B*. *ACA′C′* is a rhombus.
Properties: The diagonals of a rhombus are perpendicular and their point of intersection is a center of 180° rotation symmetry.

Method: Construct a circle *AB* and point *C* on the circle. Bisect angle *BAC*. Construct circle *BA* and point *D*, the intersection of this circle and the bisector. *ABDC* is a rhombus.
Properties: The sides of a rhombus are equal and the diagonals bisect the angles.

Each of these methods has a corresponding example custom tool.

© 2002 Key Curriculum Press

Properties of Isosceles Trapezoids (page 97)

Prerequisites: This activity introduces the term *trapezoid*. Students should know the term *isosceles*.

Sketchpad Proficiency: Intermediate

Activity Time: 25–35 minutes

Example Sketch: Isosceles Trapezoid.gsp

Sketch and Investigate

Q1 An isosceles trapezoid has one line of reflection symmetry. This line connects the midpoints of the two bases.

Q2 Both pairs of base angles of an isosceles trapezoid are congruent.

Q3 Pairs of angles in an isosceles trapezoid that do not share a base are supplementary. (Have students sum such a pair with Sketchpad's Calculator in order to see this more clearly.)

Q4 The diagonals of an isosceles trapezoid are equal in length.

Explore More

1. It's possible to drag this shape so that it's a rectangle. By the definition at the beginning of the activity, the rectangle is no longer an isosceles trapezoid. You may want to discuss the merits of a more inclusive definition of a trapezoid: a quadrilateral with *at least* one pair of parallel sides instead of *exactly* one pair. A rectangle has all the properties of an isosceles trapezoid.
2. The only conjecture that applies to nonisosceles trapezoids is that pairs of adjacent angles that do not share a base are supplementary.
3. See the Activity Notes for the following activity, Constructing Isosceles Trapezoids.

Constructing Isosceles Trapezoids (page 99)

Prerequisites: Students should be familiar with the definition of an isosceles trapezoid and also familiar with various properties of an isosceles trapezoid.

Sketchpad Proficiency: Beginner/Intermediate/Advanced. The more advanced the user, the more construction methods that user will discover.

Activity Time: 20–45 minutes (depends entirely on how long you choose to set students loose)

Example Sketch: Iso Trapezoid.gsp. This sketch contains the custom tools **Iso Trapezoid 1–6**, which perform the four constructions listed below, plus two bonus constructions.

The more time you give students, the more methods they'll come up with. This is probably the hardest of the special quadrilaterals to construct. Have students drag vertices of their figures to make sure their constructions are correct. Isosceles trapezoids that fall apart and can turn into other shapes are underconstrained. Isosceles trapezoids whose angles won't change are overconstrained. Here are various methods for constructing an isosceles trapezoid that is neither overconstrained nor underconstrained.

Method: Construct $\overline{AB}$ and $\overline{AC}$. Construct a line through point B parallel to $\overline{AC}$. Construct a circle with center C and radius AB. Find the point where the circle intersects the parallel line. This point is the fourth vertex of the trapezoid. (*Note:* Depending on how points are arranged, this construction may also be self-intersecting or be a parallelogram.)
Properties: An isosceles trapezoid has one pair of opposite sides that are equal and one pair that are parallel.

Method: Construct a horizontal line AB. Construct a ray AC using A as the endpoint. Mark angle CAB using the Transform menu. Mark point B as a center of rotation. Rotate line AB about point B by the marked angle. Construct a line through C parallel to line AB. Construct the intersection of this parallel line with the rotated line. This is the fourth vertex of the trapezoid. Hide all the lines and rays and connect the vertices with segments.
Properties: An isosceles trapezoid has one pair of opposite sides that are parallel and has congruent base angles.

© 2002 Key Curriculum Press

Method: Construct a triangle *ABC*. Construct a line parallel to side *AB* through point *C*. Select point *A* and side *BC* and choose **Circle by Center+Radius.** Construct the point of intersection *D* of the circle and the parallel line. Hide the circle, the line, and segment *BC*. Construct the missing sides.
Properties: An isosceles trapezoid has one pair of opposite sides that are parallel and has congruent diagonals.

Method: Construct a circle *AB*. Construct a segment *AB*. Construct another radial segment *AC*. Construct segment *CB*. Construct *D*, a point on segment *AB*. Construct a line through *D* parallel to segment *CB*. Construct *E*, the point of intersection of segment *AC* and the parallel line. Hide parts of the construction that are not sides of the trapezoid, then construct the remaining sides of *DECB*.
Properties: An isosceles trapezoid has one pair of opposite sides that are parallel and one pair that are congruent.

Midsegments of a Trapezoid and a Triangle (page 100)

Prerequisites: Students should know the terms *midsegment, trapezoid, base*, and *legs*. (Many books refer to the midsegment of a trapezoid as a median and refer to midsegments of a triangle as midlines. Both these terms cause confusion that can easily be avoided by using the term *midsegment*.)

Sketchpad Proficiency: Intermediate

Activity Time: 30–45 minutes

Example Sketch: **Midsegments.gsp**

Sketch and Investigate

Q1 *EF* equals the average of *AB* and *CD*.

Q2 The midsegment of a trapezoid is parallel to the bases. Its length is the average of the lengths of the bases.

Q3 The midsegment of a triangle is parallel to the third side and is half its length.

Explore More

1. Students should discover $A = mh$, where *A* is the area, *m* is the length of the midsegment, and *h* is the height perpendicular to the midsegment. This formula is nice and general and works for both a triangle and a trapezoid.
2. Students should find that the length of $\overline{A'C'}$ is one-third the length of $\overline{AC}$. The segments are parallel to each other. In general, if you dilate points *A* and *C* by a scale factor of *k*, then $A'C' = k(AC)$, and the segments are parallel.
3. The four smaller triangles are similar to the original triangle and congruent to one another. Each has side lengths one-half the original triangle's side lengths and each has area one-fourth the original.
4. Successive triangles get smaller and smaller, but each smaller triangle is still similar to the original.

© 2002 Key Curriculum Press

Midpoint Quadrilaterals (page 102)

Prerequisites: To make conjectures, students should be able to identify *parallelograms* and other special quadrilaterals. To explain their conjectures, students need to know that the segment connecting the midpoints of two sides of a triangle (the *midsegment*) is parallel to the third side and half as long.

Sketchpad Proficiency: Beginner

Activity Time: 25–40 minutes

Example Sketch: **Midpoint Quadrilateral.gsp**

Sketch and Investigate

Q1 The quadrilateral whose sides connect the midpoints of any quadrilateral is a parallelogram. The measurements support this conjecture because they show that the opposite sides of the midpoint quadrilateral are equal in length and that opposite sides have equal slope (and therefore are parallel).

Q2 A diagonal divides the quadrilateral into two triangles. Two sides of the midpoint quadrilateral are midsegments of these triangles. This means they are both parallel to the diagonal and half as long. If one pair of opposite sides of a quadrilateral are both equal in length and parallel, the quadrilateral is a parallelogram. (Students might construct the other diagonal and use a second pair of triangles to show that the other pair of sides of the midpoint quadrilateral are also equal in length and parallel.)

Explore More

1. A midpoint quadrilateral of a midpoint quadrilateral is still just a parallelogram. Successive midpoint quadrilaterals are alternately similar; that is, the third midpoint quadrilateral is a parallelogram similar to the first, the fourth is similar to the second, and so on. These parallelograms converge on the point of intersection of segments connecting midpoints of opposite sides.
2. The area of the midpoint quadrilateral is half the area of the original quadrilateral. (As an extra challenge, ask students to prove this is true.)
3. The conditions under which a midpoint quadrilateral is a special parallelogram are not obvious. In general, the midpoint quadrilateral of a trapezoid is a parallelogram, that of an isosceles trapezoid is a rectangle, that of a parallelogram is a parallelogram, that of a kite is a rectangle, that of a rhombus is a rectangle, that of a rectangle is a rhombus, and that of a square is a square. See the next activity, Special Midpoint Quadrilaterals, for more discussion.
4. The example sketch **Special Midpoint Quads.gsp** illustrates the most general quadrilaterals whose midpoint quadrilaterals are special parallelograms. This sketch is the subject of the next activity, Special Midpoint Quadrilaterals. The midpoint quadrilateral of any quadrilateral whose diagonals are equal is a rhombus. The midpoint quadrilateral of any quadrilateral whose diagonals are perpendicular is a rectangle. The midpoint quadrilateral of any quadrilateral whose diagonals are equal and perpendicular is a square.

© 2002 Key Curriculum Press

Special Midpoint Quadrilaterals (page 103)

Prerequisites: Students need to know properties of special quadrilaterals such as isosceles trapezoids, rhombuses, rectangles, and squares. It would be helpful for students to know that a midsegment of a triangle is parallel to and half the length of the corresponding base. This knowledge is necessary to answer Explore More 1.

Sketchpad Proficiency: Beginner

Activity Time: 15–30 minutes

Required Sketch: Special Midpoint Quads.gsp

Sketch and Investigate

The *Show Hint* action button reveals the diagonals of the quadrilaterals. It is the relationships between the diagonals in each quadrilateral that determine the properties of the midpoint quadrilateral.

Q1 a. A quadrilateral whose midpoint quadrilateral is a rhombus has congruent diagonals.

b. A quadrilateral whose midpoint quadrilateral is a rectangle has perpendicular diagonals.

c. A quadrilateral whose midpoint quadrilateral is a square has congruent and perpendicular diagonals.

Explore More

1. Each diagonal divides the outer quadrilateral into two triangles. The sides of the midpoint quadrilateral are midsegments of the triangles that share a common base (each diagonal). Each of these midsegments has length one-half the length of a common base and are parallel to the common base. If the diagonals are congruent, the four midsegments are congruent and the midpoint quadrilateral is a rhombus. If the diagonals are perpendicular, one pair of midsegments is perpendicular to the other pair and the midpoint quadrilateral is a rectangle. If the diagonals are congruent and perpendicular, the midpoint quadrilateral is a rhombus and a rectangle and is thus a square.
2. The easiest way (if it can be called easy) is to start each of these constructions with the special diagonals. It's also possible to construct a special quadrilateral and then construct an outer quadrilateral around it whose midpoints are the vertices of the special quadrilateral.

Summarizing Properties of Quadrilaterals (page 104)

Prerequisites: This activity works well as a summary, after students are familiar with the definitions and properties of rectangles, rhombuses, squares, parallelograms, kites, and isosceles trapezoids. Students will gain practice using these properties to locate the shapes on the grid. If you run out of computer time during this lesson, have students complete the chart on the second page at home without Sketchpad.

Sketchpad Proficiency: Beginner/Intermediate

Activity Time: 45–60 minutes for all properties of all six shapes

Example Sketch: Quad Summary.gsp

Sketch and Investigate

Q1 and **Q2**

	Rect	Rhm	Sq	P′ grm	Kite	Iso. Trap.
Opp. Sides ≅	Y	Y	Y	Y	N	N
Opposite ∠s ≅	Y	Y	Y	Y	N	N
Consecutive ∠'s sum = 180°	Y	Y	Y	Y	N	N
Diagonals ≅	Y	N	Y	N	N	Y
Diagonals ⊥	N	Y	Y	N	Y	N
Diags. bisect each other	Y	Y	Y	Y	N	N

Q3 Rectangles, rhombuses, and squares are also parallelograms. These shapes have all the properties of parallelograms, in addition to some of their own. Any row in the chart above that has a "Yes" in the parallelogram cell also has a "Yes" in the rectangle, rhombus, and square cells.

Q4 Any property that belongs either to a rectangle or to a rhombus also belongs to a square. Any row in the chart above that shows a "Yes" for a rectangle or a rhombus also shows a "Yes" for a square.

Q5 The answer to this question depends on your definition of *trapezoid.* If you define a trapezoid as having *exactly* one pair of opposite sides that are parallel, a rectangle cannot be a trapezoid. If you define a trapezoid as having *at least* one pair of parallel sides, a rectangle is a special case of an isosceles trapezoid.

© 2002 Key Curriculum Press

Exterior Angles in a Polygon (page 109)

Prerequisites: Students should know (or be introduced to) the terms *exterior angle* and *convex polygon.*

Sketchpad Proficiency: Beginner

Activity Time: 25–40 minutes

Example Sketch: Dilate Polygon.gsp

Demonstration Sketch: Exterior Angles.gsp

Sketch and Investigate

Q1 The sum of the measures of the exterior angles in any convex polygon is 360°. Make sure students try this investigation with other polygons in addition to the pentagon shown in the example. They could actually manipulate their pentagon into a quadrilateral or triangle, making one or more angle measures disappear.

If students print out their polygons with the exterior angles, they can actually cut out the exterior angles and rearrange them around a single point to show that they sum to 360°.

Q2 As you dilate the figure toward any point, the polygon will shrink toward that point, leaving you with only the angles surrounding a common vertex. This has the same visual effect as zooming out from the polygon.

When the polygon appears to be the size of a point, the exterior angles appear as spokes radiating from the point. This provides a visual proof that their sum is 360°, or the total number of degrees in one revolution around a point.

Explore More

1. Interestingly, this same conjecture applies to concave polygons, too, if you consider the "exterior" angles that fall inside the polygon to be negative. To investigate this with Sketchpad, be sure to set Preferences to show angle measures in directed degrees. The figure above demonstrates how selection order determines the sign of an angle measure. If you think in terms of a rotation from one ray to the other, a counter-clockwise rotation is positive and a clockwise rotation is negative.

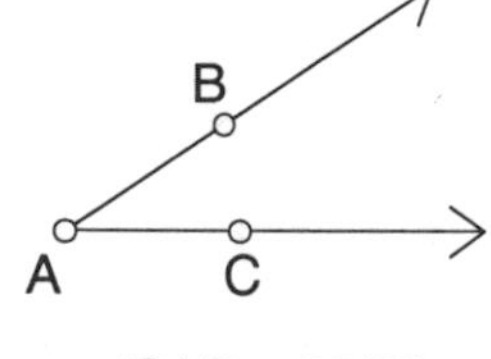

m∠CAB = 33.7°
m∠BAC = -33.7°

Star Polygons (page 111)

Prerequisites: Students should know that the sum of the angle measures of a triangle is 180°. It will help if they can find the sums of angle measures for any n-gon.

Sketchpad Proficiency: Beginner/Intermediate

Activity Time: 35–60 minutes. This is a rich problem and can easily lead to further investigation. Students may want to continue to explore the topic as a project or for extra credit.

Example Sketch: Star Polygon.gsp

Sketch and Investigate

Q1 and **Q2**

# of star points	Every 2nd point	Every 3rd point	Every 4th point
5	180°	180°	540°
6	360°	0°	360°
7	540°	180°	180°
8	720°	360°	0°
9	900°	540°	180°

Encourage students to record any patterns they observe as they fill out the chart. These could include shortcuts for drawing and measuring as well as algebraic generalizations. You also might ask students to try to explain *why* their observations are true for any given case. Some observations are described (in abbreviated form) in the chart above. Here are a few more:

The sum of the measures of the angles in an odd-pointed star is a multiple of 180°.

The sum of the measures of the angles in an even-pointed star is a multiple of 360°.

Students should see a pattern in the chart. They may wish to extend the chart (to the left and right, as well as down) to see the pattern more clearly. Students who are strong in algebra might generalize the pattern with this formula: For a star polygon with n vertices and every pth point connected, $180°\,|n - 2p|$ gives the sum of the angle measures of that star.

© 2002 Key Curriculum Press

Polygon Angle Measure Sums (page 112)

Prerequisites: None

Sketchpad Proficiency: Beginner

Activity Time: 35–50 minutes

Example Sketch: **Polygon Angles.gsp**

Sketch and Investigate

Q1 No. The angle sums should remain constant as long as the polygon is convex.

Q2 The angle sum increases by 180° with each additional side.

Q3 The diagonal of the quadrilateral divides the quadrilateral into two triangles. Each triangle has an angle sum of 180°, so the sum of the angle measures in the quadrilateral is 2(180°) = 360°.

In the case of the pentagon, the two diagonals create three triangles. So the sum of the angle measures in the pentagon is 3(180°) = 540°.

Q4 The sum of the angle measures of an n-gon is $(n - 2)180°$. $n - 2$ is the number of triangles created when you "triangulate" the n-gon.

Explore More

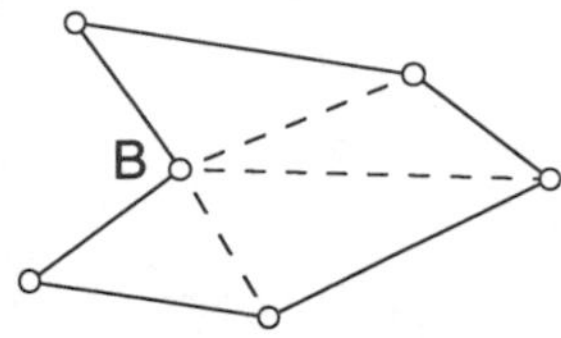

1. The sums of the interior angle measures are the same for convex and concave polygons, if you allow the angles to measure more than 180°. A concave n-gon can still be divided into $n - 2$ triangles. The hexagon shown above is concave at vertex B but still contains four triangles, showing that its angles total 720°. For some concave polygons, it's not possible to draw all the diagonals from a single vertex, but it is always possible to divide a polygon into $n - 2$ triangles.

Constructing Regular Polygons (page 114)

Prerequisites: Students should be familiar with the different polygons and their names. This activity introduces students to the terms *regular polygon, central angle,* and *interior angle.*

Sketchpad Proficiency: Intermediate. If you want students to save custom tools of their work, they will need to know how to make and save custom tools. For tips on making and using custom tools, see the appropriate sections in the help system. (Choose **Toolbox** from the Help menu, then click on the Custom Tools link.)

Activity Time: 15–60 minutes, depending on how many custom tools you want students to save. You might ask them to make custom tools for at least the equilateral triangle, the square, and the regular hexagon, since these could come in handy later. Keep in mind that custom tools for all these shapes are already on the disk that accompanies this book, as well as the disk that comes with Sketchpad, so students may already have access to them.

Example Sketch: **Polygons.gsp**. This sketch contains tools for constructing regular polygons. It's the same sketch included with the program.

If students are saving custom tools, it helps to make clear exactly where they should save them and what they should name them. Since students often save many versions of different things, tell them you will look only at custom tools with the required names, saved in the required places.

Polygon	Central angle measure	Interior angle measure
Equi. triangle	120°	60°
Square	90°	90°
Reg. pentagon	72°	108°
Reg. hexagon	60°	120°
Reg. octagon	45°	135°
Reg. nonagon	40°	140°
Reg. decagon	36°	144°
Reg. n-gon	$360°/n$	$(n - 2)180/n$

Continued on next page.

© 2002 Key Curriculum Press

Constructing Regular Polygons

Continued from previous page.

Explore More

1. Students should use Sketchpad's Calculator to calculate 5*180°/7 or 900°/7 for an interior angle, or 360°/7 for a central angle. They must choose **degrees** in the Units pop-up menu in the Calculator so that Sketchpad will recognize the calculation as an angle measure. Then they can select this measurement and choose **Mark Angle** in the Transform menu. Now they can construct the regular heptagon by rotating by this angle.

   900/7 (or 360/7 for the interior angle) is a rational number with an infinite repeating decimal. If students try to rotate by a fixed angle, they can enter only a decimal approximation in the Rotate dialog box. After seven rotations, the error of this approximation will become evident and the resulting polygon won't be perfectly regular.

2. Euclid's Proposition 1—Constructing an Equilateral Triangle, in Chapter 1 of this book, shows one Euclidean construction. It is possible to construct all the other regular polygons in this table using only the Euclidean tools. The regular pentagon is perhaps the biggest challenge. (It is not possible to construct a regular heptagon using only Euclidean tools.)

Constructing Templates for the Platonic Solids (page 115)

Prerequisites: Students should know the terms *polyhedron (polyhedra)* and *regular polygon*. To create the templates, students should understand reflections and rotations and know how to perform them with Sketchpad.

Sketchpad Proficiency: Intermediate. It is helpful if students can use and access custom tools for regular polygons. Beginners can use the example sketches.

Activity Time: 50–150 minutes. If you actually have students make templates for all the solids, print them, and then build the solids, this could be a several-day project. If you have students color the solids and hang them around your classroom, you have wonderful mathematical decorations!

Example Sketches: **Platonic Templates.gsp** contains templates for all the Platonic solids. **Polygons.gsp** contains tools for constructing regular polygons. It's the same sketch included with the program.

Try to let students figure out their own templates. The images below show some samples.

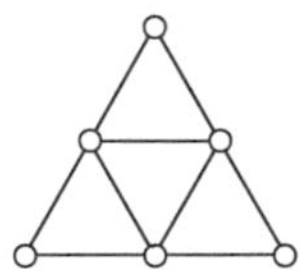

Tetrahedron

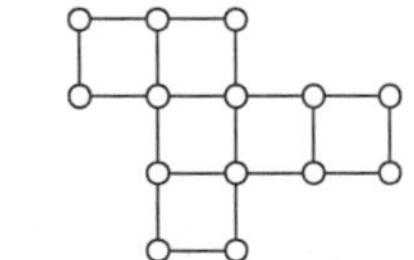

Cube

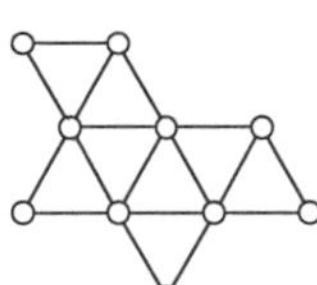

Octahedron

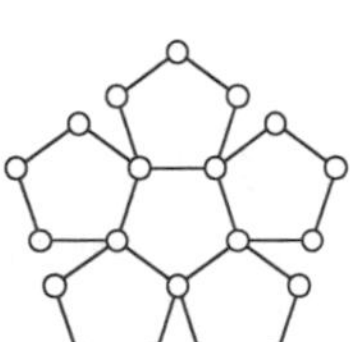

Dodecahedron (two of these needed)

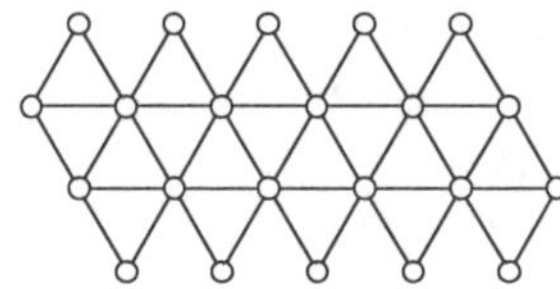

Icosahedron

© 2002 Key Curriculum Press

Explore More

1. To make a cylinder, use a rectangle with two congruent circles. Make sure the length of the rectangle matches the circumference of the circles.
2. Archimedean solids have faces that are regular polygons, but the faces don't all have to be the same kind of regular polygon. The polygons meet at each vertex in exactly the same way. There are thirteen Archimedean solids.
3. People have believed the Platonic solids to have mystical as well as scientific properties. For example, Kepler believed the orbits of the planets to be defined by Platonic solids inscribed in one another. Students can also use their solids to discover Euler's formula for polyhedra: $F + V = E + 2$, where F represents the total number of faces, V the total number of vertices, and E the total number of edges. This formula applies to any polyhedron that does not have a hole through it.

Introducing Circles (page 119)

Prerequisites: None

Sketchpad Proficiency: Absolute beginner. This activity is designed as a possible first Sketchpad activity.

Activity Time: 25–45 minutes

Example Sketch: **Introducing Circles.gsp**

Sketch and Investigate

Q1 Dragging control point B changes the size of the circle. Dragging control point A moves the center. Moving the center changes the location of the circle and can also change its size.

Q2 True.

Q3 Infinitely many circles can share the same center. For this reason, it is often more convenient to name a circle after two points than only after its center point. Naming a circle by its center point only does not always uniquely identify the circle.

Q4 Answers will vary. Two circles are congruent if they have the same radius.

Q5 A diameter is a chord that passes through the center of the circle. A diameter is the longest possible chord in a circle.

Q6 The diameter of a circle is twice as long as the radius.

Explore More

1. Construct a circle AB. Construct $\overrightarrow{BA}$. Construct point C where this ray intersects the other side of the circle. Construct $\overline{BC}$ and hide the ray. $\overline{BC}$ is a diameter.

   Another method: Construct $\overline{AB}$ and midpoint C. Construct circle CB. $\overline{AB}$ is a diameter.

© 2002 Key Curriculum Press

Chords in a Circle (page 121)

Prerequisites: Students should know or be introduced to the terms *arc, perpendicular bisector,* and *congruent*. It will also be helpful if they are comfortable interpreting graphs.

Sketchpad Proficiency: Intermediate

Activity Time: 40–50 minutes for the whole activity. If you're short on time, you can stop after Q2. If you want students to get to the conjecture in Q4 and are short on time, you can skip the graphing section, jumping directly from Q2 to step 15.

Example Sketch: Chords.gsp

Sketch and Investigate

Q1 The perpendicular bisector of any chord of a circle passes through the center of the circle.

Q2 The closer the chord is to the center of the circle, the longer the chord. The chord is longest when its distance to the center is zero. This chord is a diameter of the circle.

Q3 At the point where the locus intersects the y-axis, the length of $\overline{BC}$ is zero (its minimum value) and the length of $\overline{AD}$ is the radius of the circle (its maximum value). Likewise, at the point where the locus intersects the x-axis, the length of $\overline{BC}$ is the diameter of the circle (its maximum value) and the length of $\overline{AD}$ is zero (its minimum value).

As point G moves from left to right, its y-coordinate decreases in value, showing the chord $\overline{BC}$ moving closer to the center of the circle (and also becoming longer).

Students may notice that the locus shows a portion of an ellipse in the first quadrant. This ellipse is centered at the origin and has a major axis of twice the diameter of the circle and a minor axis of twice the radius of the circle.

Q4 If two chords in a circle are congruent, the chords are the same distance from the center of the circle. (The converse is also true.)

Explore More

1. When $HI = BC$, the plotted point (length of $\overline{HI}$, distance from $\overline{HI}$ to the center) is coincident with point G.
2. After constructing the arc, construct two chords anywhere on the arc. Construct the perpendicular bisectors of both these chords. Their point of intersection is the center of the circle.

Tangents to a Circle (page 123)

Prerequisites: The activity introduces the terms *secant* and *tangent*.

Sketchpad Proficiency: Beginner

Activity Time: 25–40 minutes

Example Sketches: Tangent.gsp

Sketch and Investigate

Q1 As you drag point C toward point B, the angle between the radius and the secant approaches 90°. If you drag slowly, you can tell when points C and B coincide, the secant becomes a tangent, and $\angle ABC$ measures 90°.

Q2 A tangent is perpendicular to the radius at the point of tangency.

Q3 Select the radius and its endpoint on the circle, then, in the Construct menu, choose **Perpendicular Line.**

Explore More

1. To construct an internally or externally tangent circle, first construct a circle and a tangent line. Extend the radius to a full line and construct a second circle with its center on that line and its radius endpoint the same as that of the first circle (the point of tangency).

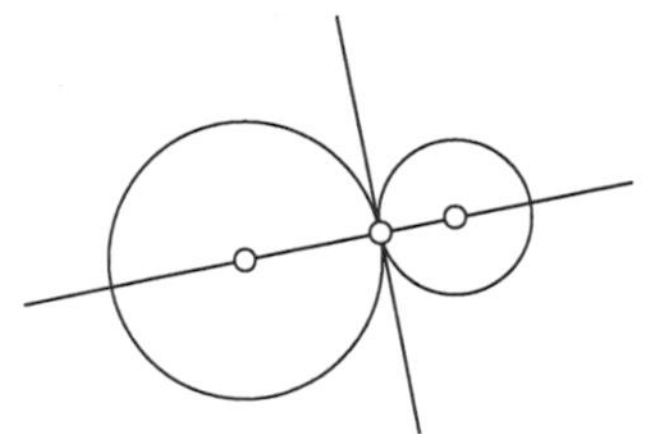

© 2002 Key Curriculum Press

Tangent Segments (page 124)

Prerequisites: Students should know the term *tangent*.

Sketchpad Proficiency: Beginner

Activity Time: 15–30 minutes

Example Sketches: **Tangent Segments.gsp**. This sketch contains the custom tool **Tangent Segments**.

Sketch and Investigate

Q1 Tangent segments to a circle from a point outside the circle are congruent.

Explore More

1. The right triangles *ABD* and *ACD* are congruent by Hypotenuse-Leg. (*AB* and *AC* are radii of a circle and $\overline{AD}$ is congruent to itself.) Thus, $\overline{DB}$ and $\overline{DC}$ are corresponding parts of congruent triangles and must be congruent.
2. This is a tough challenge. The diagram below shows the necessary construction. Circle *A* is the original circle and point *C* is the point outside the circle. Point *D* is the midpoint of $\overline{AC}$. The lines are perpendicular to the radial segments because they create angles inscribed in semicircles.

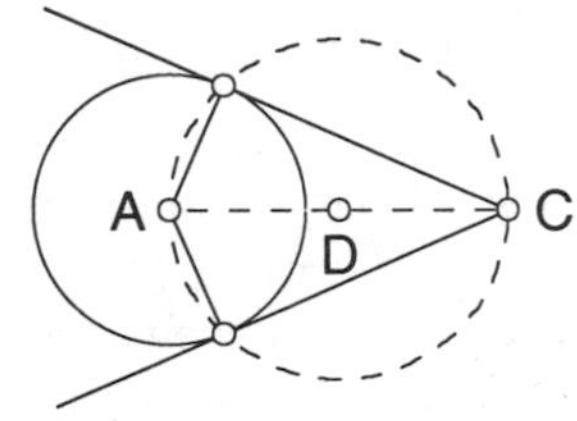

3. Construct a circle and a tangent to the circle. Construct another point *P* on the tangent and construct a perpendicular line through point *P*. Then construct a circle centered on the perpendicular with point *P* its other control point.

Arcs and Angles (page 125)

Prerequisites: It will help if students are familiar with the terms *major arc, minor arc, inscribed angle,* and *central angle,* but all these terms are also introduced in the activity.

Sketchpad Proficiency: Beginner

Activity Time: 35–45 minutes. You can also stop at the bottom of the first page after Q2 for a shorter lesson on central angles only (but not on inscribed angles).

Example Sketch: **Arcs and Angles.gsp**

Sketch and Investigate

Q1 The measure of a central angle in a circle equals the measure of the minor arc it intercepts.

Q2 The measures of the central angle and the major arc it intercepts sum to 360°. (The measure of the major arc is equal to 360° minus the measure of the central angle.)

Q3 The measure of an inscribed angle is always half the measure of the arc it intercepts. (Notice that if you drag *C* beyond *D*, the arc measurement no longer shows the measure of the arc intercepted by $\angle CDB$.)

Q4 All inscribed angles intercepting the same arc are congruent.

Q5 Every angle inscribed in a semicircle is a right angle.

Explore More

1. The expression below is equivalent to the length of the arc. The first part of the expression calculates the fractional part of the circle used by the arc. This fraction multiplies the entire circumference of the circle to find the length of the arc.

$$\left(\frac{\text{arc angle a1}}{360}\right)\cdot(\text{Circumference } \odot\text{AB})$$

2. Construct $\overline{AB}$ and midpoint *C*. Construct circle *CB*. Construct $\overline{AD}$ and $\overline{BD}$, where point *D* is on the circle. Triangle *ADB* is a right triangle because $\angle D$ is inscribed in a semicircle.

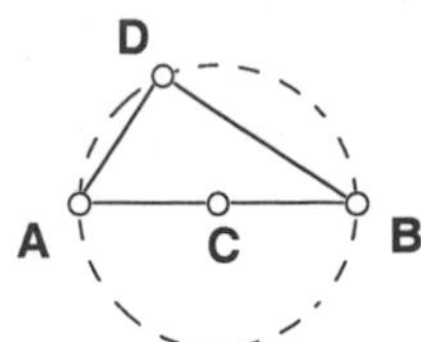

© 2002 Key Curriculum Press

The Circumference/Diameter Ratio (page 127)

Prerequisites: Students need to know the terms *circumference* and *diameter*. It will be helpful if they already know that the circumference/diameter ratio is π, in which case this activity serves as a review of this concept, using a graphical approach.

Sketchpad Proficiency: Intermediate

Activity Time: 35–50 minutes

Example Sketch: Circumference.gsp

Demonstration Sketch: Circum Diameter.gsp

Sketch and Investigate

Q1 The points lie in a line and fall in the first quadrant.

Q2 The slope of the ray is π. The ratio of the circumference to the diameter in a circle is also π. Slope shows the ratio of rise/run. In this graph, the rise (y-axis) shows circumference measurements and the run (x-axis) shows diameter measurements. This is why the slope shows circumference/diameter. You can use **Preferences** in the Edit menu to show the slope measurement (or π) to the nearest thousandth (go to the Units panel and change Scalar Precision).

Q3 The fact that all the plotted points lie on this ray signifies that the circumference/diameter ratio is the same for each of the different circles in the table.

Q4 $\pi = C/D$
$C = \pi D$

Q5 $C = \pi(2r)$ or $C = 2\pi r$

The Cycloid (page 129)

Prerequisites: Students should be able to find the *circumference of a circle*.

Sketchpad Proficiency: Intermediate. Students create action buttons and use the Trace and Merge features.

Activity Time: 40–50 minutes

Example Sketch: Cycloid Tracer.gsp

Sketch and Investigate

Q1 See the three traces below.

Inside the circle:

On the circle (the sketch should show cusps):

Outside the circle (the sketch should show loops):

Q2 When point G traces two cycles, the circumference is one-half the length of the segment. When it traces three cycles, the circumference is one-third the length of the segment.

Q3 If the circle has a radius of 1 cm, then its circumference is 2π cm. Because the rolling wheel travels a distance of exactly one circumference before it repeats itself, the period of the corresponding cycloid curve is also 2π.

Q4 The position of point G on the wheel does not affect the period.

Explore More

1. This construction is very similar to the one described in the activity, with a circular path replacing the segment path. One tricky part is constructing the rolling circle so that it's *outside* the other circle. The drawing below shows one possible solution.

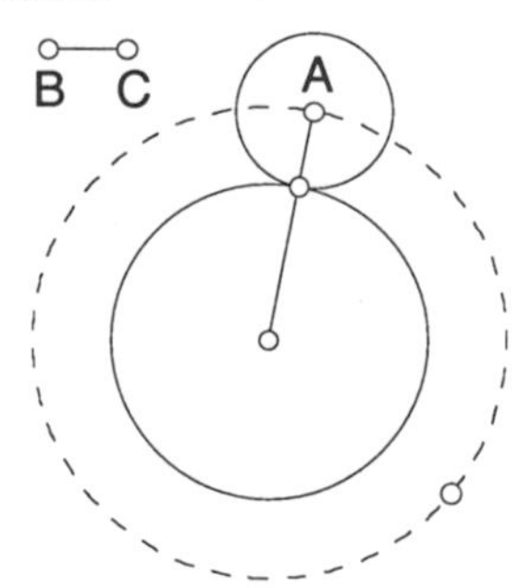

© 2002 Key Curriculum Press

2. More realistic models will more accurately portray the speed relationships between the various bodies (i.e., 365 lunar revolutions for every earth revolution). Also, consider pasting imported graphics of the sun, earth, and moon to the appropriate points for added flair.

Areas of Parallelograms and Triangles (page 133)

Prerequisites: Students should know the terms *area* and *parallelogram*. They should know the terms *height* and *base* as they apply to parallelograms and triangles. No previous understanding of the concept of *shearing* is required. This activity can serve as an introduction to the area formulas for a parallelogram and a triangle, or, if students are already familiar with these concepts, the activity can serve as a review.

Sketchpad Proficiency: Beginner/Intermediate

Activity Time: 40–50 minutes. If you want students to save construction time, have them start with the example sketch instead of constructing it themselves.

Example Sketch: **Parallelogram Area.gsp**

Demonstration Sketch: **Triangle Area.gsp**

Sketch and Investigate

Q1 The area of the parallelogram remains constant under shearing because the height and base of the parallelogram stay constant, and the area depends on only those two measures. Changing the base or the height of the parallelogram changes its area.

Q2 The area of the parallelogram equals $(EH)(DF)$.

Q3 $A = bh$

Q4 The area of the triangle is exactly half the area of the parallelogram.

$A = bh/2$

Explore More

1. During the animation, the area of the parallelogram should not change because neither the height nor the base change. Area remains constant under shearing for any figure because every cross section parallel to the shear line remains a constant length.

© 2002 Key Curriculum Press

A Triangle Area Problem (page 135)

Prerequisites: Students should know how to find the area of a triangle. It is also helpful if they are familiar with the triangle midsegment theorem that states: The segment joining the midpoints of two sides of a triangle is parallel to the third side and half as long.

Sketchpad Proficiency: Beginner

Activity Time: 25–40 minutes

Example Sketch: **Area Problem.gsp**

Sketch and Investigate

Q1 Answers will vary.

Q2 The sum of the areas of the triangles equals the area of the quadrilateral.

Q3 The shaded triangles each have 1/2 the height of the large triangle *ABC*. The sum of their bases is the base of the larger triangle, so together they make up 1/2 the area of the larger triangle. Thus, the quadrilateral must make up 1/2 also, and must be equal in area to the sum of the areas of the small triangles. This is easiest to see when you try special cases: When *F* is at the midpoint of $\overline{AC}$ the small triangles are identical, each with 1/4 the area of the large triangle. When *F* is dragged to *A* or *C*, one of the small triangles disappears, leaving the other with base $\overline{AB}$ and height half that of the large triangle.

Explore More

1. No answer necessary.
2. The two segments share an endpoint at a vertex of the square. The other endpoints should be one third of the distance away from the opposite vertex along the opposite sides.

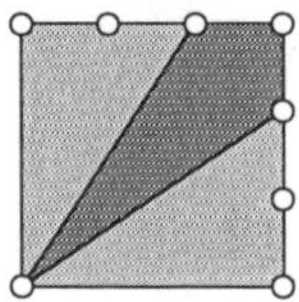

Triangle Area/Perimeter (page 136)

Prerequisites: Students need to know how to find the area and perimeter of a triangle.

Sketchpad Proficiency: Beginner/Intermediate

Activity Time: 30–60 minutes, depending on how long you allow students to explore. This problem can make a good project or long-term assignment. You might ask students to make electronic presentations of their work, showing different constructions and cases, using color, text, and animation.

Example Sketches: **Area and Perimeter.gsp**

Sketch and Investigate

Q1 It is possible for two noncongruent triangles to have the same area and perimeter. In fact, there are infinitely many noncongruent triangles that have the same area and perimeter. The explanations for Q2, below, show some illustrations of this fact.

Note: You might want to have students change the precision of their measurements on the Units panel of Preferences (in the Edit menu) to **tenths**. If the precision is very exact, students can lose track of the larger problem as they spend time dragging points one pixel at a time to try to get measurements to match to the nearest thousandth.

Q2 There are many different ways to approach this problem. Probably the most common one initially is to construct two unconstrained triangles and their interiors and drag vertices to try to make their area and perimeter measurements match up. This can get frustrating. Here are two more systematic methods. In both methods, triangle *ABC* was constructed first, and its area and circumference were measured and left fixed.

Method 1: Match areas first, then match perimeters. (See the first page of **Area and Perimeter.gsp**.)

© 2002 Key Curriculum Press

Area $\triangle ABC = 0.4$ cm^2

Perimeter $\triangle ABC = 3.9$ cm

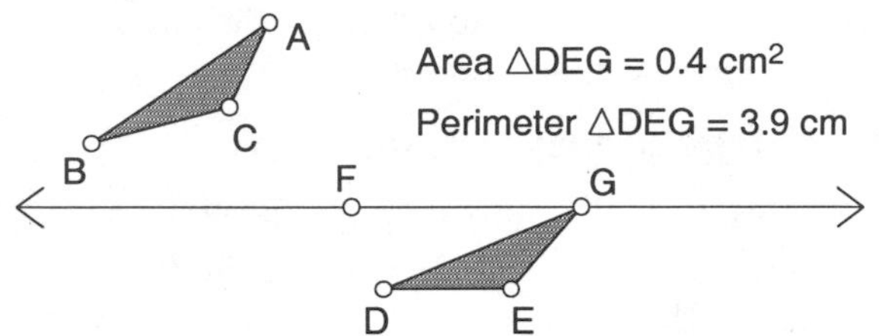

To create the diagram above, construct a line parallel to $\overline{DE}$ through F. Construct triangle DEG and its interior using a new point G on that line. Drag $\overline{DE}$ until the areas of the triangles match, then drag G (this doesn't change the area) until the perimeters match.

Method 2: Match the perimeters first, then the areas. (See the second page of **Area and Perimeter.gsp**.)

Area $\triangle ABC = 0.4$ cm^2

Perimeter $\triangle ABC = 3.9$ cm

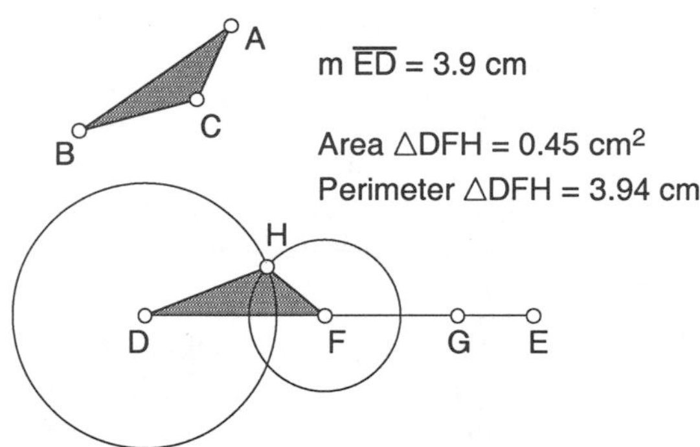

Construct $\overline{DE}$, measure its length, and drag E until DE equals the perimeter of triangle ABC.

Construct $\overline{DF}$, $\overline{FG}$, and $\overline{GE}$, where F and G are on $\overline{DE}$. $\overline{DF}$ will be one side of the triangle. FG and GE will serve as lengths for the other two sides.

Construct a circle with center D and radius FG and a circle with center F and radius GE.

Construct H, one intersection of these circles.

Construct the interior of triangle DHF. Its perimeter is already equal to the perimeter of triangle ABC. Move points G and F until the areas are equal. (By the way, if you trace the locus of point H while dragging point G, you get an ellipse!)

A Square Within a Square (page 137)

Prerequisites: Students should know how to find the areas of squares and triangles.

Sketchpad Proficiency: Intermediate/Advanced

Activity Time: 50–60 minutes. If you run out of time, Q1 is a natural place to break. If you do stop at Q1, you can ask students to explain the ratio they find there as homework. Also, to save the construction time required in this activity, you can always use the example sketch.

Example Sketch: **Square in Square.gsp**

Sketch and Investigate

Q1 The ratio of the area of the larger square to the area of the smaller is 5:1. Students might initially guess a 4:1 relationship between the larger and smaller square, partly because the midpoint suggests a power of 2. For a visual "proof" of this, have students print the sketch and cut out the nine pieces. The other eight pieces can fit together to form four squares congruent to the center square.

Q2 The area ratio for the 1/3 point is 13:1.
The area ratio for the 1/4 point is 25:1.
The area ratio for the 1/5 point is 41:1.

Q3 Students may observe these patterns:

Side ratio	Area ratio
1/2	5 = 1 + 4
1/3	13 = 4 + 9
1/4	25 = 9 + 16
1/5	41 = 16 + 25

So the logical guess for a side ratio of 1/6 is 25 + 36 = 61. If students don't notice the pattern (that the area ratios are the sums of squares), they may still see a pattern in the differences of the area ratios. The ratios 5, 13, 25, and 41 increase by 8, 12, and 16. So the next ratio would be 20 more than 41, or 61.

Explore More

1. When the side ratio of the large square is $1/n$, the area ratio for the squares is $(n-1)^2 + n^2$. This matches the pattern in the chart above.

© 2002 Key Curriculum Press

A Triangle Within a Triangle (page 139)

Prerequisites: Students should have some idea of how to find the area of a triangle.

Sketchpad Proficiency: Intermediate

Activity Time: 25–40 minutes

Example Sketch: Triangle in Triangle.gsp

Sketch and Investigate

Q1 Students are likely to guess a 6:1 or 9:1 ratio between the larger and smaller square. (The trisection will suggest a multiple of 3.) In fact, the larger square has 7 times the area of the smaller.

Explore More

1. The triangles are not similar. It's possible for the outer one to be acute and the inner one to be obtuse.
2. Dividing the triangle sides into fourths yields an inner triangle whose area is 4/13 that of the outer triangle.
3. Dividing the sides of a quadrilateral into thirds yields an inner quadrilateral whose area is 2/5 that of the outer one.
4. This method yields an outer triangle whose area is 7 times that of the original.

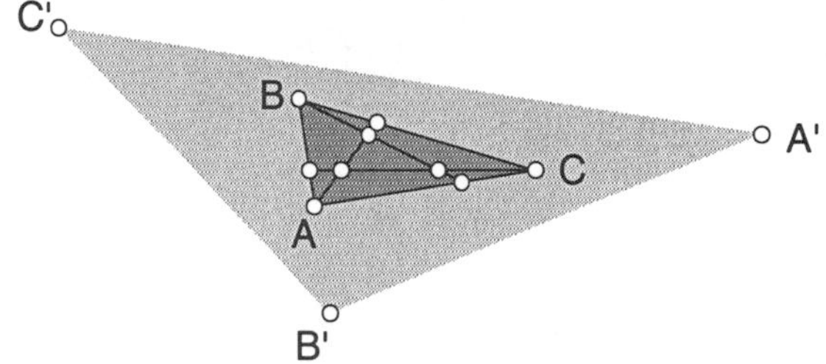

A Rectangle with Maximum Area (page 140)

Prerequisites: Students should know the terms *rectangle, square, area,* and *perimeter.*

Sketchpad Proficiency: Advanced

Activity Time: 40–50 minutes. If you are short on time, you can stop after Q2. This leaves out the exploration of the problem using the maxima and minima of a graph.

Example Sketch: Max Area Rectangle.gsp

Sketch and Investigate

Q1 As students drag point *C*, they should notice that the area of the rectangle changes but its perimeter remains constant. Because *CB* and *CD* are radii of the same circle, the sum of two sides of the rectangle, $AC + CD$, is equal to *AB*. Thus, *AB* is half the perimeter of the rectangle. As long as this length is kept constant, the perimeter of the rectangle will be constant.

Q2 A square is the rectangle with the greatest area for a given perimeter.

Q3 The coordinates of the high point of the graph show the side length and area of the maximum-area rectangle. The side length at this point verifies that the rectangle with the maximum area is a square.

Q4 The low points on the graph show where the area of the rectangle is zero. This happens when *AC* is zero and when $AC = AB$.

You might want to discuss with students why the locus graph of (side length, area) of a rectangle is a parabola.

Explore More

1. Regular polygons have maximum area for a given perimeter. Polygons with more sides are more efficient. The circle is the closed planar figure that gives maximum area for a given perimeter.
2. The area of the rectangle can be represented by the equation $A = x[(1/2)P - x]$. The graph is a parabola with roots 0 and $(1/2)P$. So the *x*-value of the maximum point is $(1/4)P$. Since the side length of the maximum area rectangle is 1/4 the rectangle's perimeter, the rectangle must be a square.

© 2002 Key Curriculum Press

The Area of a Trapezoid (page 142)

Prerequisites: Students should know the terms *height* and *base* as they refer to a trapezoid. They should know how to find the area of a parallelogram.

Sketchpad Proficiency: Beginner

Activity Time: 35–50 minutes. If you are short on time, have students stop after step 14 and ask them to use the measurements of the bases and height of the trapezoid to build an expression that equals the area.

Example Sketch: Trapezoid Area.gsp

Demonstration Sketch: Trapezoid Area 2.gsp

Sketch and Investigate

Q1 The two trapezoids combined form a parallelogram.

Q2 The parallelogram formed by the combined trapezoids has a base of length $b_1 + b_2$.

Q3 $A = (b_1 + b_2)h$ is the area of the parallelogram.

Q4 $A = (1/2)(b_1 + b_2)h$ is the area of the trapezoid.

Q5 $\dfrac{((m\,\overline{AB}) + (m\,\overline{CD}))\cdot(\text{Distance C to }\overline{AB})}{2}$

Students must use parentheses when they sum the two bases.

Explore More

1. $A = mh$, where m is the length of the midsegment, gives the area of the trapezoid. The length of the midsegment is the average of the lengths of the bases.
2. In the figure below, $\triangle LJK$ has half the area of the trapezoid. I and H are midpoints of the sides and J and K lie at the feet of perpendiculars through I and H. L is any point on $\overline{CD}$, so there are many possible triangles of this kind.

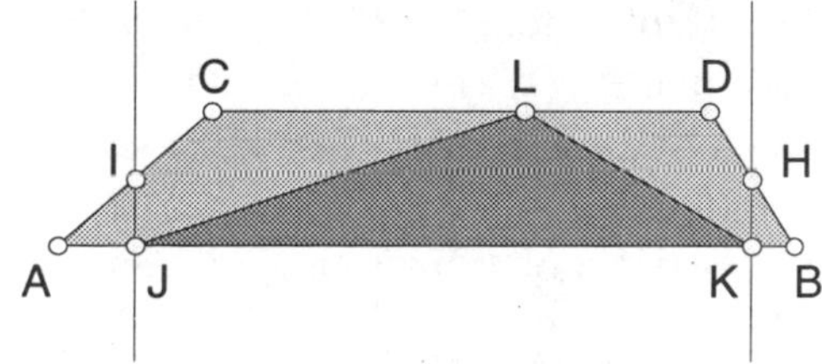

Dividing Land (page 144)

Prerequisites: Students should know how to find the area of a triangle.

Sketchpad Proficiency: Beginner

Activity Time: 10–30 minutes, depending on how long you give students. This problem can make a good long-term assignment or project. You might ask students to present their findings electronically, using animation, color, and text, or as a poster.

Example Sketch: Dividing Land.gsp

Sketch and Investigate

Students will find that the products of the areas are, indeed, equal. But that doesn't mean it's a fair way to divide the land. A fair way would ensure that the sums of the areas were equal. The product relationship can be explained as follows:

Draw altitudes $\overline{BF}$ and $\overline{DG}$. The area of $\triangle ABE$ is $(1/2)(AE)(BF)$. The area of $\triangle CED$ is $(1/2)(CE)(DG)$. The area of $\triangle BEC$ is $(1/2)(CE)(BF)$ and the area of $\triangle AED$ is $(1/2)(AE)(DG)$. The product of the areas of $\triangle ABE$ and $\triangle CED$ is $(1/2)(AE)(BF)(1/2)(CE)(DG)$. The product of the areas of $\triangle BEC$ and $\triangle AED$ is $(1/2)(CE)(BF)(1/2)(AE)(DG)$, which is the same as the product of the areas of $\triangle ABE$ and $\triangle CED$.

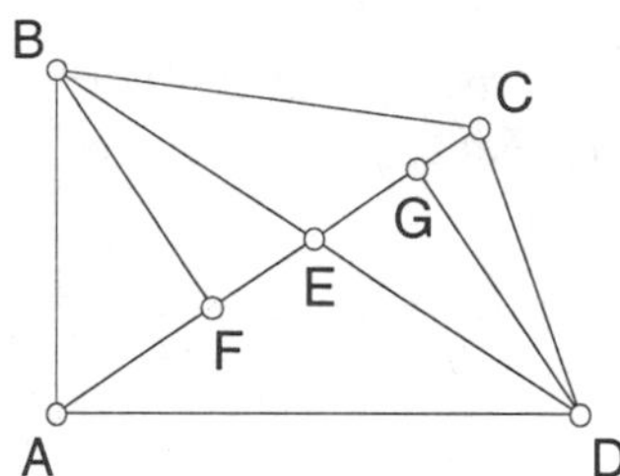

Explore More

1. Divide the quadrilateral as shown, by connecting midpoints of opposite sides. This also works for convex quadrilaterals.

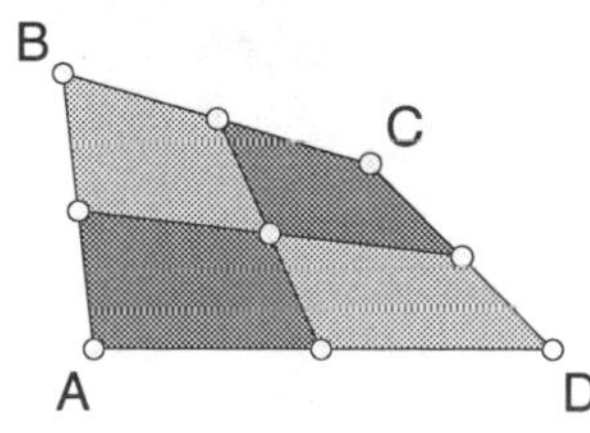

© 2002 Key Curriculum Press

Areas of Regular Polygons and Circles (page 145)

Prerequisites: Students should be able to calculate the area of a triangle.

Sketchpad Proficiency: Beginner. The required sketch provides students with the necessary constructions. Students need only use the Sketchpad Calculator.

Activity Time: 15–30 minutes. If you have an overhead projection device, this lesson works well with the whole class focusing together on the required sketch.

Required Sketch: To a Circle.gsp

Sketch and Investigate

Q1 $as/2$ = area of the triangle

Q2 and **Q3** Answers will vary. For a four-sided polygon, the expression should resemble $4(as/2)$.

Q4 $A = (as/2)n$ or $A = (1/2)(asn)$

Q5 $p = sn$

Q6 $A = (1/2)(ap)$

Q7 As the number of sides increases, the polygon becomes more and more like a circle.

Q8 As the number of sides increases, the apothem becomes more and more like the radius of the circle.

Q9 As the number of sides increases, the perimeter approaches the circumference of the circle.

Q10 $A = (1/2)Cr$

Q11 $A = (1/2)(2\pi r)(r)$

$A = \pi r^2$

New Area Formulas (page 147)

Prerequisites: Students should know standard formulas for the areas of triangles, trapezoids, and rhombuses and the term *midsegment*. (A midsegment connects the midpoints of two sides of a triangle or of the legs of a trapezoid. Many books use *midline* for triangles and *median* for trapezoids.)

Sketchpad Proficiency: Advanced

Activity Time: 30–50 minutes

Example Sketch: Alternate Areas.gsp

Sketch and Investigate

Students are not given any construction steps, the assumption being that they have enough Sketchpad experience to construct these figures. Possible construction steps are summarized below.

To construct a trapezoid, start with a segment and a point not on the segment. Construct a parallel line through the point, then construct segments from the original segment to the line. Hide the line and construct the second base.

To construct a rhombus, construct a segment and its midpoint. Construct a perpendicular through the midpoint. Construct a random point on this line, mark the segment mirror, and reflect the point across the segment. Connect the four points, hide the line, and construct the second diagonal.

To construct a kite, construct a segment, its midpoint, and a perpendicular through the midpoint. Construct two random points on this line, one on either side of the segment. Connect the four points, hide the line, and construct the second diagonal.

The first two formulas work. The formulas for the areas of a rhombus and a kite should be $(1/2)rs$.

1. In the triangle, the length of a midsegment is 1/2 the length of the base to which it's parallel. Substitute m for $(1/2)b$ in the standard formula, $A = (1/2)bh$ and get $A = mh$.
2. In the trapezoid the length of the midsegment is the average of the lengths of the bases. Substitute m for $(1/2)(b_1 + b_2)$ in the standard formula, $A= (1/2)(b_1 + b_2)h$, and get $A = mh$.
3. In the rhombus, a diagonal r divides the rhombus into congruent triangles. The height of one of these triangles is $(1/2)s$, so the area of this triangle is $(1/2)r(1/2)s$. The area of the two triangles, then, is $(1/2)rs$.
4. In the kite, the same argument holds as for the rhombus. The area should be $(1/2)rs$.

Explore More

1. Many possible answers.

© 2002 Key Curriculum Press

Pick's Theorem (page 148)

Prerequisites: None.

Sketchpad Proficiency: Beginner

Activity Time: 20–30 minutes

Example Sketch: Pick's Theorem.gsp

Warning: This activity depends on measurements matching the grid scale. If students change the grid scale, the grid units will no longer match the measurement units set in Preferences (**cm** or **inches**). In this activity, students hide the scaling point at (1, 0) in step 1. Once this is hidden, students can't scale the axes unless they accidentally show and then drag this point later on. You may want to warn students not to manipulate the axes before they hide them.

Sketch and Investigate

Q1 and **Q2** Answers will vary. It is easy to miss border points, so make sure students find and count them all. Here is a sample row for the chart:

	b	$\frac{b}{2}$	i	$\frac{b}{2}+i$	Area
Polygon	12	6	2	8	7

Q3 The last column is always 1 less than the second-to-last column, so Pick's theorem states that the area of any dot paper polygon is

$$\text{area} = \frac{b}{2} + i - 1$$

where i is the number of grid points in the interior of the polygon and b is the number of grid points on the border of the polygon.

Explore More

1. a. and b. Every triangle with height 1 and base 1 has an area of $(1/2)bh = (1/2)(1)(1) = 1/2$. Every dot paper triangle with height 1 and base 1 has three boundary points and no interior points. So by Pick's theorem, each of them has an area of $(3/2) + 0 - 1 = 1/2$. Thus, Pick's theorem correctly calculates the areas of these triangles.

   c. Every triangle with height 2 and base 1 has an area of $(1/2)(1)(2) = 1$. Every dot paper triangle with height 2 and base 1 has four boundary points and no interior points. So by Pick's theorem, each of them has an area of $(4/2) + 0 - 1 = 1$. Thus, Pick's theorem correctly calculates the areas of these triangles.

   d. Every triangle with height 2 and base 2 has an area of $(1/2)(2)(2) = 2$. Every dot paper triangle with height 2 and base 2 has either six boundary points and no interior points or four boundary points and one interior point. So by Pick's theorem, each of them has an area of either $(6/2) + 0 - 1 = 2$ or $(4/2) + 1 - 1 = 2$. So Pick's theorem works again.

   e. As you drag the top vertex of a dot paper triangle horizontally, border points trade with interior points. Since each border point trades with two interior points (and vice versa), Pick's theorem calculates the same result for each case. For larger triangles of the same base and height, there are usually several different possible combinations for the numbers of border points and interior points. Students will find that Pick's theorem calculates the correct area for each of these combinations.

   Students could continue to raise the heights and base lengths of the triangles by 1 unit to test larger triangles and continue the pattern. Still, this would only demonstrate Pick's theorem for triangles whose heights and base lengths are integers. The inductive pattern does not take into account "crooked" dot paper triangles that have nonintegral bases and heights.

2. Suppose the rectangle has dimensions $x \times y$. This rectangle will have $2x + 2y$ grid points on its boundary and $(x - 1)(y - 1)$ grid points in its interior. So Pick's theorem gives us

$$\begin{aligned}\frac{b}{2} + i - 1 &= \frac{2x + 2y}{2} + (x-1)(y-1) - 1 \\ &= x + y + (xy - x - y + 1) - 1 \\ &= xy\end{aligned}$$

   which is the correct area of the rectangle.

© 2002 Key Curriculum Press

Squares and Square Roots (page 150)

Prerequisites: Students should know what a *square root* is and how to find the *area of a square.*

Sketchpad Proficiency: Beginner

Activity Time: 20–30 minutes

Example Sketch: The sketch **Squares and Square Roots.gsp** can be used independently of this activity as a demonstration or for students to work with on their own.

Warning: This activity depends on measurements matching the grid scale. If students change the grid scale, the grid units will no longer match the measurement units set in Preferences (**cm** or **inches**). In this activity, students hide the scaling point at (1, 0) in step 1. Once this is hidden, they can't scale the axes unless they show and then drag this point later on. You may want to warn students not to manipulate the axes before they hide them.

Sketch and Investigate

Q1 A square's side length is the square root of its area.

Q2 Students should be able to find exactly 12 square roots of whole numbers less than 20. If you include the square with a side length of 0, there are actually 13 possible table entries. Their tables should look something like this:

Square	0.000	1.000	2.000	4.000	5.000
Sq. rt.	0.000	1.000	1.414	2.000	2.236
Square	8.000	9.000	10.000	13.000	16.000
Sq. rt.	2.282	3.000	3.162	3.606	4.000
Square	17.000	18.000	20.000		
Sq. rt.	4.123	4.243	4.472		

Q3 It is impossible to find the square root of every whole number using squares drawn on a rectangular grid. For example, it is impossible to draw a square with area 7 square units on a grid.

Explore More

1. The plot should look something like this:

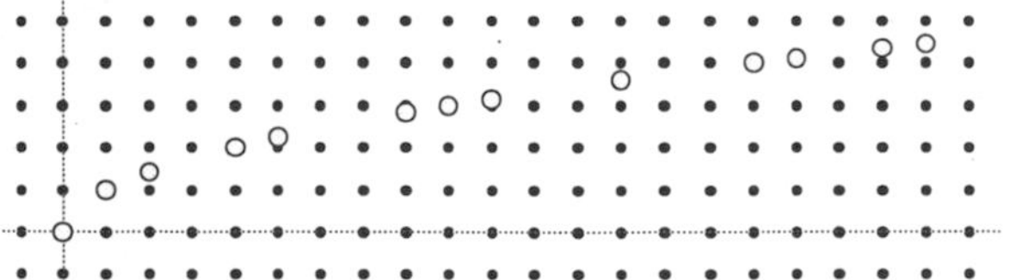

Student estimates for $\sqrt{3}$ should be between 1.5 and 2.

The Pythagorean Theorem (page 153)

Prerequisites: Students should understand the terms *right triangle, square, hypotenuse,* and *leg.* Students should know how to find the area of a square.

Sketchpad Proficiency: Beginner/Intermediate

Activity Time: 45–50 minutes, 15 minutes to construct the square, 10 minutes to construct the right triangle, and 20 minutes for the rest of the activity. If students already have custom tools to construct a square, this will save time. (They can use **4/Square (By Edge)** from the sketch **Polygons.gsp**.)

Example Sketch: **Pythagorean Theorem.gsp**

The folder **8-Pythagorean Theorem** contains several demonstrations of the theorem. One visual demonstration of the Pythagorean theorem is explained in the next activity.

Sketch and Investigate

Q1 This construction uses the following property: A square has right angles and congruent sides.

Q2 This construction uses the following property: A right triangle has one side perpendicular to another side.

Q3 The sum of the areas of the two smaller squares equals the area of the largest square. If the measurements are displayed with precision greater than the tenths place, students may not notice the relationship. It might help them to change their Distance Precision to **tenths** (under Preferences in the Edit menu).

Q4 $a^2 + b^2 = c^2$

Students already familiar with the Pythagorean theorem are likely to write this as their conjecture. You might also have them express the theorem in words.

Explore More

1. The areas of the regions built on the legs of a right triangle will always sum to the area of the region built on the hypotenuse, as long as all three regions are similar. If students have custom tools handy, they can check this easily: Try regular hexagons on each of the three sides or equilateral triangles.
2. If the areas of squares on two sides of a triangle sum to the area of the square on the third side, the triangle must be a right triangle.

© 2002 Key Curriculum Press

Visual Demonstration of the Pythagorean Theorem (page 155)

Prerequisites: Students will appreciate this more if they already have some experience with the Pythagorean theorem.

Sketchpad Proficiency: Beginner

Activity Time: 10–15 minutes. This short demonstration works well even if you have only a single computer with an overhead viewing device. You might coordinate it with any of the other activities in this section.

Required Sketch: **Shear Pythagoras.gsp**

Sketch and Investigate

Q1 In this sketch, the squares on the sides of a right triangle are sheared, without changing their areas, so that a shape on the legs is congruent to a shape on the hypotenuse. This shows that the sum of the areas of the original squares on the legs of a right triangle is equal to the area of the original square on the hypotenuse, thus demonstrating the Pythagorean theorem.

Dissection Demonstration of the Pythagorean Theorem (page 156)

Prerequisites: Students will appreciate this more if they already have some experience with the Pythagorean theorem.

Sketchpad Proficiency: Advanced. Students need to be able to use a custom tool for a square (built off its edge) and construct a right triangle from scratch. Instructions for both of these are in the activity The Pythagorean Theorem at the beginning of this chapter. Beginners could use the sample sketch and skip to step 9.

Activity Time: 25–45 minutes for the full activity; only 10 minutes if you use the sample sketch

Example Sketch: **Dissected Pythagoras.gsp**. You can use the custom tool **4/Square (By Edge)** from the sketch **Polygons.gsp**.

Demonstration Sketch: **Pythagorean Dissection.gsp**

Sketch and Investigate

Q1 The total area of the squares on the legs of a right triangle equals the area of the square on the hypotenuse (the Pythagorean theorem).

Explore More

1. No answer necessary.

© 2002 Key Curriculum Press

Pythagorean Triples (page 157)

Prerequisites: Students should be familiar with the Pythagorean theorem. They also should be familiar with radical notation for square roots.

Sketchpad Proficiency: Intermediate

Activity Time: 30–50 minutes, depending on how much time you allow for students to search for Pythagorean triples. (It's best to give them plenty of time so they don't get frustrated.)

Example Sketch: Pythagorean Triples.gsp

Sketch and Investigate

Q1 The exact length of the hypotenuse is $\sqrt{2}$.

Q2 No. If the lengths of the legs are 1 cm and 2 cm, the hypotenuse does not have a whole-number length. Its length is $\sqrt{5}$.

Q3 Students will need patience to complete all the rows in the table. If they are using a small screen, they may not find some of the bigger ones at the end of the list.

a	b	c
3	4	5
4	3	5
5	12	13
6	8	10
8	6	10
9	12	15
12	16	20
15	20	25

Q4 Any reordering of the three numbers of a triple shows a triangle congruent to the original. In the list above, (3, 4, 5) and (4, 3, 5) are triples of congruent triangles, as are (6, 8, 10) and (8, 6, 10).

Q5 In the list above, (3, 4, 5), (6, 8, 10), (9, 12, 15), and (15, 20, 25) represent triples of triangles similar to each other.

Q6 There are an infinite number of Pythagorean triples because you can multiply the numbers in any triple by the same positive integer to create another triple. For example, multiply (3, 4, 5) by 2 to get (6, 8, 10). Any triple that is not the integer multiple of another triple is called a *primitive Pythagorean triple*.

Q7 Students may check any three triples. For example,

$3^2 + 4^2 = 5^2$ because $9 + 16 = 25$

$5^2 + 12^2 = 13^2$ because $25 + 144 = 169$

$9^2 + 12^2 = 15^2$ because $81 + 144 = 225$

Explore More

1. When $m = 2$ and $n = 1$, Euclid's formula for Pythagorean triples gives the triple (3, 4, 5). Similarly, $m = 3$ and $n = 2$ generate the triple (5, 12, 13). You can use this formula to generate infinitely many Pythagorean triples because there are infinitely many choices for m and n. Euclid's formula generates every *primitive* Pythagorean triple, but it does not generate every triple that's a multiple of a primitive. For example, you cannot generate (9, 12, 15) using Euclid's formula because there are no whole-number values of m and n such that $m^2 + n^2 = 15$.

© 2002 Key Curriculum Press

The Isosceles Right Triangle (page 159)

Prerequisites: Students should be familiar with the Pythagorean theorem and should know the term *isosceles*. Students should have experience with square roots.

Sketchpad Proficiency: Intermediate. Students should know how to use a custom tool for a square. You can use the sample custom tool suggested below. If you want to build a **Square** tool from scratch, make sure the square is built off its edge. The instructions for building such a square are in The Pythagorean Theorem, the first activity in this chapter.

Activity Time: 25–40 minutes

Example Sketches: **Isosceles Right.gsp** and **Polygons.gsp**. The latter sketch contains the custom tool **4/Square (By Edge)**.

Sketch and Investigate

Q1 Triangle ABC is right and isosceles because two of its sides are sides of a square. Thus, they're congruent and they form a right angle.

Q2 Each acute angle in triangle ABC measures 45°.

Q3 The ratio is always constant at 1.414. (Decimals will vary depending on the precision students have set in Preferences.)

Q4 If each of the smaller squares has an area of x^2, the area of the large square is $2x^2$. (Each small square can be divided into two isosceles right triangles, four of which fit into the large square.)

Q5 If the legs of the isosceles triangle have length x, the length of the hypotenuse is $x\sqrt{2}$. This is because the area of the square on the hypotenuse is $2x^2$, so the length of a side of the square must be $\sqrt{2x^2}$, or $x\sqrt{2}$.

Q6 According to Q5, if each leg has length x, the hypotenuse has length $x\sqrt{2}$. Substituting these values in the Pythagorean theorem gives $x^2 + x^2 = (x\sqrt{2})^2 = 2x^2$.

Explore More

1. The discovery of the irrationality of $\sqrt{2}$ originated with the isosceles right triangle with sides of length 1. The Pythagoreans were startled to find a number that could not be represented as the ratio of two integers. The standard proof of the irrationality of $\sqrt{2}$ is by contradiction: assume the number is rational and show that this leads to impossible conclusions. The tenth book of Euclid's *Elements* contains a discussion similar to this proof. And a reference in one of Aristotle's works makes it clear that the proof was known much earlier than Euclid.

© 2002 Key Curriculum Press

The 30°-60° Right Triangle (page 161)

Prerequisites: Students should be familiar with the Pythagorean theorem and should know the term *equilateral*. Students should have experience with square roots.

Sketchpad Proficiency: Intermediate. Students need to be able to construct an equilateral triangle from scratch or with a custom tool. See Euclid's Proposition 1—Constructing an Equilateral Triangle, the third activity in Chapter 1, for construction instructions if you need them. Students also need to know how to use a custom tool for a square. You can use the sample custom tool suggested below. If you want to build a square tool from scratch, make sure the square is built off its edge. Instructions for building such a square are given in The Pythagorean Theorem, the first activity in this chapter.

Activity Time: 25–50 minutes

Example Sketches: **30 60 Right.gsp** and **Polygons.gsp**. The latter sketch contains the custom tools **3/Triangle (By Edge)** and **4/Square (By Edge)**.

Sketch and Investigate

Q1 $\angle CDB$ measures 90° because the median of an equilateral triangle is also an altitude.
$\angle DBC$ measures 60° because it is an angle in an equilateral triangle.
$\angle BCD$ measures 30° because it is half of an angle in an equilateral triangle.

Q2 In a 30°-60° right triangle, the hypotenuse is twice as long as the shortest leg.

Q3 The ratio of the area of the largest square to the area of the smallest square is 4:1. The areas have a ratio of 4:1 because the sides have a ratio of 2:1 and $2^2:1^2 = 4:1$.

Q4 a. If the smallest square has area x^2, the largest square will have area $4x^2$.

b. If A represents the area of the square on the long leg, the Pythagorean theorem gives us $x^2 + A = 4x^2$. Subtracting x^2 from both sides gives us $A = 3x^2$.

c. The ratio of the area of the square on the long leg to the area of the square on the short leg is 3:1. (If you can, check to make sure students verify this in their sketch.)

Q5 a. If the short leg has length x, the hypotenuse has length $2x$.

b. The long leg would have length $x\sqrt{3}$ because the leg is the side of the square with area $3x^2$.

c. The ratio $x\sqrt{3}:x$ simplifies to $\sqrt{3}:1$.

Q6 1.713 (Answers will vary depending on the Precision setting for calculations. Change this in Preferences in the Edit menu.)

Explore More

1. To make a Hide/Show button, select the object you want to show and hide, then choose **Edit: Action Buttons: Hide/Show**. Double-click any button with the **Text** tool to change its label. A student who finishes the activity early might make this sketch. Then you can use it with the whole class to practice calculating the missing sides for different 30°-60° right triangles.

© 2002 Key Curriculum Press

The Square Root Spiral (page 163)

Prerequisites: Students should be familiar with the Pythagorean theorem and should have experience with square roots.

Sketchpad Proficiency: Advanced

Activity Time: 40–55 minutes. This activity also makes a good project for students to work on at their own pace outside of class.

Example Sketch: **Square Roots.gsp**. This sketch contains the custom tool **Next Triangle**.

Sketch and Investigate

Q1 The Pythagorean theorem gives you $1^2 + 1^2 = c^2$, which simplifies to $c^2 = 2$, or $c = \sqrt{2}$.

Q2 Triangle $A''A'B$ is a right triangle, so you can use the Pythagorean theorem to calculate the length of its hypotenuse. Leg $A'B$ has length 1 (it's the radius of a circle with radius 1) and leg $A'A''$ has length $\sqrt{2}$. So we have $1^2 + (\sqrt{2})^2 = c^2$, or $3 = c^2$, or $c = \sqrt{3}$.

Q3 and **Q4**

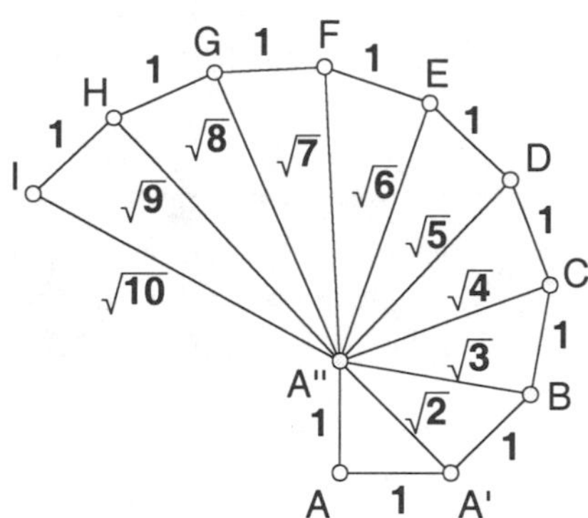

Q5

$\sqrt{2} \approx 1.414$	$\sqrt{3} \approx 1.732$	$\sqrt{4} = 2$
$\sqrt{5} \approx 2.236$	$\sqrt{6} \approx 2.449$	$\sqrt{7} \approx 2.646$
$\sqrt{8} \approx 2.828$	$\sqrt{9} = 3$	$\sqrt{10} \approx 3.162$

Explore More

1. When students have made their custom tools, this construction takes very little extra time and provides a dynamic spiral. (The original spiral is not dynamic because its purpose is to model specific irrational numbers.) It's fun for students to make action buttons to animate their spirals.

The Golden Rectangle (page 167)

Prerequisites: Students should have experience with setting up proportions, such as those used to describe relationships in similar polygons. Students will be more impressed with this activity if they've already learned something about golden rectangles and their significance. A fun activity is to have students take a poll to choose the most "popular" rectangle in a group of rectangles, one or two of which are golden. Golden rectangles tend to win hands down.

Sketchpad Proficiency: Advanced. Students should be familiar with making and using custom tools.

Activity Time: 40–55 minutes

Example Sketches: Golden Rectangle.gsp. For constructing the square, students can use the custom tool **4/Square (By Edge)** from the sketch **Polygons.gsp**.

Sketch and Investigate

Q1 ϕ is approximately 1.618. Students' answers will vary depending on their Scalars Precision settings in Preferences.

Q2 Region *DFGC* is also a golden rectangle because the custom tool for constructing a golden rectangle creates a shape that fits perfectly inside it.

Explore More

1. The proportion in the 1-by-ϕ rectangle matches the proportion at the top of the first page of the activity, except that $a = 1$ and $b = \phi$. So we have $\phi/1 = (1 + \phi)/\phi$. Cross-multiplying gives $\phi^2 = 1 + \phi$, or $\phi^2 - \phi - 1 = 0$.

   The two solutions generated by the quadratic formula are

   $$\frac{1+\sqrt{5}}{2} = 1.618\ldots \text{ and}$$
   $$\frac{1-\sqrt{5}}{2} = -0.618\ldots$$

   The positive solution gives the golden ratio.

2. $\phi^2 = 2.618\ldots$, which equals $\phi + 1$. This is verified in the quadratic equation in the last problem.

   $1/\phi = 0.618\ldots$, which equals $\phi - 1$. To prove this algebraically, start with the definition $\phi/1 = (1 + \phi)/\phi$. So $\phi = 1/\phi + 1$. Solve for $1/\phi$ to get $1/\phi = \phi - 1$.

3. The ratio of the length of a diagonal to the length of one side in a regular pentagon equals the golden ratio.

© 2002 Key Curriculum Press

Similar Polygons (page 169)

Prerequisites: Students should know what *congruent polygons* are and have experience with ratios.

Sketchpad Proficiency: Beginner

Activity Time: 20–40 minutes

Example Sketch: Similar Polygons.gsp

Sketch and Investigate

Q1 The polygons will coincide when the dilation scale factor is 1. This happens when the two segments defining the ratio have equal lengths.

Q2 Students will note that the figures are not generally the same size (so they're not congruent), but they are the same shape. Informally, this is what it means for polygons to be similar. The ratios of corresponding sides will all be the same and corresponding angles will all be congruent. Help students as necessary to arrive at the following definition:

Similar polygons are polygons whose corresponding sides are proportional and whose corresponding angles are congruent.

Explore More

1. a. Each ray through an original point passes through the corresponding image point.

   b. The ratio of the distances from the center to an image point and from the center to the corresponding original point is the scale factor. For example, the image of a point dilated by a 2/1 scale factor is twice as far from the center of dilation as the original point.

2. Answers will vary. For example, construct $\overline{DE}$ parallel to side AC. $\Delta ABC \sim \Delta DBE$.

3. Answers will vary. For example, the angles of any rectangle are congruent to corresponding angles of any square, but because the sides may not be proportional, the shapes are not necessarily similar.

4. Answers will vary. For example, the sides of any rhombus are proportional to the corresponding sides of any square, but because the angles may not be congruent, the shapes are not necessarily similar.

Similar Triangles—AA Similarity (page 170)

Prerequisites: Students should know the definition of *similar polygons*.

Sketchpad Proficiency: Beginner/Intermediate

Activity Time: 30–45 minutes

Example Sketch: AA Similarity.gsp

Sketch and Investigate

Q1 Because $\angle D \cong \angle B$ and $\angle E \cong \angle C$, angles A and F are congruent. This is because they contain the degrees that remain after you subtract m$\angle B$ and m$\angle C$ from 180°.

Q2 Triangles with two pairs of corresponding angles congruent must be similar.

Explore More

1. Neither AA nor AAA is a sufficient condition for similarity in quadrilaterals. A square and a rectangle provide a simple counterexample because they have all four corresponding angles congruent, but they are not necessarily similar. Students can prepare Sketchpad constructions similar to the one in this activity to demonstrate this.

2. The image below shows the construction. Triangle LKI and triangle LJC are similar. The pairs of angles are congruent as marked because each pair is a pair of corresponding angles. The triangles are therefore similar by AA.

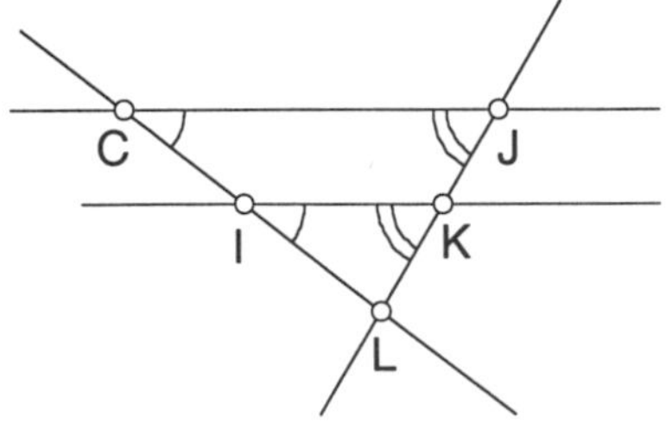

© 2002 Key Curriculum Press

Similar Triangles—SSS, SAS, SSA (page 171)

Prerequisites: Students should know the definition of *similar polygons*.

Sketchpad Proficiency: Beginner. Students manipulate a pre-made sketch and do not need to construct anything themselves.

Activity Time: 10–25 minutes

Required Sketch: Triangle Similarity.gsp

Sketch and Investigate

Q1 If two triangles have all three corresponding pairs of sides proportional, the triangles are similar.

Q2 The SSS and SAS combinations of corresponding parts guarantee similarity in a pair of triangles. The combination SSA does not. In the diagram below, $ED/BA = DF/AC$ and $m\angle F = m\angle C$. However, the triangles are clearly not similar.

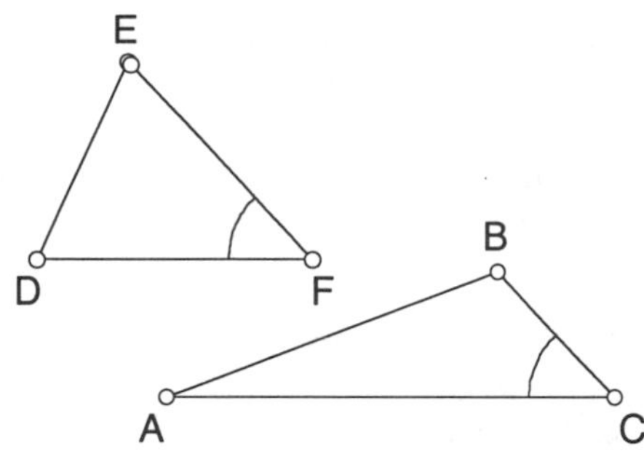

Explore More

1. ASASA and SASAS, for example, are enough to determine similarity in quadrilaterals. No combinations of four-part pairings guarantee similarity, but there are other five-part combinations that do.

The Geometric Mean (page 172)

Prerequisites: Students are introduced to the terms *geometric mean* and *mean proportional*. They need to know how to identify similar triangles and proportions in them.

Sketchpad Proficiency: Intermediate/Advanced

Activity Time: 45–55 minutes

Example Sketch: Geometric Mean.gsp

Sketch and Investigate

Q1 Triangle ABE is a right triangle.

Q2 $\Delta AEB \sim \Delta ACE \sim \Delta ECB$

Each pair of triangles is similar by AA. Every triangle has a right angle. ΔAEB and ΔACE both share angle A, and ΔACE and ΔECB share angle B.

Q3 $AC/CE = CE/CB$

Q4 The graph is half a parabola (see the graph at right), demonstrating a quadratic relationship between CE and $(AC)(CB)$. If you cross-multiply the proportion in Q3, you get $(AC)(CB) = CE^2$.

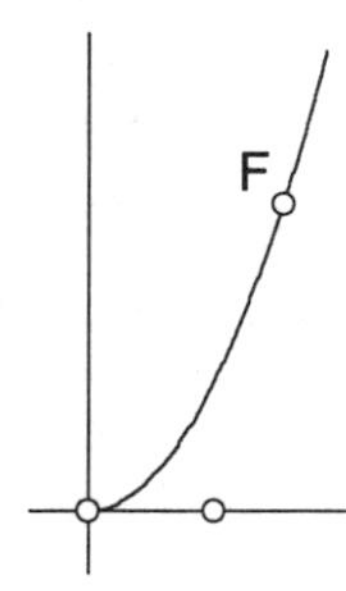

Explore More

1. In the right triangle construction in the activity, $AC/AE = AE/AB$ and $BC/EB = EB/AB$.

2. The figure at right shows the labels for the sides. The two proportions are $a/x = c/a$ and $b/(c-x) = c/b$. Cross-multiply to simplify these: $a^2 = cx$ and $b^2 = c^2 - cx$. Substitute a^2 for cx in the second equation to get $b^2 = c^2 - a^2$, or $a^2 + b^2 = c^2$.

3. In the pentagram at right, JK is the geometric mean between JL and KL. In fact, $JL/JK = JK/KL$ = the golden ratio.

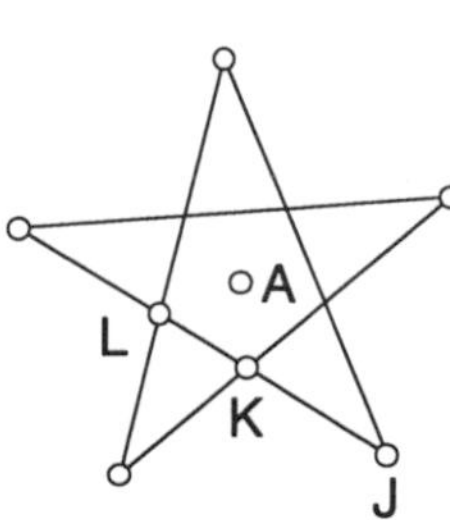

© 2002 Key Curriculum Press

Finding the Width of a River (page 174)

Prerequisites: Students should know how to identify similar triangles and write proportions from them.

Sketchpad Proficiency: Intermediate

Activity Time: 45–60 minutes

Example Sketch: River Width.gsp

Sketch and Investigate

Q1 $\triangle CDE \sim \triangle GFE$ by AA. $\angle CDE$ and $\angle GFE$ are right angles and $\angle CED$ and $\angle GEF$ are vertical angles.

Q2 $CD/DE = GF/FE$

Q3 $CD = (DE)(GF/FE)$

Q4 If you locate point E midway between points D and F, triangles CDE and GFE are congruent. This means $FG = CD$. You can find the distance across the river by simply measuring CD.

Explore More

1. The diagram below shows another model using similar triangles. You want to find x, the width of the river. Because $\triangle CGF \sim \triangle CED$, you can set up the following proportion:

$$\frac{x + a}{c} = \frac{x}{b}$$

Since a, b, and c are all lengths on the same side of the river, you can measure them and use the measurements to calculate x.

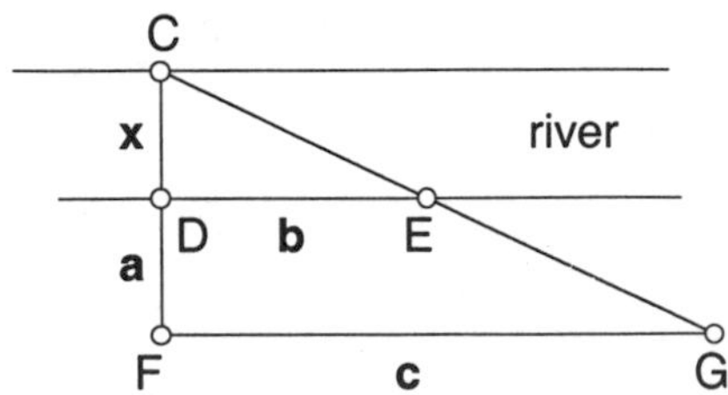

Finding the Height of a Tree (page 176)

Prerequisites: Students should be able to recognize similar triangles and solve proportions relating sides of similar triangles.

Sketchpad Proficiency: Intermediate

Activity Time: 45–60 minutes. If you can, have students use this method to measure the height of a tree, flagpole, or lamp in a parking lot or a field at school.

Example Sketch: Tree Height.gsp

Sketch and Investigate

Q1 As the sun gets lower in the sky, shadows get longer.

Q2 If you get shorter, your shadow also gets shorter.

Q3 No. Walking does not change the length of your shadow. This is because your position with respect to the sun remains essentially the same.

Q4 The triangles formed by the person and her shadow and by the tree and its shadow are similar by AA. In both cases, the angles the sun makes with the ground are congruent. Also, both the person and the tree make right angles with the ground.

Q5 Answers will vary. Students should write and solve a proportion like

$$\frac{\text{Tree height}}{\text{Tree shadow}} = \frac{\text{Your height}}{\text{Your shadow}}$$

where "Tree shadow," "Your height," and "Your shadow" are numbers measured in the sketch. To get an accurate calculation for tree height, students should use Sketchpad's Calculator. Otherwise, they'll be multiplying and dividing rounded numbers.

Q6 If students don't use Sketchpad's Calculator, calculated answers will differ somewhat from the measurement because of rounding. If students' calculations are far off from the measurement, they have made a mistake and should try their calculations again.

Explore More

1. Answers will vary. You can model one impossible situation if you drag a control point of the sun's beam of light until the sun's rays are parallel to the ground.

© 2002 Key Curriculum Press

2. The angle of the sun's rays changes continuously throughout the day, so in general, different times of day will yield triangles that are not similar. However, for each time in the morning there is a corresponding time in the afternoon when the angle of the sun is the same. If you knew exactly when two such times were, you could measure one triangle in the morning and a similar triangle in the afternoon. Also, the angle of the sun is the same at different times for different latitudes and for different seasons. Finally, it's possible to get similar triangles at different times of day with different sun angles if the sun angles are complementary. For example, suppose at one time the sun makes a 30° angle with the ground. Measure another triangle when the sun makes a 60° angle with the ground. At both times, the triangles will be 30°-60° right triangles and will thus be similar.
3. The next activity, Measuring Height with a Mirror, is devoted to this construction.

Measuring Height with a Mirror (page 179)

Prerequisites: Students should be able to recognize similar triangles and solve proportions relating sides of similar triangles.

Sketchpad Proficiency: Intermediate

Activity Time: 45–60 minutes. If you can, have students use this method to measure the height of an actual tree, flagpole, or lamp in a parking lot or a field at school. You will need metersticks and mirrors.

Example Sketch: **Mirror Height.gsp**

Sketch and Investigate

Q1 When a ray of light is reflected off a flat surface, the angle of incidence equals the angle of reflection (more simply, "angle in equals angle out"). This makes $\angle FGD \cong \angle EGC$.

Q2 $\triangle ECG \sim \triangle FDG$

The triangles are similar by AA. From Q1, $\angle FGD \cong \angle EGC$. Also, both the person and the flagpole make right angles with the ground.

Q3 If you move the mirror closer to the flagpole, you need to move closer to the mirror in order to see the top of the flagpole.

Q4 Three distances you can measure easily (with the help of a partner) are the distance between your feet and the mirror, the distance between the mirror and the flagpole, and your own height.

Q5 $DF/DG = EC/CG$

Q6 Obviously, the flagpole does not change its height if you move the mirror, so the calculations should predict the same height for different positions of the mirror. If you move the mirror, you also have to move yourself so you can see the top of the flagpole in the mirror. This adjusts the triangles so that they are similar again and so that the proportional equation still correctly predicts the height of the flagpole.

Explore More

1. The previous activity, Finding the Height of a Tree, describes a method for finding the height of a tall object using shadows.

© 2002 Key Curriculum Press

Parallel Lines in a Triangle (page 181)

Prerequisites: Students should know how to identify similar triangles and write proportions involving side lengths.

Sketchpad Proficiency: Beginner

Activity Time: 30–45 minutes

Example Sketch: Triangle Parallel.gsp

Sketch and Investigate

Q1 $\triangle ABC \sim \triangle DBE$. This is true by AA. Both triangles share $\angle B$ and $\angle BAC \cong \angle BDE$ because they are corresponding angles.

Q2 $AB/DB = AC/DE = CB/EB$. (Students may write correct ratios in other ways as well. For example, all the reciprocals of these ratios are also equal.)

Q3 $AD/DB = CE/EB$. (All the reciprocals of these ratios are also equal.)

Explore More

1. Use the proportion $AB/DB = CB/EB$ from Q2, but replace AB with $AD + DB$ and CB with $CE + EB$. You get

$$\frac{AD+DB}{DB} = \frac{CE+EB}{EB}$$

which gives

$$\frac{AD}{DB} + 1 = \frac{CE}{EB} + 1$$

This simplifies to $AD/DB = CE/EB$.

2. To check the converse, construct a triangle with an arbitrary line DE cutting sides $\overline{AB}$ and $\overline{BC}$. Measure BD, DA, BE, and EC and drag points D and E until the proportion $AD/DB = CE/EB$ holds. Then measure the slopes of $\overline{AC}$ and line DE. They should be the same, showing that the line and segment are parallel.

Dividing a Segment into Equal Parts (page 182)

Prerequisites: In order to explain why this construction works, students need to know that a line parallel to a side in a triangle divides the other sides proportionately.

Sketchpad Proficiency: Intermediate

Activity Time: 40–50 minutes

Example Sketch: Segment Trisector.gsp. This sketch contains the custom tool **Trisector**.

Sketch and Investigate

Q1 $AC = CD = DE$. These distances are equal because they are radii of congruent circles.

Q2 Angles CFA, DGA, and EBA are corresponding angles formed by a transversal and parallel lines. Triangles CFA, DGA, and EBA all share $\angle A$, so they're similar to one another. The ratios of sides AC, AE, and AE are 1:2:3, so the ratios of AF, AG, and AB are also 1:2:3. Thus, $AF{:}FG{:}GB = 1{:}1{:}1$.

Explore More

1. The construction is the same as the previous one, just using more circles. Students can generalize to see that Euclid's construction can divide a segment into n equal parts for any whole number n.

2. You can get the unit fractions with even denominators the same way, except that you start the construction with $\overline{DP_2}$, as shown below, where point P_2 is the midpoint of $\overline{AB}$.

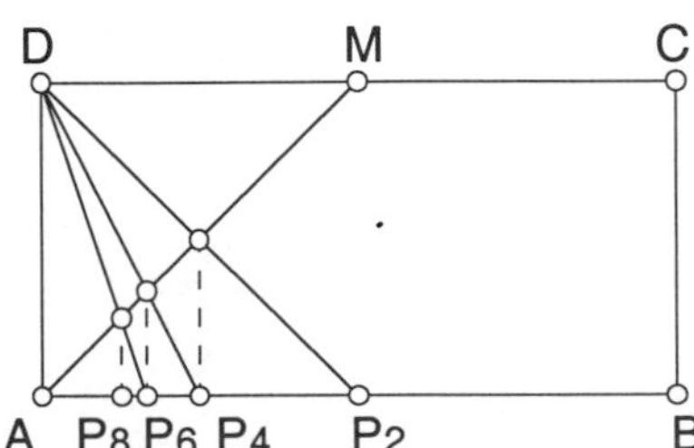

3. The two boys who discovered this construction inspired students around the country to discover similar constructions of their own using Sketchpad. This Explore More invites your students to join them in the search for more methods of dividing a segment.

© 2002 Key Curriculum Press

Spacing Poles in Perspective (page 184)

Prerequisites: Previous experience drawing with perspective may help students understand why fence posts may not be equally spaced when drawn in perspective. Ask them to think about their own experience—have them imagine a fence receding into the distance—before doing the activity.

Sketchpad Proficiency: Advanced. Students make a custom tool that allows them to make fence posts over and over again.

Activity Time: 40–50 minutes. You might want to give students out-of-class time to do this activity as a project. This allows them time to improve their sketch using other visual elements, action buttons, and color.

Example Sketch: Perspective Poles.gsp

Sketch and Investigate

Q1 The second post passes through the point of intersection of the segments constructed in step 25. These segments are the diagonals of the quadrilateral formed by post 1, post 3, and the vanishing lines. If you imagine looking at this quadrilateral head-on, it would appear as a rectangle and post 2 would appear to bisect the rectangle.

Explore More

1. No answer necessary.
2. Any triangle formed by a fence post and vanishing point *B* is similar to any triangle formed by another fence post and point *B*. This relationship is demonstrated by the ratios in the left column in the sketch below. More surprising, the ratio of (distance to vanishing point)/(distance to next fence post) increases by 1 with each successive fence post. This is illustrated by the ratios in the right column in the sketch below.

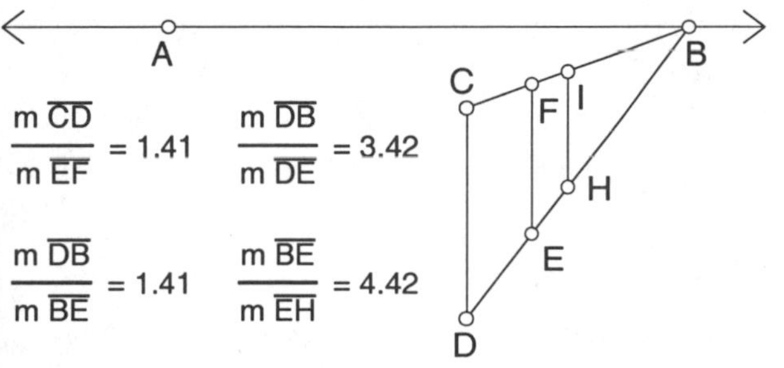

Proportions with an Angle Bisector in a Triangle (page 186)

Prerequisites: Students should know the term *angle bisector*.

Sketchpad Proficiency: Beginner

Activity Time: 20–35 minutes

Example Sketch: Angle Bisector Proportions.gsp

Sketch and Investigate

Q1 No. Point *D* is not the midpoint of $\overline{BC}$.

Q2 Point *D* is the midpoint of $\overline{BC}$ when triangle *ABC* is isosceles with $AB = AC$.

Q3 When *AB* is greater than *AC*, *BD* is greater than *CD*.

Q4 $AB/BD = BD/CD$

Q5 An angle bisector in a triangle divides the opposite side in the same ratio as the ratio of the lengths of the sides of the bisected angle.

Explore More

1. Construct a triangle with the given segment as one side and the other two sides in a ratio of 2:3. Bisect the angle formed by those two sides.

© 2002 Key Curriculum Press

Modeling a Pantograph (page 187)

Prerequisites: To understand how a pantograph works, students need to know about proportions in similar triangles.

Sketchpad Proficiency: Beginner/Intermediate. The first page of the activity is simple enough for a beginning user, but building the actual model of the pantograph requires at least intermediate proficiency.

Activity Time: 40–50 minutes, 10 minutes for the first page, then another 30–40 minutes for the rest of the activity

Example Sketch: Pantograph.gsp

Sketch and Investigate

Q1 The ratio AC/AB describes the ratio of the size of the traces. For example, if $AC/AB = 2$, the trace of point C will be half the size of the trace of point B.

Q2 To make the trace of point H twice as large as the trace of point D, drag point F so that $CE = EF$. The reason this works is that triangles CED and CFH are similar by AA. (They share angle C, and angles CED and CFH are corresponding angles.) When $CE = EF$, $CF = 2CE$, which means that lengths in the triangles and the traces of their corresponding points are in a ratio of 1:2.

Explore More

1. Students can build an actual pantograph as a long-term project. They might include with their project some information about the history and use of the pantograph, as well as their electronic Sketchpad model.

Proportions with Area (page 190)

Prerequisites: Students need to understand the concepts of *area* and *ratio*. *Dilate* may be a new term that needs explanation.

Sketchpad Proficiency: Intermediate

Activity Time: 25–45 minutes

Example Sketch: **Proportions with Area.gsp**

Demonstration Sketch: **Area Proportions.gsp**

Sketch and Investigate

Q1 The ratio of the corresponding side lengths equals the dilation ratio.

Q2

Side-length ratios	2	3	1	1/2	1/10	a/b
Area ratios	4	9	1	0.25 or 1/4	0.01 or 1/100	a^2/b^2

Q3 The ratio of the areas of two similar polygons is equal to the square of the ratio of the lengths of corresponding sides. In other words, if the ratio of corresponding sides in two similar polygons is a/b, the ratio of their areas is $(a/b)^2$.

Q4 The graph traced by the plotted point is half a parabola, implying that the area ratio is proportional to the square of the side-length ratio. If the ratios were directly related, the graph would be a straight line.

Explore More

1. To merge point B to $\overline{CD}$, select both and choose **Merge Point To Segment** from the Edit menu. To make the action button, select point B and choose **Edit | Action Button | Animation**. The button animates point B so that the ratio between the side lengths changes continuously between 0 and 1. This dilates the second polygon from being point-sized to being the size of the original polygon.
2. The center of dilation affects only the position of the dilated polygon. It does not affect the ratios between the polygons' areas and sides. These ratios are what determine the location of the plotted point L.
3. A box twice as long, tall, and wide will have eight times the volume of the original box. The ratio of the volume of two similar solids is equal to the cube of the ratio of the lengths of their corresponding sides.

© 2002 Key Curriculum Press

Trigonometric Ratios (page 195)

Prerequisites: Students should know the terms *ratio, hypotenuse*, and *leg* of a *right triangle*. They are introduced to the terms *sine, cosine*, and *tangent* as they apply to right triangles. You can use this activity at the beginning of a unit on trigonometry or as a review.

Sketchpad Proficiency: Beginner/Intermediate

Activity Time: 40 minutes, about 20 minutes for the first page of the activity, and another 20 minutes for the second page.

Example Sketch: Trig Ratios.gsp

Sketch and Investigate

Q1 When the angles change, the ratios among the triangle's side lengths also change.

Q2 When the triangle changes scale without changing shape, the ratios among the triangle's sides don't change. The different triangles produced by dragging *A* or *B* are similar to each other, so their sides remain proportional.

Q3

$$\text{sine of } \angle A = \frac{\text{length of leg opposite } \angle A}{\text{length of hypotenuse}}$$

$$\text{cosine of } \angle A = \frac{\text{length of leg adjacent to } \angle A}{\text{length of hypotenuse}}$$

$$\text{tangent of } \angle A = \frac{\text{length of leg opposite } \angle A}{\text{length of leg adjacent to } \angle A}$$

Q4 $\sin 30° = 0.500$, $\cos 30° = 0.866$, $\tan 30° = 0.577$

Q5 The measure of $\angle C$ will vary depending on the measure of $\angle A$, but the two will always sum to 90°. The sine of $\angle C$ equals the cosine of $\angle A$. This is because the side opposite $\angle C$, side *AB*, is the side adjacent to $\angle A$.

Q6 a. The sine of an angle of 0° has value 0. This is the smallest value possible for the sine of an angle in a right triangle. (The sine of angles with negative values can get as small as –1. But negative angles cannot exist in a right triangle.)

b. The greatest possible value for the sine of an angle is 1. The angle with this sine is 90°. Although students won't be able to make $\angle A$ 90° in the sketch, they can see the sine approaching 1 as $\angle A$ approaches 90°.

c. If $\angle BAC = 90°$, the triangle has two right angles, which is impossible.

d. If you drag point *C* up as much as possible, the measure of $\angle A$ approaches 90°. At the same time, the length of the side opposite $\angle A$ gets larger and larger, while the length of the side adjacent to $\angle A$ stays the same. Since the tangent is the ratio of opposite/adjacent, the tangent ratio gets extremely large, approaching infinity as $\angle A$ approaches 90°.

e. The tangent equals 1 when the ratio of opposite/adjacent equals 1. This is true when the triangle is isosceles, which happens when $\angle A$ measures 45°.

f. The cosine and sine are equal when the triangle is isosceles. This means $\angle A$ measures 45°. The two ratios are equal because the sides opposite and adjacent to $\angle A$ are the same length.

g. $\sin x = \cos (90 - x)$

© 2002 Key Curriculum Press

Modeling a Ladder Problem (page 197)

Prerequisites: Students can complete the first page of the activity with only a basic understanding of angles. For Q2, on the second page, they need to use the *inverse tangent function* to explain their results.

Sketchpad Proficiency: Beginner/Intermediate

Activity Time: 20–40 minutes

Example Sketch: Falling Ladder.gsp

Sketch and Investigate

Q1 The ratio EA/AD is 4 when EA is about 1.94 inches. This represents the ladder's reaching about 19.5 feet up the wall. The angle with the ground ($\angle EDA$) is close to 76°.

Q2 To solve the problem precisely using trigonometry, find $\angle EDA$ by finding the angle whose tangent is 4 (find $\tan^{-1}(4)$). This angle rounds to 75.96°. To solve for AE, set up the following equation: $EA/20 = \sin(75.96°)$. The solution is $EA = 19.4$ ft.

Explore More

1. If students trace the path of a paintbrush at the midpoint, they'll see that it traces out a quarter circle. What if the point isn't at the midpoint?
2. The graph of the ladder's distance from the wall versus the height on the wall is a quarter circle, centered at the origin. This means that as the foot of the ladder is pulled away from the wall, the top of the ladder starts falling slowly. But the farther away from the wall the foot of the ladder gets, the faster the top of the ladder falls.
3. Answers will vary. If you drag $\overline{AE}$ from the vertical, the model shows the ladder leaning against a slanted wall. Encourage students to add color, animation buttons, and art to the sketch to illustrate the problem they are modeling.

A Sine Wave Tracer (page 199)

Prerequisites: Students should be familiar with the *Cartesian coordinate system*. The activity is most meaningful to students who have begun studying trigonometry.

Sketchpad Proficiency: Intermediate

Activity Time: 30–50 minutes

Example Sketches: Sine Cosine Tracer.gsp and Tangent Tracer.gsp

Sketch and Investigate

Q1 As you drag point D, point F moves horizontally.

Q2 As you drag point E around the circle, point F moves vertically up and down like a sewing-machine needle.

Q3 Answers will vary. Students might sketch a path somewhat like the curve below.

Q4 The sketch will look something like this. Also, if students leave the animation running, they will probably get a series of curves like this that will start to fill in the area around the curve.

Q5 The unit circle has a circumference of 2π, about 6.28 grid units.

Q6 For the trace to repeat itself without tracing a new curve, the length of $\overline{AB}$ must be an integer multiple of the circumference of the circle. The circumference of the circle is 2π, about 6.28 grid units, so the x-coordinate of point B should be about 6.28.

© 2002 Key Curriculum Press

Modeling Pendulum Motion (page 201)

Prerequisites: Students should be familiar with the terms *pendulum* and *perpendicular*. This activity can be an introduction to periodic motion or just a fun introduction to modeling a real-world object using animation.

Sketchpad Proficiency: Intermediate (and stubborn beginners)

Activity Time: 20–50 minutes

Example Sketches: **Pendulum.gsp**

Sketch and Investigate

This activity does not require students to answer any questions in written form. To collect and assess the students' work on this activity, you can simply view their pendulums during class and check off that they completed them or collect their work electronically. Encourage students to improve their sketches according to some of the guidelines mentioned in the introduction to this book.

Creating a Hat Curve Fractal (page 202)

Prerequisites: It would be helpful if students were introduced to some fractal concepts and shown some examples before doing this construction. You could use the activity to introduce these concepts, but some prior exposure may help the construction make more sense. Students studying *infinite sequences* or *limits* can make connections with these topics and the chart in Q3. This activity is similar to the next one, Creating a Sierpiński Gasket Fractal, the major difference being which fractal is constructed.

Sketchpad Proficiency: Intermediate/Advanced. Students use the **Iterate** command to construct a multiple map iteration.

Activity Time: 40–60 minutes. 30–40 minutes for constructing an iterated image that works correctly, then another 10–20 minutes for answering the questions about the fractal. If necessary, students can answer Q2 and Q3 at home.

Example Sketch: **Hat Curve.gsp**

Sketch and Investigate

Q1 A stage 2 hat curve looks like this:

Q2 The curve pictured is at stage 3.

Q3 See entries in the second row of the chart below. The hat curve has infinite length at stage infinity, even though it is still contained in the same region of the plane.

Stage	0	1	2	3	n
Length	5/3	25/9	125/27	625/81	$(5/3)^{n+1}$

© 2002 Key Curriculum Press

Creating a Sierpiński Gasket Fractal (page 204)

Prerequisites: It would be helpful if students were introduced to some fractal concepts and shown some examples before doing this construction. Students studying *infinite sequences* or *limits* can make connections with these topics and the chart in Q3. This activity is similar to the previous one, Creating a Hat Curve Fractal, the major difference being which fractal is constructed.

Sketchpad Proficiency: Intermediate/Advanced. Students use the **Iterate** command to construct a multiple map iteration.

Activity Time: 40–60 minutes. 30–40 minutes for constructing an iterated image that works correctly, then another 10–20 minutes for answering the questions about the fractal. If necessary, students can answer Q2–Q4 at home.

Example Sketch: Sierpinski.gsp

Sketch and Investigate

Q1 A stage 2 gasket looks like this:

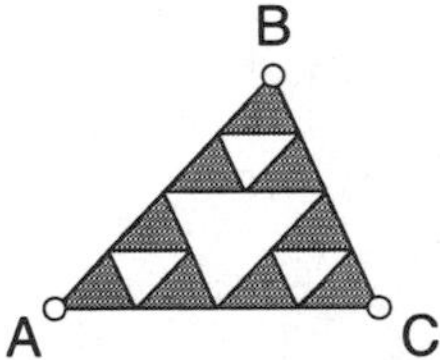

Q2 The gasket pictured is at stage 3.

Q3 See entries in the second row of the chart below. The area of the Sierpiński gasket approaches zero as the stage number approaches infinity.

	0	1	2	3	4	n
A	1	3/4	9/16	27/64	81/256	$(3/4)^n$
P	3	9/2	27/4	81/8	243/16	$3(3/2)^n$

Q4 The perimeter continues to grow without bound, so the perimeter at stage infinity is infinite. The Sierpiński gasket has the amazing property that its area is zero but its perimeter is infinite. The areas and perimeters of successive stages can be considered as infinite geometric sequences. The area sequence converges to 0 because its constant ratio, 3/4, is less than 1. The perimeter sequence diverges because its constant ratio is 3/2.

Q5 The area of a stage infinity Sierpiński gasket is zero. (See Q4 above.)

Q6 The perimeter of a stage infinity Sierpiński gasket is infinity. (See Q4 above.)

© 2002 Key Curriculum Press

Additional Explore More Suggestions

Explore More suggestions are challenging extensions to activities. Most are long-term, open-ended projects. You might have students who finish an activity early get started on an Explore More, but most suggestions cannot be completed in the same class period as the activity.

Below you'll find additional Explore More suggestions that did not fit on the activity pages. They're compiled here to save you unnecessary photocopying and to keep the book a reasonable length. You might wish to make a few copies of this section that students can borrow as needed.

Note: If the first suggestion listed under an activity title is not numbered "1," that means one or more Explore More suggestions appear on the activity page.

Chapter 1: Lines and Angles

Euclid's Proposition 1—An Equilateral Triangle (page 10)

1. Select your entire triangle and, in the Custom Tools menu (the bottom tool in the Toolbox), choose **Create New Tool**. Save the sketch, with an appropriate name, in your own personal folder of tools. (Check with your teacher if you have questions about how or where to save files.) Use your tool on two vertices of your first triangle to construct a second triangle that shares a side with the first. Keep using the tool on different pairs of vertices and see if you can fill your screen with a tessellation of equilateral triangles. Why do equilateral triangles fill the plane without any gap or overlap?
2. Find a copy of Euclid's *Elements*. Compare his Proposition 1 with the construction you did.

Duplicating a Line Segment (page 13)

1. In a new sketch, construct three unconnected segments. Now try to construct a triangle whose sides have the same lengths as the three segments.
    a. Change the lengths of the segments. Can any three segments make a triangle?
    b. Using the same three segments, construct a second triangle. Is it congruent to the first? Is it possible to use these segments to construct a triangle that is not congruent to the first?
2. Find a copy of Euclid's *Elements*, Book 1, and try Proposition 2—Duplicating a Segment using only Sketchpad's freehand tools.
3. Make a custom tool for duplicating a segment. Because the construction is only a few steps long you may not have much actual use for this tool, but it's fun to play with!

For tips on making and using custom tools, choose **Toolbox** from the Help menu, then click on the Custom Tools link.

© 2002 Key Curriculum Press

Duplicating an Angle (page 14)

2. Construct two unconnected segments and an angle. Now duplicate the angle and duplicate the segments on the sides of the copied angle. Complete the triangle. Is there more than one way to do it? Are all the triangles you can construct this way congruent?

Constructing a Perpendicular Bisector (page 19)

2. Write the converse of your conjecture from Q3. In the same sketch, investigate the converse as follows: Construct a point *G* not on the perpendicular bisector. Measure *GA* and *GB*. Move point *G* until those distances are equal. Where is the point? Explain how this demonstrates the converse you wrote.

3. In a new sketch, construct a line and a point not on the line. Mark the line as a mirror and reflect the point across it. Connect the point to its mirror image with a segment. How is this segment related to the mirror line?

4. In a new sketch, construct the perpendicular bisectors of the three sides of a triangle. Investigate their point of intersection. Can you construct a circle that circumscribes the triangle?

Slopes of Parallel and Perpendicular Lines (page 24)

1. In the same sketch, measure the equations of the two lines. Where does the slope of a line appear in its equation?

It may help to choose **Snap Points** from the Graph menu.

2. In a new sketch, show the coordinate grid. Scale the grid, if necessary, so that grid points are about 1/2 inch (or 1 cm) apart. Hide the axes. Draw a line and a point not on the line. Now construct a second point not on the line, located so that when you draw a second line through these points it will be parallel to the first line. Explain how you located the second point.

3. Confirm your parallel-line slope conjecture by constructing a line and a point not on the line. Through the point not on the line, construct a parallel line. Measure the slopes of the two lines. Drag different points and observe the slope measurements. Do a similar investigation for perpendicular lines. Explain what you did and what your investigations demonstrate.

Angle Bisectors (page 26)

4. In a new sketch, draw a triangle and construct its three angle bisectors. Construct the point of intersection of two of them. Write your observations about this point. How can you use it to construct a circle inscribed in the triangle?

© 2002 Key Curriculum Press

Chapter 1: Lines and Angles (continued)

Trisecting an Angle (page 27)

2. Here's a compass-and-straightedge trisection method many people think should work. Try it with Sketchpad: Draw an angle and a segment connecting the two sides of the angle. Find the 1/3 and 2/3 points on that segment any way you wish: it is a "legal" compass-and-straightedge construction. Draw rays from vertex *A* through these points. Does this method seem to work? Will it hold up no matter how you drag your angle?

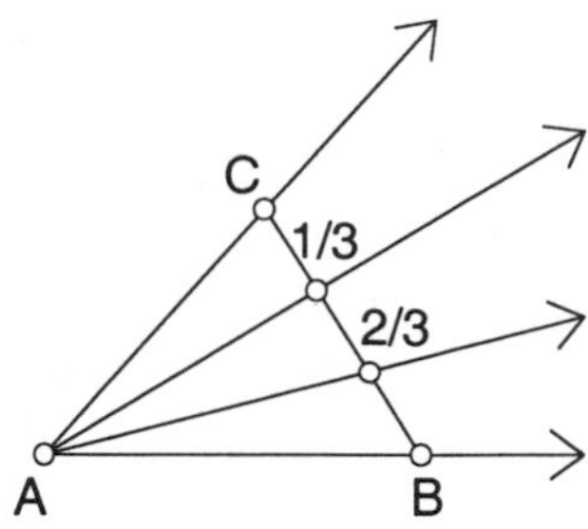

Chapter 2: Transformations, Symmetry, and Tessellations

Properties of Reflection (page 36)

3. Construct the interiors of the triangles in your sketch and print the sketch. Cut out your triangles and place them both in front of you, shaded side up. Pick up one triangle and place it on top of the other to show that they're congruent. What do you have to do with the triangle you pick up? Do they both still have their shaded sides facing up?

4. Reflect two points across a line and construct the quadrilateral with the four points (the two points and their images) as vertices. What kind of quadrilateral is this? How would you have to locate the two points to create a rectangle? A square? Can you create a parallelogram that is not a rectangle? If not, why not?

5. Construct a ray to mark as a reflection mirror. Construct another ray so that when you reflect it across the first, the reflection axis serves as an angle bisector.

6. Look in a mirror. Stand so that your nose is one ruler's length away from the mirror. How can you use the reflection of the ruler to tell whether you're measuring the shortest distance from your nose to the mirror? How far away does your reflected nose appear to be from your actual nose?

© 2002 Key Curriculum Press

Reflections in the Coordinate Plane (page 38)

2. Experiment with a reflection across the *y*-axis followed by a reflection of the image across the *x*-axis. What can you say about the coordinates of this product of two reflections? How is this second image related to the original triangle?

Translations in the Coordinate Plane (page 39)

1. In the same sketch, draw a segment from point *C* to a new point on the grid. Mark a new vector from point *C* to this point, then translate $\Delta D'E'F'$ by this new vector. You'll get a triangle $D''E''F''$ that is the result of two translations from the original triangle *DEF*. Find a vector that will translate ΔDEF to $\Delta D''E''F''$ in a single translation. How is this single translation vector related to the first two?

The Feed and Water Problem (page 42)

2. Using a process similar to that described in Explore More 1, construct a minimal path that goes first to the river, then to the pasture. Does it make any difference whether the rider feeds then waters or waters then feeds his horse? What do you think the answer depends on? *Hints:* Experiment with rays drawn from point *A*. Experiment by locating point *E* or point *D* very close to either the pasture or the river.

Planning a Path for a Laser (page 43)

2. Plan a laser path that reflects off four walls in your classroom and requires four mirrors.

Reflections over Two Parallel Lines (page 44)

2. In a new sketch, construct a figure and translate it by some arbitrary distance. Construct two lines so that you can move your original figure onto its translated image in two reflections.

© 2002 Key Curriculum Press

Chapter 2: Transformations, Symmetry, and Tessellations (continued)

Reflections over Two Intersecting Lines (page 46)

1. In the same sketch, try reflecting your figure and then its image over the two lines in the opposite order. Describe the result.
2. In the same sketch, drag the points on the lines so that the lines don't intersect any more. (The angle measures and the segments from the point of intersection should disappear.) Now how is the original figure related to the second image? What's the result of combining reflections over two parallel lines?
3. In a new sketch, construct a figure and a center of rotation. Rotate the figure about the center by any fixed angle. Hide the center and see if you can locate two intersecting lines so that reflections over them move your original figure to the rotated image.

Symmetry in Regular Polygons (page 50)

1. Construct one of the regular polygons using rotations or some combination of rotations and reflections. Explain your method and how it takes advantage of the symmetry of the polygon.
2. Explore symmetries in other figures. For example, try rhombuses, rectangles, isosceles trapezoids, or kites. Report your findings.

Tessellating with Regular Polygons (page 52)

1. Start with a single polygon that will tessellate, then tessellate by using transformations instead of using custom tools.
2. Try some semiregular tessellations, tessellations that use two different shapes—squares and equilateral triangles, for example.
3. Try tessellating with semiregular shapes—rhombuses and equilateral or equiangular polygons, for example.
4. Look for examples of tilings with regular polygons on floors, walls, sidewalks, computer screens, and other flat surfaces. Report what you find.

Tessellating with Triangles (page 55)

1. Try this investigation with any quadrilateral. Report your results.

© 2002 Key Curriculum Press

Chapter 3: Triangles

Triangle Sum (page 65)

1. Investigate angle sums in other polygons.

Triangle Inequalities (page 67)

1. Investigate inequalities among medians or altitudes in a triangle. Report your findings.

Triangle Congruence (page 68)

1. For each of the combinations of parts that do not necessarily guarantee congruence, sketch a pair of noncongruent triangles with those congruent parts. Explain why the triangles are not congruent.

Altitudes in a Triangle (page 75)

2. In your sketch, draw segments from each vertex to the orthocenter. Now you have three new triangles along with your original triangle. Choose your orthocenter tool from the Custom Tools menu and use it on each of these three new triangles. What do you notice?

3. Do you know a formula for the area of a triangle? Build three different expressions, using different altitudes and bases, that give the area of the triangle.

Angle Bisectors in a Triangle (page 77)

4. Can you inscribe a circle in any quadrilateral or only in some? What about other polygons?

Napoleon's Theorem (page 85)

2. Construct the inner Napoleon triangle by reflecting each centroid across its corresponding edge in the original triangle. Measure the areas of the original triangle and the outer and inner Napoleon triangles. Find the differences between these areas. Make a conjecture about these differences.

3. Do some research and report on Napoleon's interest in mathematics.

© 2002 Key Curriculum Press

Chapter 4: Quadrilaterals

Properties of Parallelograms (page 91)

1. Investigate the symmetry of the parallelogram. Does it have reflection symmetry? If so, where is the line of symmetry located? Does it have rotation symmetry? If so, by what angle(s)?
2. Use properties you have discovered to come up with other methods for constructing a parallelogram. Describe your methods.

Properties of Rectangles (page 93)

1. Write a paragraph comparing properties of rectangles with properties of ordinary parallelograms.
2. Investigate the symmetry of the rectangle. Does it have reflection symmetry? If so, where is/are the line(s) of symmetry located? Does it have rotation symmetry? If so, by what angle(s)?
3. Use properties you have discovered to come up with other methods for constructing a rectangle. Describe your methods.

Properties of Rhombuses (page 95)

1. Write a paragraph comparing properties of rhombuses with properties of ordinary parallelograms.
2. Investigate the symmetry of the rhombus. Does it have reflection symmetry? If so, where is/are the line(s) of symmetry located? Does it have rotation symmetry? If so, by what angle(s)?
3. Use properties you have discovered to come up with other methods for constructing a rhombus. Describe your methods.

Midpoint Quadrilaterals (page 102)

1. Construct the midpoint quadrilateral of the midpoint quadrilateral. Then construct *its* midpoint quadrilateral. Do this two or three more times. Describe any patterns you see in the midpoint quadrilaterals.
2. Construct the polygon interiors of a quadrilateral and its midpoint quadrilateral. Measure their areas. Make a conjecture about these areas.
3. What's the midpoint quadrilateral of a trapezoid? An isosceles trapezoid? A parallelogram? A kite? A rhombus? A rectangle? A square? Organize and explain your findings.
4. Under what conditions is a midpoint quadrilateral a rectangle? A rhombus? A square? See if you can construct the most general quadrilateral whose midpoint quadrilateral is one of these.

© 2002 Key Curriculum Press

Chapter 5: Polygons

Constructing Regular Polygons (page 114)

2. Find a book that shows Euclidean constructions for regular polygons and try these constructions using Sketchpad.

Constructing Templates for the Platonic Solids (page 115)

3. Do some research to learn more about the Platonic solids and their history. See if you can discover relationships among the number of faces, edges, and vertices of each solid.

Chapter 6: Circles

The Cycloid (page 129)

1. Experiment with the path of a point on a circle that's rolling around another circle.

2. Model the motion of the moon as it orbits around the earth as the earth orbits around the sun.

Chapter 7: Area

A Triangle Within a Triangle (page 139)

4. Create a triangle outside your original triangle by extending each side by a distance equal to the length of the side in a pinwheel fashion. For example, rotate $\overline{AB}$ and point B 180° about point A. Rotate $\overline{BC}$ and point C 180° about point B, and so on. Compare the areas of your outer triangle and your original one.

Squares and Square Roots (page 150)

In the Graph menu, choose **Plot Points** and enter your table values, with the areas as *x* and the side lengths as *y*.

1. Plot your table data and describe the graph. Use the graph or table to estimate $\sqrt{3}$. Check your estimate with a calculator.

Chapter 8: The Pythagorean Theorem

Dissection Demonstration of the Pythagorean Theorem (page 156)

1. Many cultures had dissection proofs of the Pythagorean theorem long before Pythagoras's time. Do some research into other dissection proofs of the theorem.

© 2002 Key Curriculum Press

The Golden Rectangle (page 167)

3. Construct a regular pentagon and one diagonal. Calculate the ratio of the length of the diagonal to the length of one side. How does this ratio compare to the golden ratio?

4. Do some research and write a report on the golden ratio.

Similar Polygons (page 169)

1. To learn more about what a dilation does, construct rays from the point marked as the center through each vertex of your original polygon.

   a. What other point does each ray pass through?

   b. How does the distance between the center and the first polygon compare to the distance between the center and the second polygon?

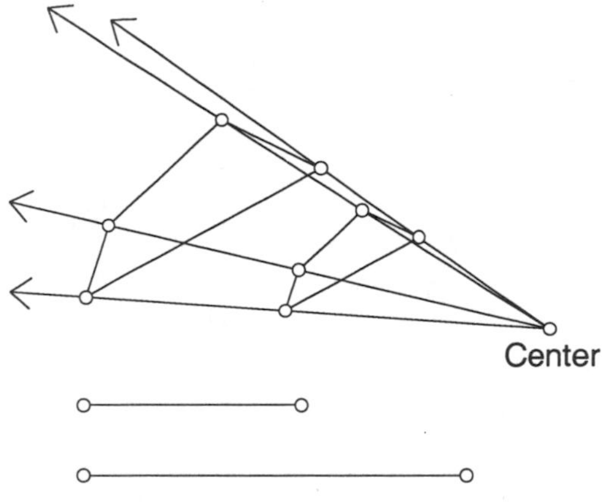

2. Construct a pair of similar triangles without a dilation. Explain your method.

3. Construct two nonsimilar polygons whose corresponding angles are congruent. Explain your method.

4. Construct two nonsimilar polygons whose corresponding sides are proportional but whose corresponding angles are not congruent. Explain your method.

Similar Triangles—AA Similarity (page 170)

2. Construct two parallel lines and two nonparallel transversals. The transversals should intersect to form similar triangles. How do you know these triangles are similar?

Spacing Poles in Perspective (page 184)

1. Make $\overline{CD}$ horizontal to change your posts into railroad ties.

2. Investigate relationships among the distances in this sketch. Compare distances between the feet of consecutive posts and distances to the vanishing point. Record your discoveries.

© 2002 Key Curriculum Press